# The Complete Traveller

# Joan Bakewell

# **The Complete Traveller**

Everything You Need to Know about Travel
at Home or Abroad

**Sidgwick & Jackson
London**

First published in Great Britain in 1977
by Sidgwick and Jackson Limited

ISBN 0 283 98395 7

Phototypesetting by George Over Ltd., London and Rugby
Printed in Great Britain by A. Wheaton & Co., Exeter
for Sidgwick and Jackson Limited
1 Tavistock Chambers, Bloomsbury Way
London WC1A 2SG

# Acknowledgements

I owe thanks to a great many organizations and people who have given me help, information and advice in writing this book. Some are working colleagues in journalism and television, many are members of travel organizations and agencies, others are simply personal friends. In mentioning them I extend my thanks to each personally: Mr G. Freeman Allen (Ian Allan Ltd.), Ivan Allen (Allen and Dunn Ltd.), Mr John Atkins M.I.T., David Attenborough, A.A., Ann Beuselinck (H.M. Customs and Excise), Barbara Bignell, Colin Briggs, David Brown (Foreign Office), James Cameron, Mr Cook (J. H. Kenyon Ltd.), John Cunnington, Margaret Deacon (National Maritime Museum), M. G. Dixon O.B.E. (Passport Office), Penelope Eckersley, Marion Edsa (Helena Rubinstein), Anna Ellis (British Waterways Board), Oliver Everett (Foreign Office), Roger Frankland (Car Ferry Enquiries Ltd.), Joanna Foley (*Successful Slimming*), John Gregg (*The Financial Times*), Prue Gearey and colleagues on the B.B.C. Holiday Programme, Bill Glenton, Sylvia Hull (*Mother and Baby*), David Halsey, Martin Jenkins, Roddy Lloyd Kirk, George Mathews (A.B.T.A.), Michelin, Mike Miller (Clifton Nurseries), Doreen Miller (Universal Beauty Club), Iain Morris (*Camping and Caravanning*), Patrick Roper (E.T.A.), Jean Robertson and Jon Swain (*Sunday Times*), Edmund Swinglehurst (Thomas Cook), W. H. Smith, Serena Sinclair (*Daily Telegraph*), Bill Stevens (B.A.), Neil Tyfield (Egon Ronay Organization), Dr Anthony Turner, David Tench (The Consumer Association), A. J. Todd, Daniel Topolski, Iris Wade (Elizabeth Arden).

I thank the Insight Team of *The Sunday Times*, the A.A., the British Tourist Authority and the World Health Organization for permission to reproduce their chart, symbols and maps on pp. 35−6, 56−9, 139−43, 202 and 206 respectively.

The maps and illustrations on pp. 42−3, 53, 54 and 98 were drawn by Ed Stuart. The chart on pp. 42−3 is taken from one supplied by the Ministry of Defence.

I am also grateful to those who helped in putting the book together: my researchers Pauline Kelly and Dorothea Phillips, my typists Christine Craven Walker, Rosalind Clarkson and Romaine Long, and my editor Jane Heller. Finally, to my family for their support, assistance and love throughout, especial gratitude.

# Contents

# Part 3: Where to Stay and What to Do

## Part 7: Coming Home

# Introduction

The entire human race is on the move as never before. More and more of us travel the world to earn our living, more and more of us want to spend our time off and holidays in places other than home. The search is on for as-yet-undiscovered holiday paradises. At the same time there are more and more ways of travelling: the Concorde, Japan's bullet train, the hovercraft, the folding bicycle.

With the increase in places to go, reasons for going and ways of getting there come all the confusions of choice. Which route? When? How? For how long? How much? An entire industry of travel and tourism has sprung up to meet these needs and answer these questions. But it does so in a piecemeal and uncoordinated way. As today's traveller you must pick your way through a forest of options and trust to luck you find just what is right for you.

This book is your guide. It tells you, not *where* to travel but *how* to travel. How to assess the different means, costs and comfort of different ways of going, staying and coming home. It does *not* spell out the prices of every possible journey: inflation and space make that impossible. Prices — where they are mentioned — are as at 1 June 1977, and are given as a guide only. Nor do I, in a single volume, go into detailed accounts of every type of travel. What I do is to offer outline guidance and point you in the right direction, and tell you where you can find out more.

This book applies to all kinds of travel, to all sorts of destinations. It is a handbook for everyone who has ever taken a plane or a train. With it you equip yourself to be the complete traveller.

I have tried to eliminate all errors from the book, but some may have survived exhaustive checking. If so, I'm sorry and apologize to you now.

Joan Bakewell.

May 1977

# Part 1

# Agents and Packages

# Chapter 1
# Do You Need a Travel
# Agent?

If you're an individualist, or very rich, and mistrust your own skills in negotiating the inefficiencies and small print of travel agencies, then, of course, you can do everything personally — or your secretary can. You can book direct through airlines: one airline will book you onto another. You can go to railway stations for tickets and through-booking across continents. You can arrange car ferries directly with the operators. You can write or telephone hotels chosen personally after much scrutiny of hotel guides. Many foreign hotels and hotel groups have representatives in the U.K. — book through them. British resorts and cities have holiday brochures that list hotels, and boarding houses, and bed and breakfast — write to the town hall.

There is much to be said for such a way of travelling. If you book through every stage yourself then you'll understand every detail — you won't simply be handed a bunch of unintelligible tickets on the eve of departure. It'll be your own fault if it goes wrong — but then you'll probably know exactly where it went wrong, and take correcting action directly and immediately.

Travelling should be looked on as a pleasure, and making your own personal travel plans is a major part of the satisfaction. Maps spread on the kitchen table, Motorail timetable at your elbow, glossy brochures in profusion to choose from, departure times to debate, cross-city connections to consult. (To avoid being trampled underfoot by religious processions or finding the museum (or shops) you went specially to visit being shut, get hold of a useful leaflet called *The Traveller's World Guide to Public Holidays,* published by Export Times, 60 Fleet Street, London EC4; telephone 01-353 7582 or 1965.) There's no doubt the accurate planning of a complicated journey brings great psychological rewards for people with a meticulous and painstaking temperament. It provides a sort of pre-echo of the journey's own satisfactions, and for a holiday it's an appetizer to the actual event.

Having said all that, the disadvantages are considerable.

You will find that the range of choices available is enormous. Information on them is enshrined in the standard reference books of the trade: weighty publications that combine and cross-refer a whole complex of options and prices. The leading ones are:

*Agent's Hotel Gazetteer* (C.H.G. Travel Publications): one volume for European resorts, one for European cities. Each place is described briefly, with lists of hotels, their facilities and location.

*The Holiday Guide* (St James Press): winter and summer editions. It lists all holiday destinations, who goes there and which hotels they use.

*Travel Directory* (St James Press): published annually and listing A.B.T.A. tour operators, travel agents, hotel groups, foreign hotels and their representatives in the U.K., coach and car hire firms.

*Travel Phone Guide* (St James Press): a miniature of the *Travel Directory* listing everyone by phone only.

*ABC Guides* (ABC Travel Guides Ltd.): the bumper reference books for journeys: *ABC Air/Rail Europe, ABC Rail Guide, ABC Shipping Guide, ABC World Airways Guide.*

*Travel Trade Directory* (Morgan-Grampian Book Publishing Co. Ltd.): an annual which lists agents, operators, airlines, coach and car hire firms, insurers, hotels and their representatives.

*The Thomas Cook International Timetable* (Thomas Cook Ltd.): a complete run-down on the world's railways and local shipping services. Published monthly.

You can look at these at central reference libraries.

It will take time to organize, write to different places and coordinate replies. That too may be part of the excitement but, unless it is, a travel agent will do it all for you, in his time, without any extra cost to you.

It could cost you more to do it yourself than booking through a travel agency, particularly if holiday air flights are involved, where packages bring tremendous savings. Nowadays package tours are very rarely highly organized, with travellers herded in groups by bossy tour-company reps. You can select a package, take the flight, arrive at your hotel and stay there throughout your visit without ever being conscious that it was a package — except when you consider the cost savings. An independently booked flight and hotel will always cost much more than the same flight and hotel booked as a package through a travel agent. Many complete holidays cost less than the scheduled return flight alone.

A package is legally required to have two components: air flight, and one other facility — e.g. accommodation or car hire — but in fact it is possible to book a package holiday simply as a cheap flight and abandon the hotel booking altogether. However, you must return on the flight specified in the package.

## Holidays and journeys to book for yourself

There are some forms of travel where the agent doesn't have much of an advantage over do-it-yourself.

## Travel in Britain

Unless you want a coach tour of Britain staying overnight at different places, journeys in Britain can easily be organized without using a travel agent. Write to a selection of hotels asking for details and brochures – a stamped addressed envelope usually encourages a quick reply. You can book trains and seats yourself, by post. British Rail offer considerable reductions for booking three weeks in advance, for students, for particular lengths of stay, and for particular days of travel. Book travel and confirm tickets in good time.

## Travel abroad

It's getting easier with the increasing numbers of car ferries and hovercraft services to pop across the Channel by car at your own whim. You can risk just turning up on the day but this is folly in the high season when you would certainly have a long wait. Otherwise book directly with the ferry firm or through a specialist such as Car Ferry Enquiries Ltd, 9a Spur Road, Isleworth, Middlesex; telephone 01-568 7343. You would be wise to take with you at least one of the major hotel guidebooks, and phone ahead to book a room for the next night before setting out in the morning. You can certainly manage such a journey without a travel agent – nor do you need one – for touring by car in Western Europe. Brave souls make it to Katmandu and even Australia.

## National tourist offices

Fifty-two foreign states have offices in London for the purpose of publicizing and popularizing visits to their countries. They often supply lavishly coloured brochures free. The superlatives can be discounted but the hard facts can be useful. Each office has lists of travel agents and tour operators who offer the best opportunities. They will also answer specific queries about motoring, food, bus routes, etc. The addresses are given in the gazetteer.

## Booking through travel agents

Travel agents exist to sell tickets for travel by air, sea or land. They are seldom allowed to charge more or less than the face value of the ticket, so there will be no booking fee for you. They get their commission from the transport and travel companies. But sometimes they will charge for getting you reservations for seats, sleepers or couchettes on Continental railways — this is allowed.

Travel agents also sell holidays as packages — inclusive tours — proffered to them by tour operators or packaged by themselves (in which case they become tour operator and travel agent in one). Most travel agents will prepare an independent inclusive tour to suit your needs, but it's likely they will channel it through one of the tours offered by other companies. In legal terms this is no 'package' — of the kind that can be covered by a bond — unless there is a brochure offer of such a holiday.

There are some 6,000 travel agents, many selling only coach tickets, currently listed in Yellow Pages. 4,000 fully-fledged travel agents belong to A.B.T.A. — the Association of British Travel Agents, 53 Newman Street, London W1; telephone 01-580 8281. This organization exists to protect and promote the interest of its members. But that involves pleasing the customer. A.B.T.A. requires certain standards of its travel agents.

They must offer all forms of travel facilities — a full travel-agent service.

They must have qualified staff, but the present qualification is something as unspecific as 'experience'. A.B.T.A. requires at least one of the people behind the counter to have three years experience and one other at least one year. That could just mean they've been selling incompetently all that time! A team of inspectors make random checks, but how can you check on satisfied customers?

Now the Institute of Travel and Tourism (same address as A.B.T.A.) offers training — in day-release and evening classes — and people qualify by examination, first as Associate Members (ATA1), and then as full Members (MTA1). This will increasingly become the job qualification for work in the travel-agency business but as the scheme is only two years old it's too soon to expect ATA1 or MTA1 staff to serve you.

A.B.T.A. expect decent premises — a counter area quite separate from other selling. Newsagents and tobacconists who also book holidays wouldn't qualify. Their packages would not have A.B.T.A.'s financial resources (see below).

Agents must submit a set of accounts each year and depending on the state of those accounts they often have to provide a *bond* to A.B.T.A. A bond is a bank guarantee or an insurance guarantee to pay certain of the agent's debts if he cannot. In the case of bankruptcy this bond goes to help repay purchasers of holidays who have been let down. The bond is the first line of financial defence holiday-makers have against their A.B.T.A. travel agents going bust.

The A.B.T.A. retailer's fund is the second line of defence for the consumer. All A.B.T.A. members contribute a sum related to their turnover to a central fund that is available to meet debts to the public of travel agents that fail. This fund, originally called the Common Fund, has no legal backing: it offers *no guarantee* to the public. It was created in 1965 after the public uproar when several travel companies went bankrupt and the public lost money. To its credit, since the fund began no member of the public booked to go on holiday has lost money through an A.B.T.A. travel agent going bust. But times are getting harder. In 1976 the fund stood at £100,000. If travel agents go out of business with debts totalling more than that, then A.B.T.A.'s resources for helping them out will be exceeded, unless their members contribute extra funds.

Some travel agents display the A.B.T.A. sign without being entitled to it. You could always ask; they could always lie. So if you're uncertain check with A.B.T.A. itself (01-580 8281) or the local chamber of commerce, major libraries or the Citizens Advice Bureau. If any A.B.T.A. travel agent provides unsatisfactory service you could write to A.B.T.A. setting out your complaint reasonably. It won't provide instant redress but it will keep the whole profession on its toes.

## Holiday guarantees

### Cook's refund

In 1976 Thomas Cook advertised on T.V. that they would give a 24-hour money back guarantee to customers who booked through them. This was Cook's guarantee against the failure of any tour operator before the date of departure. It sounded an attractive offer and in a year that saw business in the trade fall by 10% they held their sales steady. In fact, any financial loss following a failure by a tour operator is protected if you go to an A.B.T.A. travel agent. It's just that not many of them have the financial power to refund within twenty-four hours.

### Price guarantees

Competition among tour operators throughout early 1977 was fierce. Thomson Holidays, finding in January 77 that their summer bookings were 25% down, issued a virtually blanket 'no surcharge' guarantee for all holiday bookings. Only government action — e.g. an increase in V.A.T. — would put up the prices, they promised. In times of falling sterling value this is a guarantee worth having. Other companies soon followed suit and the guaranteed-price offers came thick and fast, often with slightly differing terms — some involve early payment.

It's worth asking your travel agent about guarantees. Frozen prices are good if sterling is falling in value. But they can misfire if the country of destination then devalues. Portugal did so in March 1977. Those who had already paid for their holiday *didn't* get a refund.

## Specialist travel agents

If you want a visit to one country or one area, ring the national tourist office of the country concerned and ask which agencies specialize. You may be given a number of addresses. Get all their brochures and compare.

# Chapter 2
# Packages and Tour Operators

The easiest way for the cautious first-time-abroad traveller is the all-in package. You will be confined to one hotel, with all meals in one dining-room. But a package takes away many of the problems of being abroad: language, currency, strangeness, etc. If you're merely going for sunshine, a good tan and a good time, an all-in package with other holiday-makers like yourself is ideal.

The package industry is changing. More people want more flexibility — demi-pension, just bed and breakfast, two-centre holidays, fly-drive arrangements — and the operators are adjusting to meet the demand and now offer lots more options. So if you fancy something more complex than the old straightforward package, don't assume you'll have to plan it for yourself. Your travel agent should know what other schemes are available.

## Tour operators

They organize and publicize the packages. There are 300 tour operators in Britain. The biggest are Thomson, B.A. Sovereign and B.A. Enterprise, Cosmos, Horizon and Laker.

There are many tour operators offering very specialist types of holiday either defined by region or activity. A travel agency specializing in one region or one activity will be fully informed of all the different choices available at all the different prices.

## The same holiday at different prices

It's maddening to be lying by a Mediterranean hotel pool and on comparing notes with your neighbour find that they bought the same holiday for less money. It does happen; tour operators must compete for deals with the local hotels and the prices that result can differ widely. A good travel agent should sort this out for you.

You may appear to have purchased a holiday identical to your neighbours. But you may be paying more for congenial extras, such as a room with a view, or arrival and departure times that aren't uncivilized. Being thrown out of a hotel room at 08.00 when your flight doesn't leave until 20.00 is irritating and awkward: how do you dress to meet the needs of the pool, the hot day, the journey, and the late arrival in England? If you have small children it's worse: where can they change their clothes and nappies, and have their nap? A holiday that allows you a room until time of departure may charge more for the convenience. Night flights are usually cheaper: but you feel like a dishcloth on arrival.

You may also pay extra for a choice of menu: package menus keep the choices to two or three. If you want to eat à la carte and still book the journey and accommodation, you will have to pay extra. If you book only bed and breakfast you will pay less.

Finally, you pay more for being transported from airport to hotel by car rather than coach.

## The Association of British Travel Agents (A.B.T.A.)

Membership of A.B.T.A. for tour operators depends entirely on financial stability. They must provide *an A.B.T.A. bond* against their debts. The usual amount is 10% of the annual projected turnover but if the Civil Aviation Authority agrees the amount can be reduced to 7%. This bond is the first line of defence against financial loss for chartered bookings, or contracted groups travelling by scheduled flights, coach or train. It does not cover individual journeys on scheduled flights, coach or train.

### Government Air Travel Reserve Fund

Until October 1977, this was financed by the public who paid 2% on the cost of a holiday to be protected. This only applied to inclusive *air* packages, on chartered or group bookings. When the fund reached £12.5 million in 1977 the Department of Trade suspended the levy. The fund is kept under review and the levy will be re-introduced if and when necessary.

In most cases of failure by tour operators the bond proves enough to cover, but when it does not, the Air Travel Reserve Fund is drawn on.

### British holiday packages

These are *not* protected by A.B.T.A.'s bond. They involve less risk, but do take care to book through a *reliable* travel agent and operator.

## Air Travel Organizer's Licence (A.T.O.L.)

Everyone who organizes air travel has to get a licence, called A.T.O.L., from the Civil Aviation Authority.

A.T.O.L. A means an organizer can arrange A.B.C.s (see page 18). A.T.O.L. B means he can arrange inclusive packages by air. A.T.O.L. C means he can arrange group booking on scheduled flights.

Every A.T.O.L. holder must usually deposit a bond of 15% of his turnover with the C.A.A. to repay you if he goes broke (unless he's in A.B.T.A. when his 10% A.B.T.A. bond is enough, as above).

## Brochures

Beware. These are not the level-headed consumer information sheets the operators would like you to think. They are expensively produced, lavishly designed selling magazines. They are ideal for idle browsing, cheering yourself up in winter, or even supplying the local play-school with free cut-outs. But if you're seriously buying a holiday, then read them carefully. Note the following with special care.

### Photographs

These will show the resort and the hotel in their most favourable light. If you've never been to a resort before, call in at the local library, browse along the travel shelves and flick through the pictures of the place concerned in a book that isn't out to sell. Also notice what is not shown in the picture of the bedroom. View of the sea? You might have to crane your neck round corners. Private bathroom? Is it a bath or just a shower? The more outrageous misrepresentations have now been stopped by the Office of Fair Trading. But tour operators have the right to display what they sell to its best advantage. The people in the brochures will all be young and pretty (many will have young and apparently well-behaved children). Sadly not all holiday-makers are like that. Old age pensioners may not like the noisiness of children disturbing their holiday. The young and trendy might want to be with their own kind. The travel agent might be able to help in specific cases: a hotel providing facilities for children obviously expects them. Older people often prefer holidays away from crowded beaches.

### Main roads

It is not often indicated whether a hotel is on a main road. If it is, and it's on a through route or near the local nightlife, it could be noisy when you want it quiet.

## Length of stay

If you still have a toehold on foreign soil at one minute past midnight then as far as brochures are concerned that often counts as a day abroad. A ten-day holiday can mean eight at the hotel.

## Mode of travel

The journey may be made up of air and coach. Make sure how long the coach journey is. Check on times of flight departures and arrivals at both ends. If it's a long journey will there be meals en route? Included in the prices?

## Extras

Most brochures list what is included in the price. Unless something is listed it won't be included. You may find certain options available as a supplement to the main prices. Single-bedded rooms often cost more than half a double. Beds by the pool, hire of beach towels, drinks and tips will all be on-the-spot extras.

## Surcharges

In recent years, the fluctuating value of the pound has made it difficult for tour operators to offer a competitive price when they print their brochures (up to a year before the holiday actually takes place) and yet protect themselves against unpredictable increases in cost. And the market is so competitive, they are eager to keep their advertised price down. (We've all seen enticing headlines like: 10 days in the sunshine islands – for only £xx – to discover that it means mid-week, midnight flights operating in February to the Scillies!)

In consequence, surcharges have to be made to allow for the rising cost of two things – foreign currency and fuel. At its worst in 1975 surcharges were being collected from people at airports, and even on the beach by local tour reps. This is no longer allowed by A.B.T.A. for currency surcharges, which must now be made not later than a month before you leave. Fuel surcharges can be levied later.

However, some firms – both airlines and tour operators – have now declared they will not levy surcharges. They will guarantee to hold the price on bookings made and paid in full, for holidays in a certain period. Travel agents will have full details which these are.

## Consolidations

These can come as a nasty surprise. You may have selected your holiday from the brochure, booked and even paid. They then inform you the holiday has been changed in some way. What has happened is that booking on certain holidays and flights has been very light so several holidays are being combined in one to make them economic. Inconvenience may be minimal: a flight a few hours earlier or later, a different hotel but in the same resort and similar to the one you originally chose. But 'consolidations' might involve greater changes: a different day of departure altogether, for example, or an entirely different resort. If this doesn't suit you say so at once — in writing to both your travel agent and the tour operator. They may offer you your money back. But that's tough too. You will have suffered inconvenience, and may be left with no time to arrange a replacement holiday. In such a case you should consider making a claim for damages against them.

## Cancellations

Package-tour operators will require a deposit — usually £10–£15 per person, perhaps £30 or more for a world cruise — when you book your holiday. They usually want the balance eight weeks before departure. If you change your holiday plans in the meantime and wish to select another of their packages then there is usually an alteration fee to pay. If you cancel more than six weeks before the holiday you usually merely lose the deposit. But cancellations made later cost more — a percentage of the total holiday price, excluding insurance. Traditional charges are:

   29–42 days 30% of total price
   15–28 days 45% of total price
   1–14 days 60% of total price

Cancellations on day of departure get *no refund*. Cancellation rates vary but are usually near this scale. P. & O. Cruises, for example, are higher: 15–28 days notice, 60% to pay; 1–14 days, 90%. The rates should be printed in the brochures.

# Part 2

# Choosing and Using Your Method of Travel

# Chapter 3
# Booking Air Travel

Airlines accept bookings by telephone but a booking is never confirmed until the ticket itself has been issued, and that is after the money has been paid. Until this has happened you do not have any guaranteed place on a flight or any contract with the airline. You should therefore *collect* your ticket – thus confirming your booking on the flight – well *before* the day of departure.

You can post a cheque to the airline and have them post back your ticket. This can be risky: if your cheque reaches them, but the ticket doesn't reach you in time, the airline will still have a computer record of your booking, your cheque and your ticket issue. This can be verified instantly and a duplicate ticket issued. However, if your cheque fails to reach them they are not to blame. So send air-ticket cheques 'recorded delivery' to be safe.

You can ask the airline to hold your ticket and pay on the day of flight – but you must pay in cash or by an airline charge card, not by cheque or credit card. Most airlines will hold your ticket in these circumstances, but you could put yourself at a disadvantage this way if you arrive at the last minute for an overbooked flight (see page 23).

You can call at a travel agent and ask them to issue a ticket. They have tickets for filling in, and they will usually take your cheque.

### Travicom

This is the name of a communication system which U.K. travel agents can install and rent from British Airways. It will give them a single computer terminal that can provide access to the reservation computers of up to sixty different airlines. Travel agents who have Travicom – it was new in mid 1977 – will thus be able to check out and confirm your booking with any of those airlines within seconds.

### Universal Air Travellers Plan (U.A.T.P.)

U.A.T.P. is a charge card issued to travellers by British Airways which is acceptable as payment for flights with B.A. and some 155 other airlines.

## Stand-by bookings

If the flight you want is fully booked, you can go onto a waiting list — as a stand-by — in case anyone drops out. The drop-out rate on inter-European flights is quite high. A businessman might want to fly to Paris on Monday afternoon, but have an important lunch meeting first. His secretary will reserve him a place on several flights so he can choose the most convenient. A ticket will be issued only for the flight he chooses. The rest will be available to stand-by passengers during the last thirty minutes of the check-in time.

If someone drops out in time for the airline to contact you by phone and give you a firm booking then you pay full fare. If at the time of departure you're still on the waiting list, but turn up at the airport and are lucky, then you also pay full fare.

## Last-minute bookings: I.P.E.X.

Some airlines offer cheap excursion rates on certain routes booked at the last minute. They are called I.P.E.X. fares: Instant Purchase Excursions. B.A., Air France and Sabena all offer this facility on the London to Paris, Amsterdam and Brussels flights. For Paris, you can't book before 14.00 on the day before that of departure; for Amsterdam not before 21.00; Brussels not before 19.00. There are some other restrictions but I.P.E.X. is well worth looking into for unexpected plans.

## Re-confirmation

For onward flights or return flights to the U.K. (unless within the U.K. or Europe) you must re-confirm your reservation. You should do this at least seventy-two hours before the flight. If you don't you may find your reservation cancelled.

## Cancellations

You can, of course, book by phone and just not collect your ticket. If, however, a ticket has been issued you will have paid and will be expected to turn up. Those who don't are known as 'don't-shows'. If you don't intend to show then let the airline know as soon as possible. Unless you do, you will find that when you come to claim your fare back a 'don't-show' charge might be made. The size of the charge will depend on the flight. If you cancel by phone, rather than by writing or calling in person, note the name of the person who takes the cancellation in case of a dispute about the refund. If you cancel your booking when you have sent the money, and the ticket has not been sent then ask for the locator number and quote it when making your claim.

## Stopovers

Many airlines allow you to stop two or three days at a place en route to your final destination — for example, you can break a flight from London to Sydney at Delhi. The length of stopover allowed will depend on the airline. Stopovers are often not allowed on cheap-fare flights, but only on full schedule fares. Check with the airlines covering the route before you book. Depending on the maximum allowed mileage calculated on your ticket, you may be able to deviate from the most direct route — from starting point to destination — to stop over at an intermediate point without paying any extra. A good travel agent will know all about 'allowed mileage'.

## The cheapest way to fly

Air fares are a nightmare of complexity. Even airport information staff can come up with a variety of answers to the same question. European fares are the worst of all. They are not merely confused but illogical. For example, in 1977 on the London—Malaga route there are thirty different fares, including six different types of discount. On the London—Frankfurt route there are six different fares, with seven types of discount. In 1976 it cost £21.70 *more* to fly from London to Naples — a distance of 1,002 miles — than to fly to Faro which is some 50 miles further away. The best thing is to keep your head and observe the following travelling tips.

**Book as early as you can** The earlier you can fix your dates of travel the greater your chance of price concessions. Businessmen might do well to reverse their normal procedure of making a business appointment *then* fixing the flight. Find out when the travel is cheapest and fix appointments accordingly. Bargain packages are often arranged for trade fairs and exhibitions — you don't have to go to the fair to take advantage of the bargain fares.

**Book in Britain for the entire trip** At present sterling fares are lower than those charged in other European countries. Businessmen travelling from some European cities to the U.S. are coming via London to get the cheaper London—U.S. fares.

**Packages are often cheaper than air fare alone** Several travel agents offer a package of fare and accommodation, at rock-bottom prices. The idea is that you can always scrap the accommodation and use the travel. Accommodation can be minimal. I followed up a press advertisement for ten days in Malaga for £25: the accommodation was a huge barn that served as a dormitory for eighty people!

**Shop around different airlines for quoted prices** If there's a great discrepancy then ring the costliest, tell them of the cheapest and see what they say. They may plead error and adjust their figures.

**Travelling to Asia** Consider taking an excursion fare to the city you want to visit first and then buying local short-term excursions for other destinations. Compare the cost with the through booking.

**U.S. domestic fares** are conspicuously lower than normal European fares — Australian fares are similarly only about 50% of comparable European fares. Touring across these countries need not be as expensive as comparisons with European journeys might at first suggest.

**Spouses and relations** Some airlines have special rates for accompanying spouses and family visits across oceans. They won't know unless you tell them that yours is such a visit.

## Fare construction

Businesses with travelling personnel should certainly know about fare construction. The information is in the *ABC World Airways Guide* (33—40 Bowling Green Lane, London EC1R DNE). You need to understand the fare-construction grid, fare-calculation units, and maximum allowed mileage. You can even take lessons: twenty hours of evening classes, from £65 from the Belair School, 5 Denmark Street, London WC2; telephone 01-836 1316.

Here are the basic fare structures licensed by the Civil Aviation Authority.

## Scheduled flight

The most expensive way to travel — especially if you go by Concorde when you pay extra for time saved, plus glamour and prestige. The last two may fade, but the first will always be worth money. Return schedule fares are often cheaper than twice the single. To go by air and return by sea can be less than a single flight each way — check. On ordinary scheduled flights you can break your journey at no extra cost; you may also be able to change your route and your stopovers from the originals. Ask how many places and for how long you can break your flight without the fare going up. Scheduled flight tickets are valid up to one year; you can cancel/re-book without further cost or trouble.

*First class* You get better food (choice of menu), free drink and lots of attention from the stewardesses, free cigarettes, more leg-room and quiet. The extra comfort is worth the higher fare on long journeys.

*Economy class* There are no second-class citizens, only the first class saving money. You get less leg-room and plainer food. You pay for your drinks. You sit further back in the plane where it's slightly noisier and bumpier.

## Ordinary excursion fares

These work just like railway excursions. You get reductions on scheduled routes for tickets with restrictions on time of travel. It may be that you have to stay more than twenty-one days before returning or between fourteen and twenty-one days. B.A.'s Poundstretcher for a stay of between 45 and 180 days in Australia costs £359 from London return. You will probably not be allowed to break your journey.

## Advance Passenger Excursion (A.P.E.X.)

These fares are available on scheduled flights to the U.S.A., Canada, Mexico, Malta, the Caribbean, South Africa and some parts of the Far East. However, you have to book and pay in full up to two months in advance. There's a big demand: you need to book on the first day they're available, there's usually already a queue like the last night of the Proms. How long you can stay varies from route to route. There's a weekend surcharge. Children under twelve pay two-thirds. If you cancel Australian or South African bookings you can forfeit as much as 25% of the fare, plus £5.

## European A.P.E.X.

Early in 1977 British Airways announced that they would offer reduced fares on scheduled flights to Italy, Yugoslavia, Greece and Turkey. You must book at least one month before you go; your stay must be of between two weeks and three months. The reduction is to 50% or 60% of the scheduled fare.

## Common-interest-group fares

If you travel in a large party on a scheduled flight you might be eligible for group-discount fares. But the rules on eligibility are stringently applied. They vary with locations, but you normally have to stay between ten days and a month in summer, two months in winter. You can't transfer flights.

## I.P.E.X.

See page 15.

## Advance Booking Charters (A.B.C.)

You get these tickets through a travel agent or tour operator. Not through the airline. They are currently only available on transatlantic routes to the U.S.A., Canada and the Caribbean. They may be on scheduled or special charter flights. You have to book and pay at least two months in advance. Usually you must stay for a minimum of fourteen days in summer, ten days in winter. Children go for 90 per cent of the adult fare. If you cancel within thirty days of departure you forfeit the full fare, within thirty to fifty-nine days, 50% of the fare.

Prices for the same route vary with organizer. Compare prices — in *St. James's Guide to ABC Flights*, which travel agents have. The move to introduce A.B.C.s into Europe is opposed by some tour operators. The fear is that it will upset the package bandwagon: but it's likely they'll come eventually.

## Youth fares

If you are twenty-four or under you can get special low fares to many destinations. You will be allowed such a fare on production of your passport. But between twenty-one and twenty-four years, you must also produce a letter from an accredited college stating that you are a full-time student.

## Inclusive tours

Otherwise known as package holidays (see page 7). Very good value. The flight plus full board can cost less than the scheduled flight.

## Charter flights

You can buy only the flight — or a package of flight and accommodation made up individually for you; or a charter can be organized as part of a package holiday.

## Group 3 fares

These apply to journeys to Spain and Portugal only. You must book at least fourteen days before travelling. There must be at least three travelling: a child can count as the third, but pays as much. It's still often cheaper than two ordinary excursion fares. You must stay between one and seven weeks and return on the same day of the week as you went.

## Laker Skytrain

Since 1972 Laker Air Travel Ltd have been ready to start the Skytrain service between London and New York. In February 1977 they finally had clearance to go ahead from the British government. American approval was granted in June 1977 and the service commenced on 26 September. There is no advance booking; tickets go on sale six hours before the flight. Skytrain operates from Stansted airport in this country and from J.F.K. airport in New York. Single fare for the U.K.–U.S.A. trip is £59, with the return costing $135. This does not include meals, drinks and the film, although these can be purchased at a small additional cost. Every week during the summer period (1 April to 30 September) there are eleven flights in each direction. During the winter period (1 October to 31 March) one flight leaves every day both ways.

## Airtaxis

Chartering your own plane sounds strictly for film stars and business tycoons. Well it isn't cheap but it can be cheaper than the scheduled air fare for a group of people travelling together. For example, in 1976 the scheduled return fare to Brussels was £71: a six-seater Navajo to Brussels and back in a day costs £260. If six people had to go to a one-day business meeting, chartering a Navajo would save £166 over the scheduled fare. Another advantage is that small planes can land at many small airports: 300 odd in the U.K., 500 in France, 300 in Germany. No major U.K. city is more than seven miles from an airtaxi airport. They wait for you rather than you rushing for them. You can arrive and take off within five minutes. The main disadvantage is that small planes get buffeted by the wind so you may have a bumpy ride, and it may be more cramped.

**The Air Taxi Operators Association** comprises fifty-eight British companies operating a combined fleet of over 200 aircraft including some two dozen executive jets, 170 propeller planes (all with more than one engine) plus nine helicopters. The aircraft are based at sixty airports in the U.K. and serve 300 or more airports in the U.K. and over 1,500 on the Continent. Some — mostly the jets — fly to the Middle East, Africa and Ireland. Addresses of operators can be obtained from the A.T.O.A. Secretary, Building 52, Stansted Airport, Stansted, Essex; telephone 01-599 1087.

**Safety** There have been only two fatal crashes by A.T.O.A. members in ten years: a good record for a service with a high landing rate. But not all air taxi operators belong to A.T.O.A.

## Airline Users Committee

This was set up in July 1973 by the Civil Aviation Authority to keep an eye on airline practice. Among other things they investigate individual complaints against airlines. Their address is Space House, 43—59 Kingsway, London WC2B 6TE; telephone 01-379 7311.

## The International Air Transport Association (I.A.T.A.)

This is an international trade association for airlines. Most of the big international airlines belong but not the Russian Aeroflot.

I.A.T.A. members aim at a certain amount of standardization. You can buy a ticket from one and it will be valid with another. Fares and rules about tickets are standard. Non-I.A.T.A. airlines do not have interchangeability of tickets. Domestic airlines don't need to belong to I.A.T.A. The flight purchase schemes listed above conform with I.A.T.A. rules.

## Discounted tickets: bucket shops

I.A.T.A. see discounting as an attempt to pay less than the 'appropriate agreed rates'. To you and me that means cheap air tickets: tickets for scheduled flights sold at below government-agreed fares. There are two sorts: tickets sold off by airlines quite legitimately because there is a weak demand (Cosmos 'cheapies' come within that group), and tickets sold to unqualified persons by an airline or its agents. These 'unqualified persons' offer them for sale in what are called 'bucket shops' — often advertising on the back page of *The Times*. Some are reliable, some are fly-by-nights who could make off with your deposit leaving no forwarding address.

A.B.T.A. and I.A.T.A. members are against them. Travellers like cheap prices — but run risks.

If the company advertising cheap flights has been doing so for some years you should be O.K.

Check with the airline that there is a flight at the date and time they offer. Don't pay until you are actually given your ticket.

*Remember:* your ticket will have no validity with other carriers if your journey falls through.

# Chapter 4
# At the Airport

Airports are always several miles from a city centre.

Your ticket will state on it the time by which you are required to have arrived and checked-in at the airport. Most travel agencies, on issuing tickets, will also indicate by what earlier time you should be at the city airline terminal if you wish to catch the airline bus to the airport. The cost of this coach ride will not be included in any fare already paid. In foreign countries you should expect to pay the fare to and from airports in their currency.

If you decide to go to the airport by taxi, agree the price first. It is usually a standard rate. In Britain you can find out what the standard charge is, then book in advance and agree the charge. If you're abroad inquire of the hotel porter what the standard charge is, and book in good time. If the porter's in cahoots with the taxis to up the price, there's not much you can do. If it's more than you can afford you could simply take the taxi to the air terminal: it's your responsibility to have its address.

If friends give you a lift to a large international airport to see you off, and drop you and your luggage at the terminal while they go off to park, make very specific arrangements about where and when you will see them next. Some airports − e.g. Heathrow − are huge warrens and a nearby car park may be full: the other car parks may be some distance from the terminal. They will certainly be away twenty minutes. Don't leave cars unattended outside terminals: the police are empowered to tow them away.

On walking into an airport the human animal is bombarded with information. First, visually: there are signs everywhere of all designs and colours, indicating airport facilities, flight schedules, shop fronts, banks, postal services etc. Secondly, orally: the public-address system will call departing flights, and repeat calling until that flight is closed. In foreign languages this is a nightmare: and if their alphabet is different from ours the signs mean nothing − not even sounds. Here are some obvious but important hints.

Arrive in plenty of time − businessmen on their own who are familiar with the routine can cut things fine. Being with someone else always slows you down, if with children even slower.

Memorize the number of your flight. Locate the departure board. Check your flight on it. It will say if there's a major delay.

Concentrate on the journey. This is not really the time to buy last-minute presents, exchange gossip or money, or treat the children to ice creams. Only do all or any of these if you have flight plans truly in hand.

If you go off to eat or shop − keep listening. I missed a flight call to Milan because I was gossiping over coffee in the restaurant. It took me twenty-four hours to catch up. Likewise, if you're on your own and waiting, don't get deeply into a good book or engrossed in a phone call. Keep the main track of your concentration on the journey.

Go through passport formalities and boarding routines when they are called. There's no need to rush or panic. Indeed, people who do are the most irritating co-travellers. But there's no reason to linger, so don't.

## Checking-in

You present yourself, your luggage and tickets at the counter of the airline where your specific flight destination and number are indicated. At this point you present your ticket.

Your luggage is weighed, labelled and handed over. Even if your journey

involves changing airlines, your baggage is booked through to your final
destination. Airlines accept only limited liability for lost or damaged
baggage. This may not cover their full value. Have extra insurance to
cover extra value (see p. 174). Carry personal valuables — camera,
jewellery — in your hand luggage.

Some airlines assign seat numbers on some flights. If so they usually have
a display plan of the plane and the earlier you are there the more choice
you get. You can choose a non-smoking area, or a window or an aisle. If
all the family want to sit together explain at check-in and you will get seat
places accordingly. If there is no seat allocation and you especially want
to sit with a child or children explain this now. Most airlines try to give
consideration to children — which is more than can be said of passengers!
I've seen an air stewardess ask of a crowded flight whether anyone would
volunteer to move so that a mother and child could sit together — and not
one of the 120 or so passengers has budged! So mothers be warned: start
insisting early — but gently — that you wish to sit with your child.

**Exceptions** To simplify procedures B.A. dispense with checking-in on
European flights from London Heathrow, Terminal I. In this case you
go straight to the gate. The indicator board in the departure area will tell
you which. You carry your own luggage, of course, and check in at the
airplane's side. This is ideal for day or weekend trips when you haven't
large cases. It will save lots of time at the other end.

## Overbooking

There is no such thing as a 100% firm booking on scheduled flights.
Apparently a deliberate overbooking policy is an economic necessity for
airlines — of every 100 tickets sold, only eighty turn into passengers. This
means that passengers who have booked, paid and confirmed a particular flight can be refused that flight because when it is overbooked and
everyone turns up they are 'bumped'. Exactly who gets bumped is up to
the 'station officer' in charge at the time. He has to decide who to put off.
The highest fare payers are usually given first choice: cut-price passengers of any sort will be off-loaded first. The date of ticket pur-
chase/flight confirmation might pull some weight. Personally I doubt if a
woman travelling with very small children would be bumped.

**How to avoid being 'bumped'** You can't absolutely. But by booking
early and arriving early and paying the scheduled fare you give yourself a
good start. Once the plane is boarded, late-comers, however good their
claim to a flight, might find other passengers unwilling to give up their
seat. In such circumstances the station officer cannot order you off the
plane.

**Once 'bumped'** If you've been bumped from one flight the airline must offer you a guaranteed seat on the next available flight, plus complimentary meals, accommodation and message facilities when they are appropriate. Do not leave the check-in area until this is all arranged; the more vocal your complaints the harder they'll work to get rid of you. But if you do have to hang around the airport for hours, you can claim a meal and, if overnight, a hotel room.

**Compensation: £10–£100** In the U.S.A. a compensation scheme for people denied boarding is compulsory. In Britain it is voluntarily agreed by B.A. They hedge the offer round with a number of conditions. For example at the moment it applies only to flights *from* the U.K., not to flights *into* the U.K., even if on a U.K. airline.

## Passport control

This is the next official stage. Before you go through is the time to buy newspapers and magazines, change money, post letters and cards, say goodbye to friends or, if you're in good time, have a meal. Going through passport control means you show the document to an official who gives you a looking over — he may ask you to remove a hat and sunglasses. There are always two queues — one for nationals of the country you're leaving, the other for foreigners. If you are leaving a country with rigid currency restrictions — e.g. Russia — you will have to declare how much of their currency you are taking with you. You may be asked to produce receipts for all the travellers cheques you have cashed.

## Customs control

British customs will check that you are not taking more than £25 in banknotes, or more than about £2 in coinage.

## Security checks

These are now universal at major international airports, and also on some domestic flights, e.g. flights to and from Northern and Southern Ireland. They are the most stringent in the world at Lod airport in Israel where even lipsticks will be looked into. So don't take anything that would make you blush if it were spread out on a counter for inspection!

Your handbag and hand luggage will be examined, even X-rayed. This is where packing methodically in layers will help (see page 224). You may be given a body search: women search women, men search men. I have seen a plastic toy machine gun — looking very lifelike — taken from a passenger's luggage. Searching is brisk and efficient, and though they investigate all your personal bumps and bulges, they manage to do it without it getting pornographic.

Security checks have added about forty-five minutes onto airport procedures. They are likely to be with us for the foreseeable future. For every hijacker who gets a gun through, we can expect the inspections to get more and more rigorous. At least I hope we can!

## Duty-free shops

These are supermarkets, situated beyond passport control. So you can only shop there if you are departing and have a ticket or boarding card to prove it. Here you can buy cheap goods. Most people buy duty-free when returning to Britain. You must observe the duty-free limits: beyond those limits you pay tax. But it's also worth buying duty-free going out of the country, if for example you're having two weeks holiday in a Mediterranean hotel, when drinks at the bar will be a pricey extra. Take a bottle each with you − set up your own bar in your hotel room. You'll be sipping sundowners from the tooth-mugs on your own balcony at much less cost. (But don't dilute with the local tap-water unless you know it's drinkable. Personally I still prefer not to. I go without ice for the same reason. Some of the local mineral waters are mild enough to add to whisky.)

## Boarding

When the flight is called you walk to the designated gate and then either take a brief coach trip to the steps of the plane or walk down long corridors to the plane door, where there is usually another wait. This long walk gets burdensome if your in-flight luggage is heavy. On board you find your seat and strap yourself in. You have survived the airport obstacle course!

## Delays

The spectre of a delay at an airport haunts every traveller. It is really bad news. Major causes are weather − either where you are or where you're going − and industrial action by airline or airport personnel − again in Britain or at your destination.

**Turn up** If you know delays are happening (the biggest usually make the headlines, often with pictures of airports cluttered with despairing passengers) you can phone first and ask about the situation. You may be told how long the delay is expected to be. But such an estimate is speculative. You can then decide to stay at home and wait. But if things suddenly clear, and the plane leaves without you, it's your fault. So basically − turn up at the airport.

**Resign yourself** Your own attitude will then determine how bearable the wait is. Do *not* harangue the airport staff. It's not their fault and they are usually doing as much as they can in a nightmare situation. If they seem to you calm almost to the point of indifference, it's because it's the only way they can live under such pressure. There are likely to be hundreds of other disgruntled holiday-makers like yourself. If the airport staff lost their composure they'd have ulcers and nervous breakdowns after just one week of what Gatwick was like in summer 76. So control your temper and anxiety. Add an hour to the predicted delay — and resign yourself. Only then can you think about coping with the hours of waiting.

**Food** The airline is not legally responsible for any expenses incurred because of the delay. But it may — for the good of its reputation — pay for meals and accommodation for its delayed passengers: this is generally the case for travellers on scheduled flights, who may be found rooms in local airport hotels.

On package holidays — already whittled down to the cheapest margins of cost — you cannot necessarily expect the tour operator to pay for a meal. Some do and some don't. On a flight to Palma from Luton in 1976, due to depart at 21.00, there was a seven-hour delay. One hundred passengers were given free tickets to a disco with a licensed bar in the airport spectators' building, with mini-buses to take them there. There is no record of how sober they were for the flight!

**Don't go through passport control** Beyond passport control is the area that gets most crowded and has fewer facilities. Stay outside the passport barrier and in big airports you will have more choice of eating places, magazine stalls, etc.

**Stay tuned** Do not switch off your attention to announcements. Do not get deep into a good book and lost to the airport world. Light reading, crosswords, liar dice, a drink in the bar — there's not much else to turn to.

**Children** If you expect delays and are taking small children then prepare for it. You'll know best what you need — extra disposable nappies, a bottle of feed, a couple of tins of baby food (take ones that can be eaten cold, the restaurant will be overcrowded too). Toddlers are the hardest to keep amused: take a simple jigsaw, a sucking blanket, a favourite book or toy, something familiar to them. Thankfully, children love playing the same game over and over — it's *you* who'll be screaming.

**Nurseries** Some of the biggest airports have nurseries. Heathrow has one for both Terminal 1 and Terminal 2. They are staffed by trained children's nurses and babies can be fed or changed there. Children up to the age of eight can use the play area. The service is free.

Terminal 3 at Heathrow has an unstaffed nursing mother's room, open from 08.00 to 20.00. Ask airline staff if you need it at night.

Gatwick has two — one in the arrivals hall, one in the departure lounge — Stansted and Prestwick each have one. If you anticipate a delay, ask the airline you're travelling with, what nursery facilities exist at departure, transit and arrival airports.

## Flying in

Basically the departure routine in reverse, but not necessarily in total: disembarking, passport control, baggage collection, customs, getting away.

### Disembarking

You can tell the most experienced travellers — they sit back and wait while the newcomers jump up, collect together their luggage and duty-frees — and then queue to get off. You may be on the ground but you're still a long way from arrival. At Heathrow you can have 250 yards to walk, if your plane comes in at a remote gate. There are rarely trolleys for hand luggage, so this is a tricky moment — especially for elderly people loaded with duty-frees.

### Passport control

Again divided into ours and foreigners. Transit passengers don't need to go through this: signs should indicate which direction they take. If you're entering a foreign country you might get your passport stamped, but sadly the tradition is dying out. The official will collect the form you filled in on the plane. What do they do with them all? Apparently if you overstay, get in trouble or take a job they feel they're already on your trail. At least it gives them a place to start. Otherwise, presumably they simply swell the statistics of how many came and how often to wherever.

### Baggage collection

At many airports this is still the big hiccup in your journey. For some reason flights seem to arrive at airports in bunches — so that baggage-handling facilities are stretched to the limit — and only hours later there'll be nothing to handle at all. Heathrow's Terminal 3 is a notorious black spot, the average waiting time there in 1976 was forty-eight minutes. At Heathrow on a bad day at Terminal 1 you can wait as long as it took you to fly. Baggage delay is the complaint registered most often by people who answered an airport questionnaire.

Eventually your luggage will appear on a conveyor belt or a carousel. Check it's yours: not identical but someone else's. If you take the wrong case in error you are legally bound to pay the full cost of getting it back to the owner, and getting your own back (which is what he'll feel he's doing).

*Lost luggage* If your baggage doesn't emerge, tell the airline at once. Don't panic yet. Most lost baggage is mislaid: it may have got left behind or gone to the wrong destination. This is not a rare and disastrous happening. I'm afraid it's quite common. And at least that means airlines have well-practised procedures for getting mislaid luggage to where it should be (see Emergencies p. 265). In some cases you can demand that the airline bring the suitcase to you. In Australia, one of our cases went astray and came in on a flight two hours later. We didn't hang around. They sent it by taxi to our hotel. Most airlines will take the responsibility of getting it to you.

Each B.B.C. film crew carries with it some twenty pieces of equipment: often awkward shapes and sizes and thoroughly labelled. You'd think no one could miss them. Yet it is almost routine for one of those pieces to go astray.

If you want to save yourself ulcers, you couldn't do better than copy the laconic resignation with which any hardy cameraman greets news of a loss — and somehow the stray always catches up.

If your case is irretrievably lost, then the airline must meet your claim. Moan and groan about all the inconvenience and they may give you a small cash advance for immediate needs. Now's the time you'll be glad you carried minimum toiletries and things in your hand luggage.

## Customs

If you're entering for a holiday or business most countries don't concern themselves with what you bring. Some do. In Russia, for example, you will be asked about currency and issued with a statement of how much you are bringing in. You must keep this and present it on departure together with receipts from the cashing of travellers cheques and any cheques and cash left over.

Details of the stringency of currency control should be checked with your bank or travel agent before you go.

## Getting away

*Porters* They're getting hard to find. In many European countries you pay a fixed amount per case, and there is no obligation to pay any more. But most travellers do add a little extra. Porter service at London airport, for example, is basically free of charge. But it is still customary to tip.

*Buses* Most airports run coaches regularly to the centre of their city. You must pay in local currency — so if you aren't already carrying any, cash a travellers cheque now.

*Taxis* Usually there is a going rate. But if you're a stranger in a strange land you're not to know that. You'll have to pay what he asks or go by bus. At least agree the amount before setting off. If it seems extortionate,

you can brush off the idea and head for the bus. The taxi driver may catch up and haggle. But don't bank on it. This is when you're at their mercy and so pay up cheerfully. You can't be uptight all the time.
Going rates in 1977 in Britain vary. Here are some:

Heathrow to Central London: about £7.50.
Gatwick going anywhere: there's a twenty-four-hour taxi desk at the international arrivals hall – rate 42p per mile.
Stansted to the nearest railway station, Bishop's Stortford: about £1.00.
Edinburgh to the centre: £2.20.
Glasgow to the centre: £2.00 (about).
Prestwick to Prestwick station: 35p.
Prestwick to the Turnberry Hotel (23 miles): £5.25.
Aberdeen: recommended fares given at the information desk.
Manchester to the centre: £3.00.

There's a full checklist of airport/city-centre prices (U.K. and abroad) in the complete B.A. timetable. All travel agents have them: for reference, not for sale.

*Hotels* Most international airports have hotel bookings desks where you can explain the accommodation you need and have it found for you before you leave the airport.

## International airport signs

You'd think it a simple matter to standardize airport signs. Apparently not: there are currently four manuals of differing pictograms. The International Civil Aviation Organization is trying to sort them out but it will take a while yet.

## Hiring a car

See page 62.

# Chapter 5
# In Flight

## Meals

Do not expect a meal as of right. On short flights the most is coffee and biscuits. First class you get meals and drinks free. In tourist class the drinks are at normal prices on U.K. internal flights and at duty-free prices on international flights.

You can find out about meals in advance (see p.227).

Nothing is provided on the London—Edinburgh shuttle: not even a drink. There are vending machines at the airports.

## Diets

Most airlines in the world will be able to provide a range of special diets. Many like to be notified when you book your ticket. Others will make arrangements if you notify them within twenty-four hours: check when you first make enquiries.

British Airways, typical of the major international airlines, offers the following alternatives: kosher Jewish, Kedassia Jewish, vegetarian, Asian vegetarian, Hindu, diabetic diet, fat-free diet, Gluten-free diet, low calorie, Muslim, gastric diet for ulcer sufferers, salt free, seafood.

Smaller airlines will have a shorter list. If the matter is crucial ask in advance.

El Al maintains its own kosher kitchens at London airport. But flying from the Far East to London, you might find a kosher meal difficult to order. Advise the airline you're flying and if they're coming from somewhere with kosher kitchens they can bring it out with them.

Some — not all — Arab airlines provide kosher food for their Jewish passengers. Orthodox Jewish tourists visiting Arab countries would certainly have problems in keeping the strict dietary rules.

**Alcohol** Most Arab airlines carry liquor. But Saudi Arabian Airlines is decidedly dry. You can take your own drink on board, but you are not allowed to take it into the country. So if you take a bottle you either drink the lot and arrive thoroughly drunk, or hand it over as you go in.

## British Airways Junior Jet Club

Children must be the most enthusiastic flyers. Apart from the Concorde there's little to excite a regular and jaded adult traveller. Children stay keen, watch and remember every detail of their flight.

B.A. attempt to harness this enthusiasm with their Junior Jet Club. You have to fly with their overseas division — that means outside Europe — then you get a membership badge, a personalized card and log-book in which the captain of their next flight enters the miles flown. After every 25,000 miles they get a mileage certificate. They also receive an annual magazine — *Fleetwings*.

I also happen to know that B.A. pilots are all nice chaps and if they hear there are youngsters on board will allow them in the cockpit to gaze at the gadgetry. Ask a stewardess if your child's keen. School parties are discouraged: too many to cope with.

## Killing the time

The boredom of flying is colossal. But it's surprising what people get up to, to kill the time. The following is a selection of suggestions from friends and established travellers.

**Get drunk** Personally, it's sometimes a side effect of trying to calm my flying nerves. A large brandy as soon as possible — then wine with the meal.

**Sleep** A friend of mine takes a whacking sedative, then a slug of whisky and nods away the hours. He doesn't recommend it for short hops — or you're lolling to sleep as the coach roars into Paris.

**Work** You'll need to choose a window seat, so you and your papers won't be disturbed, and you must have leg-room and a briefcase with a flat hard surface to write on. The smallest portable typewriter will just fit on the table in front.

You can carry a miniature tape recorder for dictating letters. Do your V.A.T. on a pocket calculator, review books, write speeches. There's no need to regard it as wasted time. But don't make big and final decisions — your equilibrium's disturbed and you're not yourself.

**Relax** This helps fight flight fears too. Don't just sit there — flex something. The following are a few simple exercises suggested by Marjorie Craig, Exercise Director of Elizabeth Arden: (1) Remove your shoes, place your heels on the floor, grip your toes, pull them in towards each other, up towards your knees and relax. Repeat several times. (2) Wiggling toes and gripping hands and extending fingers helps increase circulation. (3) Sit with your head relaxed, then drop your chin onto your chest and slowly move your head to the extreme left, then up, round to the right and back, in a circular movement. This relaxes your back muscles and relieves tension. (4) Take each foot at a time, extend it all full stretch, and circle slowly first in clockwise then anticlockwise direction. Do any or all of these when you are sitting with friends or next to empty seats. Other passengers might be embarrassed!

**Make love** If you make it at over 30,000 feet you qualify for membership of the apocryphal Six-Mile High Club. There's no subscription, it's simply a contemporary myth. Ideally you need a long flight, plenty of empty seats, dimmed cabin lighting and extra rugs from the stewardess. People have been arrested in mid-air for indecent behaviour — but at least it doesn't frighten the horses!

**Gossip** The altitude, the excitement, the drink, all make the tongue wag. I find people confide their private lives, bitch about enemies, tittle-tattle about friends, swop gossip about sex, dish the dirt about office politics far more uninhibitedly at 30,000 feet. It's seen me through many a boring flight. But there has to be tacit agreement that once we've all got our feet on the ground, mum's the word.

**Play games** If mere gossip fails, try crosswords, liar dice, or simply cards. If you intend a serious poker game or hand of whist, four of you will need to ask for the set of four seats facing each other. Fix it with the stewardess before you board: other passengers can be awkward about changing once they've settled in.

## Physical discomfort

Modern airliners are pressurized so you won't notice any major physical strain. However, you may experience a slight pressure on your ears, particularly during descent for landing. If so, try swallowing, pinching your nostrils and blowing. If you have a heavy head cold, tell one of the cabin staff. Babies will probably cry at the sensation: don't hush them up, it will help to clear their ears. They, and young children can be given something to suck. Sometimes stewardesses hand round boiled sweets just before the descent: they serve the same purpose.

You'll get temporary strange feelings during abnormal accelerations, when the aircraft is increasing speed or falling through an air pocket, for example. On Concorde, apparently, you feel the surge of power as you go supersonic in the pit of your stomach. The pressurizing of the average cabin gives you oxygen for normal breathing but the air may be a bit thinner than you're used to, and drier too. So wear loose-fitting clothing, nothing very tight round the waist. Shoes should be comfortably roomy. Men should wear thin socks. On a long distance flight you'll find it comfortable to change into slippers. Your legs will probably swell. Don't worry, you'll be back to normal within twelve hours. Try to drink plenty of fluid: air hostesses are advised to take a pint of water every hour. Medical advice is always to avoid fizzy drinks and too much alcohol. I agree in principle. But there's no denying alcohol can keep away fear and boredom.

For the same reason — aircraft pressurization — heavy smokers should try to keep their rate of smoking down.

## Airsickness

Prevention is better than cure so take preventive tablets in good time. However, if you're pregnant, or think you could be, then check with a doctor which medicines are safe.

In flight keep your head firmly against the head rest. Try to keep your eye on the distant unwavering horizon. Airlines usually provide a paper bag in readiness. However, not many suffer: only 1 in 1,000.

## Fear of flying

Believe me, I'm an expert! If Primitive Man's response to fear is flight:
Sensitive Man's response to flight is fear. I know every tweak of anguish,
every gulp of apprehension it is possible to feel at any point in flight. I
persist in flying because I know my fears are irrational — it's no comfort
to be told it's more dangerous driving to work — because on the whole I
haven't come to much harm yet (though wear and tear on the nerves and
heart must be registering somewhere) and because my job requires it.
So to calm you and myself down I went in search of consoling expertise to
two British Airways pilots. This is what they told me about the things
that frighten travellers.

**Sounds** The sequence of engine manoeuvres and consequent sound
changes are basically the same for all planes from Tiger Moths to
Tri-Stars. But changes in engine sound, if unexplained, can be alarming.
So here is what should happen.

There is a very loud crescendo of noise as the power is applied for
take-off. As the plane's nose is lifted from the ground this continues. Next
there is a mechanical clunk as the wheels and undercarriage fold away.
Shortly after take-off the noise reduces in force as there is a reduction in
power to bring engines back to a climb setting and because there may be
certain noise abatement procedures to observe. This is particularly vivid
on the Concorde which throttles back so dramatically you think you're
going to fall out of the sky. It does *not* mean you have had an unin-
tentional loss of power and can't manage the climb. There is another
small reduction in noise as the plane finishes its climb and levels off at its
cruising height.

Variations in engine noise and tone are greatest on the final approach,
because descent is a careful balance between engine-power reduction, to
lose altitude, and engine power being maintained to sustain level flight.
Air brakes may be applied to aid the descent — that's probably when you
feel a tendency to slide forward in your seat. The undercarriage is then
lowered: that clunking sound again. And as the wheels touch the ground
there is a sudden huge burst of sound as the engine goes into reverse to
bring the plane to a halt. The only sound then is the whispered sigh of a
hundred passengers at having touched down safely.

**Bumpiness** The first 20,000 feet are the worst: that's where the most
disturbed air currents are, where airflow rising from the ground, from
buildings, from mountains can joggle any plane — large or small — that
flies into it. The effect of bumpiness is, therefore, all tied up with heat
changes and air currents, which can be local, short-wave turbulence, or
more extensive long-wave turbulence. Going through cloud is simply the
most obvious situation in which to expect a few bumps.

T.C.T.—D

It is also possible flying at 30,000 feet to run into a patch of clear-air turbulence which can keep the plane bumping along — like driving a high-performance car over a cobbled street: they call it 'cobblestoning'. You may run into bumpiness as the plane crosses from a land mass to a sea mass — but not necessarily so. Over mountains? Yes — it's more likely. As the air hits mountains it will be turned upwards. If you're flying through that air mass, you'll go up and down with it. There's also a condition downstream of mountains, called mountain waves — these are long-term disturbance waves. If they're predicted in the general meteorological report for that area then the pilot will fly a couple of thousand feet higher to avoid them. Otherwise, there might be some rather spectacular ups and downs. Nothing to worry about mechanically: the most disturbing thing is the discomfort to passengers.

**Thunderstorms** It's often claimed that modern jets fly 'above the weather'. Quite often 30,000 feet *is* high enough to be above the weather, but not always. You can have storms up to a height of 45,000 feet even in Europe. You can only be sure of being above the weather in Concorde. So what about storms? One of the B.A. pilots said: 'I don't think any pilot with malice aforethought would fly into a thunderstorm, simply because it's uncomfortable and less safe than staying out. We would be able to identify and locate thunderstorms on our radar and fly round them. It's possible, if a storm is low to fly above it perfectly smoothly.'

However, if it so happens that the plane gets into the heart of a thunderstorm, it's likely to be very noisy, with a lot of blinding bright light. But, they explained very painstakingly, 'An airplane is an example of Faraday's cage. You can entirely surround someone with metal all electrically connected up, and then hurl a lightning strike at them — they won't get hurt.' Much trouble is taken to electrically bond surfaces, and the plane is fitted with wicks on both wings and tail, so if there is an electrical charge on it, it dissipates out through the wicks. So scientifically you're all right, but you won't like the experience. Neither do pilots — 'We go to a lot of trouble to avoid storms.'

## Collisions and crashes

The International Civil Aviation Organization gives the accident figures shown in the table below (the figures include Russia but not China):

|      | Accidents | Deaths |
|------|-----------|--------|
| 1970 | 30        | 786    |
| 1971 | 33        | 975    |
| 1972 | 44        | 1,402  |
| 1973 | 39        | 960    |
| 1974 | 30        | 1,411  |
| 1975 | 21        | 473    |

*The Sunday Times* compiled a 'twenty-five-year safety league' in 1976, and this is shown in the following table.

## Better than world average

| Airline | Nationality | Passengers flown (millions) | Passengers killed | Fatal crashes | 'Expected' crashes based on world ave. | Fatal crash record compared with world ave. |
|---|---|---|---|---|---|---|
| Delta | USA | 194 | 99 | 2 | 18 | 9x better |
| Qantas* | Australia | 10 | 6 | 1 | 6 | 6x better |
| JAL | Japan | 66 | 125 | 2 | 10 | 5x better |
| American | USA | 288 | 288 | 9 | 35 | 4x better |
| British Caledonian | UK | 21 | 101 | 1 | 4 | 4x better |
| Continental* | USA | 57 | 42 | 2 | 7 | 3x better |
| United | USA | 347 | 574 | 15 | 45 | 3x better |
| Eastern | USA | 324 | 389 | 9 | 29 | 3x better |
| Lufthansa | W. Germany | 67 | 126 | 3 | 8 | 3x better |
| TWA | USA | 203 | 623 | 15 | 35 | 2x better |
| Pan Am | USA | 139 | 557 | 14 | 31 | 2x better |
| SAS | Sweden | 69 | 54 | 3 | 7 | 2x better |
| Air Canada | Canada | 110 | 305 | 8 | 14 | 2x better |
| Swissair | Switzerland | 52 | 115 | 3 | 5 | 2x better |

## Airlines close to world average

| Airline | Nationality | Passengers flown (millions) | Passengers killed | Fatal crashes | 'Expected' crashes based on world ave. | |
|---|---|---|---|---|---|---|
| National | USA | 72 | 139 | 6 | 8 | |
| Braniff | USA | 87 | 185 | 6 | 8 | |
| Alitalia | Italy | 60 | 293 | 7 | 8 | |
| KLM | Holland | 38 | 274 | 7 | 8 | |
| British Airways | UK | 155 | 691 | 21 | 21 | |
| Northwest* | USA | 90 | 357 | 13 | 12 | |
| All Nippon | Japan | 79 | 358 | 5 | 5 | |
| SAA | South Africa | 19 | 158 | 4 | 3 | |

## Worse than world average

| Airline | Nationality | Passengers flown (millions) | Passengers killed | Fatal crashes | 'Expected' crashes based on world ave. | Fatal crash record compared with world ave. |
|---|---|---|---|---|---|---|
| Air France | France | 91 | 829 | 19 | 14 | 1½x worse |
| Iberia | Spain | 66 | 317 | 9 | 6 | 1½x worse |
| CP Air | Canada | 17 | 168 | 6 | 4 | 1½x worse |
| Varig | Brazil | 24 | 294 | 5 | 3 | 1½x worse |
| Allegheny | USA | 67 | 152 | 5 | 3 | 1½x worse |
| Sabena | Belgium | 23 | 193 | 7 | 4 | 2x worse |
| Mexicana | Mexico | 27 | 124 | 5 | 2 | 3x worse |

**Worse than world average** (continued)

| Airline | Nationality | Passengers flown (millions) | Passengers killed | Fatal crashes | 'Expected' crashes based on world ave. | Fatal crash record compared with world ave. |
|---------|-------------|------------------------------|-------------------|---------------|-----------------------------------------|----------------------------------------------|
| PIA | Pakistan | 13 | 218 | 7 | 2 | 4x worse |
| Aer Arg | Argentina | 17 | 282 | 12 | 2 | 5x worse |
| LOT | Poland | 12 | 95 | 4 | 1 | 6x worse |
| Garuda | Indonesia | 13 | 130 | 7 | 1 | 6x worse |
| Avianca | Colombia | 35 | 310 | 16 | 2 | 8x worse |
| Cubana | Cuba | 11 | 104 | 6 | 1 | 9x worse |
| JAT | Yugoslavia | 14 | 92 | 7 | 1 | 9x worse |
| CSA | Czechoslovakia | 19 | 212 | 10 | 1 | 9x worse |
| IAC | India | 29 | 322 | 19 | 2 | 9x worse |
| Cruzeiro | Brazil | 15 | 146 | 11 | 1 | 10x worse |
| THY | Turkey | 16 | 473 | 10 | 1 | 11x worse |
| PAL | Philippines | 24 | 254 | 17 | 2 | 11x worse |
| Egyptair | Egypt | 7 | 328 | 13 | 1 | 13x worse |
| Aviaco | Spain | 11 | 166 | 7 | 0 | 17x worse |
| Tarom | Romania | 7 | 173 | 8 | 0 | 20x worse |

*No crash since January 1966

Britain and northwest Europe are covered by secondary radar which identifies airliners and gives controllers their height. Systems in some African countries are much less comprehensive. All major international airports now have air radar. Ground radar is another matter.

B.A. statistician Charles Smith has computed from 1973 figures that if someone makes ten trips a year, all 12,500 miles each, he could expect to go for 38,000 years without a fatal accident. If he flew 600 hours a year then his chances would be one fatal crash every 990 years on I.A.T.A. services, or one in 260 years on non-I.A.T.A. scheduled flights. (I.A.T.A., the International Air Transport Association, is a trade association to which nearly all international airlines belong.)

## Mid-air collisions

If air traffic is on the increase, does this increase the risk of mid-air collisions? The 1975 disaster over Zagreb — a very busy airway — gave rise to much concern. At the trial that resulted, a good deal of blame was placed on the use by Yugoslavian air traffic control of Serbo-Croat rather than English. In the same airspace some six weeks later, another 'near miss' avoided collision because English was spoken. Some slight discomfort there, and also in the fact that the increase in air travel is accounted for by bigger planes carrying more passengers each, rather than a straight increase in the number of planes.

## Air traffic control

Each country has its own ground network responsible for all air movements in its airspace. U.K. airspace is regulated from Prestwick, West Drayton and Preston. Airlanes are some ten miles wide and five miles deep. Pilots report air misses to the joint air miss section which categorizes them according to degree of danger that was involved. The statistics are published in the aviation press. In 1974, air movements (civil and military) in U.K. airspace totalled $5^{1}/2$ million and there were fourteen category A (most dangerous) air misses. In 1973 the number had been twenty-two category A, out of 5,680,000 air movements. In 1975 the number was nineteen. That's the degree of risk over the U.K.

## Ground collisions

The 1977 runway collision at Tenerife was the biggest accident in aviation history: the official death toll was 576. How could it happen? It is by no means common for airports to have ground radar. America has twenty or thirty valve radar systems that were installed twenty or so years ago. But the most advanced system – AS.M1 – is made by Decca Radar Ltd in Great Britain and is very expensive: from £200,000. At the moment it is installed only at Heathrow, Orly (Paris), and at two Rome airports. Turin and Milan have Decca systems not yet operational. Zurich and Schipol (Amsterdam) have their own non-Decca systems. Since the Tenerife disaster concern about ground radar has increased. Decca have been receiving more and more enquiries. Ground radar should be a 'must' at the world's busiest airports.

## Fog

Most airports are equipped to deal with planes landing and taking off in category 2 fog – that means visibility between 800 and 400 metres (875 to 437 yards).

It's quite a normal manoeuvre for a plane landing in fog to come in low over the runway on a trial run, and if the fog proves too bad to decide to pull out of it at the last minute. This means a sudden acceleration and climb just as the passengers are expecting to touch down. It's alarming, if you are not expecting it.

The best facilities for flying in fog are on B.A.'s Tridents between Heathrow, Charles de Gaulle in Paris and Glasgow. These planes and airports are the only ones equipped to handle landing automatically in *total* fog.

## Hijacking

Naturally you do exactly as the captain tells you throughout. The captain is the person in charge of the plane. Even when it is hijacked he is still in charge of the passengers. Obey him: don't try any heroics. Once a plane is hijacked, the country of origin sets up an emergency unit and sends someone to be in the control tower where negotiations are proceeding. They will have passenger lists, and inform your relatives. There's no action for you to take.

A journalist who was hijacked over America told me she was not conscious at the time of being afraid, but pulling out her notepad to take down the story as it happened, she found she'd lost the capacity to write. There was much smoking, long queues for the loo, and everyone talking together. She found the most depressing things the wailing and prayers of the more demonstratively religious, and the Vietnam veteran who said he'd rather be back there. The most cheering: the relaxed and friendly student who simply declared: 'Well, I've always wanted to see Cuba!'

# Chapter 6
# Time Zones, the Date Line and Jet Lag

## Earth time

Days and nights are created by the rotating earth going round the sun. The measurement of time has been devised by man and reckoned from the sun's apparent movements. Once it was simple: wherever they were, people got up at sunrise and went to bed at dusk. So man naturally began measuring his time by the sun and moon. Then things got more complicated: along came civilization, clocks and travel. We can tell from the logs of those who first circumnavigated the globe that they knew and accepted the variations in time. Francis Drake, writing on his return, put it thus: 'The 26th of September which was Monday in the just and ordinary reckoning of those that have stayed at home in one place or country, but in our computation was the Lord's Day or Sunday – we safely, with joyful minds and thankful hearts, arrived in Plymouth, the place of our first setting forth.' (*The World in Compass*, published 1628.) He had travelled westward round the world, thereby losing a full twenty-four hours of time. The way to remember it: 'going west, a day goes west'.

In 1884 an international convention was held to standardize the system of measuring the world's time, to introduce the International Date Line and to synchronize, as it were, our global watches. This is how it all works.

The earth rotates on its axis once every twenty-four hours moving from west to east, bringing every part of its surface directly under the sun in the course of that time. So the sun rises earlier in Britain than America, earlier in Sierra Leone than Brazil, earlier in Israel than Spain, earlier in Afghanistan than Turkey, earlier in Australia than in India.

## Same time

At any moment there is a line of places on one side of the earth's surface where the sun is exactly halfway between rising and setting. These are the places ranged along the same line of longitude (also called a meridian from meri-dies, mid-day). They therefore also share exactly the same clock time all day. Thus if you travel either north or south along the same line of longitude, you don't go through any time change at all. So breakfast time in Gor'kiy (44°05′E) in the heart of Russia, Baghdad (44°22′E) in Iraq, and Aden (44°45′E) is, local customs permitting, virtually the same. People sitting down to lunch in Omsk (73°19′E) are sharing their mealtime with the citizens of Lahore (80°00′E) and Delhi (77°14′E). The hour for evening eating in Greenland will be the same as in Nova Scotia, Martinique (60°37′W), Manaus on the Amazon (60°00′W), Buenos Aires (61°45′W) and the Falkland Islands (61°00′W). In terms of travelling this means that a journey from Boston, Massachusetts (71°07′W) to Santiago in Chile (70°40′W) may take an exhausting 16$^{1}/2$ hours, but there will be minimal time change (only one hour) for your body to cope with. Similarly a flight from Capetown (18°28′E) to Stockholm (18°00′E) lasts 22 hours — but you live through each one of them at the normal rate. There's just a one-hour time difference.

## Opposites are easy

Obviously the side of the earth directly under the sun experiences midday at the same time that the point directly opposed to it experiences midnight. So that midday in Britain is midnight in Fiji (175°00′E), midday in Leningrad (30°20′E) is midnight in Tahiti (149°30′W), midday in Philadelphia (75°13′W) is midnight in Hanoi (105°50′E), midday in Shanghai (121°27′E) is midnight in Trinidad (61°12′W). It's what happens in between that gets tricky.

## Time zones

If the sun takes twenty-four hours to go round the earth (sorry, Galileo, it's easier to explain this way!) — that's 360 degrees — then the sun will move across one degree of longitude in four minutes, fifteen degrees in sixty minutes, etc. Thus if you travel either due east or due west through fifteen degrees of longitude then you move one hour out of your original time system. However, we can't all be continually adjusting our watches by two minutes every time we go twenty miles due west. It would make chaos of industry, timetables, broadcasting and life in general. So the 1884 international convention mapped it out for us. They agreed to divide the world's 360-degree girth into twenty-four time zones, each fifteen degrees in width. They drew vertical lines on the map of the world and declared that within each zone the same time would prevail. Each zone would be one hour ahead of the zone to its west and one hour behind the zone to its east. The starting point was to be maintained at Greenwich, London, the designated 0 degree meridian. From then on time zones would be expressed as Greenwich Mean Time plus or minus any number of hours (see chart on p.42−3 ).

## The International Date Line

Clearly if you measure out time in fifteen-degree lots both east and west of Greenwich, something very sticky happens at 180 degrees east and 180 degrees west. They coincide. It's where east and west would meet were one not twenty-four hours ahead of the other for the rendezvous.

If we travel along the equator, starting from the Greenwich meridian at 08.00 on Wednesday, 9 December, and measure out time going eastwards, then we arrive at 179 degrees E to find that the time is 19.56, Wednesday, 9 December. Measuring time westwards from Greenwich we arrive at 179 degrees W at 20.04 on Tuesday, 8 December. Take a further stride of one degree both further east and west and at the spot where you stand (or swim, you're in mid-Pacific) it will be either 20.00 on Wednesday, 9 December, or 20.00 on Tuesday, 8 December.

The convention of 1884 set up the International Date Line running north−south at 180 degrees but with a few bumps to take account of political entities. And it is at this Date Line that the jump occurs. A traveller going east reaches 179 degrees E on Wednesday, but on crossing finds himself back in Tuesday with Wednesday still to come. Travelling westward and reaching 179 degrees W on Tuesday evening he then crosses the Date Line to find it is Wednesday evening, Wednesday having vanished, and the next day is Thursday. Apart from anything else the arrangement allows the human race much scope for jokes about babies conceived on a day that wasn't there, debts, drunkenness and all forms of licence indulged in on a date without record. Even what happens should the last post sound is now an exhausted topic of jest.

## The people problem

Unhappily all wasn't solved with straight lines. This neat and tidy system got spoilt by people. After all, imagine the difficulties if one of the dividing lines happened to pass right down the High Street, putting those on one side perpetually an hour behind the others. Human communities had to be allowed for. Also human politics. If the Date Line can be wiggled to keep the entire Aleutian Islands in the American time zone and the tip of Siberia in the Russian, then the boundaries of time zones could be dented here and there to accommodate other situations.

This is the result: America's four standard time zones set up in 1883 — Eastern, Central, Mountain and Pacific — are the same today. The U.S.S.R. divides into eleven time zones. China is one simple zone: Greenwich Mean Time + 8. Most countries of Continental Europe (not Bulgaria, Greece, Romania, Turkey and U.S.S.R.) are G.M.T. + 1. But Ireland and Iceland are with the U.K. on G.M.T.

## Summer time

Throughout the summer Britain practises daylight saving by moving its clocks forward one hour thus synchronizing us with all the G.M.T. + 1 countries. Which would be fine if they stayed at G.M.T. + 1. However in Europe, Spain, Portugal, Italy and France all have summer-time periods of their own. France's scheme was particularly obtuse in 1976 chiming neither with U.K. summer time nor that of the E.E.C. countries round her. The E.E.C. Commission are now proposing that summer time in Europe should run regularly between agreed dates and should be one hour ahead of each country's winter time. Countries that do not have daylight saving time will not be affected. If you are making rail/air connections in, say, Paris, check timetables carefully.

## Time zone chart

The chart on the following pages shows the system of zones for time-keeping at sea and on land.

*Greenwich Mean Time* To convert zone time to G.M.T., the number of hours as given by the zone number is added to or subtracted from the zone time, e.g. in Zone −4 the time kept is 4 hours in advance of G.M.T. and so at 20.00 local time (2000D) it is 16.00 G.M.T. (1600Z).

*Standard Time (Legal Time)* In most cases Standard Time is that of the zone in which the country mainly lies. Countries having a longitudinal

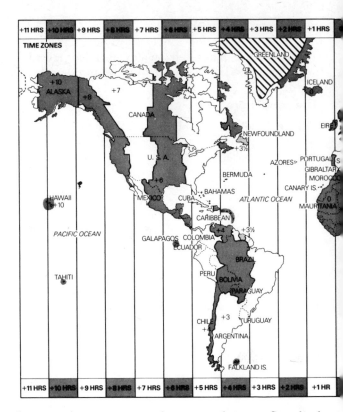

extent greater than one time zone may adopt more than one Standard Time.

Countries having the Standard Time of an even-numbered zone are shown in light grey shading.

Countries having the Standard Time of an odd-numbered zone are unshaded.

Countries in which the Standard Time differs from the zone time by a fraction of an hour are shown in dark grey shading, and those in which Standard Time has not been fixed by law are shown in line shading.

*Daylight Saving Time (Summer Time)* During Daylight Saving Time, introduced to prolong the hours of daylight in the evening, the Standard Time of the zone to the eastward is normally adopted.

*International Date Line* is shown by a dotted line. When crossing the Date Line on an easterly course, assume yesterday's date; and when doing so on a westerly course, assume tomorrow's date. Where Standard Time in the vicinity of the Date Line is described as −13h, it signifies that the clock time is that of Zone +11 but the date is the same as that of the zone west of the Date Line.

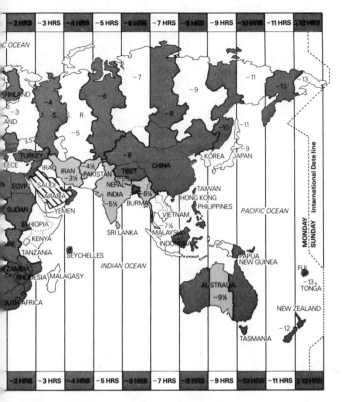

## What happens when you travel

Moving from time zone to time zone doesn't matter if you're sailing with Drake and taking '2 years, 10 months and some few odd days' to get round the world. But when the human body goes from London to New York in 7 hours, 40 minutes then there's a problem. The clash is between the world's clock and your body's.

## Circadian dysrhythmia

That's medical talk for jet lag. The body has its own rhythm — circadian rhythm (circa — around, dies — day) which tells you when to wake, sleep, feel hungry, go to the loo. It plays a major part in deciding whether you're very alert, or at a low ebb, whether you feel moody, exhilarated or sexy. It has a hand in regulating breathing, pulse rate and temperature. The human circadian rhythm beats in time with the earth and the sun, day and night. Muck about with the day and night by rushing across the globe and your own particular circadian rhythm takes time to catch up. So though you arrive physically in a new place your insides are still tuned to back home. It takes some four days to catch up after a major journey westward, six days if you go east.

## Adjusting to jet lag

If you're sensible you'll adjust gradually. A seven-hour flight west will put you right out of joint. Your body will want to go to bed just as your hosts want to take you out to dinner.

You have two choices:

1   Resist the social pressures. Go to bed as early as possible the first night. You'll wake very early next morning. Don't worry: put the time to good use. The second night go to bed an hour later — you'll sleep later too. And so on until your body's back in time.

2   Force yourself to stay up late on your first night, deliberately making yourself very tired so that you will sleep late the next morning. You'll still wake early by the clock; but again stay up the full evening and again, from tiredness, hope your body will oversleep. After several days your body will have caught up. This is the more stressful method, but probably more customary.

# Chapter 7
# Motoring

### Improve your car

It's rare that any car can't be improved in some way. If you face a long journey promise your car an improvement before you go.

### Roadworthiness

This is not any kind of extra: it is a legal requirement and a moral responsibility. A good service is essential. If you're going abroad tell them so. Don't leave it until the week before you leave; it should be carried out a month before you leave to give the car a chance to settle, and spare parts may have to be ordered. Allow time and save worry. Consult a good Continental motoring guide and study it before you go. The A.A.'s is excellent. What follows is taken from their advice on servicing.

**Tyres** If the tread looks likely to be more than three-quarters worn before you get back, better replace them. In some Continental countries drivers can be fined if tyres are badly worn. (Incidentally I've seen touring coaches with smooth tyres: always worth checking.)

**Tubeless tyres** In some Continental countries they're not in general use and may bewilder a garage if you have a puncture. It is a good idea to take an inner tube of the right size and type so it can be fitted if all else fails. When this is inserted, it's wise to put it on the rear axle in case of a blow-out — then drive at moderate speeds only until the tyre's repaired. If you're heading for snow, many authorities insist on wheel chains, spiked or studded tyres or snow tyres. They can be hard to get, so allow plenty of time.

**Warm-climate touring** In hot weather and at high altitudes, excessive heat in the engine compartment can cause vapour lock. If you are touring a caravan consult the manufacturers about the limitations of the cooling system and the operating temperature of the gearbox fluid if automatic transmission is fitted (fit a cooler if necessary).

**Cold-weather touring** Make sure you fit a high-temperature (winter) thermostat, that the plug heads are in good condition, and have really good connections, and that you put in antifreeze before you go. Antifreeze mixtures are normally alcohol or glycol based — know which yours is. If glycol based, carry some reserves as these aren't as common and you may be stranded without. If heading for mountain tops, get the strength of the antifreeze correct for the low temperatures you can expect.

**Mountain touring** If you're heading for mountainous country like the Alps a check on brake fluid is a must. If the fluid has been in the car for eighteen months (twelve if a caravan is towed) it should be changed before you leave. The reason for this being that heat generated under heavy braking can cause the brake fluid to boil away, rendering the brakes useless — a dangerous state of affairs if you're descending an Alp!

**Brakes** It's absolutely crucial to have them thoroughly inspected. If they're more than half worn, and you're going a long way have them renewed. You'll save lives without ever knowing how many. Check your brake fluid.

**Engine and mechanical** Drain and refill with fresh oil and fit a new filter. Deal with any leaks by tightening up loose nuts and bolts and renewing faulty joints or gaskets.

Check valve clearances, sparking plugs and contact-breaking points. Make sure the distributor cap is clean and dry. Check the fan belt for signs of wear. If the signs of wear are just beginning to show on any part take the correct spare with you. The A.A. spares kit covers everything prone to failure, including fuel pumps and bulbs. Your local A.A. office will give you details. Clean all filters — and a well used electric fuel pump should be replaced. The cooling system should be checked for leaks and any perished hoses and rusty clips replaced.

**Electrical** Check throughout, tracing any small fault. You don't want to get lumbered with a flat battery or malfunctioning headlight.

**Lights** Left-dipping headlights are not permitted on the Continent. There are a variety of adaptors you can use: headlamp-beam deflectors may do the job adequately. Or you may need to change the bulbs or even the headlamp units. The French use yellow headlights: but white lights are acceptable everywhere. In Sweden they keep sidelights on through-out the day. It's a legal requirement. Their batteries are adjusted to take the strain. Make sure your own is up to it.

**Dazzle** Don't set your lights with the car empty. It could mean that once it is heavily loaded the lights hit the treetops. So ballast the car, put the tyres up to loaded pressures — then set the lights.

**Vibrations** Vibration from badly balanced wheels can be tiring on a long journey. If noise is a problem put an additional layer of felt under the carpet — better still, get your wheels properly balanced before you leave.

**Spares** The A.A. provide a spares kit and that could save you time. They suggest you also take: a pair of windscreen wipers, a length of electrical cable, an inner tube or correct tyre, a tin of gasket-sealing compound, a roll of insulating or other adhesive tape, first-aid kit, car compass, warning triangle, documents in their own wallet, emergency lamp (flasher unit), a tin of radiator-sealing compound, a fire extin-guisher, a tow rope, temporary windscreen, tyre-pressure gauge, hose, fan belt, bulbs, fuses, distributor cap, fuel-pump kit.

Pack all the compact things in a grocer's cardboard box and keep it permanently in the boot. Then you only need to check it out for each subsequent journey.

**General** Satisfy yourself you have enough rear-view mirrors. Those adequate for town trips aren't really wide enough for touring. Besides they may furnish the only view the driver has of the landscape behind him.

Safety belts must be secure and not damaged. They are now compulsory everywhere in Europe except Malta.

## Check list

*Tyres* Check: correct match of tyres, treads for excessive or uneven wear, inner and outer walls for damage, valve cores and fit caps, wheel rims for damage, the spare wheel for all the same.

*Automatic transmission* Check: oil level, operation of all gears and parking lock.

*Suspension* Check: greasing points, load springs for broken leaves, spring shackles and U-bolts for wear and tightness, rubber bushes, hydraulic damper effectiveness.

*Brakes* Check: footbrake and handbrake, level of fluid in master cylinder, wheel cylinders, linings, drums or discs, oil seals for leaks, freedom in 'off' position.

*Steering* Check: level of oil in steering box, swivel (king) pins and bushes for wear, steering wheel for free play, retaining nuts on steering box, wheel nuts, all joints and assemblies.

*Clutch* Check: for unusual noise or judder, for correct amounts of free movement in pedal.

*Electrical* Check: battery-acid levels, battery terminals, wiring — not frayed or exposed, wiring — for dirty or loose connections, fan-belt tension, fuel pump (if not mechanical), to make sure the generator voltage regulator and starter motor are working properly and that the lighting system complies with Continental regulations.

*Bodywork* Check: door and boot locks — lubricate if necessary, door hinges, bonnet-release catch, seat belts, roof rack secure.

*Gearbox* Check: oil level — renew if necessary, for excessive noise, operation of overdrive.

*Engine* Check: oil level — renew if necessary, oil pressure — gauge/warning light, all joints and gaskets, valve (tappet) clearances, radiator for leaks, coolant level — replace if dirty, water hoses and clips, core plugs for leaks, carburettor adjustment, fuel pump (if not electrical), clean out sediment, plug leads, distributor head — clean, distributor points — renew if pitted, lead to coil is tight and well insulated, even running.

*General* Check: rear-view mirror, seat belts, loading — that trailer and roof-rack complete with luggage comply with regulations.

Keep the manufacturer's handbook and servicing record with you.

Alternatively:

1 Pay a reliable garage to do all this for you.
2 Ask a reliable and friendly garage to take you slowly through the whole procedure. Pay for this lesson — it'll be worth it every time after that.

## Documents

**Green card** This is an international certificate of insurance relating to liability against others for damage caused in an accident. It is not required in E.E.C. countries, or in Austria, Czechoslovakia, Finland, the G.D.R., Hungary, Norway, Sweden and Switzerland, because U.K. insurance policies are automatically valid throughout the E.E.C. But it is still a good idea to have one in these countries; they provide comprehensive cover and are a very convenient way of proving that you have adequate cover. Apply for a green card to your broker or insurance company at least a month before departure. Tell them where you are going and the dates of departure and return. The green-card system does not operate in all countries and you may have to pay special premiums to cover travel in some areas. Most countries have laws about compulsory insurance and if you do not have the correct cover you may be forced to buy insurance (usually expensive) at the border or port of entry.

**Other insurance** Your broker or insurance company will give you a quotation for insurance against breakdown, theft, fire or damage. They may insist on an inspection by an approved garage for mechanical soundness and are very unlikely to give cover for a car more than twelve years old. The A.A. Five Star Insurance, however, has facilities for cars of all ages.

**Driving licence** Your full British licence is valid in most countries of Europe. In Spain you also need an International Driving Permit (available from the A.A. or R.A.C.). Italy demands an official translation of your driving licence. You can get it through the A.A. or R.A.C. if you belong – or from the Italian State Tourist Office – free of charge.

**Age-limits vary** In most of Europe you cannot drive if you are under 18, but in Sweden and West Germany the limit is 17.

**International Driving Permit** This is needed in addition to your driving licence in many countries, including Spain, German Democratic Republic, Hungary, Iceland, Poland, U.S.S.R., Morocco and Turkey. Apply to the A.A. or R.A.C. The A.A. will issue one over the counter on the strength of your U.K. licence.

**Vehicle registration book and GB plate for car** If the car is hired you won't have it's registration book. Instead, take the hired-car registration certificate. Get it from the A.A. or the hire company concerned.

The GB plate must be of the approved oval type with black letters on a white ground, displayed at the rear of the car *and* at the rear of a trailer. Checks are quite frequent and you'll be fined for irregularities. The attractive chrome ones won't do!

**Bail bond** This is strongly advisable for Spain. If you're in a road accident there, and the authorities think it's your fault, the car can be impounded and you can be put in jail, unless there is a deposit paid to cover any liability or fine. The bond, which will cost about £1.50, provides a guarantee of about £1,000. But the amount of any fine will have to be refunded to your insurers.

**Carnet** If you're motoring further than Western Europe you should enquire — to the A.A. or R.A.C. — whether you need a carnet. Certainly one is needed for Eastern Europe, and African countries. A carnet is an offer of some guarantee that when you enter a country with your car, you intend leaving with it so you do not have to pay import duty. Buy your carnet before you go. Things can get difficult if you have to pay on the frontier: you could have to hand over the import duty which can be colossal. The cost of the carnet depends on where you buy it. The A.A. and R.A.C. issue them, and their standard carnet costs £3.40.

**Maps** You will also need good road maps and city maps. Don't settle for jazzed-up tourist maps with pictures of local sights blocking half the town. Take advice from the national tourist agency or the A.A.

## Loading the luggage

Don't leave it until the morning of departure. At least fit all the cases — empty — to see how the jigsaw will piece together. Give thought to how much weight there will be and how it will be distributed. It could affect the handling of the car; and a heavy load will send up fuel consumption. So make allowances for that when calculating likely petrol expenses.

**Inside** Maps, Thermos flask, food for the route, tissues, a polythene bag with a damp flannel for cursory cleanliness. A pack of pads impregnated with toilet water for freshness.

**Roof-rack** Basically, do not overload. A top-heavy car will affect the steering and could put up your fuel consumption by 25%. So pack heavy objects in the lower part of the car: keep the roof-rack for picnic chairs, Li-Los and push-chairs. Strap them well down and cover with a water-proof sheet. Don't let the cover flap in the wind — it will annoy other drivers and could be dangerous if it works loose. Or wrap the cases individually in heavy-duty polythene seed sacks.

## Improve your motoring

Driving yourself daily to and from work is no preparation for crossing a continent with a family of four and a load of luggage. You need to be and stay physically fit — and your motoring could do with a check.

*High-performance courses* are run by the British School of Motoring Ltd and other motoring schools. Take a single lesson from a local motoring school (licensed) — you may find you need more than one.

Apply for the *advanced driving test*. Your lessons may include a chance at the local skid pad; you'll certainly be taught how to handle emergencies.

T.C.T.—E

The new driving test (it was due in August 1976 but has been delayed) was due to include a testing of theory. Once it's in practice    you will have to understand your engine. Meanwhile ask at a local garage – or enquire about local night classes.

Watch the B.B.C.'s programme 'Motor Care' beginning 2 October 1977. There is a booklet to go with the series.

## Setting out

Don't set out on a long holiday drive after a hard day at work. If you're frantic to leave at 18.00 on Friday night, then try to share the driving with someone else.

Plan the route beforehand: try to avoid bottlenecks. Give yourself a reasonable time schedule – not one where the slightest traffic jam can put you late and fray your temper and sweet holiday spirit.

Question seriously whether an overnight drive is the best way to start a holiday – every summer the lay-bys of the M5 between the Midlands and the West Country are jammed with cars with a prostrate figure at the wheel snatching thirty winks before taking once more to the crowded roads. At the end of July, the exodus from Paris is like a stampede of lemmings heading for the Mediterranean. If you insist on travelling by night take the following precautions:

Have a light but nourishing snack before you start. You'll need energy; but a three-course meal will incline you to be sleepy.

Stop if you feel hungry or thirsty. Stretch your legs, get a breath of fresh air regularly. Carry packed food and drink if you're on one of the 'lemming' routes.

Keep the car well ventilated: don't shut all the windows and turn up the heater – it causes sleepiness, headaches, and even sickness.

*Don't* take pep pills or alcohol to ginger yourself up.

Keep alert: motorways are monotonous. The family may well fall asleep. Try to keep someone awake at any one time to talk to. Or play the radio loud. In rain, the windscreen wipers can be hypnotically lulling; try changing their speed. In a crisis I have been known to wind down both windows and sing hymns very loudly into the night. Why hymns? – there are plenty of them and I know the words and the tunes. The sentiments are frequently rousing. 'Onward Christian Soldiers' goes well down the M4!

## Long-journey games

If the family won't join a singsong I suggest other car games:

*For motorways – number-plate words*: as each car overtakes, or you overtake them, note the letters of the number-plate and the first person to think of a word incorporating those letters in that order scores a point.

*For non-motorways — the legs game*: each passenger takes it in turn to notice an inn sign. They then score to their credit the number of legs on that sign, e.g. The Green Man — two, The White Hart — four, The King's Head — none, The Coach and Horses — twenty-four.

*Counting*: from a given point, each passenger is on the lookout for churches (or pubs or garages) en route. The first to spot one claims a point. This keeps children occupied but noisy. The driver must not play.

You'll find other games listed in several children's paperbacks:

*Travel Games* by Maurice Pipard, price £1.25 (Collins, 1974).

*Games for Trains, Planes and Wet Days* by Gyles Brandreth, price £1.95 (William Luscombe, 1974).

*How to Amuse Yourself on a Journey* by Judy Allen, price £1.25 (Studio Vista, 1974).

*Fun on Wheels* by Mary Danby, price 20p (Armada, 1973).

## Distances

Don't push your luck. If you're not used to long drives give yourself a brief stop every 200 miles. Apart from the danger of driving when you are overtired, if you set too high a target for daily mileage you'll spend your holiday recovering for the return trip! Stop even more often with children. You need ten minutes' break for every hour's driving. Don't arrive later than 18.00 at hotels, or much after 20.00 at restaurants (22.00 in Spain). It's easier on you, more convenient for the hotels.

## Carsickness

Carsickness very rarely affects a driver. A Japanese scientist maintains this is because a driver spontaneously sways *into* the turns the car makes while passengers, not so in touch with the cars' motion, bounce all over the place. Medical men say it is the upset of the labyrinth of the inner ear.

Various cures have been tried, some more superstitious than medical. For example, it is claimed that a chain dangling from the back of the car will leak the 'static' away from the vehicle. Other people sit bolt upright and clutch a coin or key — difficult to keep up for long.

## Advice

Avoid fatty and fried foods immediately before driving.

Take a tablet one to two hours before the journey: Maryine, Dramamine, Benadryl, Sea Legs and Phenergan are all effective — Maryine should *not* be taken by pregnant women. Side-effects can include drowsiness, so whoever takes them should not drive. Keep the tablets well away from children, an overdose could be fatal.

Children may be sick from all sorts of other causes — especially anxiety and excitement. Tablets for children are often orange flavoured. Phenergan is also made up in a syrup for very small children. In general all these tablets have a mild sedative effect which can send children to sleep — both my children have slept through a Channel crossing in a force 9 gale. We call it the Mickey Finn treatment, though, of course, nothing more than the prescribed dose should ever be given.

Don't look at the road or passing verges, keep your eyes steady towards the horizon or sky (unless you're driving).

Stop the car occasionally to read maps or walk about.

## Motorail

Cut out the long-distance drive by taking your car by train; it travels chained on a wagon (often open to the elements), you have a compartment seat, meal, overnight sleeper.

British Rail is not prepared to accept any legal responsibility for your car. Your own comprehensive car insurance should cover you for damage in transit. But it might be worth informing your insurer.

Maximum permitted height is 2.13m (7 feet) including roof-rack. On certain routes the maximum height is 1.67m (5$^{1}$/2 feet); towed caravans may not be taken.

The car travels on the same train as you. They are more common overnight. I enjoy travelling by Motorail: tucked up in a sleeper overnight, knowing I'll wake in some wonderful landscape and be able to drive away in my own car.

By Motorail you arrive fresh instead of exhausted by long hours of driving, often overnight on strange routes you aren't used to. You have your own car throughout the holiday. Your car may have facilities a hire car would *not*, e.g. radio, roof-rack. Its familiarity may be reassuring. If it's a motor caravan you may plan to sleep in it.

When costing, remember if you drive all the way, you'll have to pay for overnight stops. If you're going to be away a month or more taking your own car may be cheaper than fly-drive or hiring.

Compare the following for London—Nice, fourteen nights:

Fly-drive: £190—200 (without accommodation).
Motorail: £299.70 (without meals en route and petrol: add £30).
Package and own car hire: £308.25.
Independently booked flight/hotel/car: £396.25.

# U.K. Motorail Services

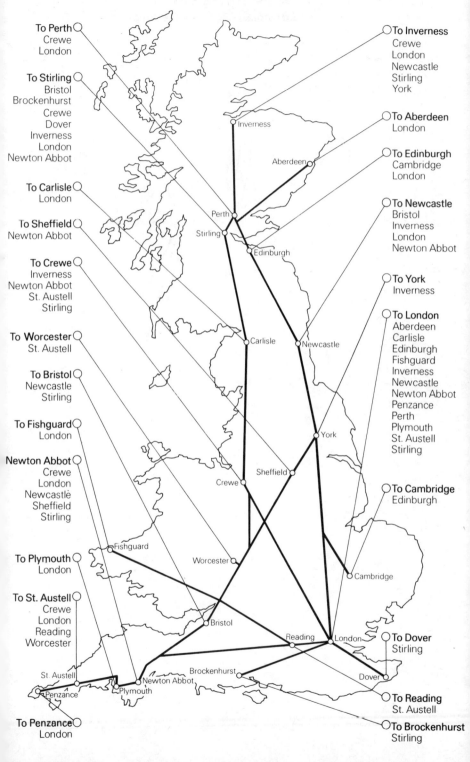

To Perth
Crewe
London

To Stirling
Bristol
Brockenhurst
Crewe
Dover
Inverness
London
Newton Abbot

To Carlisle
London

To Sheffield
Newton Abbot

To Crewe
Inverness
Newton Abbot
St. Austell
Stirling

To Worcester
St. Austell

To Bristol
Newcastle
Stirling

To Fishguard
London

Newton Abbot
Crewe
London
Newcastle
Sheffield
Stirling

To Plymouth
London

To St. Austell
Crewe
London
Reading
Worcester

To Penzance
London

To Inverness
Crewe
London
Newcastle
Stirling
York

To Aberdeen
London

To Edinburgh
Cambridge
London

To Newcastle
Bristol
Inverness
London
Newton Abbot

To York
Inverness

To London
Aberdeen
Carlisle
Edinburgh
Fishguard
Inverness
Newcastle
Newton Abbot
Penzance
Perth
Plymouth
St. Austell
Stirling

To Cambridge
Edinburgh

To Dover
Stirling

To Reading
St. Austell

To Brockenhurst
Stirling

Inverness
Aberdeen
Perth
Stirling
Edinburgh
Carlisle
Newcastle
York
Sheffield
Crewe
Fishguard
Worcester
Cambridge
Bristol
Reading
London
Brockenhurst
Dover
St. Austell
Newton Abbot
Plymouth
Penzance

# European Motorail Services

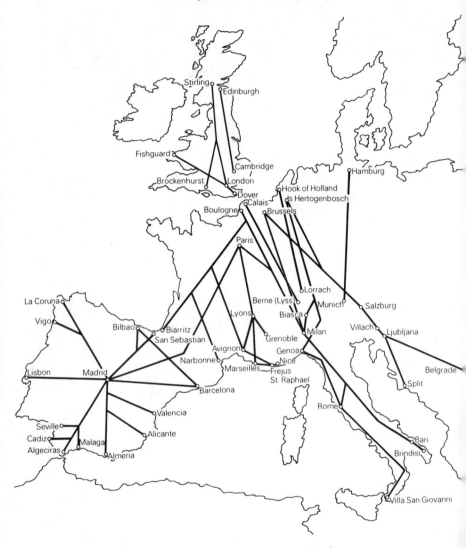

The maps on p.53−4     show Motorail services in the U.K. and Europe.

Motorail services to European cities for travellers from Britain start from the Continental port, Paris, Brussels or 's Hertogenbosch. Overnight journeys can be in sleepers, or couchette (a six-berth compartment with pillow and blanket). On very long journeys two motorail routes may be linked up. But you will have to change trains for yourself. For example, going from Paris to Naples you will have to transfer from one train to another at Milan. Sealink Car Ferries provide links with rail services to and from the ports.

## Disadvantages of Motorail

It takes longer than flying (but there are very few car-air ferries nowadays). It may be more costly over a short period than fly-drive. The maximum number of people taken at Motorail rates is four adults, or their equivalent. Extra adults are charged ordinary fare when applicable.

## Motoring in foreign countries

For ten minutes it will seem strange to be on the right-hand side of the road. Then you'll feel you've always driven like that. Pay special attention at junctions, roundabouts (especially roundabouts where our priority *is* different) and exits from garages. Traffic signs differ from ours: a selection is shown on p.56−9. Study a good motoring handbook. Seventy cent of Continental motoring holiday breakdowns happen within 100 miles of Channel ports.

## Traffic signals

In most cities and towns they operate as in the U.K. but may be suspended overhead in the middle of the road. There is usually only one set on the right hand side some distance before the road junction. Stop with enough distance to see them change. The lights themselves are often dimmer than ours. Keep your eyes peeled.

Flashing signals may mean different things in different countries − e.g. a flashing red light may mean no entry or stop at level crossing. A flashing amber light may mean dangerous intersection or obstruction. Check.

## Priority from the right

This rule is most common in France but exists to some extent in many other European countries. It's the most unnerving of all rules for the British driver. Happily it does not apply on motorways. Otherwise traffic from the right − even from a minor road − has priority. So watch carefully as you thread your way through towns. Never depend on receiving right of way at intersections. Always, in any country, it's wise to give way to military vehicles.

# European road signs

These signs are found in more than one country

Priority road

End of priority road

School-crossing patrol

Sight-seeing

Weight limits for military traffic only

Wheel-chains compulsory

Traffic prohibited (this sign may have a yellow centre)

STOP

"Stop" sign

Oncoming traffic has priority

Priority over oncoming traffic

Place names denote the beginning and end of built-up areas; speed restrictions apply. The signs may also be blue or white

Priority only at next intersection with minor road

Street lights not on all night

No through road

Direction of priority road

EINBAHN

One-way street

Umleitung

Diversion

Take care (yellow or white triangle)

Road for motor vehicles

End of road for motor vehicles

Prohibition signs used in conjunction with other signs

Restricted 08.00-17.00hrs Mon-Sat, public holiday, and preceding day

Restricted 08.00-14.00hrs Sat and day preceding public holiday

Restricted 08.00-13.00hrs Sun and public holiday

This is a selection of signs which, although not international signs, are relevant to the following countries; they may also be seen in other countries in which case they have a similar definition.

## Austria

End of two-way traffic

Tram turns at 'yellow'

Federal highway with priority

Federal highway without priority

## Belgium

Traffic restricted during period of thaw

Beginning of Blue Zone parking area

Beginning of Blue Zone parking area

Left turn from right-hand lane only

Stopping or parking prohibited—on left on odd-numbered dates and on right on even-numbered dates

End of Blue Zone parking area

Traffic in parallel lanes

One-way road or end of two-way traffic

Compulsory lane for lorries 0 2km ahead. lasting for 2 2km

Beginning of 1 hr parking zone

End of 1 hr parking zone

## Denmark

Compulsory lane for lorries

Overtaking prohibited

## Finland

Stop before entry to priority road

Diversion due to road works

Throughway in city or town directing to a numbered main road

# France and Monaco

Irregular stretch of road

Use of horn prohibited

Yield to traffic from right

Crossroads protected by stop signs on side roads

# Germany

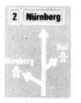

Road with directions to motorways

No overtaking for lorries, coaches, and cars with caravans

Detour for vehicles over 5.5 metric tons

Emergency motorway traffic diversion

# Italy and San Marino

Left to right: overtaking lane, normal lane, and emergency lane

No overtaking for vehicles towing trailers

Coaches have priority on mountain roads

Obligatory lane for slow commercial traffic

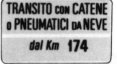

End of restriction

Wheel-chains, spiked or studded tyres, or snow tyres compulsory at 174km

# Netherlands

Cycle crossings

Danger-trams crossing

Front view of traffic pillar: motor vehicles may pass on either side; other traffic on right only

No stopping or parking 08.00–10.00hrs. Stopping permitted for private vehicles 10.00–17.00hrs (Sat 15.00hrs)

Road merges

Slow lane for heavy vehicles

# Norway

Stopping place
(on narrow roads)

Zone with special parking
and stopping regulations.
Parking restricted to 2 hours
08.00–18.00hrs
(Sat 08.00–16.00hrs).
No restrictions at other times

# Spain

End of restrictions of sign
on left

No entry

Turning permitted

Sightseeing

# Sweden

Zone in which vehicles may
park for a limited time only

End of no-parking or
stopping zone

55yds distance between
vehicles

Passing place
(for oncoming traffic)

Width of carriageway

Caution–blind
person
(signs worn on clothing)

Caution–deaf
person

# Switzerland

Mountain postal coach route:   End of route
coaches have priority

Prohibition sign
(showing exceptions)

Passing place
(for lorries)

Warning of road conditions on mountain passes:

eg pass closed;
road open as far as Realp;
wheel-chains, spiked,
studded, or snow tyres
compulsory

Göschenen – Andermatt open;
Gotthard – wheel chains compulsory.
Furka closed;
Oberalp – wheel-chains, spiked,
studded, or snow tyres compulsory

Exit road

Slow lane

## Turning

In Italy, Switzerland and Yugoslavia you often turn in front of traffic turning in the opposite direction. Not behind as we do here.

## Speed-limits

Keep strictly to them at all times. Police can fine on the spot and you must pay up. They are also empowered to impound licences, so it could spoil your entire trip.

## Horns

In built-up areas you must not use a horn unless safety demands it. In many large towns and resorts as well as in areas indicated by the international sign (a black horn with a line through it), the use of the horn is totally prohibited.

## Roundabouts

Except in Greece, Malta and Yugoslavia give priority to cars entering the roundabout. This can be tricky for British drivers who are also trying to adjust to going anticlockwise. Keep in the outside lane on a roundabout; it'll make your exit easier.

## Crash-helmets

All riders of motor cycles irrespective of the engine capacity of their vehicle should wear crash-helmets.

## Drinking and driving

This is very strictly controlled and severely penalized by fines and/or imprisonment. Don't. The Swedish are enormously disapproving and will tell on you if they suspect. The Austrians can confiscate your licence for any alcohol offence. The French limit is the same as ours but you can be imprisoned for ten to thirty days.

## Level crossings

Almost all are indicated by international signs. Most guarded ones have a lifting barrier, sometimes with bells or flashing lights to warn of an approaching train.

## Hazard warnings

If you have to stop your car where it could be a hazard to others, use direction indicators flashing on both sides of the car, as well as the warning triangle placed on the road at the rear of the car.

## Overtaking

On a road with two lanes or more in each direction, signal in good time, complete the manoeuvre and return to the inside lane. Do *not* remain in any other lane. If your car's right-hand drive you need a reliable passenger (children should be in the back anyway) to lean to their left and give you advice on whether it's safe. Work out a good system between you: safety depends on you both.

## Parking

Police can be very strict, and rules can vary. You must park facing the direction of the traffic. Some cities issue special parking discs: call at the town hall for one. Keep a beady eye for all signs indicating no parking: they're international.

## Priorities

Trams take priority over all other vehicles, and must be overtaken on the right except in one-way streets. Give way to ambulances, fire-engines, police or military vehicles with flashing lights, bells or sirens.
The blind and disabled, funerals or marching columns must be given right of way.

## Tolls

These are common on the Continent on roads and bridges. If you take a motorway route across Europe the cost can mount up. If you're costing your journey very tightly check with a motoring handbook where the heaviest costs will fall.

### Club membership

**The Automobile Association** offers advice and rescue service to its members. The Relay Service (extra fee on top of membership) will get you to your destination and your car to a garage: it only applies on mainland U.K. Full membership: £10; associate membership (for spouses): £2; enrolment: £2.50; Relay: £6.50.

*Leading publications: Annual Handbook; Guide to Continental Motoring; Guide to Hotels and Restaurants; G.B. Road Atlas; Road Book of Europe.* Plus numerous lavish books on touring and the countryside which are cheaper to members than to the general public.

*Address* See local phone book. In London: Fanum House, Leicester Square; telephone 01-957 7355.

**R.A.C.** The Royal Automobile Club has an advice and rescue service. Joint husband and wife membership: £9 annually plus £2 joining fee. Recovery charge is £5.

*Leading publications: Great Britain Road Atlas;* guide and handbook with some 4,000 recommended hotels and restaurants; Continental handbook and guide to Western Europe; and guide to Scandinavia and Eastern Europe. Available to the general public at higher prices than to members.

*Address* In any local phone book, or Box 100, R.A.C. House, Lansdowne Road, Croydon; telephone 01-839 7050.

# Chapter 8
# Hiring a Car Abroad

A package holiday can tie you to one resort or make you dependent on group excursions to see the local countryside. You may want to hire a car for one or two days. Or you may want a car for extensive use for your whole stay.

If you're on business you may want to travel between cities, hiring a car in one and leaving it at the next. There are three ways of doing this: book before you go, hire when you arrive, or hire when you've settled in.

### Booking before you go
You can do this through your travel agent, or through the offices here of the big international car-hire firms: Hertz and Avis are the biggest. Godfrey Davis operates in Britain, Holland and Spain and has licencees in forty other countries. You can arrange the place where you pick up the car: it can be brought to the airport or station to meet you, or delivered to your hotel.

### Hire when you arrive
The big international firms have offices at airports. This way you risk not getting the car of your choice, or being landed with a big and expensive one, or not finding one at all.

### Hire when you've settled in
In this case your hotel will be able to advise on the rates of local firms: or you can consult a holiday rep, or go direct to a local garage. They may be more suitable and cheaper than the international firms. On the other hand I've been landed with a bone-shaker in Malta and had to make do.

If you want to be fully sure and specific book in advance.

### Fly-drive

Fly-drive holidays are growing in popularity. You pay one price for a flight and car rental. It frees holiday-makers from the restrictions of the package. It is a great money-saver if you intend to do a good deal of touring but is not worthwhile for a day or two's excursion.

## Snags

**Not there** If you've booked in advance, the car may still not be there to meet you. Go to the airline or station desk and complain. If you are dealing with a small local firm, have their phone number handy.

Car-hire firms are eager to help. On some airlines the stewardess will get the pilot to order a car to meet you at the airport.

**Not in good order** Some firms ask you to sign a statement that the car is in good working order and free from any defect. How are you to know? Do *not* accept this. Cross out the condition and substitute: 'No defects apparent on inspection and it appears to be working normally'. If there is a defect or damaged bodywork but you are willing to accept the car, make sure the hire company has details so that you are not blamed.

You need the hire contract, the vehicle registration forms and, if you're going across a frontier, a green card.

Get a list of the company's offices, with telephone numbers, in places you intend to visit.

Check you can find switches for lights, wipers, fan heater, windscreen wipers etc. Make sure you can adjust safety belts and seats and that you know how to open bonnet, boot and petrol filler cap. If the car has a steering-wheel lock then get the hang of that too. If the girl behind the counter gets impatient, get on with the check for yourself and go back if anything's wrong.

Check there's a spare wheel — pumped up and with good tread — and tools for changing the wheel.

Inspect indicators, wipers, washers, horn, handbrake, brake lights and the tread on the tyres.

As you drive off look out for excessive noise, shaky steering, weak clutch, dodgy foot brakes. Go back if you're unhappy and ask them to change it. A motorist's phrase book will help if you have any complaints. The A.A. issue a *Car Components Guide* in twelve languages — it really does give the Danish for rear axle casing and crankshaft bearing cap!

## Cost

Generally, unless you pay with a credit card or a fly-drive voucher, you are expected to put down a deposit.

There are alternative ways of charging:

A straight hire charge at a daily, weekly or longer rate which will not vary with the mileage you do. If you're going very long distances, this is likely to be the cheaper way.

The mileage rate – you pay a basic hiring mileage and then something more for every mile you travel beyond that. Note the mileage on the clock in writing; agree it with the company's representative.

A combination of the other two: straight hire charge up to a given mileage, say 200, but extra payment per mile beyond that.

There may be a pick-up and delivery charge. If you don't collect your car at one of the hire firm's offices, then you may have to pay them to bring it to the hotel, station or airport.

Unless you have fly-drive, or a car hire as part of a package, you will have to pay in local currency, travellers cheques or credit cards. This will come out of your £300 allowance, except payment by credit card.

If you pay by credit card you may be asked to sign a blank credit-card voucher. Don't. Fill in the amount the total rental should come to, then make out another slip, if it's necessary, when you return the car.

You will probably be given a car with a full tank. You will have to pay to refill it on return. Fill it yourself to save any argument or overcharging.

If you have put oil in get a receipt so you can get your money back.

## Insurance

Included in the hire charge will be third-party insurance. *But* the hire charge may not cover insurance against liability for damaging other cars in an accident, injury to your own passengers, or damage to the hire car. Even if you have a comprehensive car insurance this is unlikely to cover you for a hired car.

Read the 'conditions of hire' carefully and ask the representative. If the provided insurance does not cover damage to other cars or injury to your own passengers then make separate insurance arrangements for this.

## Driver and hirer

Normally hire is made to one person. If you want to share the driving with someone else, say so at the start. You will have to pay extra. Otherwise the other driver will be committing a criminal offence for driving uninsured.

## Breakdowns and accidents

The cars hired out by the big international companies are rarely more than a year old. However, many of them do take a pasting, so they may be more badly worn than a year-old domestic car. Also the overhaul they should have between trips is often very cursory. I hired a car one morning only to realize that a previous passenger had been sick in it, and the evidence only superficially removed.

If your hired car develops a fault, get it repaired at a garage. Keep the receipt and claim the money back. That's usually no problem.

If you crash take the names of others involved, car numbers and details of witnesses and call the police as you would normally. Draw a sketch plan with measurements. Take photographs. Don't admit liability. Get in touch with the hire company straight away.

*In Spain*: motorists in an accident can be imprisoned. You need a bail bond to get out. So if hiring in Spain, check this is included in the hiring formalities.

# Chapter 9
# Car Ferries

Car ferries are booming. New routes open up each year, new car ferries are being designed and built. So in the coming years car-ferry business will increase in its scope and complexity. In 1977, for example, there are twenty-one different routes for taking your car to Europe. Two of those are new routes: Sheerness to Dunkerque and Portsmouth to Le Havre.

Even from the heart of England the motorist from Birmingham is only 128 miles from Southampton. No one in England should be more than three hours from a car ferry. In terms of value for money even British motorists can now compare and select from a considerable list. It's something of a buyer's market.

Car-ferry business is highly competitive. All the companies (see Yellow Pages) are out to tempt the motorist with bargain offers. Choosing 'best value' can be complicated, particularly as price structures depend on different things. Some companies let the car go free if there are four adult passengers on a five-day trip, most let children go half-fare. The size and length of car determines rate: but rates aren't uniform. Weekend and night crossings have different rates, as do different seasons and package deals of ferry crossing and accommodation together. Groups and short excursion trips are other ways to get bargain value. Sealink's businessman's package isn't just for businessmen! If you're cycling or Youth Hostelling there are special offers for you. If you rent camping or caravan equipment from some ferry lines you'll get a reduction. Crossing from Felixstowe on a Monday comes cheaper, too. The network of options can make you dizzy. It threatens to become as complex as European air fares.

**Time at sea** The longer journeys can be rough. If anyone is particularly liable to seasickness, take the shorter routes. Alternatively, those who enjoy spray and white gulls overhead would enjoy the longer trips.

**Cabins** If you make a crossing by night with a cabin you save on more expensive overnight hotel accommodation. Choose a crossing that gives you enough time for a good night's sleep.

**Already there** Cross to Brittany and St. Malo and your holiday starts the moment you're off the ferry. Rotterdam and Dieppe won't give you quite the same feeling: there's still a good distance to drive before you're in true holiday country.

**Boat or hover** Hovercraft are certainly faster than boats, still a novelty, but rather bumpy. Ideal for a quick start if you've a long way to go. The children will love it.

**Booking advice** Any good travel agent should know his way around the timetables. Otherwise go to the specialists: Car Ferry Enquiries Ltd; telephone enquiries to 01-568 7343; telex 8812465. Postal queries to 136 Oxford Road, Cowley, Oxford. Since 1970 they have published a booklet annually, *The Lazy Way to Book Your Car Ferries*, price 25p from either of the above addresses.

**Return bookings** One-way singles could cost you money. Tickets cost more abroad than in the U.K. Once your return is booked over here, the tickets on shorter routes can usually be transferred; unused open-dated tickets can be refunded.

## Insurance

When booking check who is responsible for accidental damage; usually cars travel by sea at owner's risk. Still, most car-insurance policies cover a sea voyage of not longer than sixty-five hours. If you're apprehensive and don't want to lose a large no-claims bonus, take out a separate policy for the voyage.

An average car insurance won't cover a car being taken by air. Usually the air-ferry firm takes responsibility, but check this is so.

## Ferries from the British Isles, 1977

### England to France

Dover—Boulogne: 1 hour 40 minutes; four times daily.
Dover—Calais: $1^{1}/_{2}$ hours; twelve crossings daily.
Dover—Dunkerque: $2^{1}/_{2}$ hours; three times daily.

Folkestone—Boulogne: 1 hour 40 minutes; three times daily.
Folkestone—Calais: 1 hour 40 minutes; three times daily.
Sheerness—Dunkerque: $4^{1}/2$ hours; twice daily.
Southampton—Le Havre: $6^{1}/2$ – 7 hours; four times daily.
Newhaven—Dieppe: $3^{3}/4$ hours; six times daily.
Weymouth—Cherbourg: 4 hours; twice daily.
Portsmouth—Cherbourg: 4 hours; twice daily.
Portsmouth—Le Havre: $5^{1}/2$ hours; twice daily.
Portsmouth—St. Malo: $8^{1}/2$ hours; once daily.
Southampton—Cherbourg: 5 hours; twice daily.
Plymouth—St. Malo: $8^{1}/2$ hours; once daily.
Plymouth—Roscoff: $6^{3}/4$ hours; once daily.

## England to Spain

Southampton—Santander: 36 hours; twice weekly in high season.

## Ireland to France

Rosslare—Le Havre: 20 hours; every two days in season.

## England to Belgium

Dover—Ostend: $3^{3}/4$ hours; up to nine times daily.
Dover—Zeebrugge: 4 hours; up to six times daily.
Folkestone—Ostend: $3^{3}/4$ hours; up to nine times daily.
Felixstowe—Zeebrugge: 5 hours; three times daily in summer.
Hull—Zeebrugge: 15 hours; daily.

## England to Holland

Hull—Rotterdam: 14 hours; daily.
Sheerness—Flushing: 8 hours; twice daily.
Harwich—Hook: $6^{1}/4$ hours by day; $7^{3}/4$ hours by night; up to three
times daily.
Felixstowe—Rotterdam: primarily freight but six passengers on each
crossing; $6^{1}/2$ – 8 hours; twenty sailings weekly.
Great Yarmouth—Scheveningen: 7 – 8 hours; up to three times daily.

## England to Denmark

Harwich—Esbjerg: 19 hours; daily.
Newcastle—Esbjerg: $18^{1}/2$ hours; twice weekly.

## England to West Germany

Harwich—Bremerhaven: $16^{1}/2$ hours; every other day.
Harwich—Hamburg: 20 hours; every other day.

## England to Norway

Newcastle—Bergen: 19 hours; twice weekly; one calls at Stavanger.

Newcastle−Stavanger: $17^{1}/2$ hours; one a week.
Newcastle−Kristiansand and Oslo: 20 hours; one a week.
Harwich−Kristiansand: 22 hours; three times fortnightly.
Harwich−Oslo: 31 hours; once a fortnight.

## England to Sweden

Felixstowe−Göteborg: 24 hours; three times weekly.
Immingham−Göteborg: 24 hours; twice weekly in summer.

## Scotland to Faroes, Norway, Iceland

Scrabster−Thorshavn: 14 hours, then to Bergen, Seydisfjördur.

## England and Wales to Ireland

Fishguard−Rosslare: $3^{1}/4$ hours; twice daily.
Holyhead−Dun Laoghaire: $3^{1}/2$ hours; up to four times daily.
Liverpool−Dublin: 9 hours; twice daily in summer.
Swansea−Cork: 9 hours; daily.

## England to Northern Ireland

Liverpool−Belfast: 9−10 hours; daily.

## Scotland to Northern Ireland

Stranraer−Larne: 2 hours; six times daily.
Cairnryan−Larne: $2^{1}/2$ hours; five times daily.

## England to Channel Islands

Weymouth−Guernsey: $4^{3}/4$ hours; twice daily.
Weymouth−Jersey: $6^{1}/2$ hours; twice daily.

## Isle of Man

Fleetwood−Douglas, Liverpool−Douglas, Ardrossan−Douglas,
Belfast−Douglas, Dublin−Douglas: summer timetables variable;
some crossings for passengers only.

## Scotland to Orkney and Shetland

Scrabster−Stromness: 2 hours; three times daily.
Aberdeen−Lerwick: 14 hours; twice weekly.

## England to Poland

Hull−Gdynia: 3 days; fortnightly all year.
Ipswich−Gdynia: 3 days.
Manchester−Szczecin: 5 days.
(Also: Dublin−Szczecin: 5 days.)

Members of H.M. Forces get concessionary fares for themselves and
their families on some lines.

Travellers without cars can use all car-ferry services.

Disabled drivers belonging to the Disabled Drivers' Association or the Disabled Drivers' Motor Club can apply to be carried *free* by most of the companies operating shorter routes.

## Hovercraft

Dover–Boulogne: 30–40 minutes; seven crossings a day.
Dover–Calais: 35 minutes.
Ramsgate–Calais: 40 minutes; up to twenty-seven crossings per day.

## Jet-Foil

This started in June 1977 and caters for foot passengers only. It will take you from Tower Bridge, London, to Zeebrugge in $3^{1}/2$ hours. From Zeebrugge there are coach links to Bruges station — it takes about 20 minutes. The single fare is £30, £27 off season (after October 77). Travelling this way your total time to, say, Brussels would be around 5 hours.

## Europe: North and South

We aren't the only seafarers. Another network of ferries criss-crosses the Baltic linking Finland, Sweden, Denmark, Poland and Germany. And the busiest waters of all are probably those of the Mediterranean. At the last count (*Tourist Magazine*, Summer 1976) there were fifty-eight car-ferry routes sailing primarily from Italy, France, Yugoslavia, Spain and Majorca to all shores of the Mediterranean including North Africa.

Full world lists of all cruise and sea-crossing operators can be found in the *ABC Shipping Guide*.

# Chapter 10
# Coach Travel

Private motoring helped end the supremacy of railway transport, but public motoring — the bus and coach systems of the country — never seriously rivalled trains for convenience and speed. Nowadays, however, coach travel as a means of transport (not holiday touring) is drawing off from the railway system those travellers who can no longer afford the rising rail fares.

National Express — a subsidiary of the publicly owned National Bus Company — now offers coach services on over 900 routes in the U.K. Full timetables of National Express services and those of other bus companies operating in the U.K. and across to the Continent are in *National Express Service Guide,* published winter and summer from any of the five area offices of National Travel (N.B.C.) Ltd (see Yellow Pages for address).

Coach tours as holiday packages are also popular for their cheapness and their convenience for seeing the sights.

Cosmos are leaders in Continental coach-tour holidays from Britain. Wallace Arnold are the biggest operators of holiday tours in Britain. And then there are the great treks, masterminded by Pennworld. They call theirs Overlanders: they include London to Katmandu in seventy-two days, Rio to Lima in thirty-six days and Cairo to Nairobi in thirty-three days.

## Is it really cheaper?

People using coaches as transport for travel do so for one reason: *economy.* So make sure it really is cheaper. Compare the journey with the cheap package holidays that lump flight and student accommodation together for real bargain prices — e.g. a week on the Costa del Sol for around £50 for a return flight and spartan accommodation.

If your coach journey is so long that it involves overnight stays at hotels then the cost will rise steeply: three or four days and it clearly could be cheaper to fly. Besides that, I'm told there's the psychological pressure to cope with. Once you've broken the one-day limit the urge to stop off at cafés and markets becomes almost a compulsion. The sheer tedium of the coach drives you to depend on breaks for relief, and an epidemic of shopping quite often breaks out. Before you know it, fruit drinks, coffee, wine, buns, trinkets are all cramping the space and emptying your pocket. The fare that was bargain price with no extras is now swelling under the impulse of holiday travel. On long-haul journeys fraught with such risks, it might have been as cheap to fly direct.

## Medium haul: best value

Overnight London—Paris is certainly cheap. So is the London coach that connects to the Ramsgate hovercraft and then from Calais to Paris. On overnights you don't buy things on the way: if you do it's merely 'duty-frees' that save money anyway. And a one-night journey — if you set out to make it restful — won't ruin you for the next few days. Such coach journeys — over medium hauls — are indeed good value.

## Long journeys for fun

Touring by coach allows you to see and explore the route you travel. In this case the bargain price won't matter as much as the way a coach can take you off the beaten track, land you into the heart of strange cultures, drop you off for a wander round mysterious markets or antique ruins. Usually such tours keep prices to a minimum — and can benefit from travelling in places not yet thoroughly geared to holiday parties.

## Tips for a more comfortable journey

Whether you're merely bombing up the motorway from London to Manchester in four hours, or committing yourself to eleven countries in ten weeks, there is some advice that applies to all coach travel.

Space is really at a premium. Less even than in a motor cruiser, a caravan, or a tent. National Express usually run fifty-three-seaters on their shorter fast trips. For their longer tours the buses seat forty-five to forty-seven and can recline. You will have to sit in one position most of the journey. What are called 'comfort' stops happen at prearranged times on journeys over $2^{1}/2$ hours. The National Express coach to Athens had the option of installing a loo or fridge on board; they chose the fridge, and rely on stopping for loos. The journey's less smelly and they have cool drink throughout. For really long journeys approach the different companies and ask about the type of coach they run: is it air-conditioned, does it have blinds, plenty of leg-room, reclining seats, opening roof?

Unless you're really used to buses your body will feel the strain. Take travel-sickness pills for a start. Only read if you're sure you can take it; the motion of the coach could make you feel sick. You may find you get headaches and leg cramp. On long hauls you would be wise to break your journey with one overnight stop. Otherwise you'll take a week to recover. Find out if there's a scheme for connecting coaches: e.g. London to Paris, say, then Paris to Marseilles.

In hot weather, the side of the coach that gets the sun can be crippling. It's worth arriving early to claim the comfortable seat out of the sun. Once the journey's begun people naturally stick to their original seat — even if it's uncomfortable. Something to do with animal territory.

Watch what you eat and drink. The experience of sitting on a coach is curiously enervating. You'll get peckish. Take things to nibble: *not* chocolate, but biscuits, sweets, crisps and suchlike. Antacid tablets even, to keep your tummy settled.

You will also feel very thirsty, especially in hot countries. Do *not* drink alcohol, it'll dehydrate you further. Don't drink great quantities on long hauls — rather a little that is refreshing at a time. Take barley sugars and gob-stoppers to suck. Do *not* eat loads of fruit, it might prove too loosening, and in foreign parts the skin might not be clean. Long-haul tour leaders warn against any fruit at all on the journey.

Take a cushion: the aerated kind they give to invalids are best. If not, try foam rubber. Blow-up rubber ones get hard and sticky. If you're going where the temperature drops at night enquire whether the coach has blankets.

You're living at very close quarters with forty or so other people. Personal hygiene must be immaculate. Three essentials: a good deodorant, cologne to cool and splash you and keep you smelling decent, and a moisturized cleanser for the skin. You can buy tins of impregnated tissues or swabs. If desperate halfway through the day try the army trick of swapping socks. Better still, go without, wear flip-flops and use a foot-dusting powder. Chemists sell disposable paper pants and knickers: pack a few handy for journeys that go on for days.

Wake refreshed: if you're on an overnight drive, in the morning you'll stop somewhere where there's running water. Washing out your mouth will help freshen you up: chemists now supply disposable toothbrushes with their own toothpaste. Take several.

Men can shave best with a battery-operated electric razor: any other kind and you'll have problems finding the right point. Otherwise, take a Bic disposable razor and some shaving soap.

Dress comfortably: the less things clinging round your waist the cooler. No nylon. Cotton bell-tent dresses, kaftans, or loose shirts. Jeans can be very hot: but at least they soak up the sweat. Never wear heavy or tight shoes. If you're travelling in cool weather take stretchy moccasin-style slippers. If the weather's hot — flip-flops.

Boredom can set in even among the most dazzling scenery. The trouble with landscapes is they go on for a long time. Take plenty of distractions: pocket chess, liar dice, Mastermind, crossword books etc. Someone else on the trip will be glad you did, too. But be careful of games that need close attention, especially over a bumpy road — you may get travel sick.

All the things I've mentioned call for a good well-organized holdall: lightweight, compact, with plenty of pockets on the outside. How often do you see people using plastic bags that end up torn and scruffy?

# Chapter 11
# Railways

The invention of the railway provided the universal traffic boom of the nineteenth century. And it began in Britain.

In 1830 the first public passenger railway operated by steam opened between Liverpool and Manchester. Nine years later came the first edition of Bradshaw's *Railway Guide* to inform the travelling public where and when they could go by train. By the 1840s the inter-city stage coaches were in decline and Britain's railway network in the ascendant. The fever spread — in America the Baltimore—Ohio track opened in 1830, and across Europe first Belgium, then Germany, Switzerland and France developed railway systems too.

Railways moved people: but they also moved goods, food and soldiers. So railways were part of the great colonial years. In 1846 Robert Stephenson visited India: seven years later its first lines opened. India's railways were to bind the continent together, promote its national spirit, and run on into the 1970s, the rather ramshackle legacy of British influence. At its peak the first-class Indian railway coach was two-tier: an upper sleeping-living room for passengers, room below for their servants.

In Africa, railways also followed colonial development: a series of unconnected lines running inland from the ports. Rhodes had a dream of pushing a railway through from the Cape to Cairo — he never realized it. But Britain, France and Germany provided their colonies with isolated systems on different gauges. They were to hamper trans-continental traffic and reinforce political divisions. Meanwhile, North America had been forging ahead: in 1869 the Central Pacific and Union Pacific joined across the continent, others followed. By 1920 America had one-third of the world's total track. China came later to railways: Japan's first opened in 1872.

From the 1870s onward was the heyday of the railways. In 1873 the first sleeping cars were introduced. In 1879 came the first restaurant cars: prior to that passengers had been disgorged at the stations for meals. Both Swindon and York were in their day busy dining centres. It was the era of the great long-distance trains: in 1883 the Orient Express linked Paris to Istanbul. (The trip from Boston to San Francisco took eight days on the Pullman 'hotel car', publishing its own newspaper en route. By 1914 there was a weekly Moscow—Vladivostok link: it took nine days.) Calais—Nice—Rome, Ostend—Vienna, Paris—St. Petersburg — these were the great journeys of the Compagnie Internationale des Wagon-Lits. Accommodation was often opulent: carpeting, writing tables, marble-tiled bathrooms. On the St. Petersburg—Cannes Express passengers changed for dinner.

By 1900 the world had half a million miles of track: the new form of travel had transformed the political and economic nature of the planet.

In the twentieth century the massive destruction of two world wars, the invention and mass availability of the car and the aeroplane have put railways in the shade. World coverage reached its peak in 1936 with three-quarters of a million miles of track. By 1959 America had less mileage than in 1906: in 1968 Britain's mileage was reduced by half. The railways seemed on the way out.

## Staging a come-back

However, the joys of the car and the plane have not proved unalloyed. Traffic chaos on the ground, delays on flights with long journeys at either end, have given railways a new chance. Many countries are now trying to maximize that opportunity.

## 160—500 km (100—300 miles)

This is the distance at which the advantages of car or plane are being challenged by the train. There's little in it, in time taken, for example, whether you fly between London and Manchester or go by train. Similarly central Brussels to central Amsterdam by air and surface transport takes 2 hours 40 minutes. By fast train you cover the same ground in less than 2 hours 30 minutes, direct — without all the inconvenience of bus/aircraft changes.

Railways are now out to gain custom by offering city centre to city centre service, greater comfort, and much more reliable punctuality — trains don't have the aeroplane's problems with weather and delays where they happen are shorter than with flying. Comfort and personal services are more easily available — on some Continental expresses you can have your hair cut, use a telephone, or hire a secretary's services.

Many countries now aim to price their railway service competitively with flights. So before you decide to fly — check comparisons.

## Trains are getting faster

The world's fastest train is the Tokyo—Osaka 'bullet' which does 560 km (350 miles) in 3 hours 10 minutes. It handles fifty departures a day. British Rail's High Speed Train, now operational between London and Bristol, is capable of doing 200 km per hour (125 m.p.h.). At this rate railway operators are starting to feel they could challenge air flight's supremacy in journeys up to 650 km (400 miles).

France will be opening a brand new Paris—Lyon line in 1982. Trains on it will travel at an average speed of well over 160 km per hour (100 m.p.h.), sometimes at 300 km per hour (185 m.p.h.). The London—Glasgow route, now five hours, will be reduced further by the Advanced Passenger Train when it comes into operation in 1979. This will make it highly competitive with the B.A. shuttle which only takes one hour in the air, but at least a further hour at each end.

## Timetables

You will find a comprehensive timetable of all the trains known to run in the civilized world in: *Thomas Cook International Timetable*.

It's a comprehensive work listing every train. European services give every train a number: this number is used in timetables and station notice-boards. The train's number remains with it across frontiers, as long as the entire train crosses. But beware: many international journeys are made in through-coaches which are passed from one train to another. Numbers make reading the timetable easier. It needs to be: there are plenty of notes to be decoded for almost every route. That's simply because on the Continent some Saturday and Sunday services differ from weekdays, and summer and ski seasons differ from the rest of the year. Don't take a train for granted on any particular day. Check: it's all in the Cook's timetable.

## On the debit side

Long distances still take a long time: Paris to Rome by plane and connecting buses takes about 4$\frac{1}{2}$ hours — the fastest train takes 14$\frac{1}{2}$ hours.

Trains get crowded, whereas a plane can only be full. Head south on the Paris—Rome Express in summer, for example, and you'll find second-class accommodation packed like sardines with itinerant Italian workers. The strain such crowding puts on the corridors, buffet and toilet facilities is huge. The fastest Paris—Rome night train is the all-sleeper and couchette 'Palatino'.

Several countries charge extra for speed. Italian and German inter-city trains and France's Rapides all charge a supplement; they are faster, and probably more comfortable too, than other trains.

Rolling-stock doesn't wear out easily: so it gets used up on local trains. Some of it can be very ramshackle and dirty — and not just in out-of-the-way places. Some London suburban lines suffer from ageing trains.

Train buffets can be grubby and the service churlish. It's not always so — but the lapses damage the repute of railways as the attractive form of travel they once were. By contrast with Britain, buffet cars are relatively few and far between on Continental railways. You're more likely to get a modern self-service arrangement, or an attendant wheeling a hot/cold drink and snack trolley up and down the corridor.

## Trans-Europe-Expresses (T.E.E.)

These provide a network of de-luxe trains linking more than 200 cities in nine countries: France, Italy, West Germany, Netherlands, Belgium, Luxembourg, Switzerland, Austria and Spain. Customs and frontier formalities are completed on the train to save delays.

These use eight different kinds of train — but they are all air-conditioned with full restaurant facilities. All are daytime trains and each has its own name. Some run within just one country — e.g. the Mistral (Paris—Nice) and Adriatico (Milan—Bari) — others through several. The Edelweiss runs from Zurich to Amsterdam via France, Luxembourg and Belgium. They are all first class only — plus a special supplement. You must book in advance. These are the crack troops of Europe's railway revival. They are for those who want to enjoy the journey for itself: rather than for travellers who only expect their enjoyment to begin when they reach their destination.

## Night travel

### Sleepers

Wagons-Lits still have 850 cars in service. There's no sign of business declining on the Continent, though increased speeds within Britain could make them redundant. Already passengers complete their night's sleep at the station platform having reached their destination by 06.00. But there's something adventurous about hurtling through the night tucked up in clean sheets and knowing you'll wake to strange scenery and delicious coffee. It's a romantic way to travel. But it can be wakeful: you may need a pill to help you sleep. Lock your door from the inside against intruders. Most overnight trains have sleepers.

## Couchettes

You can sleep as easily, but not as luxuriously in couchettes. The railway seats convert to beds, you get a pillow, blanket and small towel. First-class couchettes have four to a compartment, second class have six. It'll often mean you're sleeping with strangers: decide for yourself whether to undress or not. I've travelled with passengers who've gone in for the entire pyjama/toothbrush routine, and others who've just removed their shoes. Personally I find losing consciousness in the company of total strangers an uneasily intimate thing to do. But for a family of four or a group of friends, couchettes are ideal.

## Meals

For the future, full restaurant service is on the decline for all but the T.E.E.s. Most railway systems find high standards of cooking and service hard to maintain. And high prices are cutting down demand. Instead we can expect more cafeteria-style catering, with self-service, microwave ovens, etc. French railways are the only ones so far to go for airline-style catering with trays of food.

If you don't fancy it then take your own with you. Travelling as a family of four we've dined on our own hot soup, chicken salad, yogurts and coffee. Paper plates and plastic cutlery can be dumped at the journey's end.

## Stopovers

Book a rail ticket from London to Rome and you can hop on and off at any station en route. This is far easier than stopping over by plane, and a cheap and cheerful way of seeing Europe.

## Stations

In my view Britain has the most glorious railway architecture — St. Pancras, Marylebone, Paddington, Temple Meads in Bristol, York, Newcastle, and hundreds of picturesque smaller ones. St. Pancras has a grade I listing with the Department of the Environment, which puts it in the same class as St. Paul's. Abroad: Venice, Milan, Paris's Gare du Nord, Rome are all distinguished cathedrals of nineteenth-century expansion. It would be sad to see them go. However, new stations — when they happen — are being built as complete communities in themselves with shops, cinemas, hairdressers etc. Montparnasse in Paris is one. Britain lags behind in such developments; only Euston and Birmingham New Street can compare with the major rebuilding of stations in Frankfurt, Cologne, Munich and in the Netherlands and Scandinavia.

## Eurrail pass

This is a ticket sold to people visiting Europe — excepting France and Britain — and offers unlimited rail travel for twenty-eight days. This offers a terrifically cheap way of seeing the Continent, for there is no limit to how many times or where you can stop off.

## Bargain rail tickets on British Rail

B.R. has four main fare reductions: economy return — you must book one week in advance; day return — usually second class only; weekend return; monthly return.

There are also Runabout and Awayday offers, and each region's own bargains. If you plan to see Britain by rail, ask in advance. Paying full fares is expensive and avoidable.

## World survey

The best passenger services, overall, throughout the world are in Western Europe. British Rail are as good as any for their punctuality record. Italy's railways, however, don't always run on time: not up to the French, Dutch and British standards. In Switzerland each canton is proud of its own railways; they are a well-financed part of the social and commercial life of the country, especially in winter.

The old romantic trains like the Orient Express have now passed totally into fiction. Russian trains tend to be crowded: they have 'hard' and 'soft' classes as opposed to first and second.

Turkey has reasonable trains. Iran has recently bought turbo-trains from France. India's trains are more a cultural experience than a mode of transport. As a train leaves the station 'extra' passengers rush from the shadows and cling onto the carriages despite the use of batons by police attempting to drive them off. Speeds are leisurely. The train stops at a selected station while everyone disembarks, eats in the local restaurant and returns in their own time before the train continues.

America in the 40s had some of the most luxurious, streamlined, highly staffed railways in the world. During and after the war, aviation took over. Nowadays, the same rolling stock is dingy and under-staffed, but Amtrak — a government-supported corporation — has taken over an agreed network of long-distance services and is currently trying to salvage the best. The Boston—New York—Washington corridor has been brought up to date. With President Carter's election the track from Plains, Georgia to Washington was improved for the sake of the Peanut Special. Recently-announced building orders from Amtrak should have all the principal services modernized within a year or two. Mexico bought up some of America's old de-luxe rolling-stock which now runs on Mexican lines.

Japan has the world's fastest train. Australia has cross-continental lines, but basically the distances are too great: from Perth to Sydney takes three days and three nights by what is claimed to be the third most modern train in the world.

South America has the world's highest station at Toclio in Peru. The Peruvian Central climbs in twenty-four hours from sea level at Lima to Huancayo in the Andes reaching 4,900m (16,000 feet) on the way.

# Chapter 12
# Overlanders

Almost all the white-beaches/blue-surf/hot-sun areas of the world are, by now, being packaged and marketed by the holiday industry. But there are still vast tracts of the planet that are relatively untouched by modern change. And there are still plenty of people who set out to see them like that. Such people are often young, usually hard-up — not necessarily either — and endlessly resourceful. They're known as overlanders. The overland attitude to travel is that of the great adventurers: a mixture of curiosity, challenge, adaptability, informality and enormous energy. Before you join them you need to know something about yourself as well as about their form of travel.

## Outlook right

Unless you're really suited to overland travel you'll face misery, boredom and disappointment for yourself and be a pain in the neck for everyone else. You must understand that overlanding means adventure which means the unpredictable. If you want a tidily organized journey, with a punctual schedule, recognizable mealtimes and hot and cold water, stick with the more conventional package offers. Overlanders look upon breakdowns, delays and hold-ups at frontiers not as avoidable disasters to be greeted with anger, frustration and other symptoms of Western hysteria, but as part of the flawed pattern of life, that one must expect to happen and be prepared to handle — and which must not be allowed to spoil that peace of mind they set out to search for in the first place. If you insist on total planning and organization, keep away from overlanding.

On the other hand, plan wisely and thoroughly when you need to —
which is before you set out.

## Avoid the avoidable: illness

If you travel by van to Katmandu, hitch across Africa or foot-slog
through India then it's unlikely you'll avoid getting ill at all. But you can
try. Before you set out have all the jabs you might ever need: take a
medical supply of tablets for all likely afflictions (see p. 199). Remember
tablets for sterilizing drinking water, malaria tablets to take before and
while you're in infected areas and, if you're a woman, the pill (hard to get
and expensive abroad). Have your health fully checked out, your chest
X-rayed, and note your blood group. Take a copy of your spectacle
prescription. If you're going for long, consider a second pair of false
teeth. En route, always ask before swimming in stagnant water — it may
harbour bilharzia.

## Thieving

Anyone from the Western world seems rich beyond dreams to the
millions of urban poor and destitute peasantry that people large areas of
the earth. Sometimes whole classes of people are destitute to the point of
desperation. Child mortality is high and everyone is always hungry.
And, of course, everywhere has its share of villains. It's not surprising
that thieving is widespread in certain countries. What is ironic is that
thieves are no great problem to the wealthy package tourist, who is
insulated from such direct contact. But thieving is a constant menace to
the travellers who can least afford it — the overlanders.

So expect to have to be constantly cautious about absolutely vital pos-
sessions — and philosophical about occasionally losing the rest.

## Time-scale

A friend who once took a year off in the sun from his writing life told me
the first thing you give up is your daily engagement diary, the second is
the calendar, the third your watch.

The rest of the world — by which I mean the non-urbanized, non-
industrial world — moves at a different pace, and I'm sure it's us who are
mad — not them. So you'll need to adjust to a new time-scale. Learn to
measure the day by sunrise and sunset, to expect that the next bus will be
in three or four days. If you tackle overlanding at the frantic pace of a
busy executive, you'll give yourself more ulcers than he has. If you
temper your travelling to the rhythm of things around you — you may
not clock up so much mileage, but you'll gain in other directions.

## Politics

At any one moment, there will be political ferment, even violence, in several countries of the world. Again the advice is obvious: avoid the avoidable. To set out as a lonely traveller into disputed territory where guerrillas are known to be active is patently unwise. Either don't go at all, or at least inform the nearest British consulate and the police of your intended journey and route, and travel in convoy with others.

It is unlikely you will come upon a country in open conflict without the possibility of such trouble being already known to you. In that sense newspapers and telephones have made the world much safer for travellers. Headlines and reports usually have enough detail to give you guidance — take note of them. Local people are usually friendly and pleased to welcome visitors.

## Tips

Many travellers set out to see the world and come home to write books about it. Often those books are full of useful tips for those who come after. Theresa and Jonathan Hewat's *Overland and Beyond*, Dan Topolski's *Muzungu* are just two. From them and from the invaluable *Globe*, published by Globetrotters (see later), I have culled some introductory advice.

**Money** Make adequate plans before you go to have money sent out regularly; either by your bank manager or a reliable friend. If you're going for several years you may need to get permission from the Bank of England. Always carry a mix of cash and travellers cheques. A credit card can be useful at times.

Carry a reserve of money in a money belt under your clothes — and never leave it off. The U.S. dollar and the metric system are standard for overlanders.

**Baggage** Secure real essentials or valuables to your person. A friend of mine who tramped round most of Africa carried his essentials (camera, film and documents) in a 600 × 300 × 300 mm (2 × 1 × 1 feet) army bag and in remote places used it as a pillow. When he slept he had a string linking it conspicuously to his waist. But lest that failed to deter he had a secondary and secret attachment out of sight. Clothes — T-shirts and jeans — he carried in another shoulder bag; money in a special money belt around the waist. That was all — except one white shirt and one pair of reasonable trousers — for going to embassies. Overlanders report various treatment from British consulates and embassies: they can be dismissive of young scruffs in jeans. However, they do have obligations to all British passport-holders. So in any emergency you must look to them for help. It might simply be tactful to go looking as acceptable as possible.

T.C.T.—G

**Drugs** There are plenty of countries where smoking cannabis is no crime. However, taking drugs across frontiers almost always is. Don't try: the punishments can be very heavy indeed. And if you've picked up a hitch-hiker, insist he crosses the frontier independently of you.

**The vehicle** Most popular is the VW bus. Diesel is for obvious reasons getting more popular. Pick up maps en route (best places: border posts, tourist offices, petrol stations). Have small gifts handy — matches, ball-point pens, small mirrors, sweets for children.

*Driving documents* You may need green-card insurance; it'll see you some way into Asia and Africa. After that third-party insurance — compulsory in some places — can be obtained at the border. A *carnet de passage* is essential. Enquire of the R.A.C., A.A. and B.I.T. for information in good time before you go. An International Driving Permit lasts one year: the R.A.C. and A.A. issue them for £1.50. See also Chapter 7 on Motoring, p. 44.

*Driving styles* They're best in the U.S.A. and Canada, supposed to be worst in Brazil, lethal in Tehran, frantic in Israel. You'll need to adjust. If you knock someone over in Asia, vast and excitable crowds gather very quickly. Far safer not to stop but drive at once to the nearest police station and report the accident.

## Where to

The route to Katmandu was the hippy pilgrimage of the 60s. It's the easiest of all the overland routes; best time is between October and February. Sadly the freakier dregs of hippydom have brought white travellers into disrepute and women can be catcalled or insulted in some places. Learn Farsi numerals before you reach Iran. Burma is not open for overland travel. North America has the best facilities for motoring. South America is the most variedly interesting — with landscapes and ancient ruins and cities but some of the worst poverty. In Africa travellers can hire a lift in a lorry. Any lorry park in the morning usually has people bargaining the cost of a lift to the next village or even much further. You travel perched on the goods in the back and are subject to the driver's personal whim about meal breaks, delays etc.; apparently a delightfully informal and sunny way to travel.

South America has the world's worst roads and a chaotic postal service. Both call for extra time. In Asia you should insist the stamps on your letters are cancelled in front of you: lest the stamp is stolen! Have your mail directed either poste restante to local post offices, to the British embassy or consulate (though they're not keen), or to American Express offices where they exist. Everyone speaks of the people of Southeast Asia as the friendliest.

## Overland advantages

Easy to enumerate cheapness and freedom as fundamental. But there are packages that offer both. What is unique to overlanding is first the chance to come as close as possible to the people you visit. Apart from going to live with them, overlanding is the nearest you can get to seeing and occasionally sharing their way of life. Second is the chance you have to be changed by such a major experience. Ten-day package tours return you from a sunny resort much as you set out. True overlanding will change you, will influence your attitude to yourself, other people and the planet in general. It offers not merely sights and new experiences, but a new horizon on your own life.

## Overland packages

The genuine overlander moves in pairs, or alone. He tends to sneer at Benidorm-style packages, idle sun-worshipping, and pre-arranged travel details. However, because so many people yearn for the more adventurous holidays, overlanding itself is offered on package by several companies who deal in it exclusively.

## Overland organizations

It's a reckless adventurer indeed who locks the front door of his suburban semi, climbs in the car and heads for Katmandu. Every such traveller needs advice — there are organizations and books in plenty available to give it. Here are some:

*The Globetrotters Club* BCM/Roving, London WC1V 6XX. This was founded in 1945 by two young men who wanted to travel. They claim that the one characteristic of all members is 'an anaemic wallet' and their idea is to spread useful information on how to travel cheaply in all parts of the world. Each year they publish six editions of *Globe*: a news-sheet full of tips, addresses, accounts of remote places or unusual contacts and invitations from members for others to join their proposed journey; Globetrotters often meet up on overland trips and stay in each other's homes. Altogether a friendly and helpful set-up. Back home, local groups meet for talks and slide shows. London meetings are at the YWCA, Gt. Russell Street, at 16.00 on the first Saturday of each month.

*Wexas* 45 Brompton Road, Knightsbridge, London SW3 1DE; telephone 01-589 0500/3315. This is a club (membership £5 annually) that offers travel information and services for its members. You get published stuff: a handbook packed with useful references and a glossy bi-monthly magazine called *Expedition* with accounts of remote places. You also get the chance to purchase jet flights to 276 destinations at low-cost fares, mostly on scheduled services. The travel programme also offers adventure holidays, and an overland booking service. Wexas has been going six years, has impressive names like Blashford-Snell, Knox-Johnston, and Alec Rose as Honorary Presidents. It offers its cheap fares by bulk-buying air tickets available under the A.B.C. and A.P.E.X. fare structures.

*Royal Geographical Society* Kensington Gate, London SW7; telephone 01-589 5466. This is the golden oldie — founded in 1830, it has sponsored and helped famous explorers from Livingstone and Stanley to Fuchs and Hillary. It still does. It also has the largest private map room in Europe — half a million sheets — and a library of over 100,000 publications. It's the focal point of geography in Britain. You can join for £8.50, associate members under 24 for £3. It is a registered charity, organizes educational occasions, publishes the *Geographical Journal* three times a year, and is closely associated with the monthly *Geographical Magazine*.

*B.B.C.* On 31 March 1976 the B.B.C. closed the offers on the 1977 expedition/camera scheme in which, in collaboration with the R.G.S., it selected six outfits of young explorers who were setting out to interesting places and had a competent photographer in their number. They were given a three-day course in camera technique, some film footage, extra equipment and a £500 grant. The films they bring back are for transmission on the B.B.C.'s 'World About Us' series. The idea was thought up by Mike Andrews, a B.B.C. producer who got his first professional chance the same way. If the idea works he says they'll do it each year. Office: B.B.C., Whiteladies Road, Bristol.

*Young Explorer's Trust* 238 Wellington Road South, Stockport, Cheshire SK2 6NW; telephone 061-477 0898. An educational charity that helps young people with little experience — school parties, youth groups — to plan their expeditions. It's keen on safety and fieldwork — and has links with several conservancy and exploration organizations. They do not organize their own expeditions or make travel bookings.

*The Scientific Exploration Society Ltd.* Home Farm, Mildenhall, Marlborough, Wiltshire; for telephone enquiries ring 01-218 4574. Formed in 1969 by a group of explorers to organize further expeditions and help schools and universities to do the same. It mounts its own expeditions and has 250 members, many expert explorers themselves. You have to be proposed and elected: subscription £3 a year.

*Trail Finders* 48 Earls Court Road, London W8; telephone 01-937 4569/3336/2429. Travel agents who know the entire trekking field and book overland packages from all the major companies. What's more they guarantee money back if things go wrong: not all trekking companies are members of A.B.T.A., so that's a worthwhile guarantee.

They also publish books of advice both for overlander motorists and those overlanding by public transport. You get the books direct from them — not at bookshops. Their clientele are largely young, adventurous and, they emphasize, very fit. But they also get the energetic retired who've decided to see the 'world.

*B.I.T.* 15 Acklam Road, London W10; telephone 01-229 8219. It stands for Binary Information Transference — but don't let that put you off. It is an information exchange service — descendant of the newspaper *International Times* — that publishes nomadic guides for travelling rough, mostly for young people and full of 'alternative society' tips and contacts. They like you to help the feedback of information so they can keep constantly up to date and publish supplements as and when they're needed. Existing titles: *Overland through Africa, Overland to Central and South America, Overland through India to Australia.* Soon: *European Address Network.*

If you're planning a long and haphazard journey it's worth phoning them and talking it over. Their approach is thoroughly informal. They man a twenty-four-hour telephone service and have a Drop-In Service: you can call round any time, though after 22.00 they lock the door to drunks and undesirables. Knock — and they'll open.

*Magic Bus* 74 Shaftesbury Avenue, London W1; telephone 01-439 0557. This is a bargain-offer agency advertising in London's *Time Out.* They run several coach services under spartan conditions and at rock-bottom prices. They also sell tickets for other coach companies.

London—Athens by bus
£25 single, twice a week in summer, Saturdays only in winter. 3½ days, virtually non-stop, travelling day and night: no overnight stops. You are advised to take a supply of food and a sleeping-bag. You can book for destinations en route. Arrangements are vague: they don't guarantee any times of arrival (but neither does British Rail) nor even departure times. Buses leave from various parts of London: check the day before you go. Other European routes: London—Paris, £10 single; London—Venice, £21 single; London—Tangiers, £47 single. Don't expect any concessions to luxury. This is one of the cheapest ways to go. And you may not think it's worth the exhaustion and strain you feel by the time you get there. But you can go further.

London—Delhi by bus
Most frequently towards the end of summer. Some day-and-night driving, sometimes stops for two days, when it's up to you to find your own accommodation. The journey can take from four to six weeks. Single booking only. Return arrangements must be made in Delhi. Istanbul £38. Delhi £70.

*Magic Train* 74 Shaftesbury Avenue, London W 1; telephone 01-439 0557. London to Holland in ten hours by day, twelve hours by night. Single £10, return £20. A service available only for those under twenty-six.

*A.A.* Fanum House, The Broadway, Stanmore, Middlesex; telephone 01-954 7355.

*R.A.C.* Touring Services, P.O. Box 92, R.A.C. House, Lansdowne Road, Croydon CR9 9DH; telephone 01-686 2314.

Both the A.A. and the R.A.C. offer a route-planning service and a number of publications for the motorist abroad. Allow at least six weeks for them to prepare routes.

## Book a lift

Hitch-hiking was once the cheapest and friendliest way of getting around: but you also risked getting robbed and injured. Some governments got anxious and made hitch-hiking illegal. Yet it still goes on and the risks are still there. But another lift-giving service now exists:

*The Lift Exchange Centre,* 14 Broadway, London SW1; telephone 01-834 9225. It runs rather like a dating service for travellers. Would-be passengers phone and pay £1.00 to register, and have their journey put on file for offers. You can phone and ask to register for a lift to Afghanistan in three months time. You can also phone and ask whether they have a lift on offer to Edinburgh tomorrow morning. Similarly motorists phone in their offers: driving to Benidorm in July, or Swansea next week. And your amiable contact man, Mike Carter, links up the two.

When I spoke to him he had more offers than requests on his books: lifts to Sri Lanka or India were going begging. A teacher planning to start a school in Andorra was happy to take people along on his monthly journey there.

Lift Exchange is not a commercial operation; other than the £1.00 registration no money changes hands. But those being given the lift would obviously buy their share of the petrol wouldn't they? This sort of thing should be sorted out before you set off.

Passengers offered lifts have to sign a disclaimer saying that Lift Exchange is not responsible if things go wrong. After all, divorcees don't sue marriage bureaus. So it's up to you to decide who to trust.

*Provoy* This is a hitch-a-lift service, like Britain's Lift Exchange but operating from Paris. You pay 5 francs to join. Then a further 12 francs to ask for a ride. Each year they get some 10,000 passenger enquiries to match with some 6,000 drivers. They also do lifts by private plane: 1,000

passengers a year go with around 100 pilots. There's an implicit under-
standing that you share some of the cost. By car it's usually a private
agreement with the driver. By plane, usually more standard: e.g. Paris to
Nice for 400–500 francs, the cost of the first-class rail return.

Contact them at: 14 rue du Faubourg-St.-Denis, Paris 10$^e$; telephone
Paris 246 0066.

# Chapter 13
# Bicycling

Next to walking, cycling is the cheapest way to get around: the fuel is free.
Cycling is also healthy and offers a relaxing change from the tensions of
urban life. *But* you must be fit. It is no good embarking on two weeks
cycling – however modest – if you haven't cycled for years.

You must like the feeling of exercise, and of being outdoors. You must
expect to feel tired by the end of the day. For some it will be a euphoric
tiredness of achievement and well-being. The rest should go by car.

If you don't want to be too energetic, cycle for short distances in flat
country, stay at hotels, eat in restaurants and take trains for the major
journeys.

If you can face a harder trip take a sleeping-bag, lightweight tent or
tarpaulin, a small stove and cooking set. The ultimate in freedom and
economy, it could also be a hardship holiday if you're not the type. You
can stay on private land (ask permission first) or organized camping sites
(see page 146). Alternatively stay at Youth Hostels and travel from one
to another (see page 157).

## Preparation

Give yourself six to eight weeks to get in trim. Start with ten minutes
cycling a day. After a week, extend to half-hour rides. At weekends try to
fit in two half-hour rides a day. After another week you should be
through the first barrier: your seat, back and legs will no longer be sore.
Then plan a first day-long trip. Make it about twenty miles. You can
holiday happily without ever going further than that in a day.

If you're embarking on longer distances you'll need more advanced
techniques: consult other cyclists, books on the subject, and cycling

clubs — the British Cycling Bureau, 70 Brompton Road, London SW3, telephone 01-584 6706 (they have a small touring department); the Cyclists' Touring Club, 69 Meadrow, Godalming, Surrey, telephone 04868 7217.

Books: *Bicycle Touring in Europe* by Karen and Gary Hawkins (Sidgwick and Jackson, £1.25); *The Maintenance of Bicycles and Mopeds* (Readers Digest Guide, 50p); *Richard's Bicycle Book* by Richard Ballantine (Pan Books, £1.25).

## Advice

Get the right bike: a single speed won't do. You need gears, under-slung handlebars, centre-pull brakes, toe clips, water bottle, kick-stands — the lot. Take time and care — buy from a specialist cycle shop in a big city. The price can go into three figures: try to get one second-hand.

Start where there is little traffic. Tour on quiet roads — it's prettier anyway.

Never push yourself to exhaustion. What's wrong with ten miles a day? Dedicated cyclists might sneer, but let them if you're enjoying yourself on the cheap.

If you're cycling with someone respect their fitness and limitations too. Don't force their pace — they'll be lousy company in the evening!

Women might find the physical demands harder initially. They'll also be less inclined to go for record-breaking distances, so don't match yourself against men when getting into training, measure yourself against yourself. Once in trim you might even out-distance him; but don't think of it as a competitive endurance test.

Take a try-out weekend away first to check out difficulties and unexpected problems.

## Information

*British Cycling Federation,* 70 Brompton Road, London SW3 1EN; telephone 01-584 6706. Will give information and route maps. Its handbook costs 65p and has a list of repairers and accommodation. There is a touring section at the back.

*Cyclists' Touring Club,* Cotterell House, 69 Meadrow, Godalming, Surrey; telephone Godalming 7217 (S.T.D. code 04868). Its handbook lists bicycle-hire centres.

## Bicycles by rail

Since the summer of 1977 British Rail have allowed bicycles to travel free: a victory for the cycling lobby and a big boost for rural holidays. It must be carried in the guard's van, padlocked and labelled. It's probably wise to load and unload it yourself.

# Chapter 14
# Travel by water

The land is getting so crowded that more and more people are taking to boats. If you do, make sure your insurance covers all particular hazards that might arise on the water. Means of staying afloat vary from the canoe adventure holiday to cruising on ocean-going liners. Each of them has its individual problems; there are some common to all.

## Swimming

You should never try canoeing unless you can swim at least 25 metres. Canoe clubs and organized group activity centres will insist you can. Similarly many sailing clubs and teaching establishments will insist on you being able to swim. To get a Royal Yachting Association Proficiency Certificate you must be able to swim 50 yards in sailing clothes. Practise swimming in old pyjamas and sweaters, and worn-through plimsolls. Children should not be allowed in a boat unless they can swim.

If you do have small children and non-swimmers in the party they should wear life-jackets and buoyancy aids. Often these will be hired to you by whoever hires the boat.

Get the booklet, *On the Water in the Water* from the Royal Society for the Prevention of Accidents, Royal Oak Centre, Brighton Road, Purley, Surrey.

Hotel boats, Thames barges and cruiser liners are on the way to becoming floating hotels. You'd look barmy dining at the captain's table in a life-jacket. Nonetheless, if you go on one of the big cruise boats, you should know where there are lifebelts, life-jackets and lifeboats. Since the *Titanic*, nothing's considered unsinkable. It's up to you to check out the basic precautions for survival.

## Clothing

To be obvious, life on water is cooler and wetter. You won't get stung by
sea spray on a liner — but almost anything less that's seagoing will call
for special protection. Luxury cruising calls for special clothing too: all
the finery you've got, plus anything you can scrounge from friends.

## Space

All boats have limited space, even the *QE2*. Small boats impose a close,
almost claustrophobic way of life. You must be temperamentally suited
to it: otherwise you'll hate every minute and your fellow travellers will
hate you. These points help to ease the strain.

**Tidiness** A boat, like a caravan, is built with no waste space. Everything
has its place: keep it there. Fold and tidy beds once you're up — even if
you just throw covers back in place. Stow things away when they're not
in use; even on quiet inland waterways, a bump or wake of a passing boat
can wreak havoc in the galley.

**Temperament** Loud noisy personalities, however jovial, need space.
On a boat they don't have it. Calm your natural exuberance to the scale
of the living area — otherwise you'll drive everyone else nuts.

**Captain** Someone must be in charge of a boat. He must know what he's
doing, and be trusted by the others. They must do what he says.
Arguments and discussion can cause accidents. Boats don't have brakes
to screech to a halt. If you stop to debate a decision, you could cause a
collision. If you insist on equality, take it in turns to be captain day by
day.

**Moorings** Take the chance to escape the closeness of the boat: go
shopping, stop for a pint, a landmark, a chance to explore. It releases the
tensions of living on top of each other and extends the scope of the
holiday.

**Relax** Private boats are popular with tycoons and executives just
because they are supposed to offer instant relaxation. But that's up to
you. If you bring the strains and drive of the boardroom to the deck you'll
ruin it all. Don't set yourself targets of mileage, speed or achievement.
Enjoy the moment for itself, relish the slow pace, wallow in *not* being in a
hurry. Learn to waste time.

**Share the work equitably** Don't let the same people hog all the most
glamorous jobs and leave others with the chores.

## Canoeing

There are several types available: sea canoeing, Canadian canoeing, sail canoeing, and, the most popular, canoeing on inland waterways and rivers. The shape of canoe is different for each type.

As well as the canoe you will need paddles, life-jacket and spray deck. If you go to an adventure centre the cost of the holiday will include hire of equipment and instruction.

A life-jacket must be worn. The best are those that have maximum buoyancy on the chest and neck, and so float you face up automatically. Fit buoyancy bags in bow and stern and be sure that they are properly fastened in. Carry a repair kit.

A spray deck is a waterproof cover that fits round the cockpit and prevents water entering. It keeps you dry and warm below the waist. Other clothing you'll need will be shirt, shorts, light rubber-soled shoes or sandals and an oilskin jacket for wet weather.

The British Canoe Union, 70 Brompton Road, London SW3 1DT, governs canoeing in England. It publishes a list of clubs for enthusiasts, BCU publications, and a list of courses and canoeing holidays available in Britain. See, too, the B.T.A.'s *Activity Holidays*.

## Safety

In tidal waters always canoe in groups. Get weather and tide information.

Have a safety informant: the Coastguards are ideal. Boat owners complete and post a pre-paid card (CG66A) giving the Coastguard a description of their craft and their area of activity. These are kept by the Coastguard as a reference.

For longer journeys, fill out card CG66B giving details of the proposed route. Lodge a duplicate with a friend or relative; then if the boat is overdue, they contact the Coastguard station named. If you return late or make an emergency landing elsewhere − tell at once. You can get these cards at Coastguard stations, yacht clubs and marinas.

Carry distress signals − such as the Mars red hand flares − in a waterproof packet and stowed to hand.

A strong light line should be attached to both bow and stern of the canoe and specially secured so they don't tangle when capsizing.

In the event of capsize do *not* attempt to right a canoe; instead swim with it *across* the stream, *not* downstream. Only leave the canoe if it is approaching danger. If you can't reach the bank, stay with the canoe, it will support you and help rescuers to see you.

## Cruising on inland waterways

### Long narrow boats

With sleeping accommodation for ten, central heating, showers, etc. These are ideal for youth groups and parties. You do your own catering and usually your own crewing. But some do have a boatman.

### Four- to six-berth boats

You do it all yourself, converting the table into bunks and back again night and morning. The Broads and the Thames teem with them. There are even some on the Caledonian Canal. Ideal for beginners: a child could steer them.

### Hotel boats

These are for the leisured life. There's usually a crew and resident chef, fitted carpets, hot and cold water, bath, shower, public rooms, often with bar, and private bathrooms. The boats are usually converted barges plying on major waterways. My personal favourites take you through Burgundy, or along the Canal du Midi.

*Continental Waterways,* 22 Hams Place, London SW1; telephone 01-584 6773. They have seven hotel boats in all: three in Burgundy (one is charter only), two on the Canal du Midi, one in central and eastern France (charter only), and one on the Thames.

**Norfolk and Suffolk Broads** This system has three main rivers, Bure, Yare and Waveney, plus tributaries and many lakes: about 185 km (115 miles) of main waterways. Tidal, without locks. The tidal currents are very placid until you get to Great Yarmouth. On one occasion, we failed to tie up our dinghy securely overnight. Next morning it was missing. It turned up, floating out to sea at Great Yarmouth! The main towns are Norwich, Lowestoft, Beccles and Great Yarmouth.

**River Thames** The non-tidal 200 km (125 miles) from Teddington Lock to Lechlade are open to hire boats. There are forty-three locks, each managed by a lock-keeper. The area around is rich in places to see: Hampton Court, Windsor, Cliveden, Sonning, Pangbourne, Goring, Marlow and Henley-on-Thames. The banks offer easy access to good eating places: so take one or more of the published eating guides (see page 125). The main towns are Oxford, Abingdon, Henley-on-Thames, Maidenhead, Staines, Chertsey, Weybridge, Walton-on-Thames, Kingston upon Thames, Teddington, Twickenham, Richmond, Isleworth and Brentford.

**Caledonian Canal – Scotland** From Inverness to Fort William, the canal links Loch Lochy, Loch Oich, and Loch Ness. The scenery is wild and beautiful: the traffic very light. There is a series of locks at Fort

Augustus with lock-keeper. Don't swim in Loch Ness — the water is glacially cold: you'll die of hypothermia in no time. The towns on the canal are Fort William, Inverness and Fort Augustus.

**Fens** Cruising here centres on the Nene through Peterborough and the Great Ouse: a network of drainage channels connects them, but you can't cruise here without experience and special permission. The countryside is wide and airy — less busy than the Broads. Main towns are Northampton, Wellingborough, Peterborough, Wisbech, St. Neots, Huntingdon, St. Ives, Cambridge and Ely.

**Waterways and Canals of Central England and Wales** These come under the jurisdiction of the British Waterways Board which has two hire-cruiser fleets, at Nantwich and at Hillmorton. Locks are normally operated by holiday-makers. Don't be put off by waterways with locks. Locks offer interest, excitement and a chance to meet other boats and sometimes shop at lockside stores. They aren't too difficult to manoeuvre. It shouldn't be one person's prerogative either: everyone should — indeed must — lend a hand. The Board publishes five guides to the waterways at £1.50 each. Write to: Willow Grange, Church Road, Watford, Herts; telephone Watford 26422; or Melbury House, Melbury Terrace, London NW1; telephone 01-262 6711.

## France

The Canal du Midi is the most renowned, crossing southern France via Carcassonne and Toulouse. You can hire your own boat or take a hotel boat. The route is an old one, full of the picturesque and the traditional. But all French canals are well maintained: and some lock-keepers are women.

## Holland

Canals constitute one of Holland's main traffic systems — so there are plenty to choose from. The landscape's flat — so there are no locks to handle. The countryside looks much like the Broads, but the local fishing villages are old-style Dutch. Motor cruising and hotel boats are popular.

## Germany

Canals here are mainly commercial: where they are not, boat prices are high. Enquiries to the German Tourist Information Bureau, 61 Conduit Street, London W1; telephone 01-734 2600.

## Denmark

Plenty of small harbours and islands to visit; expect changeable weather, possibly blowy.

## Ireland

The Shannon is navigable for 225 km (140 miles) — very beautiful, and still unspoilt. There are ruined castles and medieval remains along its banks. Several companies hire motor cruisers.

## How to book

Write direct to the boat-hire company. The boating press will be con-
fusingly full of names and pictures of boats. If it's all too much ask an
agent:

*Boat Enquiries Limited*, 7 Walton Well Road, Oxford OX2 6ED; telephone
Oxford 511161 (S.T.D. code 0865), covers a vast area, but is especially
good on Thames and the Midland areas, and abroad. The firm publishes
a helpful *Lazyman's Guide to Holiday Afloat* very cheaply, and has a
twenty-four-hour answering service for queries — and from January to
March a twelve-hour booking service. Hirers don't pay for the booking
service.

*Hoseasons*, Oulton Broad, Lowestoft, Suffolk; telephone 0502 64991.
Agents for over 18,000 boats on all the popular waterways of Britain,
including the Norfolk Broads, Fenland waterways, the Thames, the
Caledonian Canal, Scotland, the River Shannon and the canals and
rivers of England and Wales.

*Blakes Holidays*, Wroxham, Norwich NR12 8DH; telephone 060 53 2141.
Agents for: 1,200 boats on the Broads, including 75 yachts and 50
houseboats, the rest cruisers; 20 boats on the Shannon; 56 on the
Thames; and 160 on canals throughout England. They are also agents
for companies with boats in France, Holland and Switzerland. They
publish boat-handling guides in French and German for visitors to the
Broads.

*National tourist offices*, including our own, will supply details of canal
holidays available in their countries.

## What to take

### Clothing

Extremely informal. You can get by with a rag-bag of old, outdated
clothes but they should each have a function. Trousers and jeans and
sweaters are the most common and most convenient combinations.
Women in skirts won't find clambering around either easy or discrete.
For a week's holiday I suggest, for both men and women:

 3 pairs trousers
 6 T-shirts — thin and easy to pack
 2 shirts
 2 good bulky sweaters: if it's very chilly, then wear one over the other.
    At Loch Ness in June, I've had to wear three at once. So have a
    super large one; women can borrow a man's.
 plenty of underwear: I favour cotton fabric. Also paper knickers: use
    and throw away. Then you don't build up a heap of dirty washing.
    Take a plastic bag for the rest.

7 pairs socks

shoes: at least two pairs — one might be plimsolls, another rope-soled espadrilles. This is no place for stacked soles, fashion heels etc. But if you care about fashion you will, of course, ignore the warning.

wellingtons: good for up and down the bank, wading in water if you get grounded. Not a good idea for clambering over the boat in mid-stream. If you did fall over, they'd fill up and drag you down.

nightwear: expect to be colder than at home. Take winceyette pyjamas or nighties. You might need thick socks, too. A heavy sweater will do duty as a dressing-gown. Small motor cruisers are no place to insist on privacy and modesty. Be prepared to dress, undress, sleep and wake in sight of everyone on board. If you're shy about it: either change your friends, or go on a bigger boat.

outerwear: anoraks and windcheaters are best. They may look thin but buy a size big enough to take bulky sweaters underneath, and come well down your thighs. Dress in layers and peel off as the day hots up. You must have a complete rainproof top, which covers your head. So unless your anorak has a hood, you'll need a water-proof hat or cap, just the garment to indulge your fashion fantasies: it'll cheer everyone up when it's raining.

for evening outings: women might like to have one dress with them. Men might want something kept neat and crisp for an evening meal out somewhere. But jeans and a crisp top will do it. Waterside pubs and hotels are pretty informal. So keep dressing up within modest limits.

don't: go in for washing clothes. It takes up water and space. And you're on holiday. Take a thick plastic bag for all the dirties.

## Other essentials

Compass, string, scissors, medical box, torch and spare batteries, sewing repair kit, keys from home and car (string them with two or three corks, so if they go overboard they'll float), tin-opener, corkscrew, bottle opener, asbestos mat for gas cooker. Baby items: a small baby won't get much fun out of a boat. But there's no reason why they shouldn't go along. You'll need to take special care and special equipment, e.g. disposable nappies and tins of baby food.

## Optionals

Pack of cards — or other games, paperbacks, scrapbook (it'll keep children happy if ever the going's a bit dull for them), transistor (but play it quietly — most people choose boats for tranquillity).

## Supplies and supplied

Most hire firms supply stoves, crockery and cutlery, and blankets. Sometimes you have to ask specially for linen (when booking) or bring your own: check on things like tea-towels. Sleeping-bags are ideal.

Check the number and condition of life-jackets and buoyancy aids before setting out. Check also there's a fire extinguisher, anchor, bucket and bilge pump.

## Food

Take a store of tinned and packaged food — waterways don't always go near shops. Many hire companies will put through a grocery order for you and have it waiting on your arrival. If your small children are fussy or you're particular, take some supplies with you. For some items, like olive oil, it's not worth buying small quantities specially, so take some from your home stock in a suitable container.

## Drink

Waterside stores and pubs sometimes charge more for bottles of beer, whisky and wine, than local discount stores at home. You're paying for the convenience of having it to hand. Save money by taking it with you. With children, take orange squash in 5-litre plastic containers.

## Fuels

**Diesel** is more economical and safer from risk of fire. But a diesel engine is slightly noisier and creates more vibration than a petrol one. A full tank will usually last at least two weeks. Don't turn off the supply of diesel fuel unless there is a fire.

**Petrol** is less economical so you will have to refuel at fuel stations. Remember no smoking or naked lights. Turn off the engine, and make sure any spilt drops are wiped up before restarting the engine. Do not store petrol below decks.

**Gas** Bottled gas (butane or propane) is generally used for heating and cooking. Turn it off at the bottle after use in case of leakage from the pipes. The gas is heavier than air and will sink to the floor. It has a strong smell. If you suspect a leak make up a soapy solution, smear it round the pipes and watch for bubbles. If this confirms a leak, open doors and windows, lift the floorboards and waft the gas out by fanning with a towel.

## Cooking

The bottled-gas flame is much hotter than household gas so it cooks faster but makes simmering on a low light difficult. Take an asbestos mat to reduce its heat.

Light your match before turning the gas tap. Make sure they're well and truly turned off when you've finished.

## Meal tips

Grill rather than fry — it saves fat splashing.
Take special care to keep saucepan handles turned away.
Use silver foil to keep utensils clean.
For quick cold lunches and no washing up use paper plates.

**Water** The tanks only hold a limited quantity: you stock up at filling points. But take care not to run out in between.

## Plumbing

### Lavatories

No, it doesn't flush away into the canal or river; that's illegal. Boats either have Elsan-type chemical toilets, which you empty at indicated points on the bank, or, more usually now, flushing toilets with a holding tank — out of sight and smell — that is cleared by suction process by the boat company responsible. So there's nothing 'nasty' for you to do.

### Other plumbing

Water from sinks, showers and baths is not considered polluting. So this normally drains from the boat into the waterway.

## Rules of the river

### Symbols

See p. 139 for a comprehensive list of symbols.

### Traffic

Anywhere on water, power always gives way to sail. On inland water-ways always keep to the right, and overtake on the left. The speed limit is usually 4 m.p.h. (6.4 km per hour). You have the space to do more on waters like Loch Ness. Otherwise you will see your wash breaking on the banks: that damages them, irritates fishermen and drives away birdlife. Slow down before moored boats, bends in the waterway and bridges.

### Tying-up

Don't moor near water points or at sanitary disposal stations. Others need access.

Don't moor on the outside of bends; large boats will need the space to negotiate the turn.

Don't moor near bridges or blind curves.

Don't plant your tying-up stake so that your rope lies across the towpath. It could cause accidents. Use bollards and rings where you can.

### Operating locks

See the accompanying illustration.

T.C.T.—H

## Going down

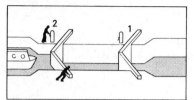

1 Make sure the bottom gates and paddles are closed.
2 If the lock is empty, fill it by raising the top paddles.

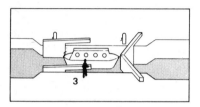

3 Open top gates and enter lock.

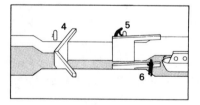

4 Close top gates behind you and lower the paddles.
5 Raise bottom paddles to empty lock.
6 Open bottom gates and take your boat out.

REMEMBER TO CLOSE THE GATES BEHIND YOU AND LOWER THE PADDLES.

## Going up

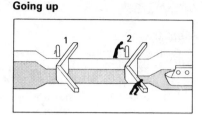

1 Make sure the top gates and paddles are closed.
2 If the lock is full, empty it by raising the bottom paddles.

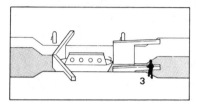

3 Open bottom gates and enter lock.

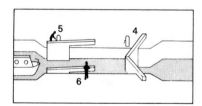

4 Close bottom gates behind you and lower the paddles.
5 Raise the top paddles to fill lock.
6 Open top gate and take your boat out.

REMEMBER TO CLOSE THE GATES BEHIND YOU AND LOWER THE PADDLES.

## Cruises

Cruising used to be only for the rich and leisured. If you're already either of these, you probably know about cruising already and this run-down is not for you.

As the numbers of rich and leisured dwindle, cruises have adapted their style, their range, their length, and their cost to attract the moderately affluent for different time-spans: from as little as three or four days port hopping in the Med. to three-month round-the-worlders. So the first thing to know about cruising is the choice.

There are 100 cruise ships currently operating round the world. In 1977 80,000 berths were on offer for cruises setting out from the U.K., 50,000 of them on P. & O. ships. No new passenger cruise ships are being built at all apart from one or two new Russian vessels. The boom has moved elsewhere: to car ferries. However, 100 ships and 80,000 berths can't be bad. Certainly, some 200,000 people travel on pleasure ocean voyages annually from the U.K.

**How to find the right one for you** Of Britain's 4,000 travel agents, about 400 are strong on cruising. If you want to be directed to your nearest, you send an s.a.e. to: The Passenger Shipping Association, Russell Chambers, Covent Garden, London WC2. This is a trade organization which will also help with any tough queries — e.g. which cruise ship will take a wheelchair, which cruise calls at Tonga? But don't go to them for generalized information. That's for your travel agent to provide.

*Cruises and Sea Voyages* is an A.B.T.A.-approved booklet which costs 25p from travel agents only and gives cruise details.

*The A.B.C. Shipping Guide* comes out monthly and is the travel agent's bible. It lists everything that sails, and where to. Get your hands on one if you won't take anyone else's word. Try libraries.

If you're prepared to research even further afield, the book to go for is: *Cruise Ships* by Gary Bannerman, which is detailed and comprehensive, and is published by Saltair Publishing, P.O. Box 2003, Sydney, British Columbia, Canada.

You can read all the listings in the world and be spoilt for choice, unless you decide your own preferences. These are some of the differences that might weigh for or against.

**Age groups** Cruising is popular among older age groups. They have both time and money. The older tend to converge on the longer cruises, and especially in the winter months. Some are old hands and disembark from one to embark on another. Many couples meet up regularly with friends made on other cruises. Families and younger couples go for shorter cruises and more usually in summer months. Two weeks in Europe obviously attracts those without the money or time to go further.

**Children** Some cruises don't take any: some have age limits. If you're thinking of taking a toddler get full details of what help you can expect.

**How sociable are you?** Cruises are not suitable for people who want privacy and quiet. Cruises are highly structured floating hotels with heaps of organization (from mealtimes to fancy-dress parties), heaps of facilities (numerous bars, cinema, pool, etc.) and lots of opportunities for chumminess and making new friends. Single people will find plenty of company: there are many more unattached women than unattached men.

Some ships have more organized activities than others: bingo, lectures, keep fit, cookery demonstrations, old-time music-hall. Church bells will ring for Sunday service. You may have a daily events list pushed under your door each morning. There may be a ship's newspaper and information hand-outs before you arrive in each port. Your role is clear enough: you must enjoy yourself with whichever combination of activities or non-activities appeal to you. You must allow yourself to be catered for and to: you are a pampered consumer of the leisurely life. Try to be anything else, and you rock the boat.

**Aboard and abroad** One of the delights of cruising is the chance to see many different places. If it's your first reason for going, then you should take a cruise that gives maximum time on land, and merely uses the ship as an overnight hotel. The trade calls these port-hopping cruises. Ask how long you're allowed in each place: five or six hours is only adequate, ten or twelve gives you more scope. The Holland America Line allow thirty hours in Bali: and it still isn't enough. Alternatively, you can cruise to a destination, say, the Canaries, stop off for a week and cruise back: or combine a cruise there with a flight back. There are hundreds of variations: so persist with enquiries.

**Size and space** Once on board you can't get away. So you need elbow-room. As a quick calculation divide the number of passengers into the gross tonnage: if the answer is 40 or more you're alright, 25–30 is fair, 15 or less means cramped – O.K. for port hopping, too choked for longer distances.

Some conversions of boats from two classes to one have not been successful. The two separate sets of accommodation were adequate for one class each. As converted boats they have no public room large enough to take all the passengers, so dances and cabaret events can be very crowded. Ask if the disco is well out of earshot for sleeping: is there a self-contained reading-room or library?

**Steward/passengers** On expensive cruises you can expect one steward to every three passengers. One steward to every ten is normal; one to every twenty is poor. The crucial question: do they serve breakfast in the cabin?

**Accommodation** The price differential is huge: the cheapest cabins have no shower or toilet. The costliest are an entire suite. Ask about size, whether the beds are bunks, air-conditioning, electric sockets, toilet facilities, lifts, laundries, telephone and radio.

**Nationalities** Cruising is an American passion and that's where the money is. So more and more cruises slant their appeal to the American passenger and the American dollar. 90% of passengers on a Caribbean cruise will be American. Europe's fly-cruises attract a mix of Europeans. Ithaca for some reason attracts almost 100% British. If you have private prejudices, keep them private, but ask your travel agent about the international mix you can expect on different cruises.

**Seasickness** Passengers usually get their sea-legs after two days. In the meantime you may need travel pills or an injection (10 dollars each on the *QE2*). If you're easily queasy, choose a boat with good stabilizing, or take a fly-cruise that cuts out the Channel and the Bay of Biscay. And avoid old converted freighters, and seas known to be stormy. The Eastern Mediterranean can turn rough, even in August.

**Cost** Cruising was costly, is getting cheaper, but still costs a good deal. The cheapest daily rate for P. & O. cruises from the U.K. in 1977 was £20 per person full board. But there are extras: bar drinks, excursions, shopping and tipping.

*Tipping*: rates vary around £1 per day for cabin and table steward — paid at the end of the voyage. Tip for drinks as you go. It adds up. Russian boats run slightly cheaper cruises and don't accept tips. They're less grand, more informal.

*Excursions*: organized by coach from the port of call. An expensive extra. It's almost always worth two or four of you clubbing together to pay for your own taxi. Go where *you* want at your own pace.

*Duty-free area*: Your limit of £300 travellers cheques applies abroad — not on board. You can pay drinks bills and for shopping in your own cheques on a British ship: save the £300 for souvenirs of distant places. Cigarettes and spirits are cheap at sea, wine about the same as on land.

*Economies*: You can choose a cabin without its own bath or W.C. and hop along the corridor. Indeed this is common on quite pricey trips. You can share a cabin or have one on the inner corridor. Some cruises keep the price down by berthing in remote parts of the port or out in the bay.

**Social life** The idea is to wine and dine in leisurely comfort. This isn't so easy in two sittings. Also the ship's officers will give small parties for passengers: the cocktail hour hums with activity. You'll be expected to dress up a bit at night. Some boats are more formal than others: rarely 100% dinner jackets, but the ladies usually put on a show.

Dressing up is part of the fun. Take all you've got and more — you can borrow. Cruise-wear departments in stores will show the way. It's usual for women to wear something different each night: if it's a strain, take one long skirt and a variety of tops — sitting at table, no one can tell. On cultural cruises: e.g. Swans Hellenic — not so much display is expected.

**Menus** Eating is one of the main pastimes of cruising. Meal after meal is set before you: the temptation to overdo it is huge. Have seltzer, liver salts, etc., in readiness. The food will be standard international, with perhaps a few dishes of the same nationality as the shipping line. Special diets — e.g. vegetarian or kosher — can be provided on some cruises.

### Illness and death

With ageing passengers cruising through different latitudes and climates for several months, it's not surprising people get ill. Sometimes a virus can sweep an entire ship. Ships usually carry ample medical staff, supplies and facilities. In fact, if you're going to have a heart attack, you couldn't choose a better place than on board: they'll reach you with emergency equipment in less than five minutes. Still a passenger list decimated by infection is a glum affair: you may want to take your own vitamins and simple medicine.

If there's a death on board, the captain and crew know what to do (see page 273).

## Chartering a yacht

This is increasingly popular — especially with yacht owners who see hiring out their expensive toys as the best way of paying for maintenance costs. So for the weeks when owners are not personally on board they put their vessels on offer to the rest of us. It doesn't have to be a millionaire's holiday — but it certainly can be if you can afford it.

### Agencies

The Mediterranean and the Caribbean are thick with charter firms: the people who organize the hiring out of the boats on the owners' behalf. It is the owner's responsibility to see that his boat is seaworthy, equipped with safety needs, flares, life-raft etc. The agency negotiates the hiring agreement and hands the boat over to the hirer.

### U.K. chartering

The main British yachting centres are the Solent, the Clyde, the Thames estuary and the harbours of the southwest like Salcombe and Torquay. For addresses of established charter firms look in the yachting magazines or consult the Yacht Charter Association, 33 Highfield Road, Lymington, Hampshire; telephone Lymington 72472 (S.T.D. code 0590).

The oldest in the business, so they say, is Blackwater Yacht Charters based at Maldon, Essex. Besides hiring by the week they also do three-day weekends — at half the weekly rate. Boats are fully kitted out: you simply arrive and sail away. Good charter firms will always tell you what they provide so you know what to bring of your own — sheets, soap, groceries, etc. Charter firms also usually ask you to sign a previous-experience form.

## Warning

Never sail in tidal waters without experience. Estuaries can be very tricky with strong tides and wind and no room to manoeuvre — in some ways even more dangerous than mid-Channel where you at least have plenty of sea room.

The Dover Strait is one of the world's busiest seaways. Some 300 to 500 ships use it every day. To avoid risk of collision a Traffic Separation Scheme was set up in 1967. The number of collisions declined. The Channel Navigation Information Service gives regular radio broadcasts of navigational information, including information about 'rogue' vessels. Details from H.M. Coastguard, Marine Survey Offices, Room 306, Gaywood House, Great Peter Street, London SW1P 3LW.

## Crewed boats

These are bigger craft and can go further afield. Many will have a captain, mate and cook to take care of the sailing for you. Thames barges come into this class. Anglian Yacht Services even operate some cruises specially for bird-watchers or painters and on those trips you simply hire yourself a berth, and meet fellow travellers on board.

## World charter

This is the big time! You can hire either a sailing or motor yacht fully crewed and live like kings on the high seas. These charters involve flying to and from the port of hire. Although charter yachts can and do cross the oceans it's rare for charterers to go with them. Instead the charter firm will quote you an inclusive price for flight, yacht and crew hire.

**Cost** It doesn't have to be astronomical. Halseys — Britain's prime charter specialists with offices in U.K., France and Greece — quoted me £137 per person, without food or any extras, for a week's charter in April of an 18.9m (62-foot) sailing yacht with crew of three, and equipment that included deep-freeze, fridge, dinghy with engine, water-skis and fishing gear. It gets pricier in the high season: two weeks in July or August on the same boat with airfare, food and fuel added would be about £600 per person. If you want luxury they have it: the sort of millionaire's yachts that are furnished with French antiques, and their own internal telephone system, and fold-away bicycles for remote exploring. These are costly: a 340-ton yacht with a crew of ten, taking up to eleven passengers rents at around $17,500 per July week. But even in this market you need to know what you want — and to say so very clearly to the broker. 90% of luxury-yacht hirers enter into the arrangement without seeing the boat. So decide first, do you want a formal or informal life? Sail is less formal because the crew mix with the holiday-makers — they have to sail the boat, remember. But a motor yacht can be as formal as you like, with the crew remaining up front and boarding on the port side, while the charterers come aboard on the starboard side. Many of these motor yachts have crews straight out of Wodehouse — men who have been stewards for twenty years. Usually most crews speak English: the captain certainly will. And usually they try to arrange that one crew member will be a woman — not to oblige a boat-load of bachelors but for 'those feminine touches' or personal attention.

This style of sailing is, of course, the ideal of luxury and relaxation — it's much favoured by harassed executives, the sort who work ulcer-hard all year in order to afford it. A vicious or delicious circle! Some fifteen years ago it was the sport of film stars, then property developers got rich and it was their turn. Nowadays clients are often from oil countries. David Halsey's more recent bookings show a revival of American interest. He takes it as evidence that the economic decline is over. If it suits busy men, wives won't get bored either. For a yacht can moor somewhere different each night, visit noisy ports or tiny harbours with markets and restaurants, or make for sleepy bays just round the corner of tourist cities. From the sea you can find unspoiled coastline even along the crowded South of France or Majorca: beaches and bays that are inaccessible by road.

But to get right away, join your charter at the Seychelles or the newly opening up Maldive Islands. Southern Turkey is still unspoilt. Alaska sounds an unlikely spot, but in summer it is apparently warm, empty and beautiful.

Life on board probably wakes around 7 each morning when early birds go for a swim or water-ski. By 9.30 or 10 everyone else is probably up too, for a leisurely breakfast while the yacht gets under way. It may cruise for two or three hours, then stop for swimming, snorkelling or fishing before visiting a harbour for lunch ashore. Three or four hours afternoon cruising will take you to another port to visit. Dine on board or on shore as you please — visit a night-club or a disco — or cruise on to a secluded bay for the night. I don't know why I'm telling you all this. You don't need persuasion: you need the money!

**Snags** Yes, at least the rich can be miserable in comfort. But you won't be relaxed if the crew is quarrelsome or argumentative. If the weather's bad you stay in port: choose one with indoor local interest — a museum or casino. If the weather's rough at sea the crew can handle the boat, while you cope with your own problems. It can get pretty bumpy in the east Mediterranean.

## Yacht charter clubs

These are organizations that charge a price for membership and devote that money to purchasing and maintaining their own yachts for hiring out to members. They are not in it for commercial profit but as a way of making available to ordinary sailing enthusiasts the sort of holiday that would be costly for an individual to organize on his own.

### The Yacht Cruising Association

This was founded four years ago, with six boats and now has fifty-four sailing in the Mediterranean. It is affiliated to the Royal Yachting Association. In 1977 some 2,500 members and their families are expected to take sailing holidays on the Association's yachts. It also runs its own sailing school in the U.K.: beginners are advised to take a three-day course at Chichester or near Southampton (beginning either Tuesday or Friday) in preparation for a sailing holiday.

### Flotilla cruising

These are holidays organized by the Yacht Cruising Association, in which groups of their boats sail together — in flotilla — round the islands of Greece.

By cruising in company, the less experienced sailors can depend on the others. Each boat takes up to five or six people: the Y.C.A. like one of them to be at least able to sail a dinghy or small cruiser in sea or estuary conditions. Subscription for membership is £3.

You fly from Gatwick to Athens or Corfu. You then travel by bus and ferry to the point where you join your boat and meet the Association staff of three who sail in a pilot yacht. The route is planned for you: the average sail is about four or five hours. Once at anchorage your yacht is entirely yours for independent exploring and sailing. Combines luxury style with reasonable cost.

For further details contact: Yacht Cruising Association, 9 The Broadway, Crawley, West Sussex; telephone 0293 26512.

### The Island Cruising Club

This has its centre at The Island, Salcombe, Devon; telephone 0544884 2445. You pay £10 to join and then have a joint share in their eight cruising boats — from 9.5m to 21.3m (31 to 70 feet). You then book and pay to join the cruises: £55–£90 per person depending on the season. Children have special weeks to themselves, without parents, at Easter and summer (£45–£55).

The four largest cruisers go across the Channel to the north of France. In 1977 two will venture further, round the coast of Brittany and their 50-ton schooner will go to the Azores. The smaller boats stay in local waters. Membership stands at 2,500 and is always open.

## Further flotillas

Commercial companies provide flotilla sailing too. Mediterranean Charter Services (22 Woodstock Street, Bond Street, London W1R 1HF; telephone 01-408 2170) has nine boats sailing Greek waters, sleeping up to six each, and in company with an 18.3-m (60-foot) mother ship that acts as a guardian and social centre. High-season all-in prices around £279 per person.

Likewise, Aegean Flotilla Holidays, operating from Knutsford, Cheshire, have a fleet of Snapdragons and Mirages. You'll find details of these and other operators in the yachting press.

# Part 3

# Where to Stay and What to Do

# Chapter 15
# Booking and Paying for Accommodation

Any roof over your head — even a tent — is a substitute for the one you know best, usually known as 'home'. But then home, itself, may be a landed estate, a council house, or a student's digs. So how you judge accommodation will be dependent on a mix of many variables: do you want it to imitate home, help you forget home, fulfil an escapist fantasy of high or low living, or offer efficient but immemorable service for your busy way of life?

Your scale of judgement will be unique to yourself: you may hate having to pop along the hotel corridors in a dressing-gown to a bathroom shared between several rooms; you may have a phobia about fires and refuse any accommodation above the first floor; you may hate baths and prefer showers. Lovers separated by long distance set high store by a bedside phone: so do businessmen doing deals, and gamblers buying bets — you can't shout intimacies about sex or money from the public phone in the foyer. People on holiday are supposed to be particularly choosy about the view from the window: businessmen couldn't give a damn, but care more about the promptness of early calls and the reception staff's capacity to find taxis and hire cars instantly. Women may be pleased to know they can borrow a hair drier or have something ironed at the last minute. Personally, I'm often grateful for the loan of a typewriter and a warm towel-rail to dry the overnight wash.

If you're travelling with children you'll certainly need extra personal attention for bottle warming, cot facilities, etc. and other guests will wish to sleep as far from you as possible! Penniless students out to see the world and older, impoverished, but keen, travellers, will be happy to lay their sleeping-bag anywhere: flat roofs, hostel dormitories, even caves.

The first thing about accommodation, then, is to know exactly what you want, what facilities you *won't* go without and what you can dispense with. That set of requirements, set against the money and time available provides the formula by which you or your travel agent can find the right accommodation.

To make the most of your travel, it's no longer enough to book a hotel room or a guest-house plucked virtually at random from a travel brochure or town's tourist guide. Decide what you want and read the details of what you might get in an impartial publication (see page 125). Remember a glossy marketing brochure is primarily out to sell. That means that within the limits of the Trade Descriptions Act, they will make things sound as attractive as possible. If you find their descriptions inadequate, ask for more. If you find them actually inaccurate complain immediately and follow it up when you get back (see page 115). But better to sort out your expectations and choices before you go. You can choose from the following:

International hotel groups
Hotels of different categories as designated by the national travel authority
Guest-houses: also graded by the national travel authority
Farmhouses
Bed and breakfast: usually locals operating a freelance service
Hostels
Self-catering
House swopping
Caravan and camping
Boats

## Booking

**By letter** When you write to any accommodation make it clear whether your letter is merely a preliminary enquiry or a firm booking. If you write: 'I should like to know whether you have a double room for the weekend of 7/8 January' – don't expect it to be booked in your name when you arrive. You must either follow up such an enquiry with a confirmation, or write firmly from the start: 'I wish to book a double room for the weekend of 7/8 January; please confirm this booking in writing.' If you enquire, then don't want to confirm, write and say so. You don't have to but it may make someone else's booking easier. If you want to be absolutely sure where you stand, keep a carbon copy of your own letters of confirmation. If things go wrong, it won't make an occupied room suddenly available, but it might make the management sheepish, and encourage them to find you alternative accommodation. Fanatics for tying up all loose ends will send confirmation letters by recorded delivery.

**By telephone** Many hotels take phone bookings and accept the fact that at the last minute, or with present postal delays, letters of confirmation might not arrive in time. Take time making a phone booking: insist they take down your name, home address and especially telephone number, so that if they realize overnight there's been a muddle, they can phone and tell you. There often are muddles — Basil Fawlty lives! — but many could be straightened out if the hotel manager could ring up his intending guests before they set out.

**Abroad** You are more likely to get a reply sooner if you enclose an international reply coupon. Buy them at the Post Office: price 20p.

Clear and simple English is usually the acceptable language in the international travel industry. However, if you're writing to a French farm or a Portuguese fisherman keep the English very simple indeed, or ask your child's teacher to translate the letter for you. Remember, they'll have to translate the reply too.

**Deposits** Many hotels and tourist operators will want a deposit. In the event of you cancelling this is forfeited: it is meant to cover the cost of the administration. If, however, the hotel or tour operator rebooks your room and flight, then he is not entitled to recoup more than that administrative cost. You can send a deposit direct to a hotel abroad by money order, or your bank can transfer it for you.

**Cancellations** Always cancel the moment you know you must. It's a good idea to give a reason: children ill, or sudden business demand. The hotel must then offer your room for rebooking. If it cannot do so you may be liable for a cancellation fee. Amounts vary: if you're booking a family of four for two weeks it would be worth checking what you stand to lose if the unforeseen happens. They can't make you pay for meals you haven't eaten or linen you haven't used.

## Overbooking

It is currently standard practice for most large U.K. hotels to overbook by up to 25%. Hoteliers say it is to cover themselves against losses from no-shows. The alternative would be to increase prices by some 15–20%. By some fluke — or managerial judgements — the system rarely leaves customers without beds. The practice, however, may soon be made illegal: it is being investigated by the Department of Prices and Consumer Protection.

## Booking by bribery

Business travellers will find that in many countries it is customary to bribe your way to a hotel room, a taxi or special services. Booking is an erratic affair in the Middle East: new arrivals are wise to have $10 bills in readiness when tackling reception desks.

In West and Central Africa bribery is rampant: the word is 'dash' in English-speaking countries. It can occur at hotels, customs, immigration and health checkpoints, border posts and airline ticket offices. It's part of the way of life and there's no point in complaining to the police. Simply

have plenty of small-denomination notes — especially dollars — always
to hand.

## Farms

It suits the farmer if his wife can earn a little extra serving huge farm
breakfasts to visitors. It suits city man to get back to the country, if only
for a very cushioned stay. So farm accommodation is available right
across Britain. It is characteristically small scale, informal and modest.
You are a paying guest in someone's home. Families with small children
often like the chance for them to see a working farm, even feed and handle
the animals. All sorts of additional country pleasures may be involved:
riding, fishing, hay making, shooting.

Meals are usually breakfast and an evening meal. Often they'll provide
packed lunches. Best to check the extent to which they expect you to join
the family — do they want you off the premises during the day? Do they
allow and enjoy you sharing the family sitting room — and television — in
the evening? A phone call before you book would settle such matters. If
they hesitate to make things clear, try elsewhere.

Check too for distances from tarmac road, fire certificate and indoor
plumbing. Make it clear whether or not you want to join in the farm
work.

## Beds

People who do not worry too much where they lay their heads, still
basically expect it to be in comfort: that usually means clean sheets,
reasonably sprung mattress and two pillows. But unless you're a mis-
anthropic businessman who only ever goes to bed with a good book, the
main question is:

### Double or single

A double room used always to mean a double bed. A 'matrimonio' it's
called in Europe. But very often, nowadays is means a twin-bedded
room. The theory behind such a trend is that twin-bedded rooms can be
rented to brother and sister, two friends, two men. It gives the hotel
booking more flexibility. Where does that leave married, or just loving
couples? One technique is to move the single beds together, fixed head-
boards permitting. In which case the staff dutifully open up the gap
between you each morning, either separating the beds or making up each
bed separately so you have to strip the bedding first. There's always a
danger you'll slip through the gap in the middle of the night: not the most
romantic climax to an evening's wooing.

Or you can go visiting from bed to bed. But then you face the do-we/don't-we decision and either sleep in a squashed tangle in one bed, or someone has to go back to their own — cold and lonely — to get some real rest.

There are some ways you can deal with twin beds.

Falling through the middle can be solved by taking a plastic bed sheet, with an elasticated edge and covering the two beds with it. This won't gape, and hotel staff will get the message.

Ask the hotel to push the beds together and cross-mattress them.
Specify a double bed when booking: most good-class hotels everywhere have *some* double-bedded rooms, but they go to those who ask.

Here's a quick rundown on what to expect where:

*Classier chains*: Hiltons and Holiday Inns have only double beds. A twin-bedded room means two doubles.

*Luxury hotels*: expect them to offer you a choice. Worth asking. Many have lavish décor with four-posters, testers, etc.

*Standard tower blocks*: always twin-bedded. Here you need to be quite firm if you want them made up together.

*Germany*: the Germans themselves prefer twin beds, perhaps something to do with those voluminous bedspreads. Hotel rooms will be twin-bedded too.

*Spain and Italy*: their own people sleep in double beds, so in older establishments, inns, etc., you can also expect a matrimonio. In newly developed resorts, however, there will be only twins.

*France*: here you can expect the traditional double bed still to hold sway, certainly in older hotels, auberges, logis and small-scale accommodations.

*Guest-houses*: farms and rented cottages usually have a choice. You may even be lucky enough to find a sumptuously soft feather bed.

### Four-posters

These are for specials — first and second honeymoons, making up quarrels, reward for coming through a bad patch, livening up a dull spell, or embarking on a new romance. Or that's how the British Tourist Authority think of them: they've gone to the trouble of compiling a list. The West Country has most: sixteen hotels there have them; only five in London and 141 hotels in the rest, including the Channel Islands, Northern Ireland, Wales and Scotland. Information sheet *free* from the B.T.A., 64 St. James's Street, London SW1.

### Bills

Wherever you intend to stay, you should find out the basic charge for accommodation before you book. The source of information may be your travel agent, a holiday brochure, or correspondence with the hotel, guest-house or hostel. Ask early, because the basic rate may well be only the beginning. In any accommodation ask whether the following are charged extra and how much: private bathroom, sea view and balcony, single room, ground- or first-floor room, baths and soap, tennis court, poolside daybeds and towels, umbrellas, telephone, garaging, service charge as extra to basic tariff, hotel and local taxes.

## Expected extras

Drinks, laundry, excursions.

## Checking the bill

When the bill is finally compiled, at your departure, you can ask for an explanation of every item. You won't look mean, querying everything at the counter. It's usually reckless expense-account businessmen who pay without looking.

The best, though unfashionable, system is to pay for extras like drinks, in cash as you go along. It may look more knowing to sign the bill, or wave a dismissive arm saying, 'Put it on the bill'. The fact is that the more you drink the more the arm-waving can get out of hand. And you'll have no record, or memory, of what you drank. Also, it's not unknown for guests' drinks to become confused and wrongly charged.

**Abroad** What we think is cheap may be expensive there. I've been charged over 50p for a cup of tea and a bucket of ice (separate orders: separate occasions). Check early in your stay how much you're clocking up. Ask what the locals drink and keep to that. Drinks brought to your room will often cost bar prices plus room service. You can save money by buying your own bottles (take them in as duty-frees) and using the tooth-mugs.

**Service** This is a thorny problem. For years hotel staff have been paid meagre wages on the principle that it would be made up by tips. When that was universally so, then you had to tip as you went along: porter, chamber-maid, room service etc. Then the system changed: but only slightly and only in some places. Because staff not directly in contact with guests never had the piece of silver slipped into their palm, it was felt to be unfair. The idea then prevailed of a staff tipping fund: staff who were tipped were expected to hand over their haul, and discrete boxes marked 'for the staff' appeared on reception counters. The next move was for the management to take over the organization of the system and simply put a 15% service charge on the bill.

This was the amount for redistribution to the staff. In fact it has in many cases ceased to be a separate handout. Managements' explanation is that

T.C.T.—I

by putting 15% service on the bill they are able to pay their staff a better wage. Tipping has turned into a service charge, and has in turn been transmitted to a wage rise.

Where does that leave the guest? I'm afraid the answer is: back at the beginning. Any traveller in any land will find it is still the universal truth that service staff in high and low establishments will always be grateful for a tip. And they will be more willing to put extra effort into finding a taxi, a table by the window, or bringing breakfast before it's stone cold, if there is the prospect of tangible gratitude.

**What to do?** Ask clearly at the reception desk — on *arrival* — what is their policy regarding tipping (service charge if the honest phrase sticks in the gullet).

If you think management are pocketing tips for themselves, ask the girl who brings the morning tea. There's no substitute for an honest and direct enquiry, and no substitute for honest and direct thanks.

*N.B.* No one tips proprietors: the profit goes to them. But in guest-houses and bed and breakfast where they're particularly friendly, and caring, you show your thanks as a friend would. A teenage daughter who's helping out wouldn't be insulted by a small gift.

## Telephone calls

Hotels in Britain frequently make a surcharge on the Post Office rate for a call. This, they explain, is to meet the cost of operators' wages and installing phone extensions and switchboard equipment. Sometimes, they tell you: there will be a card above your extension saying how much you will be charged per unit. But this will rarely indicate how much their surcharge is. Here are some current surcharge rates (The standard Post Office unit is charged on private telephones at 3p):

> The Hilton: 6p per unit.
> Holiday Inns: 7p per unit.
> Anchor Hotels: 8p per unit for the first 10, then 4p per unit; maximum surcharge £1; local calls 15p.
> Trust Houses Forte: 7p per unit; maximum surcharge £6; local calls via operator 25p.
> Metropolitan Hotels: local calls 12p.

There are at the moment no rules limiting how much extra hotels can charge. So you could unwittingly run up quite a bill. If there's no information, ask when you arrive what their rate is. Or save yourself any of this fuss by using a coin-operated phone. There may be one in the hotel foyer: or, if you've the cheek, ask at reception where you can find the nearest.

## Dissatisfaction

If you have booked accommodation and arrive to find it's not what you expected, then consider who is at fault. Did the brochure, on the faith of which you booked, seriously misrepresent facts? If so you can decide to say so and walk out and go elsewhere. But you must do this at once. To stay may be construed as acceptance of what is provided and your legal position becomes that much weaker.

If you are on a package tour then you should contact the tour operator's representative on the spot. The fact that you are dissatisfied and can say why, will make them eager to meet the requirements you expect. What you are doing is declaring that any contract entered into between you and the tour operator is not valid because they are not providing what they promised to provide.

**It might be you** You must be realistic about your expectations. Sins of omission are hard to fight in the courts of law. If a brochure failed to mention that there was a factory chimney outside your window, or a main uphill road where all the traffic changed gear noisily below your balcony, it would be hard to prove they misled you. If, however, the hotel promised 'quiet, secluded peace' and a local disco is blasting away until dawn, then you can claim the description was inaccurate.

Holidays are the idealistic peak of everyone's year. You want it to be perfect: like the ads but more so. Be realistic with yourself, and try to judge fairly. I have seen tour operators' representatives being abused and blamed when people's disappointment was personal and psychological. They thought they'd booked for Paradise. I've also seen neglectful reps, who try to fob off genuine, if petty, complaints. However, if you think your complaint is justified then make it. The travel industry is more likely to improve its services if it hears from consumers what they think is wrong. See yourself as part of the great consumer army:

*Belong*: the Consumers' Association, 1 Caxton Hill, Hertford SG13 7LZ is in the forefront of consumer protection. Associate membership is £6 annually. It publishes *Which?* monthly – dealing with a broad range of consumer products and services. *Holiday Which?* – a further £3 – is published four times a year and gives consumer advice on tours, packages, different countries, currencies, insurance etc. If you wish the Consumers' Association to act on your behalf in any complaint you can join the Personal Service, for about £5 a year. Most good libraries carry back numbers of the Association's publications.

*Take notice*: if you're motoring through, don't stop over in a modest wayside hotel without taking note of what standards it claims (A.A. stars, or R.A.C., etc.) and what it delivers.

*Report*: if you are in the A.A. or R.A.C. or buy any of the standard guides — tell them if you think their standards aren't being maintained.

*Recommend*: word of mouth survives in this media-glutted world as one of the most reliable ways of supporting the best. Friends usually share values and standards and can most accurately assess what each other would like.

*Speak out*: people like thanks; and you should voice any complaints, don't slink off hugging your grievance to yourself — if you're firm without being angry they're more likely to remedy matters.

## Compensation

If you haven't paid you're in a strong position. If the accommodation isn't as you expected, but you stay, explain your complaint to the management. Put it in writing and keep a copy if you can. If you were promised hot and cold water and only get cold, and if you complain, and if it still isn't remedied, then you might be justified in withholding some payment. If you intend to do this, make sure you handle your own luggage — or load it into the car before declaring your intention. Otherwise the staff could hold onto your luggage in the face of what they see as a refusal to pay (see 'Rights and Wrongs', p. 274).

**The law of distances** The further from home base and home customs the less able will you be to impose your own standards of 'the way things should be done'. In many parts of the world their way of doing things may be vastly different. We once descended into a precipitous, damp and dark cavern in the mountains of Crete, led by a local guide with whom we had not bothered to agree, beforehand, a price for his half-hour tour. Only at the bottom when, without him, the way out and up would have been treacherous indeed, did he state his prices: £2 for each of us. We groaned, agreed and put it down to experience. And in true British fashion we paid up like lambs when we got out again. What we should have done was re-open negotiations, and got a reduction!

## Hotel discounts

This does not apply to private individuals but to companies or trades or professional associations who can offer enough business to an individual hotel or a chain to make it worth their while to offer a discount. Chances of negotiating a discount will be highest where they are expecting to have spare hotel capacity and a struggle to fill it. This is more likely to be the case in North America and Southeast Asia than in London, Frankfurt, Johannesburg, Tokyo or the Middle East. Still nothing ventured, nothing won. It is always worth making an approach.

## Hotel chains

The best they're likely to offer is 'a guaranteed commercial rate'. This means that if you have enough business to offer them, and undertake to place it with them, then they will agree to your paying only the rate applicable on 1 January of that year. You thus avoid any increases imposed on casual customers as the year goes by.

Though they won't admit it, in some instances, chains will also offer an additional 'incremental discount'. This means that if your company spent £100,000 in one year with a certain chain, come the next year you set out in some detail what business they can expect from you in the next twelve months and ask what terms they offer for keeping the business. They may then offer a percentage reduction of all the business you bring, above the earlier year's £100,000.

These discounts are usually made only on bookings directly negotiated and not if you book through a travel agent or an airline.

The hotel may decline to take credit cards as a means of payment: after all that facility is already costing them a percentage. On the other hand they may be willing − if financial references are good − to supply monthly accounts and thirty days credit instead.

There is a risk: an individual manager or franchisee within the chain may turn away a discount customer with a reservation in favour of a casual visitor who arrives earlier.

## Individual hotels

Some companies find they have more success dealing directly with a particular hotel, whether or not it is a member of a chain. It may, for example, be a way of establishing goodwill for a new hotel in a city that already has plenty of rivals. In dealing individually, plan your case. Deal at assistant manager/sales manager level − or even with the general manager.

Set out how many employees or associates are likely to spend how many nights in their city in the next year.

Discuss which form of payment they prefer: will they extend credit to your employees?

Are there high-peak booking periods when the discounts would not apply?

Is there someone your employees should approach by name, who will know of the discount arrangement?

Ask what their attitude will be if a full-paying customer arrives ahead of your employee who has already booked.

Once the arrangements are settled, have the relevant documents photostated and give one to each travelling employee.

Employees who pay discount rates when travelling for you may want to return as private individuals, maybe with wife and family. Will your negotiated discounts apply in these cases? Such arrangements could be an untaxed fringe benefit.

# Chapter 16
# International Hotel Groups

Hotel groups are in the travel industry: they mass-produce hotel facilities in which the consumer is one of many fed into a system and serviced as efficiently as is economically viable. They are the hotels of the future, spreading rapidly across Greece, Turkey, the Middle East, into Africa and South America.

In this category come the tower-block hotels, the sprouting forests of the Costa Brava, Costa del Sol, Majorca, Tenerife and Rimini. Their basic achievement is to offer a standard product in huge units: 200, 300, or 400 bedrooms.

You can expect certain things: a neat, spacious room with its own bathroom and toilet. The bathroom may only have a shower and will rarely have a window so it will be electrically lit and a ventilation unit will operate as you put on the light. It's no place to put on make-up if you're going out into sunlight. You will have a tea- and coffee-making unit, with packaged tea and coffee supplies, and a carton of milk. Your breakfast tray will have pre-packaged butter, packaged jam in single helpings. It feels like a luxury factory farm.

Your bed linen will usually be changed daily. There will be a telephone and a radio by the bed, possibly even a television.

*You cannot expect*: individual rooms, highly personal attention and getting to know the staff. Room service, phone bookings etc. will be slow, because such a big machine can only respond at a certain pace to the demands of lots of guests.

I sometimes think you could live and die there without being noticed. If the staff do smile and greet you then it's because they've been trained in courtesy response. This is the mass modern product: ideal for business and conferences, serviceable for visiting families, depressing to human individualism and local idiosyncrasies. It's no way to get to know a foreign country. It's a guaranteed way of being sure of certain international standards.

## The world's biggest six

### Holiday Inns

The biggest judged by number of hotels: at the latest count (June 1977) 1,709 in fifty countries, averaging around 300 rooms. They used to boast there was a new one every fifty-two hours: when I phoned to ask, they consulted each other — 'How many do we have this morning?' So expect more.

They produce an absolutely standardized package: it's their boast that a Holiday Inn room in Plymouth, Papeete in Tahiti, or Colombo in Sri Lanka, has the same specification with minor variations in décor.

Every room will have ample space, wall-to-wall carpeting, its own bathroom with bath, shower and W.C., television, individually adjustable central heating/air conditioning, Holiday Inn soap and towels (much of which is manufactured at the central complex in Memphis).

There are no single beds: a twin-bedded room will have two double beds.

All Holiday Inns, but one, have a swimming pool; in Johannesburg it doesn't because although it's a mixed hotel, mixed swimming is still illegal.

There'll be free ice on every floor, and a Bible beside your bed: staff are instructed to leave it open.

The hotel service will provide baby-sitting (they refer you to an agency: you pay the agency direct), secretarial help (by the day, they will call on an agency), conference rooms, free car parking, currency exchange, laundry and dry cleaning, room service, doctor and dentist on call and a computer booking facility direct to any other Holiday Inn in the world. Children under 12 can stay free in their parents' room in all the Inns, and about 1,000 of the Inns allow 'children' under 19 to stay free in their parents' room. Cots are free but a rollaway bed is charged. They will loan you an ironing board, iron, hair drier and deposit box — FREE.

### Ramada Group

Ramada has 700 hotels, 600 in the U.S.A., sixteen in Europe, the rest worldwide including Bombay and Bahrain. There are none in the U.K. at present.

Each room has its own bathroom and W.C., air conditioning/central heating, colour television, bedside phone, radio.

Service includes: baby-sitting, children under 18 free in parents' room, free parking, restaurant and coffee shop, swimming pool (except in Brussels), laundry, conference facilities. Most take pets. Computer booking for all the other hotels.

## Inter-Continental Hotels

A wholly owned subsidiary of Pan American World Airways — the group also includes Forum Hotels. The two U.K. Inter-Continentals are the Portman Hotel, 22 Portman Square, London W1, and the Inter-Continental, Hyde Park Corner.

The group has a total of eighty-one hotels — all with a difference, so they claim. They are first-class hotels aiming to keep the atmosphere of the country in which they're built: but they all have the usual international standards of comfort.

## Trust Houses Forte Group

The group owns 888 hotels in thirty-three countries with a huge range of styles and facilities, ranging from five-star luxury — Grosvenor House, Park Lane, London, and George V, Paris — down to small country inns — once coaching inns — like the Saracen's Head, Great Dunmow, which has fifteen rooms (three private bathrooms), and the Speech House, Forest of Dean, with fourteen rooms (three private bathrooms), and chalet holiday villages in Sardinia and St. Ives.

The Post House chain is also in the group. There are twenty-nine in Great Britain. They offer the mass-catering product on the lines of Holiday Inns.

Trust Houses Forte also own the Travel Lodge group — 474 motels across the U.S.A. and Canada.

Service charge is included in all accounts.

## Hiltons

There are 237 in all: three in the U.K., but the empire is divided into two companies. The Hilton Hotels Corporation covers the U.S.A. only and is still under the personal eye of Mr. Conrad Hilton. Hilton International is a subsidiary of Trans World Airlines Inc. and is responsible for the rest of the planet.

Hiltons aim at a standard international level of service at central or important locations in major cities. The service includes: spacious bed-rooms (never anything less than $2.74 \times 2.74$ metres; $9 \times 9$ feet), twenty-four hour room service, porter service, radio and colour television, each room has a bathroom and W.C., car parking, conference facilities, a coffee shop and at least one other restaurant. Individually controlled central heating/air conditioning. Free ice on each floor — not essential in Britain, but regarded as a 'must' by good-living Americans.

Apart from accommodation, many Hiltons, like many American hotel chains, aim to provide for conferences. For example, the New York Hilton can provide conference facilities for up to 3,000 at one go.

## Western International

An American firm with headquarters in Seattle and fifty hotels in four-teen countries; none in the U.K. These are de-luxe hotels with the same high standard everywhere: e.g. Plaza, New York, and the seventy-three-storey Peachtree Plaza hotel in Atlanta with revolving restaurant. Attempts are made at individual service: the butter isn't packed. The ice in each hotel comes from its own purification plant, so it's safe in the drinks, which is important in places where the water's suspect, e.g. Mexico.

# Chapter 17
# Guides to Accommodation

How on earth can one measure and compare hotel facilities and standards in different parts of the country, let alone different parts of the world?

The big chains establish their own multinational standards. Below and alongside are all the other millions of hotels jostling for attention and custom. Grouping them into categories and awarding stars is now a major industry, both in the public and private sector. Annually hundreds of books pour from the presses offering accommodation advice. The trick is to find one you can trust and stick to it.

## State-organized classifications

Hotel ratings made by national tourist offices are most common in Western Europe. There are no internationally agreed criteria, simply a common-sense view of hotel standards. The U.S.A. has no national hotel classifications: instead it has independent, privately assessed systems run by Mobil and the American Automobile Association.

National categories are usually seen as descriptive rather than incentive awards to spur the industry to do better. Nonetheless, the more stars, the better the facilities. Moreover, if you stay in a three-star hotel and get what you consider two-star service, you can write to the star-awarding authority and say so. They won't change their entire scale for one individual: if several complain they'll notice, if hundreds moan they'll start asking questions.

## The star system

The following is an outline of the facilities offered in one European country with star ratings for hotels, hostels and pensions. Classifications laid down by national tourist offices vary: those listed below should be used as a working guide only.

### Hotels

*5-star* or *de luxe* Air conditioning in all public rooms and bedrooms; central heating; two or more lifts; lounges; bar; garage; hairdressers; all bedrooms with complete bathroom; some suites with drawing room; laundry and ironing service; telephone in every room.

*4-star* Air conditioning in all public rooms and bedrooms unless climatic conditions require only central heating or refrigeration; lifts; lounges; bar; garages; 75% of bedrooms with complete bathroom and a shower in the rest; telephone in every room; hot and cold running water; laundry and ironing service.

*3-star* Permanently installed heating; lounge; lift; bar; 50% of bedrooms with complete bathroom; 50% with shower; laundry and ironing service; hot and cold running water; telephone.

*2-star* Permanently installed heating; lift in four or more storey buildings; lounge; 15% of bedrooms with complete bathroom; 45% with shower and W.C. and the remaining with shower; hot and cold running water; laundry and ironing service; telephone.

*1-star* Permanently installed heating; lift in five or more storey buildings; lounge; 25% of bedrooms with washbasin, shower and W.C.; 25% with shower and washbasin; 50% with washbasin; hot and cold running water; bathroom to every seven rooms; laundry and ironing service; telephone on every floor.

### Hostels and Pensions

*3-star* Permanently installed heating; lift if the establishment is on the third or higher floor; lounge; 5% of bedrooms with complete bathroom; 10% with W.C., shower and washbasin; 85% with shower and washbasin; bathroom on every floor; hot and cold running water; laundry and ironing service; telephone.

*2-star* Permanently installed heating; lounge; laundry and ironing service; one bathroom on each floor for every 10 rooms, with hot and cold running water; telephone.

*1-star* Rooms with washbasins and cold running water; one bathroom per 12 rooms with hot and cold running water on every floor.

**British Tourist Authority,** 64 St James's Street, London SW1A 1NF; telephone 01-629 9191. Promotes holidays in Britain.

## Britain's National Tourist Boards

These cater for foreign visitors to the U.K., and all residents here who have holiday queries. Between them they publish up to 100 different items a year, from free hand-out leaflets to books and guides on sale at booksellers. Their *Where-to-Stay Guides* cover different parts of the country. They cost 40p each, the West Country 50p. They are basically listings of accommodation, no judgements or preferences are indicated. They carry information as supplied to them by hotels; they do not criticise or add their own comments. Their addresses are:

*English Tourist Board*, 26 Grosvenor Gardens, London SW1W 0DU (written enquiries only).

*Scottish Tourist Board*, 5 Waverley Bridge, Edinburgh EH1 2AD; telephone 031-332 2433 (personal callers and telephone enquiries only).

23 Ravelston Terrace, Edinburgh EH4 3EU (postal enquiries only).

London address: 137 Knightsbridge, London SW1X 7PN; telephone 01-589 2218.

*Wales Tourist Board*, Welcome House, High Street, Llanduff, Cardiff CF5 2YZ (postal enquiries only).

3 Castle Street, Cardiff; telephone 0222 27281.

*Northern Ireland Tourist Board*, River House, 48 High Street, Belfast BT1 2DS; telephone 0232 31221/36609.

London address: 11 Berkeley Street, London W1X 6BU; telephone 01-493 0601.

*Isle of Man Tourist Board*, 13 Victoria Street, Douglas, Isle of Man; telephone 0624 4323.

London address: Manx Information Centre, 14 Dover Street, London W1X 3PH; telephone 01-491 1452.

*States of Guernsey Tourist Committee*, P.O. Box 23, St Peter Port, Guernsey, C.I.; telephone 0481 24411.

*States of Jersey Tourism Office*, Weighbridge, St Helier, Jersey, C.I.; telephone 0534 31958 (information), 24779 (accommodation).

## Regional Tourist Boards

There are twelve in England, set up by the English Tourist Board, local government and commercial interests to promote tourism on a more local basis. Their addresses are:

## England

*Cumbria Tourist Board*, Ellerthwaite, Windermere, Cumbria LA23 2AQ (written enquiries only).

*East Anglia Tourist Board*, 14 Museum Street, Ipswich, Suffolk IP1 1HU; telephone 0473 214211.

*East Midlands Tourist Board,* Bailgate, Lincoln LN1 3AR; telephone 0522 31521.

*Heart of England Tourist Board,* P.O. Box 15, Worcester WR1 2JT; telephone 0905 29511 (written and telephone enquiries only).

*London Tourist Board,* 26 Grosvenor Gardens, London SW1W 0DU; telephone 01-730 0791.

*Northumbria Tourist Board,* Prudential Building, 140-150 Pilgrim Street, Newcastle upon Tyne NE1 6TQ; telephone 0632 28795.

*North West Tourist Board,* The Last Drop Village, Bromley Cross, Bolton BL7 9PZ; telephone 0204 591511 (written and telephone enquiries only).

*South East England Tourist Board,* Cheviot House, 4-6 Monson Road, Tunbridge Wells, Kent TN1 1NH; telephone 0892 33066 (written and telephone enquiries only).

*Southern Tourist Board,* Tourist Information Centre, Canute Road, Southampton, Hampshire SO1 1FH; telephone 0703 20438.

*Thames and Chilterns Tourist Board,* P.O. Box 10, 8 The Market Place, Abingdon, Oxfordshire OX14 3HG; telephone 0235 22711.

*West Country Tourist Board,* Trinity Court, 37 Southernhay East, Exeter, Devon EX1 1QS; telephone 0392 76351.

*Yorkshire and Humberside Tourist Board,* 312 Tadcaster Road, York YO2 2HF; telephone 0904 67961 (written and telephone enquiries only).

## Scotland

There are nine regional councils or boards responsible for tourism in Scotland:

*Borders Regional Council,* Department of Planning and Development – Tourism, 3 Exchange Street, Jedburgh, Roxburghshire; telephone 083 56 2227.

*Central Regional Council,* Tourist Department, Viewforth, Stirling FK8 2ET; telephone 0786 3111.

*Dumfries and Galloway Tourist Association,* Douglas House, Newton Stewart, Wigtownshire DG8 6DQ; telephone 0671 2549.

*Fife Tourist Authority,* High Street, Leven, Fife KY8 4QA; telephone 033 32 3327.

*Grampian Regional Council,* The Leisure, Recreation and Tourism Department, Woodhill House, Ashgrove Road West, Aberdeen AB9 2LU; telephone 0224 23401.

*Highlands and Islands Development Board,* Bridge House, 27 Bank Street, Inverness IV1 1QR; telephone 0463 34171.

*Lothian Regional Council,* Department of Recreation and Leisure, 40 Torphichen Street, Edinburgh EH3 8JJ (postal enquiries only).

*Strathclyde Regional Council,* Department of Leisure and Recreation, McIver House, Cadogan Street, Glasgow G2 7QG; telephone 041 204 1881.

*Tayside Regional Council,* Tourism Division, Department of Leisure, Recreation and Tourism, Tayside House, 28 Crichton Street, Dundee; telephone 0382 23281.

## Wales

There are three Tourism Councils for the North, Central and Southern regions of Wales:

*North Wales Tourism Council,* Civic Centre, Colwyn Bay, Clwyd; telephone 0492 56881.

*Mid Wales Tourism Council,* Owain Glyndwr Institute, Maengwyn Street, Machynlleth, Powys; telephone 0654 2401.

*South Wales Tourism Council,* Darkgate, Carmarthen, Dyfed; telephone 0267 7557.

## Tourist Information Centres

These are even thicker on the ground; some 360 local centres, in virtually all major towns, cities and points of entry. They offer publications for sale and free personal advice on local matters.

Refer to them for information on such topics as the following:

Hotels near airports
Hotels with 4-posters
Hotels with golfing facilities
Hotels for senior citizens
Hotels with fishing facilities
Health farms

## Egon Ronay Organisation Ltd.

Publishers of *Egon Ronay's Lucas Guide*, £3.50. The 1977 edition covers 1,233 hotels, 145 inns, thirty pensions, 1,014 restaurants, thirty-five wine bars, 247 economy restaurants and thirty pubs.

There is an annual re-inspection of the bulk of entries. Inspectors book in their own name, pay their bill and only then make themselves known to the management. Suggestions come from readers' recommendations, the hotel itself (if you give a good service, nothing wrong in having it tested) and the trade press. Inspectors work different regional journey cycles and meet every four weeks for discussions. Assessments are made of twenty-two factors: efficiency of reception, appearance of staff, room service etc. More emphasis is given to bedrooms than public rooms. Creature comforts count a good deal.

In 1977 the guide awarded three stars to only two restaurants:

Thornbury Castle, near Bristol, and Inverlochy Castle, near Fort William. Two stars were awarded to eight London restaurants and two provincial restaurants. It made an especially strong attack on 'catering for the crowd' and named Hampton Court, Regent's Park and Hyde Park as appalling. It also called for a boycott of cellophane-wrapped sandwiches — surely expecting too much.

**Egon Ronay's 1977 Lucas Guide to Transport Cafés (95p)** Six inspectors recommended 341 cafés for food, and 81 for accommodation, out of 430 inspected. Holiday areas come off best: West Country, Wales, Cotswolds, the Lake District. Scotland scores the highest for home cooking. Motorway cafés are not included. Accommodation is mentioned only when it reaches a certain standard. The guide indicates which places are suitable for the general public.

**Egon Ronay's Pub Guide** Published every few years. The 1977 edition (£2·95) covers 600 pubs, including 53 pubs on the Continent, of particular merit as regards atmosphere, amenities, draught beers and snacks, and architecture.

### Financial Times World Hotel Directory

Primarily for businessmen: lists such facilities as secretarial help, conferences, parking, telex, etc. Published annually, the 1977 edition costs £9. It sells around 3,000 copies and can be found at leading central libraries. It lists around 3,500 hotels in 155 countries, mostly in de-luxe, five-star and four-star categories.

In countries where the national tourist offices have established categories — mostly Western Europe — these are mentioned. (Watch out for Holland: they have two systems working in contrary order of stars, so a top hotel can be four-star in one system and one-star in the other.) Otherwise the information is mainly taken from questionnaires to individual hotels, tourist offices and *Financial Times* contacts. No judgements are made.

### Hotel-booking bureaux

These exist at all major airports and rail terminals. They are ideal for emergency arrivals when all else has failed. They will match what you need with the best they can offer and phone the reservation for you then and there. The service is usually free.

### The AA

Motoring organizations have a major interest in recommending places to stay to their members. The A.A. also has a considerable publishing business. You don't have to belong to buy. The best of its guides is *The*

*AA Guide to Hotels and Restaurants*, which lists nearly 5,000 approved restaurants and hotels in Britain and Ireland. Stars are black, red and white: black for standard rating, red for those of outstanding merit within the normal rating, white for motels and roadhouses, more functional than personal. Rosettes are awarded for fine cooking. There are separate listings of country-house-style hotels, conference hotels, hotels with sports facilities, and hotels equipped for children. It also has good maps and 150 town plans.

## The Good Food Guide

Published annually and now in its twenty-sixth year, it awards approved restaurants and hotels, pass, credit and distinction ratings for their food. Accommodation is secondary but mentioned where it exists. There are no inspections of rooms, so no judgements are made. But *The Good Food Guide*'s style is one of lively comment: its descriptive texts for each place are longer than in other publications. So you can judge whether the atmosphere of a place sounds attractive as somewhere you would like to stay. Cross-check for details with accommodation guides.

## The R.A.C.

Their *Guide and Handbook* is published annually; price to members is £2 plus postage, non-members, £3.50 plus postage. Accommodation is rated one star to five stars, after inspection. Restaurants are rated for amenities from one to five knives and forks; rosettes indicate outstanding food. They have classifications for grill inns, country-house hotels and hotels suitable for the disabled. Hotels under construction are mentioned in areas which are short of accommodation. These have obviously not been inspected, but they might prove useful if you're in a tight spot. There is a helpful section on 'Motoring in Great Britain' which is good for all-round reference.

## Michelin

The most famous and popular: a universal bible made by another motoring interest, Michelin tyres. Some people won't cross the Channel without at least *The Guide to France*. There are Red Guides to the following countries: France, Germany, Italy, Spain, Portugal, Belgium, Holland, Luxembourg, Britain and Ireland. It's a popular misconception that their first priority is food. Usually two-thirds of their entries are hotels, a third are restaurants with rooms. Inspectors with a three-month training make the rounds at least once a year. Basic accommodation standards must be good wherever they are — from Palermo to Perth. Gastronomy comes next.

The information is all given in symbols so it looks rather austere on the page. None of Egon Ronay's friendly chat. But its rosettes for fine cooking command international respect.

## Herald Advisory Service Publications

A family business, now twenty-five years old, and employing some eight central staff and part-time agents throughout the country. Their address is 23a Brighton Road, South Croydon, Surrey; telephone 01-681 3595. Their publications are cheap, dealing with accommodation that is reasonable down to inexpensive: but they are partly commercial listings, partly recommendations, so make sure which you're reading — paid-for advertisements or lists of accommodation that's had an inspection.

**Children Welcome** (1977 — 60p) The only one of its kind. 400 entries per year. Each entry earns its place by inspection. The first entry is free. After that, they're expected to pay a subscription. There is a valuable section on holidays for unaccompanied children: thirty-eight entries, of which two are in the French Pyrenees and the rest in Britain.

**Wayside Inns of Britain and Country Hotels of Britain** Some 400 recommendations in each, plus a directory of listings, some 800 more.

**Pets Welcome** Sells some 50,000 copies. 1977 is its seventeenth year. Some recommended hotels, some commercial listings. A good selection of inspected kennels and catteries.

**Complaints** Herald say they're glad to hear of any complaints concerning advertised accommodation. They will attempt to mediate; if this fails they will inspect. If all else fails they will threaten to drop the advertisement though naturally they do this reluctantly.

## Farm Holiday Publications

This organization produces ten brochures of country accommodation, originated in 1946 by a tough old Scot called David Murdoch. They sell ten million annually — and are distributed in Europe and North America by the British Travel Authority.

**Entries** They list some 6,000 places at modest prices. There are roughly 3,400 farms, and bed-and-breakfast places cost around £3 per night.

All places pay to be listed; but first they must supply names and addresses of six recent visitors. Entry depends on their recommendation. Recently Reader Diploma Awards have been instituted. In 1976 they had 1,000 recommendations: seven awards were made.

**Complaints** On receipt of a complaining letter an inspector is sent incognito to stay and report. If the place doesn't satisfy, the entry is dropped. If the editor feels the complainant deserves compensation, he says so in writing to both reader and owner.

**Titles.** Their publications include: *Farm Holiday Guide* (English, Scottish and Welsh editions), 68p; *Bed & Breakfast Stops,* 43p; *Furnished Holidays in Britain,* 43p.

## Abroad

It's impossible to compile a comprehensive list. But for individual countries the best general advice is to apply to two sources: the national tourist office (see the Gazetteer, p. 288); or the cultural attaché of the embassy.

*Remember*: accommodation guides are of two kinds: descriptive — these are listings and do not offer any endorsement or judgement of standards; and assessments — these usually have their own inspectorate, and their own reputation to maintain. Go for the second type of guide where possible.

### Leaders in the field

The A.A. (see p. 126), Financial Times Directory (see p. 126), Michelin Guides (see p. 127).

### Logis de France et Auberges Rurales

This is published by La Fédération Nationale des Logis de France, 25 rue Jean Mermoz, 75008 Paris. The 1977 edition costs £3.80. Covers France only. Basically the very best of France's simple but comfortable hotels. The price will be reasonable, the cooking often very good. The list was compiled by a non-profit making organization, aiming to promote the medium-sized French hotels: these are the Logis de France. Auberges Rurales are smaller, offering slightly simpler accommodation and are not graded. The logis, however, are graded from one star to four, and de luxe.

### French Farm and Village Holiday Guide

By J. Henderson McCartney, published by BHAM Books, 12-14 Whitfield Street, London W1. The 1977 edition costs £1.50. It covers 1,000 holiday houses in France, prices from £20 a week.

### Relais de Campagne et Châteaux hotels

The plush end of the market in twenty-one countries, published by and for the French government. Basically it's an amalgamation of four groups: Relais, Châteaux, Relais de Montagne, and Relais Gourmande, so France gets the biggest slice of the book with 152 entries. Britain, Italy, Belgium, Spain have a good handful each. Japan, Haiti, Canada, one each; U.S.A., two.

This is really a de-luxe selection. You can expect attractive locations, lavish facilities and, most of all, superb food. Top prices too!

T.C.T.—K

# Chapter 18
# Fire and Security

## Fire

Fire risk is increased by a combination of factors: large numbers of people living at close quarters; abundant, well-ventilated corridors of air in which fire can spread freely; building and furnishing materials that are highly flammable; the absence of any coherent alarm system. In many countries the law imposes minimum standards on these matters, and you can make your own checks.

**Great Britain** All hotels, boarding- and guest-houses and places with accommodation for more than six people are governed by the Fire Prevention Act 1971.

The legal requirement is that the local fire authority must be satisfied that fire precautions at the premises are adequate. Since 1972 all such premises are supposed to have been inspected by the local fire authority. Any improvements should then have been made before a re-inspection and if that's satisfactory, the issuing of a fire certificate. Many guest-houses state in their advertisement that they have a fire certificate.

Building laws in this country are now stricter than anywhere else. So new buildings are fire safe from the beginning. This means that if a fire does start it will be confined to the floor and area of the outbreak.

**Your own checklist** Ask to see the hotel's fire certificate which is your guarantee of the local fire authority's approval: inspection will have been by the local fire brigade.

Each room should display a set of fire rules. They're usually on the back of the bedroom door. Some of these can be so banal — 'Make for the nearest exit, as speedily as possible'; 'Do not use the lift' — as to be virtually useless. I sometimes suspect they're manufactured in bulk and distributed high and low with no further regard to the hotel's individual layout.

So ask: what will the fire-alarm sound like? Where are fire extinguishers kept? What are the means of raising the alarm if you find a fire?

Personally check where there are staircases, fire exits and escapes. I have a weak sense of direction and some of our Olde Englishe hotels are mightily convoluted. So I either study the hotel ground plan — there should be one — or take time to memorize the route to stairs, etc., carefully. Notice the 'Fire Exit' signs.

**Abroad** Each country is governed by its own legislation. In Europe a group of eleven countries have a standing Conference of Fire Protection Associations, so you can expect standards in these countries to be on a par with our own: Austria, Belgium, Denmark, France, Finland, Germany, Holland, Norway, Sweden, Switzerland and the U.K.

**Don't start one** Fires in hotels are often the fault of guests. Smoking in bed and falling asleep is a common cause. Also when people have drinks brought to their rooms and have a few friends in, that's the time cigarettes may not be put out, or may be tossed in flammable waste baskets. If you go in for this kind of jamboree, check for safety once your chums have left.

**In the event of fire** As a guest your main responsibility is to evacuate yourself and your family from the premises. It is for the staff, who should be trained in these matters, to assist you. The putting out of the fire is not your concern: the hotel alarm system should be connected to the fire brigade. Leave it to them. It's the smoke that'll kill you. You may burn in the end but you'll have asphyxiated long before that. So take smoke seriously: there's no smoke without a danger. Especially is this true of the toxic fumes caused by man-made fibres used in ceilings, carpets, upholstery, etc.

If you do find yourself cut off from the means of escape, by smoke, then close your bedroom door, jam the crack round it with eiderdowns, pillows etc. Raise the alarm by telephone or the window. And wait to be rescued. You'll find it easiest to breathe near the floor: a wet towel or hanky will keep the air cool.

**The towering inferno** The worst hotel fire in living memory is a case history of fire risks and lack of safeguards. So you'll know what to watch for when you book into some anonymous tower block — here's a brief account of the inferno.

The fire happened on Christmas Day, 1971, in the Tae You Kak Hotel in Seoul, Korea. The hotel had 223 guest rooms extending from the fifth to the nineteenth storeys. The twentieth storey was a Sky Lounge. The door from the Sky Lounge to the roof is thought to have been locked. There were approximately 200 guests and seventy employees of the hotel in the building when fire broke out at 10 o'clock on Christmas morning. Many guests were still in their rooms. The fire started in the coffee shop next to the hotel foyer. Liquefied petroleum gas from a 20 kg cylinder supplied a two-burner stove on the counter. There was an explosion that killed three waitresses. The fire rapidly engulfed the coffee shop and foyer, on the first floor, cutting off escape down the hotel stairs. Interior finishes on the walls included rice-paper, rice straw and wood panelling. These burned fast.

The internal walls — between rooms and corridors — were made of 200 mm (8 inch) concrete blocks — but the rooms had wooden suspended ceilings, below the concrete floor slabs. There were horizontal openings above these suspended ceilings into the corridors. This allowed the fire to spread horizontally. The automatic fire-alarm was not connected to the fire brigade. The fire spread up the hotel stairs, then through vertical heating and air-conditioning shafts. It soon reached the Sky Lounge. By midday there were forty fire-engines, 530 firemen and 750 police in attendance. They could not reach the trapped. 163 died, 121 were recovered from the building, thirty-eight died jumping, two fell from rescue helicopters, sixty people were injured.

One guest on the fourteenth storey made a rope from two bedsheets and climbed down to the thirteenth storey. He entered a room there and repeated the same climb, this time to the twelfth storey, and so on until he reached the sixth storey, where they got a lifeline to him. If that story cheers you, then take note that he didn't panic, didn't suffer from vertigo, and must have been very fit.

## Security of valuables

It is unwise to take the family diamonds on a hitch-hiking journey to Katmandu. Indeed the best way not to lose valuables is to have none. However, you can't expect holiday-makers, letting rip on an annual two-week spree, to leave at home their favourite, possibly most attractive jewellery.

Second best advice is to wear it; all of it, all of the time. It needs to be very classy stuff to carry that off — solid gold chains (several), bracelets (numerous) and rings (valuable). A glamorous girlfriend, not a million miles from the B.B.C.'s Holiday programme, wears all of hers like that, even in bed. Her only fear is when in remote and dangerous terrain, that some barbarous tribesman won't stop and take the time to thieve, but simply sever her hand at the wrist and make off with the lot!

Third best, but most likely advice is to take enough care to put the responsibility for loss on someone else.

**Hoteliers** The law puts hoteliers under quite severe obligations, a result of the days when innkeepers were in cahoots with highwaymen. Today's operative law is the 1956 Hotel Proprietors Act, which makes him liable for loss or damage to the property of resident guests, even though the loss was not his fault. No hotelier can escape that responsibility: but he can limit his liability.

Many hotels display notices referring to the Hotel Proprietors Act and limiting liability for valuables lost or damaged. If they use the right notice (a general disclaimer is no good), this means that liability for loss of valuables taken or missing from your room is limited to £50 per article and not more than £100 overall. It seems inflation has left these relatively modest amounts well behind. There is no such limit to their liability for valuables placed in their care. This responsibility does not apply to cars, and does not cover private hotels.

**Keys** To reduce the risk of his being so liable, most hoteliers issue keys to each room. If he can show you have failed to lock your room, he might claim that the loss was your fault and not his responsibility. So use your key on all comings and goings from your room. In big, impersonal city hotels, it's a good idea to lock from the inside too.

**Abroad** Each country's laws differ. If you lose valuables you should, of course, report it. But the local laws, plus the foreign language and a hesitant proprietor might thwart your attempts to claim liability. In this case your best policy is to be thoroughly covered by insurance.

**Insurance** Details of highly valuable individual items which you are taking with you should be itemized on your insurance policy. This should include watches, cameras, all jewellery, furs.

# Chapter 19
# Caravanning

There are basically two types of caravanners: the addicts and those who see caravanning as a convenient way of taking a family holiday.

Addicts are committed to their vehicle, its facilities and its gadgetry. They attend caravanners' trade exhibitions and take several of the seven consumer publications devoted to their interests. They organize and attend rallies, go caravanning as often as possible, and are familiar with all the sites. Like all other enthusiasts — whether for cars or camping or budgerigar breeding — they are a race apart. Their social life too will revolve round their hobby: organized singsongs, bingo, fancy-dress competitions. If you want to join them, apply for membership of the

Caravan Club, East Grinstead House, London Road, East Grinstead, West Sussex; telephone East Grinstead 26944 (S.T.D. code 0342), and start buying the magazines.

Other people see in caravanning a convenient method of travel combining maximum range and flexibility with minimum cost. Their interest in their caravan will be confined to how well it serves their travelling purpose. Caravans are miniature homes so it's not hard to slide into a preoccupation with the interior − colour schemes, gadgetry, etc. But as a functional way of getting around the simplest is usually the best.

If you're considering a caravan − as a purchase or a holiday − bear the following points in mind.

## Touring caravan or motor caravan?

Both have their champions. The advantages of touring caravans include the fact that they have lots more space to move around in. You can stand up in comfort. You can unhitch a touring caravan and leave it behind to reserve your site pitch, while you drive around sight-seeing. You've a wide choice for parking because levels can be adjusted.

The disadvantage is that you must have a suitable touring car, and you're limited to 50 m.p.h. (80 km per hour) in the U.K. You have less manoeuvrability and can't travel in the van while you're on the move.

The advantage of a motor caravan is that it is faster, and easier to handle: it can go virtually anywhere a car can go. It is cheaper crossing the Channel because you save on length. You can live in them as you travel, feeding children and getting meals ready.

On the other hand, motor caravans are very cramped for space: O.K. if the weather's fine and you've an outside awning, but a strain on wet days, especially with children. They're pretty heavy on petrol and don't double well as the family's year-round car. Also, you'll have to leave something behind to reserve your pitch on any campsite when you go off on an excursion for the day.

## Touring caravan checklist

Don't buy or hire a touring caravan any larger than you really need; 75 mm extra width is more trouble handling round corners etc., than an extra 300 mm in length. But parents who are buying and have tiny children should bear in mind that they'll get bigger − and need more space.

Check brakes by backing up a slight slope without the reversing stop in position: the brakes should go on hard. Brakes will be smoother and gentler if the over-run mechanism is controlled by hydraulic damping.

A loaded caravan should be slightly nose-heavy: follow the manu-facturer's guidance.

If car wing mirrors are wider than the caravan, they'll provide a good measure. If they can get through so will the caravan. It's a legal require-ment that you can see behind. There are various gadgets available which will give straight through vision.

When assessing storage capacity don't be impressed by lots of tiny pigeon-holes: some are useful, but you also need larger simple enclosed spaces.

It's safer if the loaded weight of the caravan is no more than three-quarters the loaded weight of the car. That way, there's no risk of 'the tail wagging the dog' — a situation in which the caravan starts to swing from side to side and takes over from the car. This is particularly dangerous on a downward slope of motorway. If it starts to happen, take your foot off the accelerator, then give a sudden but slight burst of speed to get the car back in control. The slipstream of a passing articulated lorry can also start off such a movement.

Essential effort, like making-up the bed, cooking and washing-up, should require the minimum of conversion and effort. If the equipment looks fancy — however ingenious — it could take more of your time.

The tow bracket fitted to your car must be beyond reproach. Go to a specialist.

You must have indicators on the back of the caravan; they are connected to your car's indicator system by a special seven-point plug. To avoid overloading you will need to fit a heavy-duty flasher unit. Check the legal requirements governing caravan lights. Always check brake lights, sidelights and reflectors before moving off after any stop.

You must display the weight of the caravan on the chassis and the weight of your car on the vehicle.

Warning: keep a check on the storage of gas and on the piping. Turn it off *at source* each night. Carry a fire extinguisher in the caravan.

## Touring

*Packing* must be systematic. Designate a place for everything and keep it always there. Breakables need to be held in place. You need to stow everything before each move. Keep heavy stuff at a low level: the centre of gravity should be low. Pack weight over the wheels; lighter stuff on top shelves. Once the system's set out, give each one in the family a list of things to be responsible for. Pin a checklist — in plastic cover — to the door.

*Join the Caravan Club* for at least three immediate benefits: their handbook and lists of sites, their insurance scheme, and more chance of getting on certain sites — for example, the Forestry Commission has leased five sites to them exclusively. The address is East Grinstead House, London Road, East Grinstead, West Sussex; telephone East Grinstead 26944 (S.T.D. code 0342).

For abroad the Club's Foreign Touring Department will supply country-by-country advice and they have a foreign handbook and directory.

*Moving on*: don't make it everyday. Every other day is often enough. Do the major part of a journey by midday — finish off the distance at a more leisurely pace in the late afternoon. That way there's no panic about arriving in reasonable time. Follow strenuous mountain drives by staying put for several days to recover.

*Homework*: sort out guidebooks and maps before setting off. Decide the basic route and which sites you're aiming for. But allow enough flexibility for changed plans or routes.

*Eating habits*: if you're on the move eat before and after. That's a good breakfast before setting out and a major meal in the evening (this can be home cooking or eating out). Don't open up your cooking arrangements midday: pack a lunch before setting out, or make do (fruit, cheese, bread) by buying things as you go along.

*Booking* is increasingly necessary. Popular sites — especially in Britain — are booked up early. In the West Country I have seen strings of beleaguered caravans wandering siteless looking for somewhere to spend the night. Often they use lay-bys and grass verges in their desperation — but they risk being moved on by police. If you're stuck for a site try asking at a Post Office, the local police station or local A.A. and R.A.C. posts.

*Parking:* avoid hollows, where water might collect. The best choice is level but fairly high ground, sheltered from prevailing wind and the stares of outsiders. If you can park so there's a wonderful view from your window all the better. Take a spirit-level and be tireless in getting your van absolutely straight. The slightest slope can have you slipping down the bed. Fore and aft levelling is straightforward enough with a jockey wheel. Lateral levelling can be achieved with wooden blocks, suitably tapered: remember to take them with you and make sure when you get them that they are wide enough for your caravan type. If you're staying several days cover the tyres against the heat.

*Lavatories*: most caravans have chemical closets similar to those on boats. They don't flush but strong chemicals take care of smells. Use one that is acceptable to main drains: Elsan Blue and Racasan are two makes commonly used. They have to be emptied every so often — how often depends on use but it's unlikely to be daily. Many caravan sites have lavatories.

*Claustrophobia*: caravans are fine-weather vehicles: a coloured awning, an open door and wide-open windows will all minimize the sense of cramped space. In good weather you can eat outside, play and sit around, almost continually, out of doors. So the fact that you're living in a large box won't worry you too much. But in bad weather it can be very depressing and oppressive to be cooped up so close to other people — even family, especially family! It means everyone must be extremely judicious about throwing their weight about — psychologically and physically.

One windy autumn night on a site near Stratford-on-Avon we took it in turns to go for blowy walks outside the caravan to sooth down our sense of brooding hostility: much as lions in the zoo must feel.

One way to avoid it is to have a 'rainy-day plan' already laid. So the moment it sets in, you can either get out on visits to stately homes, cinemas, shops or nearby towns; or settle in for the eliminating rounds of the chess or Mastermind tournament. But remember, towns in busy caravan areas soon get clogged with people in wet weather. Either way you avoid half a day spent bickering about what to do, and the next half not long enough to do it in.

*Behaviour*: some caravan sites are bristling with noise and life late and early. You don't have to join in — but you might not sleep too well. If, however, you arrive at a quieter site, keep to the mood of the place yourself; don't spoil things. If you find that cramps your style a bit, and you have to tone down both the transistor and the children's natural boisterousness, the best thing is to cut your losses and move on as soon as you can to a site more in key with your lifestyle. If you take the dog don't let it worry others. Many sites require them to be on leads.

*Choice of sites*: how do you judge a site from the brochures? Some sites are like holiday camps or a small housing estate with plenty of facilities and action in the evenings: shops, social club etc. Usually the number of caravans allowed is your best indicator of both scale and style. But you will find other things offered: swimming-pool, shops, showers, hot baths, laundry, television, restaurants, toilets, mains-water connection, gas sales. The choice of how developed a site you want is a matter of personal preference.

*Castels et Camping-Caravanning*: these are sites within the grounds of French châteaux. Ask at the French Tourist Office, 178 Piccadilly, London W1, for their most recent brochure. The sites are in beautiful settings, so they don't permit many visitors: rarely more than twenty places. They also request that there is quiet after 22.00. Dogs are not admitted.

*Horse-drawn caravans* — *France*: write to the Office Départmental de Tourisme, 16 rue Wilson, 2400 Perigueux for details.

## Country style

If you come from the city and aren't used to country life, you'll need to observe their way of doing things. If you're keen there's a booklet called the *Country Code*, free from the Countryside Commission, John Dower House, Crescent Place, Cheltenham, Glos; telephone Cheltenham 21381 (S.T.D. code 0242).

The basic point is simply to respect farming activities. 'Countryside' isn't just spare space round the edges of cities: in Britain it's usually intensively farmed agricultural or pastoral land. The fact that it looks like a painting by Constable shouldn't lead you to think it's not being used.

**Gates** Leave them as you find them. Obvious really, but you can either be negligent and leave open gates that should be closed, or over-eager and shut gates that the farmer intended to stand open. And keep your eyes skinned. The countryside is not necessarily safe. The Ramblers Association have recently asked that it is made illegal for owners to graze dangerous animals — bulls — in fields crossed by public footpaths. So far it isn't. And they claim 'walking is becoming more and more dangerous'. So watch out.

**Fields** Walk round not across fields. Even if it looks like a field of grass. It will be — mowing grass — and that's a crop like any other (keep to paths through farmland). Don't break through hedges or break down branches for fires.

**Fires** In high summer, the countryside is like tinder. You will hear warnings against fires on the radio. In such a case don't light anything and be scrupulously careful about cigarettes. In other circumstances you can light fires but ask permission if you're on someone's land, don't light a fire near abundant dry grass, choose a sheltered but elevated spot (not too windy or wet) and set the limits of your fire either with large pieces of timber, bricks or stones found nearby or by clearing a circular area of ground. Any of these will hinder the fire from spreading.

**Produce** Farm-fresh eggs, milk, butter, etc. can often be bought from the farmer's wife. No one minds you asking.

**Dogs** It might look like a marvellous chance to let them off the rein to enjoy a completely free run — but is it? Farmers go mad with rage at the way city-dwellers let their dogs roam free. Even on the high Yorkshire moors — wild and unenclosed — I've heard farmers complain that visitors' dogs worry sheep and can lead to losses at lambing time. Some

# Amenity Symbols

| | | | | |
|---|---|---|---|---|
| Abbey | | Caravans for hire | | |
| Advertisement in Guide | | Caravan site – touring | | |
| Aerial activities | | Castle | | |
| Aerodrome | | Cathedral | | |
| A la carte | | Central heating in bedrooms | | |
| Ancient Monument | Stonehenge | Chapel or small church | | |
| Antiquity – Roman | Fishbourne Palace | Chemical/Sewage disposal unit | | |
| Antiquity – Other | Rollright Stones | Childrens facilities/ playroom | | |
| Arboretum/Botanical Gardens | | Childrens play area | | |
| Art Gallery/Museum | | Children – special rates for | | |
| Athletics | | Church – Protestant | | |
| Baby minding facilities | | Church – Roman Catholic | | |
| Ballroom (for hire) | | Cinema | | |
| Battle – site of | 1066 | Collection and delivery of mail | | |
| Beach | | Communal lounge | | |
| Bed and Breakfast only | | Communal wash basins not under cover | | |
| Boarding House/Guest House/Bed and Breakfast | | Communal wash basins under cover | | |
| Boating activities | | Conference facilities available | | |

| | | | |
|---|---|---|---|
| Cooking facilities/ availability of Stoves | | Ferry — pedestrian | |
| Country park | | Ferry — vehicular | |
| Craft centre | | Field games | |
| Cycle path | | Field study centre | |
| Cycling | | First aid post | |
| Deer stalking arranged | DS | Fishing on hotels private water | |
| Diabetic and/or vegetarian diets | V | Food shop | |
| Dogs not admitted | | Footpath | |
| Double/twin bedded room | | Ford | Ford |
| Eating Place | | French and at least one other language spoken | |
| Electric cooking | | Fridge | |
| Electric points for caravans | | Games and sports area | |
| Electric points for razors | | Garage/parking facilities on the premises | |
| Electricity/gas bought by meter | M | Garden | |
| Entertainment centre/ theatre | | Gas cooking | |
| Evening entertainment | | Gas cylinders available | GAS |
| Farm produce available | | Go-karting | |
| Fenced and guarded camp | | Golf | 9  18 |

| | | | |
|---|---|---|---|
| Hairdressing | | May be booked through travel agent/commission paid | T |
| Historic property | | Meter charge for bedroom heating | M |
| Holiday camp | | Midweek bookings accepted | MW |
| Horse riding facilities/ pony trekking | | Mini golf | |
| Hotel | | Motel | |
| Individual cubicles with wash basins | | Motor caravans accepted | |
| Industrial archeological site | | Motor cycling | |
| Information | i | Motor racing | |
| Laundry/valet service | | Mountain resort | |
| Licensed club on site | | Native fortress | |
| Lift | | Natural attraction | |
| Lighting throughout camp | | Nature reserve | Slimbridge |
| Local crafts/cottage industry | | Nature trail | Gwyddon |
| Long distance path (for pedestrians) | Offas dyke | Narrow gauge railway | |
| Long distance path (for horse rides) | South down way | Night porter | |
| Loudspeaker/P.A. system | | No caravans | |
| Mains sewage connection | | No children | |
| Marina | | No coach parties | |

|  |  |
|---|---|
| No drinking water | Reduced rates for old age pensioners |
| Only accessible by foot | Refuse disposal |
| Packed lunches provided | Repairs workshop (plus distance) |
| Parking | Residents lounge |
| Parking not permitted | Restaurant |
| Parking area for private boats and trailers | Rock Climbing |
| Petrol pump (plus distance) | Rooms with Bath/Shower |
| Picnic site | Rooms regularly equipped for family use |
| Place of interest — Stourhead | Rooms set aside for non smokers |
| Power boating | Rowing — see canoeing/rowing |
| Power cruising | Rural settings |
| Potholing | Sailing |
| Public House | Sand yachting |
| Public telephone on site | Sauna bath |
| Pursuits centre | Seaside Resort |
| Radio in bedrooms | Service/cover charge added to bill |
| Railway station — Terminus | Shooting arranged |
| Recreation/games room | Showers — Cold |

| | | | |
|---|---|---|---|
| Showers — Hot | | Unlicensed | |
| Single room | | Viewpoint | |
| Skiing (arranged) | | Washing and ironing facilities | |
| Slipway for boats | | Washing machine | |
| Snacks | | Water — cold | |
| Some bedrooms without hot and cold water | | Water — hot | |
| Special Christmas programme | | Water supply | |
| Subaqua activities | | Water drainage for caravans | |
| Suitable for wheelchairs/ disabled guests | | Water points for caravans | |
| Swimming Pool | | Water skiing | |
| Swimming Pool — Indoor | | Wildlife park | |
| Target sports | | Working farm | |
| Telephone (in bedrooms) | | Youth hostel | |
| Television in bedrooms | | Zoo | |
| Tennis courts | | | |
| Tents for hire | | | |
| Toilets (with water closet) | | | |
| Toilets (without flush) | | | |

farmers will even shoot a dog if there's no owner in evidence. And the law's on their side. So keep dogs under control. Not necessarily on a rein but within call and obedient if called to heel.

**Lambs** Don't assume you know the farmer's job for him. If you find a newborn lamb, nestling alone in a hollow, don't assume it's been abandoned by its mother, and take it thoughtfully to the nearest farmhouse. The farmer won't thank you. The mother sheep probably knew perfectly well where she'd left her offspring, and he will now have to restore it to her. If your soft city heart is stirred, then leave the lamb where it is, and call at the nearest farm to tell them.

**Litter** Surely the message has got through by now. Litter spoils the country for others — and that means you on a return visit. Take large plastic bags for any picnic or snack wrappings you may have. Leave the site as you would hope to find it.

**Locals** People not pubs; though you'll probably meet the former in the latter. Country people talk to strangers more easily than city folk. So ease up. It's customary to bid good day to people you meet on walks. They're probably as curious about you as you are about them. Don't be reticent and you'll find them happy to make friends.

**Lanes** Motor accidents have happened to hiking groups. Always walk towards oncoming traffic; don't bunch; listen for approaching vehicles.

**N.B.** Farming is an industry: respect all signs referring to diseases, e.g. foot and mouth disease requiring dips.

### Symbols

The symbols shown on pages 139 to 143 are gradually being introduced throughout the U.K.

# Chapter 20
# Camping

The attractions of self-sufficiency and economy are bringing a boom in camping holidays. This should mean continuously changing and improving standards of both sites and equipment. You need lots of information and practical guidance; I can tell you where to find it, and offer a brief summary. Then it's up to you. One of the most comprehensive guides to camping sites is the *Guide to British and Continental Camping and Caravanning*, published by Letts Diaries and R.A.C. It covers over 4,000 sites in 32 countries.

**Practise first** Don't plunge into the expense of buying equipment or booking full-scale holidays until you've sampled life under canvas. Take a few days at the children's half-term or Easter — a long weekend — to see how it suits you. You can rent the equipment.

Assess your reactions to open-air cooking, basic sanitation, rain and wind on the roof, and the varying facilities of different sites: some can be like canvas holiday centres, others primitive, remote and peaceful. Judge for yourself just how much back to nature you want, or just how much camp community life you need.

**Renting** Look up camping specialist shops in Britain in the Yellow Pages: most of them hire out. Blacks of Greenock at Sidcup have thirty-two U.K. branches. For the Continent, you can hire from cross-Channel ferry firms; you can pick up the equipment as you drive on board at Dover, Southampton, Portsmouth or Felixstowe. Check with the ferry company concerned. For example, Sealink have a five-day scheme — you pick up the pack at Dover, Newhaven or Sidcup. Take advice books and magazines to help you get the tent up: if you're renting en route you won't have practised. An expert can put up a frame tent in half an hour. Take time to learn how.

**A tent of your own** The collapsible tubular frame tent has made camping a far less primitive affair than it used to be: they cost from £100 to £400. Go for the best you can afford. Camping shops are often staffed by enthusiasts: chat over with them how easy each is to stow and to erect, and how much interior space and headroom they have. Buy a tent one size larger than you think you need. Watch out for weakness at joints, corners and zips: check ventilation and rust risks. If you're heading south consider mosquito netting and opening-out sides. Do you want awnings, roof insulation and sewn-in groundsheets? Variations are innumerable: and half the fun is picking and choosing. But go to expert shops such as:

> Binleys Camping Centre, Kettering. Mail order catalogue — colourful, comprehensive — 25p.
> Pindisports, 14 High Holborn, London EC1.
> Blacks of Greenock, Ruxley Corner, Sidcup, Kent.
> Raclet, 24 Lonsdale Road, London NW6.
> Camping Centre, 20 Lonsdale Road, London NW6.
> South London Camping, 211a New Kent Road, London SE1.

Magazines to consult: *Camping*, *Practical Camper*, *Camping Club Magazine* (members only).

T.C.T.—L

Good-quality camping gear costs around £350 to £500. A good tent will last ten years. The investment's well worth it if you'll be camping regularly. If not, you're buying expensive lumber.

If you intend touring give some thought to speed and ease of stowing away. A roof-rack and car boot may not be enough: a small trailer will help out and take all the paraphernalia too.

**Rent-a-tent** You can save yourself all the packing or even hiring strain by taking a package camping holiday. More and more companies (see list) are offering a camping-site holiday, complete with tent ready set up and equipped, plus site, shops and showers, even an English-speaking courier.

You simply arrive and move in; they usually prefer you to arrive in the morning. There are sites across Europe: mainly France, Spain and Italy, and you can book a holiday at one or several sites. But you should book. Word's got round that they're good value.

A firm called Canvas Holidays pioneered the idea twelve years ago and are probably still leaders in the field. They offer a choice of thirty-five camps in four countries, most in France. Their brochure gives extensive details of how peaceful or luxurious the different sites are. They offer advice, insurance, car-ferry packages, even overnight hotels on the way.

## Addresses:

*Canvas Holidays*, Bull Plain, Hertford; telephone 0992 59933.

*Rent-a-Tent*, Twitch Hill, Horbury, Yorkshire; telephone 0924 275131.

*The A.A.*: book through travel agents.

*Eurocamp*, 9-11 Princess Street, Knutsford, Cheshire; telephone 0565 52444.

*Club Cantabrica Holidays*, 2-6 Verulam Road, St. Albans, Hertfordshire; telephone 56 30231.

*Continental Camping Holidays*, Ainsworth Lodge, Radcliffe (Manchester), Lancs; telephone 061-764 3118.

*Sunsites*, 1 South Street, Dorking, Surrey; telephone 0306 87733.

*Camping Club of Great Britain and Ireland*, 11 Lower Grosvenor Place, London SW1; telephone 01-828 1012. Worth joining. Has sections for advice on canoe and lightweight camping (including cycling), rucksack and mountain camping with tips on survival. Even deals with the much less rigorous touring and holiday site camping by motor. Also helpful about stove cooking, fire risks etc. The first-year fee is £7.50. The Club publishes a monthly magazine and a guide to U.K. sites. It has touring and insurance services. There are also guides to foreign sites.

## Abroad

A recent survey showed that 17 per cent of all British campers and caravanners went abroad. The most popular places are France, Germany, Belgium, Holland, Luxembourg, Spain and Italy.

## Sites in Europe

Camping is not the casual, go-as-you-please, whim-of-the-moment thing it used to be. Gypsies have discovered that to their cost. It's getting more organized and will get even more so. British sites are often the least 'developed' — more natural, back to nature. The Forestry Commission and National Trust make available stretches of beautiful countryside and discourage holiday-camp habits. European sites will at least have lavatories and running water — often far more.

The *A.A. Guide to Camping and Caravanning on the Continent* lists nearly 5,000 sites throughout eighteen countries (£2.25).

*Eastern Europe* Camp at will but observe strict hygiene rules.

*France* Over 6,000 sites of all types. Camping outside official sites is discouraged because of fire risk. Some popular sites should be booked in advance. Often they have shops, restaurants, pools. The Michelin *Camping and Caravanning in France* is a good guide (the 1977 edition costs £1.75). Some châteaux allow camping: get the *Castels et Camping* list from the French Tourist Office.

*Germany and Holland* Sites tend to be efficient, with shops, restaurants, hot showers etc. They can look like an estate of canvas suburban bungalows. They may also provide pools, tennis courts etc.

*Scandinavia* Plenty of sites. They make up in location what they lack in facilities. In Sweden you can camp at will as long as you observe strict rules of hygiene.

*Spain and Italy* Hundreds of excellent sites, many with lavish facilities, such as supermarkets, hairdressers, shops and swimming pools. Most are by the sea.

# Chapter 21
# Rented Villas and Cottages

## Some plain talking about self-catering

Renting accommodation is currently the widest, most popular trend in holidays. But before the idea completely sweeps the holiday trade off its feet and reduces tower-block hotels to a twentieth-century Acropolis, and Benidorm to a ghost town, let's consider the hard facts. There are things to be said for and against. Consider both before making your own decisions.

## In favour of self-catering

**You rent a home of your own** About eight hours after moving in, less if you're very adaptable — you feel it's your place. You hold sway there: no one else has authority over you: even the discreet authority of a hotel manager. For one or two weeks it's 'our place'.

**You gain freedom** You are entirely free of the timetables of hotel mealtimes, or even the friendly but defined arrangements of guest-houses, farms or bed and breakfast. In all these places, where people are employed to attend on you, then you have, to some extent, to follow a predictable timetable. I was once a guest in one of the country's most beautiful and distinguished country homes, only to find that my being slightly late one evening threw the perfection of their system into disarray. There was a risk that, however quickly I bathed and changed for dinner, the precise timing of that meal would be threatened. Rather than offend the staff in such an unthinkable way — or be so discourteous as to deny me my relaxing aperitif, his Lordship, himself, brought my gin to me — while I was in the bath. No holiday package can promise treats like that! Still in your own place you can drink gin to the eyeballs as long as you like before eating — or instead of eating. You can breakfast at noon; have a full-blooded fry-up at midnight; suit yourself. If that kind of freedom means a lot, then rent.

**Children aren't any problem** At least no more than they are at home. If your toddler likes blowing his cereal across the table, or tipping his orange juice over his high chair — it's irritating enough at home. In a hotel it's far worse. You'll feel torn between allowing your children their usual degree of freedom and cowering in shame from the other guests, or trying to force the uncomprehending children into unexpected patterns. 'Best behaviour' will make it no holiday for them and a nervous strain for you. In a rented place you and they will all feel less constrained and able to keep up normal family routines.

**More scope for eating** Unless you book simply bed and breakfast at a hotel, you will be committed for one meal per day to the meals they provide. These will have been costed and marketed to fit their budgets. In package-holiday terms they may be terrific value and offer enough choice to please you. But they can't offer the range of choice you can buy for yourself in local markets and stores. And very often, foreign markets are part of the picturesque place you've come to see. What was a chore at home becomes an interesting routine abroad.

**Bad-weather bonus** If the weather keeps you indoors in a hotel you'll have to clear out of your rooms while they're cleaned, there'll be queues for the hotel's pool table or table tennis. You'll feel unwanted anywhere. In your own rented place, you can please yourself.

**Noise unabated** If you're frankly a noisy lot and want to drink and shout into the early hours, far better do it in a remote villa entirely your own. You won't be welcome in a hotel. But you won't be popular in a closely knit settlement of villas either. The noise problem is solved for children too: if the baby has colic it's simply an extra worry that you're keeping the people in the next hotel room awake. Rented accommodation also allows for teenagers who can't move without a 'trannie' clamped to their ear. O.K. in a villa − if *you* can bear it!

**Cost** I list it last because it doesn't follow automatically that rented accommodation is cheaper. To rent in Spain, for example, and then have to pay for all your own food will not be cheaper than the all-in flight and full-board packages on offer. But on the whole the boom in self-catering and renting is based on the belief that it is much cheaper. Certainly in Britain, and outside the full-board package-holiday bargains it will be.

**Renting packages** It is now common to be able to buy the renting of a villa and a return flight for an all-in price. Many individuals who own homes abroad, but have them standing empty for several months, now put them in the hands of specialist firms who offer them for holiday rental. Owners Service Limited − O.S.L. − is the biggest. There are a growing number of others. *Holiday Which?*, December 1975, lists forty-nine companies renting either in Britain or abroad. Since then there has been a great increase. Consult advertisements in *The Times* or a good travel agent. Many firms issue annual brochures like any other travel operator. Even private owners can offer charter flight travel. What's more, travel companies, like Thomsons, are offering flats or villas to rent, and inclusive flights. Self-catering is the direction that much holiday travel is taking so shop around for bargain deals. They might include rent of a car, a swimming-pool of your own, maid service, a cook − or they may not. Which brings me to the snags.

## Against self-catering

Katharine Whitehorn put her finger on it when she asked, 'Who is self?' If you simply transfer your normal system of housekeeping to a different setting, it won't be a holiday in the true sense at all. You'll just be keeping house in a different place. The person who might object most is Mum: will she be expected to cook, clean, make beds, clear up after everyone as she usually does? If so, she'll need a hotel holiday to recover. There are certain modifications you can make.

Abandon all cleaning: you won't be there to notice the dust, you'll be down on the beach.

Make everyone do a share of the rest. In one family I know Dad does breakfast for all, teenage children do a salad lunch, Mum does supper. That suits them fine but it depends on how willing Dad and children are to help — staging an instant experiment for egalitarianism might not be their idea of fun. So if mother has any doubts, she should raise the 'fair shares' bogey before they set out.

Eat out — or at least out of tins. The one will be delicious and expensive, the other cheap and nasty. But a mix of both, with the family making occasional efforts is probably the best solution.

Choose a place with staff provided. If it says in the brochure 'domestic help', it might simply mean that a local girl with no English calls in to make the beds. Ask. And if necessary ask for more. You'll pay extra for longer, more for cooking.

**Isolation** The brochures call it 'secluded': but you could be miles up a cart track with no means of reaching even the nearest seedy bar, and no way of finding anyone else who speaks your language. Many people see a holiday as the time when they make lots of new friends. You won't do that up a mountain in Sicily or in a crofter's cottage on Mull. If you're used to the social life of a hotel — even if it's only a drink in the bar before dinner — you might find it leaves you a bit lonely if you're on your own. On the other hand if you've been too busy climbing a career ladder all year you might relish the chance to get to know your family again. It's a matter of what kind of family you are.

**You're on your own** when it comes to broken plumbing, dodgy electricity, and a swimming-pool full of dead flies. This is where groups can help: they often have a local representative who will come to the rescue. That, of course, means contacting him, by unfamiliar phone or gestured messages to the locals. Self-catering abroad calls for a certain resourcefulness.

**Outings** If you're not in or very near a town or village, you may well need a car. If your holiday is primarily a rest — eating, sleeping and lying in the sun — you won't mind being cut off. But there may be a famous castle just over the hill, a museum in the next town, or breath-taking scenery in the near beyond. Hiring a car as a separate enterprise is expensive. So either find a rental that includes car, or ask about fly-drive arrangements at your travel agent.

**A villa is a house: so is a cottage** The language and photographs of both brochures and owners are intended to entice you. Examine both for hard evidence. 'A villa in the sun' might be a semi-detached at a noisy intersection, an idyllic country cottage may be in a nineteenth-century terrace beside a coastguard station. Ask how far the nearest neighbours are and the nearest main road: ask about water supply, plumbing, fridge, bedding, shops, markets and doctor. Consult a tourist guidebook or map of the resort and see just where the flat or villa is situated. What happens in the area just beyond the edge of the brochure's photograph? A garage? a factory? a night-club? Or a beach? a sea view? a promenade?

## The choice is big – and getting bigger

You won't be stuck for where to rent – from individual offers on the back page of *The Times*, to commercial brochures by holiday companies, and listings from places like the Forestry Commission and the National Trust. But a few pointers might help.

## Chalet settlements

There are houses built specifically for holiday letting, often grouped in villages with shops, boating, fishing, tennis, and a social club provided. The effect is of a holiday camp where you 'do' for yourself. Some of them have chosen attractive sites, with views of sea or hillsides. Some of them actually spoil the scenery with their spread of houses. You'll find them listed in accommodation brochures.

## The Forestry Commission

In Britain they have permitted developers to follow the Scandinavian idea and build settlements of log-cabin houses in areas of woodland. There are often country pursuits within easy reach: canoeing, pony-trekking, fishing, etc. You may even be able to buy a chalet: 1976 prices were over £6,000. Write to: The Forestry Commission, 25 Saville Row, London WiX 2AY; telephone 01-734 4251; or Portcullis House, 21 India Street, Glasgow G2 4PL; telephone 041-248 3931.

## A.A. Villa Rental Service

The A.A. gives its blessing to the 376-page brochure of Swiss Chalets – Inter Home, who offer accommodation in twenty-one countries: though mostly Switzerland (one in Tunisia, one in Eire). More luxurious places are marked with a four-leaf clover.

## The National Trust

You can't actually move in on any of the stately homes, but you can come pretty close. I can personally vouch for the beautiful setting of quayside cottages at Cotehele House in Cornwall. And Doyden Castle by Port Isaac looks rather exceptional: a castellated folly on the cliff edge — not recommended for children.

The National Trust also has furnished chalets, caravan sites, adventure huts, camping sites, etc., on many of its beautiful stretches of landscape.

It is a charity, not a government department, dedicated to 'all that progressive preservation means to our island heritage'. So you should expect their accommodation to be well planned, and either with or near beautiful views.

Write to the National Trust, 42 Queen Anne's Gate, London SW1; telephone 01-930 0211. It has separate lists for different parts of the country.

## The Landmark Trust

A trust started in 1965 by John and Christian Smith to preserve small buildings — the sort the National Trust can't cope with — and to find a use for them. They have around forty lettings available. Or they were available until people in the know realized what delightfully odd sorts of places they were. They include an eighteenth-century tower folly in Hampshire, a thirteenth-century timbered house in Suffolk, the gothic temple in the grounds of Stowe School, a martello tower in Aldeburgh, and an Italianate railway station in Staffordshire. They also have seven cottages on Lundy Island. Booking is well in advance. Visitors from abroad planning a year ahead might relish the chance to live in a bit of history. The Landmark is also a charity: so it needs funds and support. Address: The Landmark Trust, Shottesbrooke, Maidenhead, Berkshire; telephone Littlewick Green 3431 (S.T.D. code 062882).

## Universities

For large parts of the year, large parts of universities — the accommodation — stand empty. Or used to. Many countries — especially those hard pushed for tourist space — have realized their universities provide ideal self-catering places to hand. Ask at the national tourist office of the country that interests you. They will probably hand you over to an agent that deals in such lettings. In Britain such a one is University Holidays Limited, Borehamgate House, Sudbury, Suffolk; telephone Sudbury 76111 (S.T.D. code 07873). They have self-catering flats and bed-and-breakfast accommodation. Universities include: Aberdeen, Aberystwyth, Bristol, Canterbury, Colchester, Dundee, Edinburgh, Exeter, Glasgow, Keele, Liverpool, London, Newcastle, Oxford, Stirling and York.

## Commercial listings

You'll find books of accommodation to let on the country's major book-stalls. Both the Farm Holiday Guides, and Herald Advisory Service do them (see p.128)

**Warning** As with hotels, make a clear distinction in guides between accommodation listed — often for a fee — and accommodation inspected and recommended. The latter is obviously preferable. Better still if you're familiar with their standards of judgement or have been recommended by friends.

## Questions to ask

Details before you set out save disappointment. So write or phone enquiring about:

**Costs** Is electricity and gas included, or must you feed a slot machine? Television is often on a slot-machine principle too: costs can mount up.

**Linen** Do they or you provide sheets and towels? Remember you bring the soap.

**Heating** How many electric fires are there? What kind of plugs? Can you light a fire in the fireplace or has the chimney been blocked off? Where do you get logs?

**Crockery** How much, and what happens about breakages?

**Gardens** Are there deck-chairs, washing lines. Can you pick the flowers? Do they want it watered?

**Security** In many country villages people leave their door on the latch. It's getting less common and after the needs for locked front doors in the city you might feel nervous. Ask what is usual.

**Problems** Will the roof leak if there's a thunderstorm? Are there any plumbing quirks — like banging pipes or a lavatory that only flushes once in half an hour? Is there hot and cold in kitchen and bathroom? Where are the water stopcock, the electricity fusebox and the gas meter?

**Contacts** Ask for phone numbers for the nearest doctor and dentist, plumber and electrician, garage and taxi. It's useful but not essential to know of a friendly neighbour. Who delivers milk, papers, bread? You may find a van comes round with fish, crabs, vegetables: find out on which days. When should you put out the dustbins?

**Damage** Suppose the toddler's sick on the rug, or the children bounce on the bed and bust the springs. Agree beforehand if and how much you must pay. You can take out an insurance against damage if yours is a particularly unruly crowd.

**Local events** You could be renting a farm in Brittany and not know about the festival in the next town. There may be a town band, a rose queen or church events.

**Opening times** Shops, banks and pubs differ in different areas: especially in remote places. Buses and ferries might only call once a day or once a week and you don't want to miss them.

# Chapter 22
# Home Swapping

This is an idea born of inflation which flourishes because of its proven success. The idea is simply to swap your home — say in the centre of one of Britain's cathedral cities — for a villa on the hillslopes around Florence. Families simply swap over and they live in yours while you live in theirs. If like swaps with like, then money doesn't change hands. The main advantage is cheapness: all you pay for is the fare and the food. And there's someone taking care of your home — security, pets, house-plants, phone calls — while you're away.

You can also swap cleaning ladies, baby sitters and cars. You feel you move into a whole new way of life, settle in quickly and feel at home Most accommodation is available at the time you want it — the holiday months. So you get maximum choice.

The main problem is that you won't find it easy to swap a cramped flat in a dingy area for a luxury seaside villa in California. Keep your expectations in scale with your own level of living. That doesn't mean you're stuck to swapping the sort of thing you've already got. An academic in London might be delighted to swap with a Welsh farmer; a semi-detached outside Cambridge might be a fair swap for a tower-block flat in Rome. It's the place that matters, not the luxury living.

You'll have to prepare your house for strangers, preferably by locking all personal things, clothes, bills and tat, away in one small room, with the rest of the house empty for them. It'll take time — and be more worth the effort — the longer the swap.

There's no moving out, or coming home early if you don't like it. Once the bargain's made and begun, you'll have to go through with it.

Their children might smash your collection of Crown Derby; they might

spill red wine on the carpet; get crumbs in the hi-fi; alienate the shopkeepers and trample on the flowerbed. Well, you do take risks. But don't
forget they know you're in their house too. Basically, it's best if families
with the same degree of housepride can swap with each other. There are
some families that take it for granted that children carve their name on
the banisters: let them swap with each other too.

## How to do it

There are agencies which publish directories carrying lists of descriptions. You pay to have your house added; and you pay for the directory.
You then select ones you find suitable and write to the owner. My advice
would be to write to several, and then write several times more to the
ones that sound best. The more information about lifestyle, standards,
interests and gadgetry you can exchange the better. Does the door fly
open on their spin-drier? Is the handle broken on your coal-scuttle? Note
down all such quirks in a notebook. Some people use a tape-recorder.

With people's jobs taking them abroad for periods of a month or more,
this seems an ideal way of taking the family too. Even swaps for six
months or a year are possible. It makes for an easier and friendlier way of
getting round the globe.

## Agencies

*Home Interchange Limited*, P.O. Box 84, London, NW8 7RR; telephone
01-262 3822. They have an associate company in New York. They began
in 1962 and now list an average 3,000 homes in thirty countries, covering
the U.K., most of Europe, North America, Canada, Australia, New
Zealand, the Far East, the Caribbean, Mexico and East Africa.

They will list you for exchange, rental or exchange hospitality. The latter
means you go as guests of a family and then they return to be your guests.
In 1977 the listing and directory cost £6.50. For a further £2.00 they will
print a photograph (80 × 120 mm; 3 × 5 inches). The directory comes
out in December, with supplements in February and March.

*Homex Directory Limited*, P.O. Box 27, London NW6 4HE; telephone
01-458 1031. There's a link with British Airways, though they don't say
what. Also in cooperation with Canadian Holiday Home Exchange,
British Columbia, Canada. The *Directory* is sent to subscribers who
supply Homex with details of their home, of where they want to go and
when. The subscribers then contact each other. Homex concentrate on
exchanges between Britain and the U.S.A. and Canada.

Listing and directory — if you're in the U.K. or surface mail to Europe —
cost £8.00 in 1977. Subscribers elsewhere pay £10.25, but get the directory by air mail. A photograph costs another £2.75.

*William Lowell Associates Incorporated*, 305 South Saint Asaph Street, Alexandria, Virginia 22314, U.S.A. They claim to offer 'a professional service for professional people', and they charge highly for it: $135 (about £80) for up to four weeks exchange on their international schedule, rising to $470 for a stay of thirty-seven to fifty-two weeks. What they offer is not just a list of exchange names but also a security service that will take up and verify all the references each side must provide: and that includes two local credit references, a credit-card reference, two personal references, and three business references. Once your application to swap has been processed you are sent a portfolio of 'pertinent information concerning the occupant designate of your home'. They also put you in touch with each other by telephone: who pays isn't clear. But the organization prides itself on minimizing the risks of house swapping.

*Handihols,* The Cottage, The Chase, Ashingdon, Rochford, Essex. This is an agency for exchanging homes between disabled people. Such homes will have adaptations made to doors, stairs, plugs and access to lavatories to make them suitable for the handicapped. If you fill in their forms and pay a £3.00 a year registration fee they will try to match your needs as closely as possible.

# Chapter 23
# Hostels and Others

## Y.M.C.A.

Young Men's Christian Associations operate in eighty-five countries. Their directory lists 1,750 addresses in those countries. Many of them have accommodation, though it may be limited, so writing ahead to book is advisable. The Y.M.C.A.s are always intended as places where people can seek help for their problems: they will usually have addresses for referral to doctors, lawyers, priests, consulates. Get the directory from: National Council of Y.M.C.A.s, 640 Forest Road, Walthamstow, London E17 3DZ; telephone 01-520 5599 (see also the Gazetteer at the end of this book.

## Y.W.C.A.

Young Women's Christian Associations operate too widely for them to list every hostel and local association. However, their annual directory (cost 60p) gives addresses in seventy-nine countries, indicating where there is accommodation for permanent and/or transient guests. As with the Y.M.C.A., the intention is to keep costs as low as possible, and to offer services of help and advice wherever needed. Get the directory in the U.K. from: Y.W.C.A. of Great Britain, Hampden House, 2 Weymouth Street, London W1; telephone 01 – 636 9722/6 (see also the Gazetteer).

## Y.H.A.

The youth-hostel movement – non-profit making – that provided so much pleasure when I was a teenager is still vigorous, youthful and cheap. There are over 4,000 hostels in all parts of the world, from Argentina to Bulgaria, from Iceland to the Philippines. There are 250 in England and Wales, 150 in Scotland and Ireland.

**Where you stay** The hostels can be a Norman castle, a water-mill, a farm or an old rectory. Some are rumoured to be haunted: many are in beautiful settings. They vary in size from twelve to 200 beds. In Britain hostels are graded as follows (number in each grade in parentheses, then overnight cost for a bed): simple (67) 65p, standard (150) 80p, superior (32) £1.00, special (3) £1.25. London has three that cost up to £1.50 a night.

**Provision** Separate dormitories for men and women. A bed, mattress and blankets are supplied: bring your own sleeping-bag. You are expected to help with the chores: conditions are spartan, informal and friendly.

Each hostel has a warden who provides simple meals which cost from 30p to £1. Allow £3.50 a day for bed, and two meals and a packed lunch. Motorists and motor-cyclists are allowed rather than encouraged.

There's a limit of three nights in any one hostel.

**Membership** You must belong to the Y.H.A., 29 John Adam Street, London WC2 (telephone 01-839 1722). That will take you to hostels in any country: the fees are modest – up to £2.00. Minimum age five years. Children between five and nine years old must be with a parent or guardian of the same sex. Children under twelve must be with a member aged eighteen or over. There's a maximum age of twenty-five years in Switzerland; twenty-seven years in Bavaria.

## Retreats

Not everyone wants to be out and about in the world. More and more people seek the chance to withdraw from it. Many of them seek to renew inner peace and calm by going to a religious retreat. 'The aim is to foster the growth of spiritual life' declares *Vision*, the journal of the Association for Promoting Retreats (25p from Church House, Newton Road, London W2; telephone 01-727 7924), which lists retreats in the U.K., the U.S.A., Canada, South Africa and New Zealand.

You can go on a retreat as an individual or as a group. You can go to study, to be silent, to take part in yoga, Zen or Christian worship. Some retreats are for women or men only, many are mixed. All houses welcome members of any denomination, but you don't have to belong to a church. They are happy to take in those who are simply weary and spiritually exhausted by life.

## The Directory of Monastic Hospitality

This is a list printed by the Poor Clares of Arundel (50p from All Saints, London Colney, St. Albans, Herts) of monasteries and convents in the U.K. that offer hospitality compatible with their traditions and their rule. There are forty-one convents and twelve monasteries. They open their doors in the hope that inmates and visitors can learn from each other. Charges are usually by donation, or around £2 per day.

## Cold comfort

You can volunteer to catch a cold at the Common Cold Research Unit, Harvard Hospital, Coombe Road, Salisbury, Wiltshire; telephone 0722 22485. You must be between eighteen and fifty years old and not on any regular drug treatment. You book for a ten-day stay and are subject to certain restrictions. You can only mix with the one or two others with whom you share a flat. (Husbands and wives, and friends can book together.) You are confined, indoors, to the flat itself. There is radio and television. Outdoors, you must stay in open countryside. No popping into wayside pubs. Ideal for a rest or the chance to study, write a novel, etc. You are given a travel allowance within the U.K., free bed and board plus 35p pocket money per day. One in three get colds.

# Chapter 24
# Activity Holidays

People are increasingly dedicating their leisure to keeping busy. This may involve travel itself as a pastime: trekking, sailing etc., or it may mean enlisting on residential courses in a chosen subject. The choice is vast — and up to you. It's not for me to enumerate the rewards of weaving or the snags about bird-watching. But I can point you in the right direction if you want to make a holiday of it. There are certain things you should always check on.

*The level of tuition you will receive at residential courses.* Always check out any holiday courses you see listed or advertised with the British authority in that particular subject (these are listed in the following pages). Otherwise, seek the advice of some educational body whose judgement is impartial: e.g. National Institute of Adult Education, 35 Queen Anne Street, London WC1; telephone 01-637 4241.

*Level of safety.* People teaching things like mountaineering or pot-holing have a special responsibility. Ask, before you or your children go, what their safety rules are and how they are applied. Also check your own insurance against injury.

*Accommodation.* Residential courses often take place in schools and universities during holidays. Some provide only single rooms; some have family self-catering facilities; some only offer dormitory accommodation. Settle before you book, which you want.

## General information

The British National Tourist Boards (page 123) publish inexpensive leaflets.

National tourist officers (see Gazetteer), usually in London, will have details of activity holidays in their particular country.

The Sports Council, 70 Brompton Road, London SW3 1EX, arranges a great number of coaching courses, both for beginners and those with experience.

Universities abroad offer courses in many subjects. See Central Bureau for Educational Visits and Exchanges, Chapter 38, page 244.

## Subject guide to helpful organizations

### Archaeology and history

Sites under the Department of Environment listed in their publication — *Historic Monuments Open to the Public.* From Her Majesty's Stationery Office, P.O. Box 569, London SE1 9NH.

Season ticket from Department of the Environment, Room 106, 25 Saville Row, London W1X 2BT.

Council of British Archaeology, 8 St. Andrews Place, Regent's Park, London NW1 4LB, publish a *Calendar of Excavations*.

## Archery

Grand National Archery Society, 20 Broomfield Road, Chelmsford, Essex.

## Arts and crafts

The Council for Small Industries in Rural Areas, 35 Camp Road, Wimbledon Common, London SW19 4UP, publishes a list of craftsmen and workshops that can be visited.

*Macklin's Monumental Brasses* (Allen & Unwin) lists 4,000 brasses in the U.K.

Federation of British Craft Societies, 80a Southampton Row, London WC1B 4BA, or any local institute of adult education.

## Ballooning

British Balloon and Airship Club, Kimberley House, Vaughan Way, Leicester LE1 4SG; telephone Leicester 51051 (S.T.D. code 0533).

## Bird-watching

There are nine bird observatories round the coast of England. Many nature reserves have bird-watching viewing points.

The National Trust, 42 Queen Anne's Gate, London SW1; telephone 01-930 0211.

Nature Conservancy, 19 Belgrave Square, London SW1; telephone 01-235 3241.

Royal Society for the Protection of Birds, The Lodge, Sandy, Bedfordshire SG19 2DL.

Society for the Promotion of Nature Reserves, The Green, Nettleham, Lincoln LN2 2NR.

British Trust for Ornithology, Beech Grove, Tring, Herts.

## Canoeing

British Canoe Union, 70 Brompton Road, London SW3 1DT; telephone 01-584 9229.

## Caving and pot-holing

National Caving Association: Secretary, Mrs. J. Potts, 3 Greenway, Hulland Ward, Derby DE6 3FE.

List of caving clubs in *Descent Handbook for Cavers* from 30 Drake Road, Wells, Somerset.

## Climbing

British Mountaineering Council, Crawford House, Precinct Centre, Manchester University, Bath Street E, Manchester M13 9RZ; telephone 061-273 5835.

## Cricket

Your local cricket club — address from the local library — will be able to put you in touch with cricket coaching courses.

## Cycling

See page 87.

## Drama

Arts Council of Great Britain, 105 Piccadilly, London W1; telephone 01-629 9495, will have a list of all festivals in the U.K.

Further details from: British Arts Festival Association, 33 Rufford Road, Sherwood, Nottingham; telephone 0602 61979.

For courses: National Institute of Adult Education, 35 Queen Anne Street, London WC1; telephone 01-637 4241.

## Festivals

Specialists in festival travel: Special Tours, 2 Chester Row, London SW1; telephone 01-730 2297. Heritage Travel, 22 Hans Place, London SW1; telephone 01-584 5201. G. W. Henebery, 22 Oppidans Road, London NW3; telephone 01-722 0866.

## Fencing

Amateur Fencing Association, The De Beaumont Centre, 83 Perham Road, London W14 9SY; telephone 01-385 7442.

## Field studies

Field Studies Council, Preston Montford, Montford Bridge, Shrewsbury SY4 1HW.

## Fishing

*Fishing Waters,* published by Link House Publications Ltd., Link House, Dingwall Avenue, Croydon, Surrey; telephone 01-686 2599.

*Where to Fish,* edited by D. A. Orton, published by Harmsworth Press Ltd., 8 Stratton Street, London W1; telephone 01-499 7881.

Any local water authority.

## Flying (aviation)

List of clubs from: British Light Aviation Centre, Artillery Mansions, 75 Victoria Street, London SW1H 0JD; telephone 01-222 6782. Also magazines: *Flight International* and *Pilot.*

## Golf

Administrative body of amateur golf in England is: Golf Union, 12A Denmark Street, Wokingham, Berks RG11 2BE.

T.C.T.—M

## Gliding

British Gliding Association, Kimberley House, 47 Vaughan Way, Leicester; telephone Leicester 52051 (S.T.D. code 0533).

## Hang-gliding

British Hang-gliding Association, Mr. C. Corston, 16 Dillons Road, Creech St. Michael, Taunton, Somerset; telephone Henlade 442595 (S.T.D. code 0823).

## Hunting and shooting

British Field Sports Society, 26 Caxton Street, London SW1H 0RG; telephone 01-222 5407.

Magazines: *The Field, Horse and Hound.*

## Orienteering

British Orienteering Federation, Lea Green Sports Centre, Matlock, Derbyshire; telephone Dethick 561 (S.T.D. code 062984).

## Parachuting

British Parachute Association, Kimberley House, 47 Vaughan Way, Leicester LE1 4SG; telephone 59778/59635 (S.T.D. code 0533).

## Pony-trekking

Ponies of Britain, Brookside Farm, Ascot, Berkshire.

## Riding

British Horse Society, National Equestrian Centre, Kenilworth, Warwickshire, CV8 2LR.

Association of British Riding Schools, Chesham House, Green End Road, Sawtry,Huntingdon, Cambridgeshire.

## Sailing

List of teaching establishments from: Royal Yachting Association, Victoria Way, Woking, Surrey; telephone Woking 5022 (S.T.D. code 04862).

List of member companies offering yachts for charter from: Yacht Charter Association, 33 Highfield Road, Lymington, Hampshire; telephone Lymington 72472 (S.T.D. code 0590).

Adventure courses in deep-sea sailing are run by: Outward Bound Trust, 34 Broadway, London SW1; telephone 01-222 2926; Sail Training Association, Bosham, Chichester, West Sussex; telephone Bosham 572429 (S.T.D. code 0243).

*Boat World*, published by Haymarket (01-439 4242) lists all sailing centres round the U.K. coast and inland waterways.

## Sand and land yachting

British Federation of Land and Sand Yacht Clubs, 2 Woodcrest, Northey Road, Blackburn, Lancs.

## Skiing: snow, dry and grass

Ski Club of Great Britain, 118 Eaton Square, London SW1W 9AF; telephone 01-235 4711.

## Special-interest courses

National Institute of Adult Education, 35 Queen Anne Street, London WC1; telephone 01-637 4241, lists residential courses.

National Trust: Acorn camps for 16$^1$/2-year-olds upwards provide working holidays helping with the upkeep of properties. £6 a week pays for keep. Enquire: The Old Grape House, Cliveden, Taplow, Maidenhead, Berkshire SL6 OH2; telephone Burnham 4228 (S.T.D. code 06286).

Volunteer work camps: The National Conservation Corps, Zoological Gardens, Regent's Park, London NW1 4RY; telephone 01-722 7112/3.

Workers' Educational Association, 4 Carlton Crescent, Southampton SO7 5UG; telephone Southampton 29810/29819 (S.T.D. code 0703). Study and summer schools.

R.V.S. Enterprises, Hilton House, Norwood Lane, Meopham, Gravesend, Kent DA1 3oYE.

## Squash

Squash Rackets Association, 70 Brompton Road, London SW3 1DX; telephone 01-584 2506.

## Surfing

British Surfing Association, 18 Bournemouth Road, Poole, Dorset; telephone Bournemouth 746154 (S.T.D. code 0202).

## Table tennis

England Table Tennis Association, 21 Claremont, Hastings, East Sussex; telephone Hastings 33121 (S.T.D. code 0424).

## Tennis

Lawn Tennis Association, Barons Court, London W14; telephone 01-385 2366.

## Underwater swimming

British Sub-Aqua Club, 70 Brompton Road, London SW3 1HA; telephone 01-584 7164.

## Walking

Youth Hostels Association, Trevelyan House, St. Albans, Hertfordshire.

Ramblers Association, 1—4 Crawford Mews, London W1H 1PT; telephone 01-262 1477.

For walking and special-interest group holidays: Country-wide Holidays Association (C.H.A.), Birch Heys, Cromwell Range, Manchester M14 6HU.

For topo-guides, booklets with maps for following signposted footpaths: Stanfords International Map Centre, 12—14 Long Acre, London WC2E 9LF; telephone 01-681 1751.

## Water-skiing

British Water Ski Federation, 70 Brompton Road, London SW3 1EG; telephone 01-584 8262.

## Safari

Africa is the land of safaris. At present East Africa is the main area: virtually the Costa Brava of safaris. Safaris are also common in Kenya, Tanzania, Uganda, Botswana, Namibia, Sudan and North Cameroon. The idea is so popular it will certainly grow. The economies of African states look to safari tourism to bring in foreign currencies. There are safaris in India too: the Chitral National Park in Nepal is one.

Allen and Dunn Expeditions, 16a Soho Square, London W1; telephone 01-734 1072, is a travel agent specializing in safaris all over the world. So they have to continually devise ones in less popular areas. Botswana has one of the most unspoilt game parks — the Moremi. But it's unlikely to stay like that until the tsetse fly has been dealt with. North of there the area called Savutti is very beautiful and further south the Okavango Swamp is marvellous for bird life.

### Cameras not guns

Hunting safari is now very expensive indeed. Just the licence to shoot at a lion in Africa will cost you £1,000. There are hunting expeditions in Botswana and south Sudan, where the slaughter of elephants for their ivory is still widespread. But international conservancy pressures are against it.

### Packages

Business is booming, especially among the Germans: chartered jumbo jets fly into Mombasa three or four times a week from Germany alone.

A three-week inclusive tour from Britain to Nairobi — two weeks on safari, one at a beach resort — cost from £400 in 1977.

You travel as a group, but stay overnight at safari lodges, along with other safari groups. These lodges are often of a very high standard: some 200 beds, swimming pools, international cooking with the odd zebra steak to add novelty. Alternatively you can stay in tented accommodation for something like half the cost. Life is highly sociable at the lodges: and you may all meet up again next day as your minibus lines up beside theirs to get a good look at the wildlife. Socially it's a white man's holiday. Groups travel together, and socialize together — so chances to meet local people are rare. And not always attractive: in the bottom of Tanzania's Ngorongoro crater there's a staged 'typical' village kept as it is, for paying tourists to visit — a totally false way for one culture to encounter another. However, it's not all like that. Masai herdsmen still roam freely over parts of Kenya and Tanzania. But they like to be asked permission before you start photographing them.

## Cameras at the ready

If you're paying to go on safari, it's worth having a decent telephoto lens to fit your camera. Plenty of game-park animals remain shy of converging minibuses and take off into the savannah. So take the best camera equipment you can afford.

Ivan Allen admits that the first thrill of photographing animals can soon pall for some people. The first sighting of the first lion is a moment of vivid excitement, but within four or five days people get very blasé. 'No I'm not photographing them — there are only three lions.' And lions can be very boring. Unless they are hungry and seeking food, or hungry and eating it, they just sit and gaze around. Still that does give a chance to those who're not so hot on the action snaps. But if you spot a female on the move it is well worthwhile waiting around a while as she may soon indicate her intention to kill. Watching her isolate a buck from the herd and then go in fast for the kill is an unforgettable sight.

## Frontiers

Safari companies from Kenya had been used to taking their groups across frontiers into game parks of other countries. Such excursions were paid for to Kenyans, in Kenya. In February 1977, Tanzania closed its frontiers to such excursions. Instead visitors to such renowned places as the Serengeti Park and other of Tanzania's 45,000 square kilometres of National Park must fly into Tanzania and buy their excursions from Tanzanian companies and pay for them into the Tanzanian economy. Check on such fluctuating frontier situations before you go.

## Books

*Field Guide to the Larger Mammals of Africa* by J. Dorst, price £2.50 (Collins, 1970).

*Field Guide to Birds of West Africa* by W. Serle and G. Morel, price £5.95 (Collins, 1977).

*The Lost World of the Kalahari* by Laurens van der Post, price 60p (Penguin, 1964).

*Out of Africa* by Karen Blixen, price £1.50 (Cape, 1964).

## A working holiday

Push an activity holiday to its limit and you get paid for it. And if you don't enjoy it — well it's only for a limited time. There are plenty of agencies to help you find work. Here are some:

**Vacation Work:** 9 Park End Street, Oxford; telephone Oxford 41978 (S.T.D. code 0865). They publish three paperbacks listing job opportunities for the summer: *Summer Jobs Abroad* and *Summer Jobs in Britain,* both £1.75; and *Summer Employment Directory of the U.S.A.* (£3.00). This last gives details of how students outside the U.S. should apply for work there. Jobs on offer vary from teaching sailing in Hawaii to wardrobe mistress at a summer theatre in New York State. Heaps of needs for summer-camp helpers.

They also publish — at nearly £5.00 — *The Directory of Jobs and Careers Abroad,* a more extensive coverage of career and job prospects in different countries, with immigration and training details.

**Fruit Picking:** Concordia (Youth Service Volunteers) Ltd., 11a Albemarle Street, London W1; telephone 01-629 3367.

**Kibbutz work in Israel:** Kibbutz Representatives, 1 King Street, St. James's, London SW1; telephone 01-930 6181.

**American Summer Camps:** Camp America, 37 Queen's Gate, London SW7; telephone 01-589 3223.

**BUNAC** (British Universities North America Club): 168 Gower Street, London NW1; telephone 01-388 0691. Students needed to teach teenagers.

**Club Méditerranée:** 5 South Molton Street, London W1; telephone 01-499 1965. Need cashiers, state-registered nurses, playgroup leaders and sport instructors. You must have fluent French and five months from May to October. Apply in writing.

**British Council:** 65 Davies Street, London W1Y 2AA; telephone 01-499 8011. Free booklet, *Teaching Overseas,* for details of one- and two-year appointments for all teachers and graduates.

## Coordination Committee for International Voluntary Service:

1 rue Miollis, 75015 Paris, France. Send three international reply coupons (from any post office) and they send a booklet of 130 organizations arranging international work camps.

**Working Holidays** (1977 edition costs 85p; £1.00 by post): Over 100 pages of suggestions with heaps of addresses, usually other agencies to put you in touch. Country-by-country details; everything from grape picking in France, milking cows in Norway, to building camps for Aborigines in Australia. Published by the Central Bureau for Educational Visits and Exchanges, 44 Baker Street, London W1M 2HJ; telephone 01-487 5961 or 01-486 5101, or 3 Bruntsfield Crescent, Edinburgh EH10 4HD; telephone 031-447 8024.

## A health holiday

If your mind and body are too exhausted and indulged even to enjoy a week on a beach, give yourself a decoke and a sense of moral superiority by going to a health farm. In Britain the leading ones are:

*Henlow Grange*: Henlow, Bedfordshire; telephone Hitchin 81111 (S.T.D. code 0462).

*Champneys*: Tring, Hertfordshire; telephone Berkhamsted 3351 (S.T.D. code 04427).

*Ragdale Hall*: Ragdale, Melton Mowbray, Leicestershire; telephone Rotherby 831 (S.T.D. code 066475).

*Forest Mere*: Liphook, Hants; telephone Liphook 2051 (S.T.D. code 0428).

*Shrublands*: Coddenham, Ipswich, Suffolk; telephone Ipswich 830404 (S.T.D. code 0473).

*Enton Hall*: Godalming, Surrey; telephone Wormley 2233 (S.T.D. code 042879).

The style is usually gastronomically spartan but lavish in every other direction to make up. Houses are grand, gardens extensive: rooms have private bathrooms and colour television. There are usually plenty of other beauty treatments on hand to fill the hours of yearning for more than a lettuce leaf. The cost is high considering what they save on catering. But they compensate for starvation by cosseting you: a psychological redress, I suppose. Those with strong wills and thinner purses can get similar results by dieting at home. But they probably won't feel as indulged or as rested. Nor will they meet the fat and flabby celebrities who go there to recover their glamour.

## Cultural identity cards

Issued by the Central Bureau for Educational Visits and Exchanges in London and Edinburgh, 44 Baker Street, London W1M 2HJ; telephone 01-487 5961 or 01-486 5101; 3 Bruntsfield Crescent, Edinburgh EH10 4HD; telephone 031-447 8024. The cards are available to nationals of Council of Europe countries, including the U.K. and Republic of Ireland. Ownership entitles you to admission free or reduced to museums, art galleries, cultural centres, etc. in member countries (everywhere in Western Europe except Portugal, plus Greece and Turkey) other than your own, but you must produce a passport.

Cards are issued to individuals not groups, and you must be of the academic fraternity — teachers, lecturers, students who already have a first degree, authors, librarians, architects, painters, musicians — a clearly defined group of intellectuals in search of further knowledge. The categories, however, are not exclusively or ultimately dependent on profession, so if you think your visit is worthy enough (holidays don't count) then get someone to back you up and send off an enquiry/ application.

# Part 4

# Preparing to Go

# Chapter 25
# Passports

A passport is a traveller's most important document. Keep it with you. Do not leave it in trust for credit or yield to a police request to hold it. You may be required to leave it with the hotel management while you are registered. Reclaim it next morning. I forgot on one occasion and only realized as I went to board my flight home. I was turned back. My return was delayed for twenty-four hours and the taxi sent to retrieve the passport cost £11. That would be as nothing compared with losing your passport in a country in political upheaval: that would be to lose your identity (see Chapter 42 on Emergencies).

You do not need a passport for travel in the U.K., the Republic of Ireland, the Channel Islands and the Isle of Man, or for 'no passport' excursions across the Channel lasting less than forty-eight hours.

## How to get one

The right to British citizenship depends on parentage and place of birth. A child born in Britain to British parents is unequivocally British. After that it begins to get complicated. The situation at the moment (1977) is as follows, but legal changes to the nature of British citizenship are currently being discussed:

A child born in Britain to a British father and foreign mother is British.

A child born in Britain to a British mother and foreign father is British.

A child born abroad to a British father and foreign mother is British.

A child born abroad to a British mother and foreign father is not British.

This is felt by many – mostly women – to be a glaring injustice, and there is hope that it will be changed.

If you are in doubt about whether you are eligible for a British passport then consult one of the Passport Offices – in London, Liverpool, Glasgow, Peterborough, or Newport (Gwent). Give yourself plenty of time, patience and stamina.

## Issue of passport

### Standard passport

You can get an application form from banks, post offices, Passport Offices, or travel agents. There are separate forms for the various types of passport:

*Form A*: for an individual sixteen and over. This passport is valid for ten years, has thirty pages and costs £10. An alternative version with ninety-four pages costs £20 and is useful if you travel a great deal.

*Form B*: for a child under sixteen's own passport. This passport is valid for five years; it can be extended without further fee on production of a new photograph. A child under five needs a separate passport only in exceptional circumstances (if it has to travel alone in the care of an air stewardess, for example). It is usual for a child to be included in the passport of an accompanying relative.

*Form CAF*: for child under age of sixteen to be added to passport of relative — cost £1.00.

*Form D*: for an extension of a U.K. passport initially issued for five years. Total possible life is ten years.

*Form G*: for an amendment of a U.K. passport — e.g. for change of name of a woman by marriage, or a new photograph if the existing one has ceased to be a true likeness.

### Post-dated passport

A woman who is getting married and going abroad at once can get a passport in her future name post-dated to the wedding date, or have an existing passport amended. The minister or superintendent registrar who is to perform the marriage has to complete a form confirming that it will take place and this has to be sent with the passport application.

### British visitor's passport

This is quicker: it can be issued to you at a post office while you wait if you've left things late. Evidence of identity will be needed: e.g. birth certificate, N.H.S. medical card or pension book.

A British visitor's passport costs £5.00 and is valid for only one year and only in certain Western European countries, Canada, Turkey and Bermuda. They are for short trips only — a maximum of three months. The Scandinavian bloc is treated as a common travel area and your visits to this area must not exceed three months in any nine months. These passports are meant for holidays, not for taking up employment or 'engaging in any other form of gainful employment'. For more extensive travel a standard passport is obviously better value for money.

## Husband and wife

With both types of passport a wife or a husband can be the main passport holder — usually it's the husband. In that case the wife can never travel alone on a passport issued to her husband for their joint use. A passport issued to a parent can have a child under 16 entered on it. But the child cannot travel on that passport when going abroad with the other parent alone. In cases of divorce and remarriage, this is a matter that needs sorting out. A child of divorced parents can be entered on both passports, but things will be easier if he or she has their own.

If husband and wife are abroad on the same passport and emergencies arise (e.g. husband on business, child at home falls ill) then the British Consul will arrange a separate passport or adequate travel documents for the wife.

## Photographs

You must provide two. Use the instant-delivery type from machines. They're the right size. Take the extra two with you when you travel — they might be useful for library membership, ski lifts etc.

Photos must be endorsed by a British subject who has known you personally at least two years and who is an M.P., J.P., clergyman, lawyer, bank officer, policeman, doctor or a person of similar standing. The rest of the population obviously aren't to be trusted. If your friends are all villains, ask at the Citizen's Advice Bureau for help.

## Collective passport

This can be issued to approved parties (not less than five, not more than fifty) of students and members of the Scout and Guide movements who are British citizens aged under 18 travelling with a responsible leader, who must be 21 and the holder of a standard passport. There is no collective passport for groups over the age of 18.

## No-passport excursions

British Rail, some airlines and cross-Channel ferries operate no-passport visits to Belgium, France and the Netherlands. So if you're holidaying on the South Coast you can cross on impulse for a stay of up to forty-eight hours. You will need an identity card with photograph which will be supplied at Victoria Station or departure ports for Channel crossings. The organization running the excursion will give you details.

## Visas

Many countries now require a visa endorsement of your passport. (See the Gazetteer at the end of this book.) These are issued by the consulate of the country concerned: inquire there for details of application, cost and time to allow for issue. Get entry, transit and exit visas if necessary. Travel agencies may advise you and help you apply: but they may charge for the service. Ask first.

## A second passport

**Arab countries/Israel** Travellers are liable to be refused visas and admittance to an Arab country if their passports show, or it is otherwise known, they have visited or intend to visit Israel. There are two ways round this. I understand the Israeli authorities will withhold their stamp if you explain why you wish your passport not to show your visit. Or a supplementary passport can be issued by the Foreign Office.

# Chapter 26
# Travel Insurance

You should insure yourself when you travel. There's no law that says you must — except in a car (see page 47) — but it would be reckless not to do so. The theory is that Lloyd's will insure anything: but the more eccentric it is, the more you'll pay. I once insured against having twins — £7 — and I didn't. My sister didn't insure and had them! You can insure against rain on your holiday. But most often people insure against: loss of luggage, loss of tickets and money, cancellation, illness.

## Independent travel

You buy insurance from an insurance company, an insurance broker or a travel agent. You can either buy a standard mass-produced form of insurance — usually enough for the average family on holiday — or purchase an individual insurance policy for your specific needs. The latter is more expensive.

If you plan to take your eighty-year-old granny snake-collecting along the Amazon, you obviously combine a highly individual set of risks. Go to an insurance broker: he will find the best bargain on the market for you.

**Watch out:** If you have any history of medical unfitness or risk, if you might be or get pregnant, if you have elderly relations whose illness might be the cause of you cancelling a holiday, then you need insurance that will cover all such cases. Many 'sausage-machine' policies have certain exclusions in the small print. So before signing *read the small print*. There is a useful article on these points in the June 1976 issue of *Money Which?*, available in many reference libraries or from the Consumers' Association, 1 Caxton Hill, Hertford SG13 7LZ.

## Proposal form

You take out insurance by filling in a proposal form. You may be required to declare that you and your family are in good health. You must declare at this point any *material facts* which might influence the likelihood of your making a claim: for example if you have a history of heart trouble you should say so. You may pay more: but you will certainly be covered if the ill-health recurs. If you don't declare previous ill-health then the insurers could argue that the policy didn't take this into account and refuse to pay up.

## Package-tour insurance

Tour operators often offer this in their brochure for you to take up when you make your booking. You don't have to. You can refuse theirs and make your own arrangements. If you accept their insurance you don't have to fill in a proposal form. But if you accept theirs and also have private insurance arrangements you can't claim twice for the same loss.

## Read the policy

Whichever way you acquire insurance, insist on having a copy of the full policy — *not* a summary. Take the documents with you.

## What can be covered by insurance

**Medical insurance** This is dealt with in detail on p. 175.

**Cancellation or return** You can be insured for what you lose if you cancel at the last minute for an acceptable reason. Reasons usually accepted: your ill-health, that of a close relative, jury service, sudden redundancy. Standard policies may not offer enough if your booking is for, say, a three-month world cruise.

**Luggage or belongings** Insurance policies set a limit to each claim for loss of luggage. Otherwise, we could all claim we dressed at St. Laurent and had lost the lot. If the limit doesn't cover what you carry, specify individual items: e.g. watch, jewellery, camera, furs.

**Loss of money** It's debatable whether it's not as sensible to carry cash and insure it as to take travellers cheques. You should be covered for up to £100, including tickets. The moment you discover a loss, report it to the local police. Try to obtain some document saying when you reported and how much.

**Personal liability** This means your liability if you injure someone or some property. It may be covered by your house insurance: find out.

**Personal accident** This type of policy usually provides £1,000 on death or other serious injury. Otherwise £4 − £10 a week for so many years. The sums always lag so far behind inflation they don't count for much. If you're serious about death or injury you should have a thoroughgoing all-time policy anyway − not just one for travel.

**Motor insurance** See page 47.

## Business travel

If you travel abroad on business, try and get your employer to pay your travel insurance. Many companies provide this fringe benefit for employees.

## Medical insurance

### State social-security schemes

The N.H.S. applies only in the U.K. You can't take it with you, or claim money back when you get home.

Reciprocal agreements exist with the E.E.C. countries and some others allowing insured nationals in this country to enjoy emergency medical facilities on the same basis as their own insured nationals. In Denmark and Ireland the treatment will be free. In other countries you may have to pay in part − e.g. for drugs.

However, these arrangements usually do not apply to the self-employed or the unemployed because their insurance is not on the same basis. Only Denmark and German Federal Republic give treatment to all U.K. nationals. The arrangements do apply to students until they have an insurance for part-time work. Speaking as one of the self-employed who have to pay very heavy national insurance, I'm glad Britain is seeking to discuss with the E.E.C. reciprocal cover for this group too. In the meantime a self-employed woman would probably qualify as a dependant of her husband.

The key to getting your treatment in E.E.C. countries is form E111. You get this by filling in form C.M.1. at the local office of the Department of Health and Social Security. They'll post it to you if you phone (you don't need it in Denmark or the Irish Republic). Ask too for leaflet SA 28.

Address: The Netherlands General Sickness Insurance Fund (A.N.O.Z.), Kaap Hoovndreef 24-28, Utrecht.

Prescribed medicines are free if you show form E.111 to the chemist. You may have to pay some percentage for dentistry.

**Austria** In-patient hospital treatment is free if you have a U.K. passport. Other medical services must be paid for.

**Bulgaria** Free treatment if you have a U.K. passport and an N.H.S. medical card. A charge is made for medicines.

**Channel Islands and Isle of Man** On the whole medical treatment is free to visitors from the U.K. There is a small charge for medicines. In Jersey, hospital, ambulance and dental services are free. Sark has no hospital. The Isle of Man is as the U.K.

**Gibraltar** Free medical treatment is available at the General Practice Health Centre if you have a U.K. passport. At St. Bernard's Hospital you will have to pay a part. Charges are made for prescribed medicines.

**Malta** All medical treatment is free though a nominal daily charge is made for hospital in-patients.

**New Zealand** Hospital treatment is free. G.P. is paid a small consultation fee.

**Norway** 80% of the cost of a G.P. or out-patient treatment at a hospital will be refunded. Ask for a receipt *(legereguing)* and take it with your passport to the Local Social Insurance Office *(Trygdekasse)*. Hospital in-patient treatment is free.

**Poland** Treatment is free if you live in the U.K., have a U.K. passport and an N.H.S. card. A doctor's visit will call for a fee. You pay 30% of the cost of prescribed medicines.

**Romania** All treatment is free, but you pay for medicine supplied by a public pharmacy. You need to show your passport and evidence that you live in the U.K. − driving licence or N.H.S. card are ideal.

**Sweden** 75% of the cost of a G.P. or hospital out-patient treatment can be refunded. Get receipted bills, and the correct form where you have the treatment. Take them with your U.K. passport to the Local Administrative Office *(Forsakringkassan)*.

Hospital in-patient treatment and certain medicines are free if you live in the U.K.

**U.S.S.R.** Show your passport. All medical treatment is free − you pay a small charge for medicines.

**Yugoslavia** All medical treatment is free. A small charge is made for medicines. You'll need to show your U.K. passport.

## Private medical insurance

If you are *not* covered by form E.111 or you want further cover, then you must take out adequate private insurance.

Medical expenses can be high. I suggest insurance up to at least £1,000 for each of the family in Europe. The U.S. Embassy suggest $10,000 per person in the U.S.A. Some policies will cover not only doctors and hospital costs but expenses of staying on at hotels, phone calls and extra travel expenses for a relation who stays on beyond the intended date. Make sure you know exactly what you can claim for, and what you're paying for. My husband lost his false teeth at sea, swimming on the incoming tide at La Baule. They were retrieved by a snorkelling son, but fractured in the process. Insurance covered all dental costs for repairs. But nothing made up for two holiday mornings wasted — except possibly our laughter.

## Skiing and other sports

Counting broken legs coming down the ski lifts, insurers would be crazy not to charge more for risky activities. This will mean a special policy. So do mountaineering, gliding etc. Ask the tourist agency and whoever you booked the holiday with. There are insurance companies that specialize in policies for this kind of risk.

All this applies to emergency treatment for travellers. If you are going abroad specifically to have an operation under foreign medical care other conditions apply.

## Europ-Assistance Limited

This is one of several companies that offer more than just simple insurance. They are service companies. This means that — instead of you having to summon help, ambulances, transport, hospitals, etc., in an emergency, then pay up and claim later — they have agents in thirty-eight European countries acting for them who leap to the rescue and do all the fetching and carrying for you. Europ-Assistance (269-273 High Street, Croydon) began in Paris in 1960, and came to the U.K. in 1972. They do contract work for the U.N., B.P. and Gulf Oil. The service costs £2.50 for a person flying, for up to twenty-one days. They have a twenty-four-hour multilingual exchange at 01-680 1234.

# Chapter 27
# Currency

Every country has its own set of exchange-control regulations. You must respect those of the countries you visit as well as British exchange controls. Some countries permit only a small amount of their currency to be exported. Some don't allow any. Infringement is considered a serious matter.

## British exchange-control regulations

### No controls

You can take as much as you like to the Isle of Man, Channel Islands and Ireland. To Gibraltar the only limit is that you can't take more than £25 in sterling banknotes.

### Elsewhere

The limits are set out in a paper called 'Notice to Travellers'. You'll get it at your bank. Read it, because restrictions do change.

Currently, each individual (over eighteen) can take, on each visit: (1) up to £25 sterling banknotes; (2) up to about £2 in coins; (3) up to £300 in travellers cheques, foreign currency, open credit or bank transfer.

This is allowed without formality by your bank. If you want more – for a world cruise – or a three-month stay, you must apply to the Bank of England on form T (from banks, travel agents or tour operators).

Of course, you can pay the cost of fares, accommodation etc. to a tour operator in this country before you go, so your full allocation can be spending money. You can't collect your holiday money and cheques more than one month before you leave. Take your passport along to the bank: the amount has to be entered in it. Copy down the numbers of the travellers cheques; then if you lose them, your bank will honour them on your return.

## Sterling banknotes

You get a poorer rate of exchange for banknotes than for travellers cheques and they're less secure: but they can be brought home again without loss of value. Don't be tempted to sell banknotes to private individuals abroad — the deal is certain to be illegal and you won't necessarily even do well out of it.

## Foreign currency

Before you go abroad you can buy foreign currency over the counter at the larger travel agents and the bureaux de change branches of banks. Other branches will need a few days notice. Everyone charges a commission on the sale of currency: check the exchange rate, the percentage commission and the amount you're given.

## Travellers cheques

Sterling travellers cheques are issued by English and Scottish clearing banks in £2, £5, £10, £20 and £50 amounts. You pay charges on each one: small units are more costly. I take mostly £10 and £20 with one or two big ones, and smaller units come in handy on the last day. You don't need an account with a bank to buy its travellers cheques. Usually you can purchase travellers cheques over the counter.

When you get abroad you can exchange them for currency at banks or bureaux de change, or pay directly in hotels, some restaurants and shops. Check on the rate you will be getting — it often pays to shop around. Hotels can be convenient but costly places to cash cheques (for their loss: see Emergencies p. 265.)

You can buy travellers cheques in many other currencies — U.S. dollars are the most widely acceptable. If you're good at predicting how exchange rates will move while you're away then you can buy the currency that will best protect the value of your money.

## Eurocheque scheme

There are banks in every country in Western Europe, and in Greece and Turkey, Bulgaria, Czechoslovakia, Romania and Yugoslavia, Cyprus and Israel, Morocco and Tunisia, which operate the Eurocheque scheme. They display an 'EC' sign in their windows. If you have a chequebook and a cheque guarantee card that also has the 'EC' symbol then you can cash a cheque for up to £30 in local currency. You mustn't use this to go over your £300 limit.

## Letter of credit

Rather an old-fashioned way of doing things. Your bank issues a letter of credit with coupons on it. You take it to a bank when you are abroad and they will set up an account for you on which you can draw up to the amount stated.

**Open credit** This allows you to cash your cheques with a particular branch of a bank abroad. All High Street banks (except the Co-op) will arrange this. Your bank will write to a specific foreign bank and ask them to honour your cheques up to a certain amount, for a specific period. Suitable if you plan to stay in one spot for some time.

**Circular letter of credit** In this case your bank writes to several banks on your route asking them to cash your own cheques to specific amounts. You must take with you two papers: (1) the circular letter itself and (2) a letter of indication bearing a specimen signature.

This system has the obvious limitation that you have to get to a specific bank at the time when it is open. Travellers cheques are more convenient certainly for short stays and holidays.

## Bank transfer

This can be a godsend if you run out of money while you're away. This is what to do: telephone, telex or send a telegram to your bank manager and tell him: (1) why you want the money; (2) how much you want; (3) whether to send it slowly (by mail) or fast (by telegraph); (4) the address of the bank where you want to collect it; (5) if you're writing to head office, the address of your own local branch.

He will then organize the transfer of money from your bank account accordingly.

## Petrol coupons

Some countries — Italy, Portugal and some in Eastern Europe — issue petrol coupons. Buy them with sterling before you go from the embassy of the country concerned or its National Tourist Office. The petrol costs less this way and you save on currency allowance.

## Post Office overseas money orders

These cannot be used to defray travel expenses or personal debts. They can only be used for cash gifts to foreign residents, for goods imported into the U.K. up to £50 in value, in payment of subscriptions and entrance fees to clubs or societies, other than for travel services, up to £50 per year, in settlement of commercial or professional debts up to £50, for maintenance payments, or to support a dependant.

## Travelling on business

Seek advice at your bank. Naturally you can take £300 per trip, and your bank can authorize up to £75 per day to a maximum of £3,000 per journey. Above that amount you must fill in forms for the Bank of England.

The exchange-control regulations are very complex: get a banking expert to guide you through them.

## Remote places

Find out from your home bank before you go who their correspondents are in the country you're visiting. Take with you the names and addresses of all those banks. Before you go overlanding, make plans with your bank manager about where and how you will be kept supplied with money. It's easier to fuss before setting out than to make arrangements over long distances and erratic postal systems.

## Credit cards

Credit cards are ideal for travel. They are safer than cash. Even if you lose a credit card, so long as you inform the issuing company at once, you are not held liable for purchases made subsequently.

You don't have to pay at once. Usually you are allowed at least a month's interest-free credit. But after that the charges climb steeply – so pay within the limit. Indeed you'll get best value if you use your credit card most in the days just after your account has been issued.

Backed by the appropriate credit card you can cash a personal cheque anywhere in the U.K. Banks also issue their own cheque-guarantee cards for purchasing goods and services up to a certain amount. You can cash one of your own cheques abroad with a cheque guarantee card.

Save your £300 foreign-travel allowance by paying by credit card abroad and have the bill delivered at home. Officially, this is permitted only when hotel and travel expenses arise 'unexpectedly'. Helpful on, say, a three-month world cruise where £300 doesn't go far. Credit cards are acceptable in cruise shops, and they are also handy for shore excursions. Also, if you deposit money with the London office of the shipping line before you go you can draw cash daily on that account.

In a financial emergency in an unsure currency situation, British cash and travellers cheques may be refused where an international credit card will be accepted.

## Plastic money

**Barclaycard** Been going over ten years now. Three and a quarter million people have them: 87,000 places in the U.K. accept them. Interchangeable in America with Americard and in Europe with Ibanco and Carte Bleu cards. Issued free, but rarely offer credit more than £500. *But*: garages selling cut-price petrol won't allow that discount if you pay by Barclaycard. Also now offers a cheque-guarantee card facility if you have a Barclays bank account.

**Access** Five years old with 96,000 outlets in this country. 1.75 million outlets worldwide, mostly in North and Central America, Scandinavia and Mediterranean holiday countries. Issued free — but credit limit may be only £100, rarely up to £500. Interchanges with U.S. Mastercharge and European Eurocard (similarly holders of Mastercharge and Eurocards can buy goods at Access outlets in the U.K.). But you can't draw cash abroad with it: it is not a cheque-guarantee card.

**Company cards** If you are a regular user of hire cars, airlines or hotels, stick with the same one or group throughout and they may think your business is worth a discount. Many car-hire firms issue their own cards, e.g. Avis, Hertz, and so do airlines — Pan Am, B.A. — and hotel groups, e.g. Trust Houses Forte. Some simply bestow credit: others, differing degrees of discount. If your business is big enough, ask round for who offers the best terms. (See also U.A.T.P., page 194.)

**American Express** Has 200,000 to 250,000 card-carrying Britons. There's no limit to the credit allowed: but after sixty days you'll be expected to pay in full. They won't declare how many outlets they have: certainly you can dine at any of 300 restaurants in Brussels, 600 in London. They have 885 subsidiary offices round the world where you get help with booking flights, hotels, etc. Buy hotel rooms, meals, airflights (on over 200 international airlines) and pay when you get back home. In the U.K. you can use your card at any Lloyds Bank for a personal cheque up to £30, or a cheque up to £125 (£20 cash, £105 travellers cheques) at American Express travel offices in the U.K. But American Express is *not* linked to the Eurocheque system. Cost of membership: £7.50 a year.

**Diners Club** 175,000 British carriers — some 350,000 outlets worldwide. But only 12,000 in the U.K. You get forty-five days unlimited free credit: pay £7.50 fee for the privilege.

**Countdown** This is a cash-card system that works the other way. Retailers and outlets pay credit-card companies a percentage on each card-carrying transaction. It's obviously good news to them whenever purchasers pay by cash or cheque. A system called Countdown has, so to speak, cashed in on this. They offer their members in the U.K. (£8.30 + V.A.T. annually) a listing of 12,000 restaurants, shops and night-clubs which will deduct 10% from the bill on showing the Countdown card with payment by cash or travellers cheque. Some 0.75 million U.K. citizens are currently paid up either as individuals or through corporate subscription.

*Visitors to Europe* If you come from America, Australia and South Africa you can purchase Countdown membership that gives you 10% off deals in eighteen European cities (Germany and Austria *not* included). There are also listings for the Channel Islands and for Malta and Gozo — again

covering restaurants, shops and nightlife. U.K. members get these too.
*U.S.A.*: 10% off. Countdown's newest scheme covers ten American
cities. U.K. members must purchase this separately. Some tour
operators or airlines offer this as a bonus incentive for their organized
tour offers. Enquiries to Countdown, 11 West Street, London WC2;
telephone 01-240 2011.

# Chapter 28
# Languages

You have been born with one huge blessing: an English-speaking tongue.
So this means you have grown gradually to command the complexities of
English grammar, and can take in your stride the inconsistencies of
English spelling. Try explaining enough/plough to a Yugoslav, or
light/write/right to a Japanese – and you'll realize your luck. Consider
the plight of foreigners travelling in Britain trying to make sense of
Altrincham, Loughborough, Chipping Campden and – my own favour-
ite – Dunchideock. They also find our signposts bewildering – why
S'hampton, B'ham? And an American friend over here in the 60s really
thought it was cool, man. 'This place really is swinging: you even have
notices in the subway saying it's Way Out.' The American word is Exit.
So, first thing to do is realize your good fortune.

Second, you can learn something of a foreign language before you go.
You can do this at varying degrees of intensity depending on the time
available, money to spend and your own enthusiasm and commitment.
The scale probably runs from the most casual efforts of your own with
phrase-books, then into co-ordinated books and recording aids, joining a
broadcast further-education series, going to evening classes or taking a
crash course at a language school.

## Phrase-books

There are plenty of them. They are usually pocket size, and they have
stopped offering translations (if they ever did) of phrases like 'The
postillion has been struck by lightning.' Instead they concentrate on
such essentials for all travellers, but especially the British, as – 'How
much does it cost?' 'Have you anything cheaper?' 'Is service included?' 'I
cannot afford so much.'

Among the most popular phrase-books are:

*Penguin*: Dutch, French, German, Greek, Italian, Polish, Portuguese, Spanish. From 6op to 75p.

*Collins*: Italian, French, German, Spanish, Russian, Portuguese, Scandinavian languages, Greek, Yugoslav, Dutch, Latin-American Spanish. All at 5op.

*Berlitz*: Arabic, Danish, Dutch, Finnish, French, German, Greek, Hebrew, Italian, Japanese, Norwegian, Polish, Portuguese, Russian, Serbo-Croat, Latin-American Spanish, Spanish, Swahili, Swedish, Turkish. 5op each.

There are serious snags to phrase-books. The major one is that once you have mastered a phrase and have studied the phonetics so that it sounds fluent to a native, the natural thing is for the person to whom you address it to answer you in a torrent of the same language, instantly assuming you understand. And it being his own, he will tend to speak fast, use colloquialisms, and he may even have a regional accent. So the phrases to master are: 'I speak very little ———', 'Do you speak any English/French/German?' 'Speak very slowly please.' It's also useful to learn foreign words for the numbers for bus, train, car and how far, how long and how much.

Other than that you have the whole range of non-verbal communication to fall back on — frowning, nodding, waving of arms. It is possible to simply shove the name of a national landmark under the nose of a passer-by and, by dint of waving and internationalese for subway and bus-stop, get the correct direction.

You mustn't be sheepish and suburban about it: and if the rest of the family snigger, insist they take it in turns. Certain phrases are understandable in any language. They can be summed up as: Oh, la, la! Bellísima cara. No, no. Basta! Stop. Go away. NON! Help POLICE! The non-verbal language is usually pretty explicit then too.

## Pidgin English

Over the colonial years many remote parts of the British Empire adapted the language of their rulers into a shorthand version of their own. By now this language — pidgin English — has developed its own grammar and language system. You would be wrong, as an English-speaking visitor, to assume you can simply string a few leading words of English together and be intelligible. What's more, you can make some whopping errors. According to David Attenborough, whose televised travels have given us, as well as himself, an insight into remote places, you need to beware of carelessly adapting English words. In New Guinea a helicopter is called 'mixmaster belong Jesus'. No harm there. But 'bokis' — derived from our 'box' — means in pidgin the female genitals; 'fightim', 'workim' both mean to copulate. You could be in trouble if your own creative attempt at pidgin got out of hand.

## Lessons on your own

There are on the market co-ordinated sets of books, records and cassettes which are designed to give you some basic knowledge of a language. Snags here are that you have to impose your own discipline, the lessons lack life and flexibility and it takes a long time to get anywhere. However, such systems are good for a family with young children all working together if you start well ahead of your holiday and make it into a game. Also, a housewife on her own all day could simply play and replay the cassette, carrying it round the house with her. Emily Brontë learnt German with the book propped behind her baking board — so why not you? To get the feel of a language, listen to it in a foreign film on television. Try not to read the subtitles. It will need to be a film you're not keen to follow for other reasons.

**Linguaphone** The most well known trade name. Their packages offer a complete twenty-one-record course and cost about £50.

**Berlitz Cassettepaks** 300 phrases on a cassette and a Berlitz phrase book. Cost £3.95. Available in: Danish, Dutch, Finnish, French, German, Greek, Hebrew, Italian, Japanese, Norwegian, Portuguese, Russian, Spanish, and Swedish. They are of limited range, but are ideal for a few weeks study before a journey abroad.

## Public libraries

You can go into any library and ask for the record lessons in the language you want to learn; they may not have them on their own shelves, but they will know where to get them. This works best in big cities. In any London borough, for example, you can go into your library, fill in a form saying which language you want to learn, and they will undertake to get the record set for you. You may have to wait. London libraries draw on the resources of the Holborn Library, 32 Theobalds Road, London WC1; telephone 01-405 2709, which stocks every conceivable language. Their catalogue starts at Afrikaans and goes through to Vietnamese. They have the costly Linguaphone records but these are giving way to the B.B.C.'s records and publications. They recommend one hour a day for twelve weeks for a solid grounding. They also have Berlitz cassettes for quick pre-holiday inklings.

There is often a waiting list for popular languages: French is most often in demand, then German and other E.E.C. languages. Businessmen are boning up on Arabic. But once your turn comes you can keep the set for three months.

## Evening classes

Now you're getting really serious. If you're prepared to commit yourself to one night or even two per week in all weathers then you're keen. Evening classes are the responsibility of your local education authority. Phone or write for their brochure, or ask at the local library. Try to enroll with a friend; then you can keep each other up to scratch, and feel some loyalty to attend. You can also practise on each other. Prices of classes vary even within Inner London. One night a week for the full academic year (thirty-five weeks) can be as little as £5.50 or as much as £10. Extra classes: 50p each. Outside London the average is 70p per lesson. Worth shopping round.

## Broadcast courses

The B.B.C. courses in major European languages are run on a cyclical basis over a five-year period. The pattern is usually of twenty-six lessons — divided into two terms — on both television and radio. There is usually a repeat of each within the week of broadcast. They have run as follows:

'Contacta' (1974/75). Beginners' course in German on both Radio 3 and television. The follow-up second-level course was on Radio 3 only. Each course involves a book and a record or cassette.

'Ensemble' (1975/76). Beginners' course in French on both Radio 3 and television. The follow-up second-level course, 'Sur le Vif', went out on Radio 3 only, in the autumn of 1976.

'Conversazione' (mid 1977). Beginners' course in Italian on both television and Radio 3 ('Bocci d'al Italia'), each week throughout the autumn of 1977. Follow-up course planned for the future.

With each of these courses the B.B.C. provides books, records and cassettes, which remain on sale after the programmes are over. Because its new courses are being used by evening classes, the B.B.C. also supplies tutorial notes and occasionally filmstrips to local education authorities for these classes.

In addition, in the spring of 1977, B.B.C. Radio 3 launched two intensive language courses: 'Get By in German' and 'Get By in Spanish'. They consisted of five half-hour programmes each night for a week and then repeated the following week.

The B.B.C. has also run courses in Russian, Arabic and Chinese. They are all taught phonetically with emphasis on speaking. There's a full supporting kit of publications and records.

For more information read the small print of the *Radio Times* or phone the B.B.C.

## Language schools

Berlitz is certainly the oldest and biggest language-teaching organization. It has 200 schools in sixty-five European cities. In Britain it has
three in London and one each in Croydon, Manchester, Leeds, and
Birmingham. Its courses range from group instruction once or twice a
week through crash courses of about two weeks, to what they call a
total-immersion course.

Total immersion is everything the name suggests. You study from 09.00
to 18.00 continuously and intensively for three to four weeks. Even over
lunch (provided), you are still expected to keep up language practice
with your teacher. There is one teacher to each pupil, sometimes two
teachers. You have homework every night. Teachers are usually nationals speaking their mother tongue. This is the bumper treatment. Ideal if
you're a film star going to film for a foreign company. You'll need that
kind of money. It's a bumper price: four weeks cost £1,750 plus V.A.T.
Berlitz say there's been a boom in all the E.E.C. languages, and now
Arabic and Farsi (the language of Persia) are in growing demand. Fine if
the company pays!

A two-week crash course in French would be less like brainwashing.
Yours for from about £500 plus V.A.T.

There are other language schools in most big cities and they are listed in
the Yellow Pages. Ask for prices and compare. But remember you don't
have to have a licence to set up privately as a language school for pupils
over 16. So there's no guarantee of the standard. If you're considering a
language course, ask what the local education authority has available
first.

# Chapter 29
# Measurements

The International Organization for Standardization is working on a
plan for similar sizing to operate in some thirty-eight countries. Currently they have agreed on a human body pictogram that will be intelligible in any language. Until this is adopted we shall just have to muddle
through. Conversion tables are given accordingly – but with a warning.
They can be misleading. For example, French dresses are labelled

according to bust measurements, but the centimetres figure is *halved* for labelling purposes.

## Men's sizes

| Collars | | Chest | | Waist | | Swimwear | | Hats | |
|---|---|---|---|---|---|---|---|---|---|
| in. | cm. | in. | cm. | in. | cm. | in. | cm. | in. | cm. |
| 14 | 36 | 32 | 81 | 28 | 71 | 26/28 | 66/71 | 5 | 41 |
| 15 | 38 | 33 | 84 | 30 | 76 | 29/31 | 74/79 | 5½ | 45 |
| 15½ | 39/40 | 34 | 86 | 32 | 81 | 32/34 | 81/86 | 6 | 49 |
| 16 | 41 | 36 | 91 | 34 | 86 | 35/37 | 89/94 | 6½ | 53 |
| 16½ | 42 | 38 | 97 | 36 | 91 | 38/40 | 97/102 | 7 | 57 |
| 17 | 43 | 40 | 102 | 38 | 97 | 41/42 | 104/107 | 7½ | 61 |
| 17½ | 44 | 42 | 107 | 40 | 102 | | | 8 | 65 |
| 18 | 46 | 44 | 112 | 42 | 107 | | | 8½ | 69 |
| | | 46 | 117 | 44 | 112 | | | 9 | 73 |
| | | 48 | 122 | 46 | 117 | | | | |
| | | 50 | 127 | 48 | 122 | | | | |
| | | | | 50 | 127 | | | | |

## Women's sizes

| | Bust/Hip | | | Waist | |
|---|---|---|---|---|---|
| | in. | cm. | | in. | cm. |
| 8 | 30/32 | 76/81 | | 23 | 58 |
| 10 | 32/34 | 81/86 | | 24 | 61 |
| 12 | 34/36 | 86/91 | | 26 | 66 |
| 14 | 36/38 | 91/97 | | 28 | 71 |
| 16 | 38/40 | 97/102 | | 30 | 76 |
| 18 | 40/42 | 102/107 | | 32 | 81 |
| 20 | 42/44 | 107/112 | | 34 | 86 |
| 22 | 44/46 | 112/117 | | 36 | 91 |
| 24 | 46/48 | 117/122 | | 38 | 97 |
| | | | | 40 | 102 |
| | | | | 42 | 107 |

## Shoe sizes (men and women)

| British | American | Continental |
|---|---|---|
| 3½ | 5 | 36 |
| 4 | 5½ | 37 |
| 4½ | 6 | 37/38 |
| 5 | 6½ | 38 |
| 5½ | 7 | 39 |
| 6 | 7½ | 39/40 |
| 6½ | 8 | 40 |
| 7 | 8½ | 40/41 |
| 7½ | 9 | 41 |
| 8 | 9½ | 42 |
| 8½ | 10 | 42/43 |
| 9 | 10½ | 43 |
| 9½ | 11 | 44 |
| 10 | 11½ | 44/45 |
| 10½ | 12 | 45 |
| 11 | 12½ | 46 |
| 11½ | 13 | 46/47 |
| 12 | 13½ | 47 |
| 12½ | 14 | 47/48 |
| 13 | 14½ | 48 |

## Distances
Metric conversion: to convert miles to kilometres take the central column as miles and read to the left. To convert kilometres to miles, read the central column as kilometres and read to the right.

## Metric Conversion

| Kilometres | | Miles |
|---|---|---|
| 1.609 | 1 | .062 |
| 8.047 | 5 | 3.107 |
| 16.093 | 10 | 6.214 |
| 48.280 | 30 | 18.641 |
| 64.374 | 40 | 24.855 |
| 80.467 | 50 | 31.069 |
| 96.561 | 60 | 32.282 |
| 112.654 | 70 | 43.496 |
| 128.748 | 80 | 49.710 |
| 144.841 | 90 | 55.923 |

An instant method of roughly converting kilometres to miles (useful for those driving alone) is to halve the number and add the first digit (i.e. 20 kilometres = 12 miles approx.).

## Capacity

| Litres | | Gallons |
|---|---|---|
| 4.546 | 1 | .220 |
| 9.092 | 2 | .440 |
| 13.638 | 3 | .660 |
| 18.184 | 4 | .880 |
| 22.730 | 5 | 1.100 |
| 27.276 | 6 | 1.320 |
| 31.822 | 7 | 1.540 |
| 36.368 | 8 | 1.760 |
| 40.914 | 9 | 1.980 |
| 45.460 | 10 | 2.200 |

## Temperatures

| Centigrade | Fahrenheit |
|---|---|
| −30 | −22 |
| −20 | −4 |
| −10 | +14 |
| −5 | +23 |
| 0 | +32 |
| +5 | +41 |
| +10 | +50 |
| +20 | +68 |
| +30 | +86 |
| +36.9 | +98.4 (normal body temperature) |
| +40 | +104 |
| +50 | +122 |
| +60 | +140 |
| +70 | +158 |
| +80 | +176 |
| +90 | +194 |
| +100 | +212 |

Conversion tables are taken from the *A.A. Continental Handbook*.

# Chapter 30
# Pets

Make plans for them when you plan for yourself. You have three choices
for your animals: leave them at home with friends; leave them in kennels;
take them with you.

## Leaving them at home

**Cats** They're easiest to leave at home. They don't get lonely or anxious.
Ask a friend or neighbour to pop in once, at most twice a day to set out
food, and change the tray. Best to leave a stock of pussy's favourite tinned
food, cat litter, old newspapers, rubber gloves and plastic bags, so your
neighbour is put to the minimum trouble.

**Dogs** They cannot be left in an empty house. They get lonely and
anxious, and may start to shred the furniture and carpets; they also bark
and neighbours may complain to the R.S.P.C.A. about the noise. Asking
a neighbour depends on goodwill. A dog is a responsibility, will need
exercise, food and affection. Only you know your friends.

**Precautions** Make arrangements before you go in case your animal gets
ill, so neighbours don't have to worry — or pay. Make it clear to them to
contact the vet — leave phone number — in case of any ailment. And
arrange to pay all bills on your return. Tell the vet too.

**Reward** A duty-free bottle of Scotch on the return flight might do it. But
remember the cost of feeding your animals is yours. Don't leave friends
out of pocket — they'll never oblige twice.

**Birds, gerbils, tortoises, etc.** Pet shops often take caged birds.
Neighbours with children might take the others. Tortoises won't come to
any harm in the garden — if it's escape proof.

## Boarding out

Book when you book for yourselves. Lists are in the Yellow Pages, or ask
friends to recommend. Get quotes from several.

**Catteries** There is no official licensing. But the Feline Advisory Bureau
has a list of approved catteries. Its address: 6 Woodthorpe Road, London

SW15. Phone them between 10.00 and 12.30, Tuesday, Wednesday and Thursday: 01-789 9553. Catteries are usually in the country, which may mean a journey for you. Most catteries will require your cat to have a certificate of vaccination against feline enteritis and cat flu.

There's a risk in catteries of respiratory infections and flu — not the fault of the cattery. A healthy cat can spread the virus. So if you go to inspect, the distance between cages is critical. My vet recommended six foot plus but you'll rarely find that in city catteries. Separate chalets are best. Look out for adequate air flow ventilation, and make sure it's in the right direction. Ask whether each cat always has the same feeding bowl and how often it is disinfected.

**Kennels** The risk of infection is less among dogs. If you visit look for size of cage, ask about exercise and what they're fed.

Most good kennels require certificates of vaccination against distemper. A dog should also be injected against leptospirosis and hepatitis every year.

## Taking them with you

If you're thinking of taking them abroad, sort out the health and customs regulations well in advance: see p. 194.

**Travelling by car** It is not a good idea to take cats to hotels, but taking them to a rented cottage would be fine. Get a good cat basket. Cats are rarely carsick; if they're due to be fed, give them only a little to eat before they travel. If you think the journey will distress them get a tranquillizer from the vet.

Dogs are more likely to be carsick: the vet will supply tablets to be given half an hour before the journey.

**By trains** Dogs can cost as much as children. I think that should mean they're entitled to a seat unless they're too large, but you'll be frowned on if it's crowded. Steel yourself to leave them in the guard's van. On British Rail, dogs and cats should travel either in containers or, leashed and muzzled, in the guard's van. They may be allowed in the compartment with you if they do not interfere with other passengers. The cost is half the adult fare to a maximum of £4.40 single, £8.80 return. Dogs are not allowed in restaurant cars or sleeping compartments.

**On aircraft** No animal is allowed in the cabin. They must be sent cargo (you can sometimes arrange that it's your plane) in a special crate (the airline hire it to you) and food must be supplied.

**Hotels** Many hotels welcome pets. Always ask — don't just arrive. The book *Pets Welcome* lists over 2,000 holiday chances, plus a countrywide list of catteries and kennels.

T.C.T.—O

**Abroad – outward bound** You can easily take animals out of Britain. The problem is getting them in anywhere else.

Coming from Britain, most European countries will let animals in with the required documentation. That may mean all the vaccinations, including rabies, with certificates possibly in two languages, and the requirements change so you'll need to check. Take a deep breath and act early.

Contact the embassy or consulate of the country concerned. Get a *written* statement of their requirements — *don't* trust information given over the phone, it's liable to be vague and misleading. Most embassies or consulates issue a form saying what you'll need and how long it'll take. Take it to your vet: he'll supply the jabs and the documentation. But certificates have to be prepared a specific time prior to travel and every country seems to have different requirements (some want blood tests), so allow eight weeks.

**Abroad – getting back home** Quarantine regulations are stringent. You should plan well ahead. See page 285.

# Chapter 31
# Gardens and House-plants

Every year more people are travelling away from home. Every year more homes are adorned with house-plants. There must often be a considerable overlap of travellers returning to shrivelled palms and withered pot plants. Unless you've got shares in the local garden centre the following precautions might save time, money and foliage.

## Outdoors

Water lawns and border areas well before you go. Lift off window-boxes and put them in a shady situation. If yours is a town garden with tubs, move them into the shade. Established shrubs will have a hard enough foliage to survive. New growth with soft foliage will suffer first in a drought.

If you fear a dry spell and want an extra safeguard for something newly planted try this trick. Remove the bottom from a wine bottle — champagne's best but it seems excessive to buy bubbly to water the flowers.

Then turn the bottle upside down and ram the neck hard into the soil until it's jammed solid with earth and stands upright. Then fill the bottle to the brim with water. It works on the principle of all self-watering devices: a reservoir of water slowly allowed to filter through to the plant. You could probably use them in window-boxes, too.

## Indoors

Plants are most at risk during a summer absence. If you're away in winter leave the plants well watered on a cool window sill, and the central heating no lower than 13°C (55°F).

In New York you can send your plants to a nursery for care. It hasn't come here yet: but why not suggest it informally to your local nursery or garden centre?

Depending on how fanatical you are about your houseplants any or a selection of the following could help.

**Palm your palm** Big palms cost a lot to buy and drink so much water that no reservoir of water could keep them supplied. So ask a neighbour to mind it. Leave watering instructions but remember if it dies it's still your loss, not their responsibility. If you want expert attention a local flower shop might take it in, to add to their décor.

**Keep cool** Take all houseplants away from sunny window sills and put them in the coolest part of the house that's still reasonably light. Dark corners will kill. Water well first.

**Leave well-watered alone** Most house-plants die of too much water. Many — like monsteras, philodendrons, dracaenas — will last two weeks with no trouble, as long as the plant pot is a good size. Water them thoroughly by standing in a sink of water until they've absorbed all they can — a dribble from a watering-can isn't enough. Never leave plant pots sitting in saucers of water or the sink.

**Tray treatment** Plants that need moisture can be set on a tray that has a layer of moist gravel. Several pot plants together will create their own local humidity, so the moisture doesn't escape from the leaf surface. This is a good system for *ficus benjamena* (weeping fig) and philodendrons but most plants would be satisfactory as long as the moisture level in the gravel does *not* touch the bottom of the pots.

**Plastic bags** Put each plant in a clear polythene bag. Trap as much air inside as possible and make airtight with a rubber band or wire. However, if there's any rot or disease already there, the sealed atmosphere will intensify it. Therefore this is a short-term measure only and is not really safe for more than a week.

**Automatic watering** On the wine-bottle principle you can buy ceramic containers that stick into the soil beside the plant and diffuse water gradually: from cheap plastic about 70p to ceramic frogs from £2 upwards.

**Self-watering containers** You can get a plant container built with a tank in the bottom and a gauge to indicate when the tank needs refilling, usually every three or four weeks. Ideal for busy city life generally, but they cost from £3.70, so they're only worth it for use all year round.

# Chapter 32
# Home Security

Advice from a friendly police officer: In Metropolitan London there's a house burglary every nine or ten minutes day or night. If you're away for a fortnight that's over 2,000 burglaries — one of them could be yours.

### Tell it in whispers

Cancel the milk, cancel the papers but not at the top of your voice so the local tearaways have full details of which house will be empty when.

Tell the local police, giving dates and an address where you can be contacted in an emergency. Tell them too if you're expecting anyone to call, otherwise they might swoop on the daily or a visiting aunt. The local crime prevention officer will call and inspect the house and give advice on security — all free. Putting in extra bolts and window locks is a once-only expense that could buy peace of mind.

Deposit a complete set of house keys with neighbours. Not just for holidays, but for when you lock yourself out. Ask them to go in occasionally to check everything. Perhaps if you're away all summer, they'd cut the grass. Or in the winter, put the light on for a while in the evening. My neighbour was almost too enthusiastic — laid a meal and left the radio on. I got back to flat batteries and what looked like the remains of a party.

Ask neighbours to be nosy and on the lookout for strangers — if men in white coats start loading the grand piano on a van (it happened once at the B.B.C.), tell them to take the registration number and ring 999.

### Getting in

Fit a special cat door for the cat, rather than leave a small window on the latch. Most casual housebreakers are youngsters on the lookout for just such an invitation. They can get through a very small space.

Secure the front door with two locks — a slam lock with dead locking — and a mortice lock to British Standards. The same for the back door. If it's not thick enough fit bolts top and bottom.

Ground-floor windows should have security locks; so should windows over the garage or flat roofs.

Lock away ladders or steps in the garden shed or garage.

If you're very wealthy, fit an alarm system. The simplest, the kind that triggers a bell when the door opens, will cost around £60-70. If you've got a Rubens, you'll need the works — and can probably afford it. Tell a neighbour what it means if the bell rings, and how to respond. We've all passed unconcerned shops with alarms screaming away and wondered whose grabbing the swag on the inside. For maximum protection book a private security firm — look up the Yellow Pages and shop around for a good price.

## If it moves — shift it

Anything small and valuable can go to the bank — jewellery, pearls, an old master. Furs could probably be left at the store where you bought them. Harrods will take in your mink (wherever you bought it) and store it at a yearly rate. The cost will depend on value: a £2,000 coat might cost around £20 a year, but that's the price for a fortnight too.

No hiding place is good enough. It is no use stashing valuables under the floorboards, in the airing cupboard or between the sheets. Burglars search carefully. If you're pushed for time then hiding is better than nothing: but be original. How about diamonds in the lavatory cistern — family heirlooms in the kitchen saucepans.

Letters clogging the letterbox could give you away. If you want your mail forwarded the Post Office will do it for as short a period as a week. Ask for form P944G; everyone whose mail is to be forwarded must sign personally. It will cost £1 for up to a month, £2.50 up to three months, £6 up to twelve months. A separate charge is made for *each* surname entered. Give the Post Office seven clear days notice.

*Absentminders Ltd*: A new company in London will do all the above for you — water plants, feed animals, check security, forward mail etc. Enquiries and quotes from 01-940 2517 and 01-736 0688.

If you've taken all the precautions then your house will require time and effort to enter. Most casual burglars will prefer somewhere else. So leave home with a quiet mind: plenty of other people aren't as careful as you.

# Chapter 33
# Planning for Health

## How fit are you?

To embark on a long journey when you are less than fit is to make things worse. A holiday may give you the chance to recover from overwork or exhaustion. But if you travel knowing you're suffering from an illness that might get worse it could be more of a problem away than at home.

Before you go discuss with your G.P. any extra precautions you might need, if your journey takes you into relatively isolated places. It might be a matter of taking extra drugs, or special advice about adjusting to the climate. Discuss it before you go − in English! Abroad you might not know the Russian word for, say, insulin, diabetic, epileptic, etc. Have your teeth checked before you go. You don't find dentistry as good as ours in every part of the world.

## General advice

**Play safe** When you're travelling keep your life as healthy as you possibly can. There's no point in courting disaster through carelessness. Be meticulous about your personal hygiene, and insist children wash their hands as a matter of routine whenever they have anything to do with food. To pick up and eat a grape that has fallen on the floor at home is one thing − you know when the floor was last cleaned − to do so in a foreign café is quite another matter.

**Water** In many places water can carry germs that cause tummy upsets or worse. Outside of major cities where you know its safe, either ask about the tap-water or drink instead mineral water, or boiled, or filtered or sterilized water.

*Mineral waters*: bottled commercially are safe, often of minor medicinal value (see the awards on the label) and come in a variety of tastes and degrees of sparkle.

*Boiled water*: Water has to be boiled for over ten minutes to be really safe. Then it must be cooled to be drinkable. You won't get that in restaurants, but it is worth arranging if you're travelling with a baby.

*Filtered water*: Filter 'candles' with fine pores will remove matter and most disease organisms found in drinking water. They should be examined frequently for leaks, and cleaned or boiled once a week. The method is not foolproof. Filters with silver sterilize as well. These are available with a hand pump and are suitable for caravanners and campers.

*Sterilized water*: Sterotabs or Puritabs from the chemist will be adequate for small quantities. One Puritab sterilizes 1 litre (1 3/4 pints). Leave it for thirty minutes before drinking. For heavily contaminated water use two tablets.

**Take information about yourself** Carry it with other documents. You should have a record of your blood group left where it can be found by the doctor if you're unconscious. Always take a prescription for your glasses or contact lenses. If you have any drug allergy, or are diabetic or epileptic then consider wearing a medical bracelet saying so.

**Jabs** Vaccination is a worldwide practice for controlling virulent diseases. Some countries will require you to be vaccinated against one or more diseases (usually smallpox, yellow fever and cholera) before letting you in. Remember that if you go to an infected area you may not be allowed back into Britain without a vaccination. Sometimes the granting of a visa will depend on having the correct vaccination certificates.

Other illnesses — such as diphtheria and polio — are also very severe, but vaccination is a matter of personal choice. Recent and quite proper concern over the risks involved with whooping-cough vaccine has had an unfortunate consequence: a decline in vaccinating for other illnesses. Though the vaccine for whooping cough is under suspicion, others are not. It is the practice of vaccination that has made diphtheria a rare disease in Britain. It isn't so everywhere. Travellers *must* keep themselves up to date with jabs, and see their children are equally protected.

## Compulsory vaccination

The World Health Organization is responsible for the control of three major diseases: smallpox, yellow fever and cholera. It designates countries as infected areas and all travellers to or from those areas have to be vaccinated. This scheme has virtually eradicated smallpox and has prevented the spread of yellow fever, but has not been a major factor in the control of cholera.

Immigration authorities can be very strict about the vaccination requirements. The best thing is to find out first what the current requirements are, then get the necessary vaccinations and make sure you have a properly signed certificate. If you have not then you may find that you have to be vaccinated at an airport and then kept in isolation for up to fourteen days.

If you have to have all three vaccinations then they should be in the order yellow fever, cholera, smallpox and you should allow at least a month for completion of the series. The smallpox vaccination becomes effective eight days after it is given.

**Certificates** A jab without a form is no good. And it must be the approved international certificate: no other will do, nor will a letter or personal certificate from your doctor. The cholera certificate is cream, the smallpox certificate is green. They are standard size — irritatingly a fraction larger than a British passport. You get them from your doctor, your travel agent or local health authority.

When you have been vaccinated by your own doctor his signature on the certificate must be authenticated by the local public health authority. This endorsement by rubber stamp is what makes the form valid. Either take or post your certificate to the nearest health authority. Your doctor will know which it is.

**Non-vaccination** If you are considered unfit to vaccinate then your G.P. must issue a medical certificate to that effect. That certificate must be stamped and countersigned by the local health department of the same area.

If you are, for ethical reasons or as a matter of personal convictions, unwilling to be vaccinated, tell your doctor. He might write a letter explaining this and stating your medical condition. But it will merely explain matters: it won't have any authority. Countries can and do insist on vaccination. If you relent at the frontier, you can usually be done on the spot.

## Smallpox

The disease is in its death throes. The latest news is that doctors in East Africa are currently waging the final attack. If they succeed it will be the first disease to have been totally eradicated by man. The World Health Organization see this as a landmark in showing the world what coordinated effort and resources can achieve.

The smallpox campaign began in 1966. It's an illness spread only by an affected person, who is contagious for only a four-week period. By 1975 only 3,949 cases were reported. In 1976 it was down to 942 known cases — most of them in Ethiopia and neighbouring Somalia. So at the moment international health officials and local surveillance agents are infiltrating tribal groups and wandering nomads there, to track down the very last cases.

Until the disease is officially declared eradicated, travellers to and from infected countries must have smallpox vaccination.

A smallpox vaccination becomes operative eight days after a successful first vaccination. From then on an adult will need to keep it topped up every three years. If you forget, and are leaving on the morrow you can rush round to the doctor: revaccination takes effect at once. The certificate is valid for three years.

*Children*: Nowadays smallpox is no longer given as part of routine childhood vaccinations in Britain. So if you are travelling with children to where a smallpox certificate is required, enquire of their embassy or national tourist office at what age a child must have a certificate. Some countries expect a child under three months to have a smallpox jab, some don't insist on it not until six months, some until a year. Ask.

*Don't vaccinate*: where there is infant or adult eczema, a failure in children to thrive, skin allergy, leukaemia, or if you are receiving corticosteroid medicine or immuno-suppressive treatment.

*Pregnancy*: It has been suggested there is an increased risk of abortion immediately after vaccination if it's done in the first three months. You'd do best to avoid vaccination altogether during pregnancy – if you can. However, if you *must* go to a high-risk area, then advise your doctor who may give a simultaneous shot of antivaccinial gamma globulin.

*Smallpox symptoms*: Headache, backache, prostration. Later a rash, which is very similar to chicken-pox, develops, especially on the face. There is a fever. The illness has an incubation period of ten to fourteen days, and is infectious from two days before the rash appears until the last scab has fallen off. The disease usually leaves permanent scars.

## Yellow fever

Immunization is compulsory for Central Africa and the disease is endemic in Panama and in tropical South America. The immunity and the certificate last ten years: vaccination is an absolute guarantee against catching the illness. People travelling by plane who disembark in the transit areas of airports in the countries affected do not usually need to worry: transit areas are not considered endemic areas, except when travelling through India and Pakistan.

The timing of yellow fever vaccination is slightly awkward. Ideally, it should *not* be given at the same time as other live vaccines such as smallpox and polio. They should be given three weeks apart. If primary smallpox vaccination has already been given, then you must wait twenty-one days before having yellow fever. If it was only revaccination for smallpox, wait at least seven days. Also there should be a gap of at least fourteen days between vaccination with a third live virus vaccine. Yellow-fever vaccination is valid after ten days.

Avoid yellow-fever vaccination in pregnancy unless the risk is high. Most countries don't insist on it for a baby under twelve months.

# Global Spread of Cholera 1961-1976

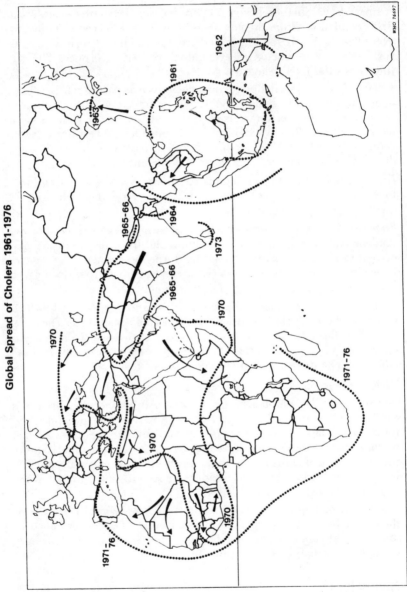

You cannot get this vaccination from your G.P. You must go to one of sixty centres round the country. Any local health authority will direct you. Phone first to make an appointment. Hours are usually between 10.00 and 17.00. There is usually a small charge.

*Symptoms*: Violent fever and severe jaundice which may cause complete liver failure.

## Cholera

Cholera vaccination certificates are less in demand than they were. In 1970 the U.S.A. ceased to demand them of travellers coming from cholera infected areas. They were the first country in the world to take this attitude. Apparently there is little evidence that cholera vaccine does any good in preventing the spread of cholera. The World Health Organization has expressed little confidence in it. However, it offers the individual partial protection, which starts six days after the injection, but only lasts for six months. A revaccination within that six months makes the protection continuous. Certificates — valid for six months — are required by certain countries.

Vaccination is advisable if you're going to tropical and subtropical countries in Asia and Africa and parts of the Mediterranean coast (see the Gazetteer at the end of this book). In 1973 there was a cholera epidemic in parts of Italy, in the summer months. But vaccination is not normally necessary for countries in southern Europe. Visitors to the Middle East at the time of the Pilgrimage will need two injections. Otherwise one injection is considered enough.

*Pregnancy*: Vaccination against cholera is perfectly acceptable in pregnancy. Countries don't usually expect children under one year to be injected.

*Symptoms*: Cholera organisms come only from the human intestine and are spread by faecally contaminated water — not by direct contact or inhalation. Raw shellfish will pick it up, and pass it on — so they could be dangerous. A sudden onset of profuse watery diarrhoea in a known epidemic area calls for urgent attention.

The disease will only be brought under control by strict observance of high standards of sanitation and personal hygiene in affected countries. In countries that have developed such personal habits and policies of public health, cholera does not spread.

## Optional jabs

### Typhoid fever, paratyphoid fevers and tetanus (T.A.B.T.)

It's a good idea to have these injections if you're travelling anywhere beyond Northern Europe. If you're going on holiday to a newly

developed resort area around the Mediterranean it would be a particularly good idea. It is absolutely essential if you are going camping or
caravanning in that area. There are risks in sudden tourist boom areas
that the strain on the public health services could lead to a sudden
outbreak.

T.A.B.T. involves three injections: the second four to six weeks after the
first, and the third six to twelve months after the second. That means
seven months to have the course. If time is too short, have one or two
injections rather than none at all. In cases of urgency the gap can be
narrowed to ten days. T.A.B.T. gives some protection against typhoid
fever for one to three years. If you get a wound from a dirty object, ask the
doctor about a tetanus booster. This gives five years' protection.

*Pregnancy*: T.A.B.T. jabs in pregnancy are quite acceptable.

*Symptoms*: Usually typhoid and paratyphoid fevers are caught from contaminated water, or from foods such as watercress and other salads, ice
cream, fruit not properly washed, milk and oysters. Flies spread it, so can
things handled by someone carrying the illness but not showing
symptoms. It takes seven to twenty-one days to develop, so you could be
back from your holidays before any sign occurs. You'll get a headache,
constipation, maybe a nosebleed. The temperature will rise gradually
over several days. Diarrhoea and abdominal pain will develop with
possibly a rash. Get medical attention immediately.

## Poliomyelitis

Don't assume the disease is over. We have it under control in Britain
because people are vaccinated. If you've been vaccinated in the past you
may need a reinforcing dose. Nowadays they give it to you on a lump of
sugar.

Vaccination is advisable for everywhere except northern Europe, North
America, Australia and New Zealand. Visitors to Spain, Turkey and
North Africa should have it, adults as well as children. Epidemics can
occur in late summer and autumn. Protection lasts five years. Children
may need a booster.

*Symptoms*: Poliomyelitis can take one to three weeks to develop. The
symptoms are fever, headache, vomiting, sore throat, stiff neck, pain in
the neck and back, sometimes diarrhoea. Usually this is all that happens.
In paralytic cases pain develops in the muscles after twelve hours and
within seventy-two hours there's paralysis. Recovery from paralysis is
common, otherwise other muscles take over — so improvement continues.

## Diphtheria

Again we should not feel smug since we don't hear of the disease much in
Britain nowadays. Vaccination is the reason why.

*Symptoms*: Pains in limbs, loss of appetite. Breath tastes foul. Sore throat, swollen neck glands. Dangerous.

## Infectious hepatitis

Highly endemic areas are Egypt and West Africa, the Indian sub-continent and farther East. It's an illness that has dogged those who take the hippy trail to Katmandu.

Travellers could consider having an injection of gamma globulin. Passive immunity lasts about five months and is not 100% effective. If you're staying longer you would need to repeat the injections for protection.

*Symptoms*: It comes on gradually with fever, a distaste for food, diarrhoea and vomiting for several days. Then the jaundice develops and the other symptoms fade.

The treatment is rest in bed and a diet that includes barley water with added glucose. Later — no alcohol for six months! (Pass the gamma globulin now!) It's slightly catching so take special care with hand-washing after the toilet.

## Time needed for vaccinations

A full course of all the various vaccinations — surely for a world tour of amazing variety — will take some three months (seven if you take a third T.A.B.T. jab). You could have a crash course of smallpox, T.A.B.T., yellow fever and cholera vaccinations in fifteen days.

## Malaria prophylaxis

Malaria kills 2.5 million people a year and debilitates some 250 million a year. One thousand cases were imported into the U.K. in 1976. It's not a danger in Europe, the Near East and North America, but in some areas malaria is actually on the increase. The death rate is higher in visiting Europeans than in the native population. It can be prevented. The daily-dosage anti-malarial drugs are best. You should start taking them the day you leave, and continue during and for twenty-eight days after visiting malarial areas. You can safely take the tablets during pregnancy, so be sure you do or you may transmit the disease to the foetus. Some are preferable to others. Consult your doctor.

**Symptoms** Malaria develops ten to fourteen days after being bitten by the mosquito that carries the malaria parasite. It brings a high fever, shivering and sweating by turns, intense headaches and nausea and vomiting. It is dangerous to the visitor who lacks the immunity of the native through years of living near the swampy land where the mosquitoes breed.

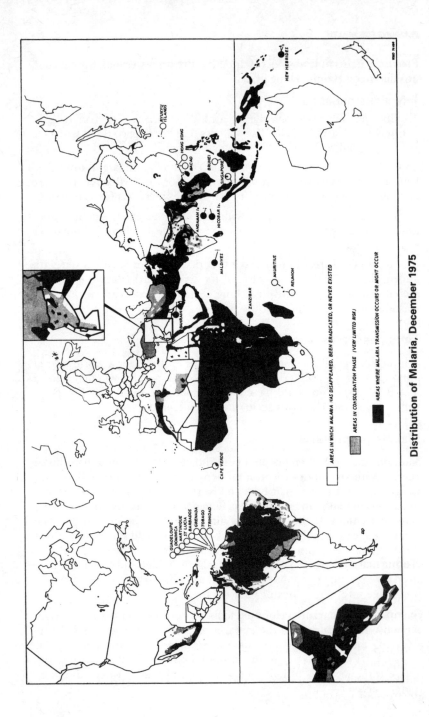

**Distribution of Malaria, December 1975**

☐ AREAS IN WHICH MALARIA HAS DISAPPEARED, BEEN ERADICATED, OR NEVER EXISTED

▨ AREAS IN CONSOLIDATION PHASE (VERY LIMITED RISK)

■ AREAS WHERE MALARIA TRANSMISSION OCCURS OR MIGHT OCCUR

RYUKYU ISLANDS
HONG KONG
MACAO
BRUNEI
SINGAPORE
ANDAMAN Is.
NICOBAR Is.
MALDIVES
MAURITIUS
REUNION
ZANZIBAR
BAHRAIN
CAPE VERDE
NEW HEBRIDES

GUADELOUPE
DOMINICA
MARTINIQUE
ST LUCIA
BARBADOS
GRENADA
TOBAGO
TRINIDAD

WHO 76-699

**Prevention during stay** Keep taking the tablets throughout, but also do your best to avoid being bitten by the mosquitoes. They bite after dark so preventive measures should include all of the following:

Dress to cover as much of your skin as possible throughout the evening and night. For men this means long trousers, long-sleeved shirts, socks. For women, too, trousers or long skirts, long-armed blouses or dresses, high necklines.

Use an insect repellent on exposed skin. There are several: whatever their trade name they will contain either diethyl tolumide, or dimethylpthalate or indalone. Look for these in the ingredients on the tube. The repellent properties of the cream last up to four hours, less if you sweat. Watch you don't get it on eyes and lips.

Sleep either in an air-conditioned room with windows and doors shut, or in a room that has mosquito-proof netting across all open windows, or under a mosquito net draped over the bed. Make sure the net has no holes in it!

As well as all these other precautions, use an insecticidal aerosol spray around the room.

The Ross Institute of Tropical Hygiene publish a comprehensive booklet called *Preservation of personal health in warm climates*, available from the London School of Hygiene and Tropical Medicine, Keppel Street (Gower Street), London WC1E 7HT, for 80p.

## Diabetics

There's no reason you shouldn't travel if you're diabetic. But you must plan. For example, if you fly across time zones, travelling west, and the day is prolonged more than four hours, you'll be offered an extra meal, and you'll need to be covered by extra insulin. Airlines and shipping companies are helpful. So is the British Diabetic Association, 3–6 Alfred Place, London WC1, which publishes a brochure called *Holidays and Travel for Diabetics*.

## Pregnancy

You will naturally be under your doctor's care and should consult him about any proposed journeys. He will also advise which jabs it is safe for you to have. Apart from the discomfort there is no reason why, if you are perfectly fit, you should not travel.

**Booking** After twenty-eight weeks most airlines will want a medical certificate saying you are fit to fly. You won't be accepted for flights after thirty-six weeks. If you disguise your condition you could no doubt get aboard, but it wouldn't be wise. Babies *have* been born on aircraft –

which usually have plenty of hot water and towels. Beyond that, their medical supplies are not geared to childbirth.

**Cruises** Although most boats have doctors on board, many lines − P. & O. for example − will not take you on a cruise that ends later than the seventh month of pregnancy. Post-booking pregnancies may cause cancellation; notify them as soon as you know to discuss what the cancellation will cost you.

**Inclusive tours** On the whole tour operators leave the decision to you. A holiday in mid-pregnancy is after all an ideal time to take a rest. But no one would be wise to go away in the last two months of pregnancy.

## Contraceptives

Take supplies with you. Several months' supply won't take much space. But if you lose your contraceptives, or have any problems about methods that need equipment and attention − the cap or an I.U.D. − you can contact a local doctor or hospital or the nearest family planning agency. There are 135 of the latter round the world, in remote as well as developed places. For example there are ten among the different island communities of the Pacific. They exist too in some of the strongly Roman Catholic countries, such as Ireland, Italy, Mexico and Brazil. Spain and Malta don't have them, but in Spain the pill is widely used among the middle classes. However, as a visitor with a British prescription you may have difficulties.

The local British embassy or consulate should be able to supply the address of a clinic. The International Planned Parenthood Federation issues a complete list with addresses, free. Their central office is at 18 − 20 Lower Regent Street, London SW1Y 4PW; telephone 01-839 2911.

## Tampax

Tampons are widely distributed throughout the world, wherever pharmacies stock Western products. But they can be expensive. If you're only going for around one month take supplies with you.

However, if you're travelling to remote places, staying several months or more, or overland trekking, it's worth knowing more. Tampax have for their own use a complete guide to world distribution and stockists. It includes information for travellers graded as: (a) take emergency supplies; (b) arrange provisional mail-order supplies; (c) arrange definite mail-order supplies.

Tampax assure me that they err on the side of caution and may be advising arranging mail order to places where, unknown to them, there is already a local stockist.

Mail order can be arranged through: Boots Co. Ltd., Overseas Despatch Department, Nottingham NG2 3AA; telephone Nottingham 56111 (S.T.D. code 0602).

# Chapter 34
# Looking Good

Traditionally concern about one's 'looks' is considered a feminine priority. Certainly in matters of cosmetics and make-up it obviously is. But travel affects the condition of everyone's body, skin, hair and general tone.

So the advice given here is not exclusively cosmetic, although it is included for the benefit of women travellers.

## Hair

Basically the hair is a barometer of your body's health. So after long and tiring journeys, long hair will flop around — just like you! There may be a slightly greater hair loss and hair will be difficult for a day or two until it gets back in form. Different climatic conditions will affect the hair.

**Dry hot climate** Hair improves in the sunshine if it's not too strong and not for too long. The Italians have always been credited with the best hair: twenty-four-inch Italian was the prime choice of wigmakers. But a hot dry climate can cause dehydration. It happens to your skin: and the scalp is skin too. For a prolonged stay, desert crossings etc., try to nourish the scalp regularly. Just a little oil on the fingertips every day is good — but don't saturate it. If your hair's greasy, apply the moisturizing lotion the night before you plan to wash your hair. Use a lotion specially prescribed for you by a qualified trichologist, a member of the Institute of Trichologists, whose General Secretary (228 Stockwell Road, London SW9) will send you a list of members and their addresses (send an s.a.e.). Otherwise use Boots E45 cream, or ask a chemist for a jar of oily cream B.P. — or second best where shops are rare, use coconut oil.

**Shampooing** Avoid shampoos labelled 'for greasy hair', they will further the dehydration. Use a bland, mild shampoo, not a medicated kind. Lanolin as an ingredient helps refat the hair and scalp. If the hair is very dry, don't shampoo too often.

**Humid hot climate** Hair likes humidity so it will flourish in a humid climate. Again too much direct sun can cause it to dry.

**Warning** Don't tint or bleach hair just before you go to the sun, or too soon after you come back. It will go brittle and break.

**Great humidity and greasy hair** These are a bad combination. Hair will go lank and unattractive. A tar shampoo might liven it up.

**Sea-water** Always rinse it from your hair before sitting in the sun; the salt is very damaging. Hotel pools provide fresh-water showers for the purpose.

**Chlorinated water** Chlorine is a strong bleaching agent. It might make a blonde blonder, but it can also make hair very brittle. Again always rinse under the shower. If you're doing a great deal of swimming, a swimming cap gives some protection. But don't drag the hair as you put it on.

**Hard and soft water** If you're washing your hair in a strange hotel, test the hardness/softness of the water first. For really scummy hard water, you could use Calgon water softener. But it's only sold in big tins and you can't easily take it with you. Most bath oils or crystals will be adequate. Avoid all soaps made for salt water.

**Central heating** What it does to furniture, it can do to you. People put out bowls of water to keep their piano from falling apart. Remember to keep your hair and scalp moisturized too.

**Diet** Sudden extreme changes of diet may affect your body. If your hair starts going wrong, dropping out etc., check the way your eating habits have changed.

**Men: baldness** The Nordic races have fine fair hair and they tend to lose it. Type and distribution of scalp hair is thought to be partly a racial characteristic. Interestingly, however, Jamaicans have a higher incidence of baldness in Britain than in Jamaica! But baldness can be a danger in strong sunshine, especially for fair skins: beware of burning the exposed scalp. Young men with a thin covering, but who still pretend they've plenty of hair, are most at risk.

**Beards** Hair grows faster in the sun. Men with a heavy beard growth may need to shave more often.

**Blacks** The habit of having the hair straightened makes it go very dry and porous. The scalp and hair will need moisturizing.

## Legs

You should keep them looking good all the time: few people do. With a journey in view the two problems for women to solve are hair and colour.

**Hair** Shave it off. Wet shaving with single-edged blades and plenty of lather is best. Dry shaving with an electric razor takes time to get used to and you're dependent on an electric point. Don't try anything new when embarked on a journey. Get used to it beforehand.

Wax it off. You can buy and apply strips of wax, wait for it to set, grit your teeth and rip it off. Simpler but more costly to get a beauty salon to do it for you: about £6 both legs, £3.50 up to the knee. If you're going on holiday and favour very brief bikinis, they'll do the 'bikini line' too (£1.50) — Ouch!

**Colour** White legs look awful with summer dresses. Either use a sun-lamp which takes time, or apply a fake tan until the sun takes over. Before a holiday you could treat yourself to a solarium visit. They'll give you an all-over tan in thirty minutes: £3.40. It's better if you have two or three sessions. You'll feel in trim from the moment you arrive. Similarly, a good pedicure gets you off to a groomed start: prices around £2.75.

## Skin

It's all a matter of the moisture in the skin which will evaporate at different rates in different conditions. Aim to keep the moisture balance correct. Replace moisture when the skin has been subjected to excessive drying, and allow the skin to lose moisture in excessive humidity. The following conditions dry the skin.

**Flying** The body is generally dehydrated. Before you fly put on a double application of moisturizer, then very little foundation. Use eye cream instead of powder shadow. Just before you land soak a piece of cotton wool in water, and use it to apply skin tonic all over your face. Then make up again. Once at your destination cleanse your face completely and take fifteen minutes rest.

**Wind** The keener, the more drying.

**Water** Especially hard, sea or chlorinated water — always rinse off as soon as possible. Add bath oil to hard tap-water.

**Central heating** Worst if coming from extreme cold. That tingling of the cheeks can cause broken veins.

**Soap** Hotel soaps aren't renowned for their cosmetic properties. If you've a sensitive skin, don't use soap and water at all, or use a specially mild one of your own choice.

**Sun** Tanning can burn and lead to flaking and increased lines. Women in the tropics have conspicuous crow's-feet for that reason.

**Snow** is highly reflective. Skin and lips need thorough protection on the ski slopes.

**Humidity** While dryness does the greater damage, humidity can also affect the skin. In an atmosphere already very laden with moisture, the moisture of the skin will evaporate more slowly. The skin needs to rid itself of some moisture to dispel impurities. So there may be a tendency for pores to enlarge and for the texture of the skin to coarsen. Help the skin by regular use of a cleanser and a skin tonic. Together they will keep the skin clean and toned up. Use very little moisturizer: never a rich one.

**Moisturizers** The cosmetic industry produces hundreds of makes, all claiming rival degrees of skin penetration. In fact any one of them will offer some moisture replacement. Choose a light-textured one for a hot climate, a richer more emollient one for the cold.

**Cleansers** A cleansing milk for hot weather, creams for cold.

## Sun-tanning

Sun-tanning promotes the body's production of vitamin D. It helps clear up spotty skins. But its greatest benefit is undoubtedly psychological. Once it was fashionable to be pale skinned and women used veils, large hats and parasols to protect themselves. Today, white-skinned women use oils and creams to promote sun-tan. The important thing is to avoid sunburn.

**Protect your skin** In an emergency a couple of drops of olive oil are better than nothing. But basically you need a *sun-screen*. Sun-screens protect the skin from harmful rays while the body's own natural protection is developing. This natural protection is the changing of the skin pigment — what we know as a tan. Leading sun-screens are Ambre Solaire, Ski-Delial, Bergasol, and Eversun. But even with a sun-screen you must still tan slowly. Beauty experts advise starting with half an hour at a time, preferably before 11.00 or after 15.00. Then increase it by half an hour a day. At that rate it'll take six days before you can lie three hours in the sun and that could be half your holiday! I think such advice is accurate but optimistic. Still you have been warned.

Tricks to cut short the whiter-than-white agony: (1) *Start early*: get what tan you can before your holiday. With recent British summers that's not hard. (2) *Fake tans*: they contain chemicals that react on the body to produce a brown colour after a few hours. They last several days before fading — but they don't give protection against sunburn. You'll need a sun-screen and to limit your sunbathing time. (3) *Sun-lamps*: they might get your skin acclimatized but they're awkward to use and you can burn easily. (4) *Beauty treatment*: for three sessions of one hour a day in a single week a beauty salon will charge around £5. You can emerge with gorgeously tanned legs.

## Warnings

*Snow*: is highly reflective. Lips are particularly vulnerable. Happily a glossy pearl lipstick gives good protection. Otherwise use Chap Stick, Uvistat L or Eversun lip protection stick.

*Topless*: The breast is a gland of the body, and very delicate. Medical people are concerned at what may happen if women going topless reveal white sensitive skin to strong sunlight. Be very careful!

*Bald heads*: burn very easily — even through thinning hair. So sun-hats are essential!

**The non-tanners** Some people are just too sensitive to tan at all. Their pigmentation just isn't strong enough. This is particularly true of red-heads with pale white skins. They shouldn't try, but there's no reason why they shouldn't go into the sun. They need a sun-block cream: one that completely checks the sun's rays. such as Uvistat, Spectraban or Eversun.

**Tablets** Sylvasun is the name of a pill containing vitamin A and calcium carbonate. Its makers claim it 'speeds up the skin's own natural resistance to sunburn'. They recommend two tablets a day for the first two weeks in the sun, combined with the use of creams and lotions. Tests in 1970 on B.A. staff indicated some effectiveness. Tests by the Consumers' Association indicated none. Case not proven.

**Sunburn and sunstroke** Calamine is cool and soothing. Apply it and stay in the shade. If the burn is blistered see a doctor.

If you get a temperature, headache, nausea and vomiting, it could be too much sun. Take aspirin or paracetamol to lower the temperature. Go to bed in a shady room, use a fan or spongeing to keep cool. Consult a doctor.

## Feet

Don't expect to wander barefoot on sand and shingle and retain soft-skinned feet. The hardening of skin when you go barefoot is functional. Don't worry about it or attempt to remove it. Time enough for that when you resume shoes. Pretty Feet will then remove the hardened skin.

## Nails

Nice to have them in good trim before you set out. If you feel extravagant and indulgent have a paraffin-wax treatment on hands and feet. Otherwise, use a vitamin E cream. Dark varnishes stain the nails yellow and don't look good in the sunshine. So two or three days before you go on holiday remove the varnish and use lemon juice to remove the stain.

**Avoid chips and splits** Frantic packing and humping luggage will bang and chip your nails. Unless the weather's boiling, wear gloves. Take with you a packet of Mendanail — patches for repairing the damage.

For persistent flaking apply colourless iodine on fresh cotton wool every day and night. Start the treatment two weeks before you set out.

**Sun and sea** Sea-water does nails and hands good. But you'll need hand cream to replace the moisture. Hands won't burn, but if they get too brown they can look leathery and ageing.

**Ice and snow** A layer of polish reduces the risk of breakage: use a non-frosty one, it will have fewer chemicals. Keep hands and feet well nourished with cream overnight: wear light cotton gloves or socks if they're getting very chapped and dry.

**Central heating** Going from extreme cold to overheated hotels is bad for the body generally. Nails suffer too. Use hand exercises — invent your own, or play an imaginary piano — to get the circulation to your fingertips.

## Sunglasses

Wherever there is glare, as from extensive snow, a white beach or a clear sunlit sea, then sunglasses can reduce the strain on the eyes. The better kind will also cut off harmful radiations.

**Coloured plastic lenses** Often cheap, but sometimes not even made with a proper lens. These simply act as a filter reducing the intensity of the light. They do not cut out harmful radiations and so will not be as relaxing as others. Keep them in a case or cover as creams and oils can make them go opaque. Also they scratch easily.

**Polaroid glasses** The label will give the Polaroid trademark. These allow light to pass through in one direction only. They can also cut off ultra-violet and infra-red radiation: so they are more protective to the eye. Glasses with lenses that shade from dark to pale are not able to cut off glare that comes from below — e.g. a beach or snow, they thus offer less protection.

**Crookes lenses** There are a whole range, many for industrial welding and such. But the $A_2$ lens would be used as a sunglass lens. It cuts down the ultra-violet and infra-red radiation, thereby reducing strain and danger to the eye.

**Zeiss umbral lenses** The best protection you can get — in two intensities: 65% umbral and 85% umbral. These effectively cut off harmful radiation. Cost from £15 to £30.

## Shaping up

Of course you intended to diet weeks ago, so that by now yours would be the slim outline of the girls on the holiday posters. Too late for a major campaign, not too late for a last-minute tapering down. I asked *Successful Slimming* to create a diet that would provide plenty of energy for that final pre-holiday scramble. I also complained of the monotony of most diets. This is what they came up with: a three- or five-day diet full of energy and originality.

## One-food-a-day-diet

### Day One — Eggs

Breakfast  Two boiled eggs, one slice of lightly buttered toast, tea or coffee without milk or sweetening.

Midday  Two-egg omelette or two eggs scrambled in a little milk.

Evening  Large green salad with two sliced hard-boiled eggs, with one dessertspoonful of low-calorie dressing; or devilled eggs (mix the yolk of two hard-boiled eggs with a little curry powder and refill whites with the mixture).

### Day 2 — Vegetables

Breakfast  Two grilled tomatoes, 85 g (3 oz) grilled mushrooms on one small slice of toast, tea or coffee without milk or sweetening.

Midday  Leeks vinaigrette or chicory, cauliflower and tomato salad, followed by vegetable stew — a selection of vegetables simmered in a little stock.

Evening  Large salad dressed with lemon juice.

### Day 3 — Fish

Breakfast  Small grilled kipper, small slice of lightly buttered toast, tea or coffee without milk or sweetening.

Midday  Baked white fish, small green salad.

Evening  115 g (4 oz) tinned salmon, tuna or crab (drained) with small helping of salad.

The diet can be extended to five days.

### Day 4 — Fruit

Breakfast  One orange and/or grapefruit, small slice of lightly buttered toast, tea or coffee without milk or sweetening.

Midday  Grilled half of grapefruit, large fruit salad (fresh fruit only) with 55 g (2 oz) hard cheese and 55 g (2 oz) cottage cheese.

Evening  Good helping of stewed or baked fruit and 115 g (4 oz) of cheese.

## Day 5 – Meat

Breakfast    Two slices of grilled lean bacon or ham, small slice of lightly buttered toast, tea or coffee without milk or sweetening.

Midday    115 g (4 oz) of braised steak, or grilled liver, small helping of green vegetables.

Evening    Six slices of cold roast chicken or boiled tongue.

The diet must be followed only for the time stated. As much water as you like can be drunk throughout – but nothing else.

# Chapter 35
# Packing

## Suit your case

People's needs differ: that's why the choice of cases is so large. The criteria differ for different methods of travel – and range from looking good to carrying light. And what's fine for a plane won't fit in the car boot. So shape and flexibility count too.

But the first consideration is weight. 'Leather looks good and lasts' was my mother's advice. Alas I took it. My fifteen-year-old cases have weathered well, sustained any amount of mistreatment and still won't wear out. But even empty they weigh as much as a full canvas holdall. Once packed and locked nothing could tear or damage them: they hold their shape. But leather is certainly too heavy for easy air travel.

*Moulded cases* are lighter and rigid, and last longer than any others. They're strong, won't break or yield under pressure and are solid reliable travellers.

*Soft-sided cases* – fabric or plastic – are getting more popular: they are very light, can look very snazzy, more flexible to pack, but need the support of straps, and are less resistant to getting banged about. So don't pack bottles of sun oil on the surface.

*Fibreboard cases* are adequate but won't last if you're a busy traveller. They don't age well, getting scuffed and tatty. But they're cheaper than many others.

*The Wardrobe bags* are supposed to save your clothes creasing. Frankly, I don't see how they can totally; why not take an iron? But I've never used one and they obviously have their devotees. But on baggage carousels they often look squashed and vulnerable. Also hanging bags are awkward to handle; only reasonable for car travel door to door, when you can hang them on the car hook.

*The carry-on bag or holdall* is today's most popular case because you can dispense with flight luggage loading and take it with you. Some are designed specifically to fit under aeroplane seats – for which they must be no bigger than 450 × 350 × 150 mm (18 × 14 × 6 inches). Most have side pockets for underwear, socks, toiletries. Ideal overnighters or weekenders. But watch a holdall with two straps – see they're firmly anchored and kept in good repair: luggage loaders often heave them singly and they tend to tear.

*Cases with castors.* Human porters being scarce you should go prepared to carry your own cases at airports. Here the sexes aren't equal, so cases with their own wheels are popular with women. Then you can scud across the airport to the taxi queue ahead of the men. But watch varicose veins and tights when humping them upstairs. Alternatively you can buy separate wheeled 'porters' to strap to any case, which cost around £8. Some of them fold up and away when you've reached the check-in or the taxi.

## Inside or outside extras

*Strong leather strap.* No harm for extra security.

*Locks.* Always lock your case. It may make it harder to burgle, though many suitcase locks seem a token interchangeable gesture. Still, insurers will be kinder to you if you did lock it – or if you say you did. Carry two sets of keys: one on your standard key-ring, another somewhere safe and secret.

*Labels.* I used to think the gaudier the better, both stick-on and tie-on; then thieves at Gatwick began stealing labels as a clue to empty houses. So use stick-on labels only and attach permanently to the *inside* of the lid of your case a clear statement of your name, home address and phone number.

*Fold-away carrier.* Clothes swell when you travel and if you pack every inch of your case on the way out, you'll have leftovers coming back. Take a flat folding canvas or straw bag, one that can do double duty for swim things and shopping while you're away, and pack it, flat, at the bottom of your suitcase.

## Air travel

*Don't* pack aerosols and fountain pens full of ink – they can leak at high-altitude pressure; carry them in your hand luggage.

*Don't* pack camera film — it may be damaged by security-check X-ray machines.

*Don't* pack or carry lighter fuel — it is not allowed on the plane.

## Baggage allowance

*On international flights*: 20 kg (44 pounds) tourist and economy class; 30 kg (66 pounds) first class.

You can buy special luggage scales. They come in handy for their domestic uses — weighing a crop of apples, or the Christmas turkey. Otherwise use the bathroom scales: think of the tourist limit as around 3 stone.

*On package holidays* Weight allowance varies, dependent on routes, airport of departure etc. It is usually 20 kg (44 lb) but is sometimes 15 kg (33 lb). They should tell you when you book.

*On European and domestic flights* British Airways policy is to phase out weight limits and adopt the 'piece system'. A traveller is allowed only two pieces of luggage free. The sum of the three dimensions of one of them must not exceed 1.7 m (67 inches) and the sum of the dimensions of the other must be less than 1 m (39 inches).

There is no free baggage allowance for infants (10% fare).

In addition to the free allowance, you are also entitled to take free of charge: a handbag, an overcoat, an umbrella or walking stick, a small camera, a pair of binoculars, infant's food for the flight, infant's carrying basket, an invalid's fully collapsible wheelchair, a pair of crutches, a reasonable amount of reading matter, and duty-free goods acquired since checking in.

## It's too much!

Excess baggage must be paid for: usually at 1% of the normal first-class fare for the whole journey — per kilo.

Air cargo is cheaper: about half the excess rates. So ask that your excess goes freight. Or you can plan to send it the day before you travel: otherwise you may be delayed at customs or waste hours — even a day or two — waiting at the other end.

Otherwise arrive early, stand by the check-in desk and watch for a passenger with spare baggage allowance. Ask if your excess can be counted on his allowance. If you persist it usually works.

## Train luggage

A British Rail passenger with a second-class or season ticket may take 110 lb (55 kilos) of luggage free. First-class passengers can take 155 lb (70 kilos). Excursions and cheap day returns, however, only allow you handbags and small personal articles.

**In advance** Where arrangements are available B.R. will collect and deliver your luggage by van. To send it in advance you must have a ticket and give them plenty of notice. Allow at least fourteen days from (say) London to Inverness. Cost: £1.90 per article, 87p supplement to the Channel Islands. The time of collection must be arranged between you and your local station: you may have to stop at home until they come.

## What to take

If you're bad at packing and usually forget something, try to be more systematic. Think of things in categories:

Toiletries and overnight
Unders
Overs
Outers
Accessories
Paperwork and extras

Two things are then true: everything you need will fit into one of those categories; however brief your holiday you will need something from every category. Categories 1 and 2 will always be standard. Thus:

## 1 Toiletries and overnight

| | | |
|---|---|---|
| *Standard sponge-bag* | — face-cloth | |
| | razor and blades | |
| | toothbrush and paste | |
| | tweezers | |
| | deodorant/talc | |
| | cologne/aftershave | |
| | nailbrush | |
| | hairbrush | |
| For women: | skin cleanser | |
| | skin moisturizer | |
| Optionals: | *Nailcare bag*: | manicure set |
| | | tissues |
| | | nail base or strengthener |
| | | polish |
| | | remover |
| | *Haircare bag*: | sachet shampoos |
| | | tail comb |
| | | rollers and rollerpins |
| | | sachet conditioner |
| | *Electricals*: | electric rollers |
| | | hair drier |
| | | iron |
| | | travelling clock |

*Medical*:        essentials only:
                  aspirin
                  antiseptic cream
                  antacid
                  laxative
                  anti-diarrhoea tablets

For women:        contraceptives
                  tampons
For men:          contraceptives

*Nightwear*: Not essential. Central heating has brought a slump in pyjama sales. Nighties are often more for glamour than warmth. If you still wear either, take the briefest.

*Dressing-gown or jacket*: Yes. Useful for hotel-room breakfasts, or where the loo is along the corridor. Choose one that will do double duty by the pool or on the beach.

*Slippers*: Use flip-flops or flat sandals instead.

## 2 Unders

For women:        bras
                  knickers: disposable paper ones are ideal for holidays
                  slips: if you wear them — an antistatic, stops jersey clinging
                  tights

For men:          vests — if you wear them
                  pants — paper ones for holiday
                  socks

How many of each is up to you: at least one set for each day; more in hot countries.

## 3 Overs

| *Men* | *Women* |
|---|---|
| shoes | shoes |
| shirts (cufflinks) | dresses |
| ties | skirts |
| suits | trousers |
| trousers | blouses |
| sweaters | T-shirts |
| casual jacket | sweaters |

*Quantities:* more the longer you stay and the hotter the climate.

## 4 Outers

overcoat
top jacket
raincoat
plastic mac, folded small

## 5 Accessories

shoes
belts
hats
scarves
gloves
bags
jewellery

## 6 Paperwork

writing paper
address books
travel documents
reading
guides
prescriptions for glasses and medicines (so you know what to ask for
if you need replacements)

### Extras

sewing repair kit
camera
small hand torch
sunglasses
folded umbrella
needle and cotton
bottle and tin opener
iron

## How much for how long

Needs vary. I prefer to take too much. But I know people who get by on
very little. Here are some suggested lists:

*Winter Weekend in Paris — Woman*

**1** and **2** standard
**3**  1 good day dress
     1 good dress for evening
     1 skirt
     2 sweaters
**4**  wear coat, pack mac

**5** wear boots; take 1 pair walking shoes and 1 pair high-heels
2 belts
2 scarves
2 pairs gloves
beads

**6** documents
reading
umbrella
sewing repair kit

*Winter Weekend in Paris — Man*
**1** and **2** standard

**3** change of jacket or suit — depending how formal
2 shirts (cufflinks)
tie
2 sweaters
1 pair trousers

**4** wear overcoat, pack mac

**5** 1 change of shoes
2 belts
gloves
scarves/hat — if you wear them

**6** documents
reading
umbrella

*Ten-day Summer Seaside holiday — Woman*
**1** and **2** standard

**3** 2 sundresses
3 day dresses
2 pairs trousers/jeans
1 short skirt
1 long skirt
6 T-shirts
2 shirts
2 tops
3 bikinis
2 kaftans or long cotton dresses

**4** cotton jacket
warm bulky cardigan
poncho or shawl
small plastic mac

**5** 1 pair flat sandals
1 pair flip-flops
2 pairs espadrilles
sun-hat — or buy one there
2 scarves
1 beach bag

**6** documents
address book
reading
camera
sunglasses

*Ten-day Summer Seaside holiday — Man*

**1** and **2** standard

**3** 10 shirts
10 T-shirts
3 sweaters
3 pairs jeans
3 trousers
2 jackets
denim or cotton suit
swimming things

**4** bulky sweater
folded-away mac

**5** 2 pairs sandals
2 pairs light canvas shoes
4 belts

**6** documents
reading
camera
sunglasses

## How many cases?

**One each** Husbands and wives should never share a suitcase. Take one each and if necessary an extra holdall for shared extras.

**Two easier than one** For your spine's sake take two small cases rather than one huge one, when you can. For European flights that means one to weigh in, and one, smaller, to take on board.

**A woman's right** Every woman is allowed a handbag. Make it as big as possible, and it'll carry enough for an overnight away: tights, knickers, sponge-bag, make-up, jewellery. This is allowed in addition to a carry-on bag of limited size. Men are only allowed the latter!

## How to get everything in

If speed of packing matters most allow yourself more space. If space is at a premium, give yourself more time. From habit I've learned to pack two cases in fifteen minutes. If you travel often, develop a regular routine.

Start with the awkward shapes: spread a medley of shoes, electrical needs (hair drier, rollers, travelling clock, iron), assorted toiletries. Wrap shoes in plastic bags. Level off with smalls and T-shirts.

Then build up clothes in even *layers*. Use large sheets of plastic half as big again as the suitcase to separate different layers of clothes. This makes packing and unpacking easy if you're moving on. It also helps at airport searches.

Take trousers and skirts on their hangers.

Break toiletries down into separate groups and pack each into its own small bag. I have one bag for nailcare (manicure set, polish, remover, tissues, nailbrush), one for hair (shampoo, rollers, tail comb, sachet of shampoo, sachet of conditioners), one for washing (minimal sponge-bag needs: flannel, soap, toothpaste and brush), one for medicines (see below). It's a good idea to keep the sponge-bag in your hand luggage — then if your case goes astray at least you're equipped for twenty-four hours without it.

Once you've strapped down the clothes, the things you may never need but which are occasionally invaluable can be fitted into nooks and corners.
Top off your case with something soft and enveloping — like a shawl, poncho or dressing gown. Try not to have to jump on the lid to get it shut!

## The medicine box

You can buy most common medicaments in most European and North American countries, but names may differ and they may cost more. It is a good idea to take prescriptions for glasses and medicines with you so that you know exactly what to ask for if you need to replace or replenish them.

How much you take with you depends on how much of a hypochondriac you are. I have a plastic box 200 × 140 × 50 mm (8 × 5½ × 2 inches) that takes the following: travel-sickness tablets, first-aid strip, plasters, cotton gauze, vitamins, insect repellent, footpowder, TCP, calamine lotion, antiseptic cream, water-purifying tablets, laxative tablets, anti-diarrhoea tablets, eye cream, nasal inhaler, soluble aspirin, indigestion tablets, anti-histamine tablets, oil of cloves.

It weighs 500 g (over a pound) so it goes in hand luggage when flying. For weekends or brief trips on my own it's certainly excessive — a case of medical overkill. But for bumper holidays, especially with children, by car, or to remote places, I recommend my package as comprehensive, easily available at any chemist, and taken in small quantities, not bulky.

## Clothes

You'll need more in summer than in winter. Winter clothes are bulky but can't crease so badly, and hang out quickly.

Summer clothes need careful choice if you want to manage without ironing. Ideal items are: cotton jersey (for men and women); cheesecloth and seersucker, or drip-dry; flip-flops (they take no space and double as bedroom slippers); Terylene suits (?); and anything with a double duty — sandals that will go with an evening dress, shirts that look good with bikini or evening skirt, interchangeable tops, trousers, skirts and shirts.

**Shoes** Take one more pair than you think you'll need. A couple of pairs might not cover a weekend — caught in a downpour the first night and an escalator the second, you'll be shopping for pricy or unfashionable replacements when you should be enjoying yourself.

## Hotel-room grooming

**Washing** If it's drip-dry or jersey try wearing it and washing it under the shower. Rinse it thoroughly, take it off you and onto a hanger. Wash and rinse T-shirts then flatten them out carefully against the side of the bath — leave them there to dry and they won't need ironing.

**Ironing** You can now buy a travelling iron that works on two voltages. So you're equipped for a great many countries. (See voltages in the Gazetteer at the end of this book.) Carry adaptors for different plug fittings. When using low voltages the iron will take longer to heat up, and ironing becomes slow and painstaking.

**Laundry** Classy hotels do it for you. Laundry services in small establishments round the Mediterranean can be excellent: white clothes hung in the hot sun to dry come up whiter and crisper.

# Chapter 36
# Countdown to Departure

The dawn of the holiday morning is a glorious moment — butterflies of excitement rather like sports day at school, Christmas or getting married. If it's the family's bumper annual holiday then plans have long been laid, money paid, and everything is ready. Or is it?

## Holiday countdown

The dawn may be glorious, but the eve will be thundery with unfinished business unless you're very skilfully organized the previous ten days. I rarely do it myself — and am found at midnight paying a stack of overdue bills, so we're not cut off in our absence, clutching a brandy and swearing the one thing that puts me most in need of a holiday is getting ready for it. A neatly circular cause and effect that I'll leave the sociologists to interpret. This is what you — and I — should do if we were organized enough.

## April to June

**Animals** If you didn't book the kennels or catteries when you booked your own hotel, do it now. They get full for the high season.

**Children** Parents are fully entitled to take their children away for up to two weeks of the school year. If they're young enough there's probably no harm done. If they're working hard for O levels, it seems hard on them. But if you plan to do so, let the school know in advance: it might be tactful to phrase it as a request rather than a *fait accompli*. You should have a good justification.

**Shopping** Go shopping now for holiday clothes even if you don't go until late August. This is when the widest choice of high summer fashions are in the shops. Sales start in early July. You might leave beach towels, walking shoes and jeans until then: they're year-round standards. But the choice of latest-style bikinis, evening wear, sandals etc. declines after early summer. For last-minute shopping, chain stores like Etam, Dorothy Perkins, C. & A., are best for keeping summer stock going.

## Two months before

Time to pay the balance on any package tour. If you leave it later than eight weeks before departure date the tour operator can cancel the booking and keep the deposit. If you cancel less than six weeks before the holiday you lose more than the deposit: if you do so within four to six weeks, you have to pay 30%, within two to four weeks 45%, within two weeks 60%. That is the scale agreed by the Association of British Travel Agents.

Any change of plan by the tour operator should reach you at least six weeks before departure date. If it is a major change — different resort, or day of departure — protest vigorously. Some tour operators offer cash compensation for any changes within six weeks of departure. Changes within two weeks of going could bring £20 per person refund.

Check all family passports, visa and medical needs — jabs — for where you're going. Start any applications necessary now: visas can take weeks to come through. If you forget and find at the last minute your passport's out of date, you can get a British Visitors Passport over a Post Office counter within a day. But you can't take a course of medical treatment. So check the family's polio and diphtheria and T.A.B.T. (advisable for Mediterranean beaches) dates in good time. Check animal jabs too; good kennels and catteries need certificates.

**Insurance** Don't fail to check it out. It may be included with a package tour. If not make arrangements where necessary through an insurance firm. Better to err on the generous side, for such things as medical expenses in America, valuable individual items such as watches, cameras. You can even insure against having to cancel.
Check house insurance. You may need to update the value of contents: are you covered for the contents of the deep freeze? Call in locksmiths for any extra security locks.

## One month before

If you plan to use any other way of taking money abroad than travellers cheques, discuss this at your bank.

If you plan to tour by car get it serviced.

If you have ambitions for intensive sightseeing and you're travelling by car, buy maps, foreign motoring guides and books and get to work.

Review your luggage — check locks, handles and straps. Take for repairs if necessary. Buy luggage wheels, extra strap, foldaway bag.

If you are strictly vegetarian, pregnant or physically handicapped advise the airline, they will tell you if they can make special arrangements. British Airways have thirteen different meals: including kosher, vegetarian, low-calorie and seafood.

Check on dental needs, and make appointments where necessary. Get a prescription for glasses or contact lenses to take with you in case of accidents.

Motorists: apply now for green card insurance, A.A. 5 Star travel packs, and arrange with the A.A. or R.A.C. if you want to rent one of their packs of spares.

Get form C.M.I. from the local office of the Department of Health and Social Security. Fill it in and in return you get form E111 which entitles you to free medical treatment in the E.E.C. countries. If you're self-employed you're excluded and must make private arrangements.

## Ten days before

Review all the clothes you intend to take. Shake them out and repair where necessary. Mend anything that looks about to go: loose buttons, dodgy hems, threatening seams. Gradually start to set aside the washed and ironed articles ready for packing. Most people have enough cast-offs and last-year rejects to wear while the holiday wardrobe is got ready. But if you're wearing everything you have, you'll face a final wash on the final day (though it won't be a large one).

Apply for travellers cheques and cash in good time.

Take shoes to the repairers, clothes to the cleaners; watch for half-day closings, Bank Holidays or their own holidays — you don't want them closed when you come to collect. Check everyone's sunglasses, the camera, Li-Los and swimming rings. Buy film: it's cheaper here.

Tell milkman and newsagent when you intend being away. They don't like last-minute cancellations: some will charge if you don't give a week's notice.

Phone cat and dog kennels to remind them of your booking. Agree with them either when they call to collect your pets, or when you take them round yourself.

Take stock of the family's health — even minor snivels and tummy upsets in small children need remedying now.

Arrange with the Post Office to refer calls to an answering service to have phone messages taken for you. Arrange with the local Post Office for redirecting mail in the U.K. It costs £1 per month, per surname: form P944G.

Get a spare set of ignition keys and stash them in a magnetized box tucked somewhere on the bodywork of the car.

Take the car in for servicing: review the security, alarm systems, and locking devices. Get roof rack fitted, yellow headlights for the Continent.

Watch daily papers for news of political unrest, airport strikes, devaluation etc. at your destination.

## Five days before

The final shopping: this should top up all cosmetic and medical needs — sun oil, prescriptions to doctors etc. — and final forgotten fancies. A 50p-a-child treat gives them something to do, and keeps them out of your hair as the tension mounts.

Decide which luggage goes where: try a first fitting into the boot and roof rack. It may mean you change this round.

Check no seasonal deliveries are due while you're away: central-heating oil, coal, window cleaner. If so cancel.

Neighbours: if they're good ones they'll water the garden, mind the cat. Give them notice now, write down special instructions, vet's address etc.

## Three days before

Check out all documents, put them in appropriate documents case ready:

> Passports (visas and vaccination forms where necessary)
> Health form E111
> Insurance cover
> Driving licence/International Driving Permit
> Green card insurance
> Car log book and GB plate
> Bail bond — for Spain
> Carnet where necessary
> Currency and credit cards
> All tickets and vouchers

Collect clothes from cleaners, shoes from repairers, travellers cheques from bank.

Call at or phone local police station giving dates of absence, and addresses for contacting. If you are touring for as long as a month arrange for poste restante address. Leave a set of keys with a neighbour — essential if they're caring for a pet or plants, but a good idea in case of emergencies. The water tank in our flat burst during one holiday, flooding the people below. They had to break glass to get in. Leave an address with relations for contacting you in an emergency.

Explain firmly to each child what luggage they will be allowed and no more: one package and one cuddly toy. A toy suitcase is a good idea: it keeps them occupied and gives them practice. It'll mean they can pack for themselves once they hit their teens.

Start to run down the fridge and all the fruit and vegetables you have.

## Two days before

Pay outstanding household bills — especially those in red. If the phone is cut off while you're away it will cost £3 for it to be reconnected — more if the lapse is a matter of weeks. If you're going to be away over a month consider having the phone service discontinued at your request. It costs £2 and saves any crisis when you get back.

Decide what to wear for the journey. All too often people travel in clothes suitable for a coach to Luton or Gatwick and for nothing else. The clothes hang unused throughout the holiday waiting for the return. Better to travel in clothes you can wear there: a summer dress and a cardigan· rather than a suit.

The British have a steadfast belief that a traveller needs a coat. Yet in summer I've travelled abroad often with no more than a cardigan as my warmest clothes (plus wool sweater in the bag for mountain tops and sudden winds). You will definitely always need a plastic mac that folds up to a small bundle.

For airflights wear loose-fitting clothes: the adjustments in pressure and the dehydration may cause a slight distension of gases in the intestine. Tight clothes might feel uncomfortable. Wear comfortable shoes. Avoid constricting elastic in clothes and shoes. Feet sometimes swell, even on relatively short flights. For a really long-distance flight take bedroom slippers. I arrived in Australia with legs like tree trunks and couldn't get my original shoes on again. Swollen ankles and legs are often a result of sitting in the same position for a long time — this was thirty hours. They should get back to normal within a day.

Take the car to a car wash or pay the children to wash it. The extra pocket money should persuade them. Don't wash it yourself. You've enough to do already and don't want to get overtired.

Take the animals to their kennels.

Give contactable address to next of kin not travelling with you.

## The day before

Make the beds and prepare meals, but let the rest of the housework go hang.

Pack slowly and methodically. Throughout the morning.

Water indoor plants thoroughly and the garden if necessary.

Plan any meals for the journey.

Load the car.

Avoid parties, lavish meals, too much to drink.

Empty and tidy your handbag: discard all the accumulated rubbish. Pack carefully with essentials only. These might include spare tights, pills, contraceptive pills, travel-sickness pills, small flask of brandy; even overnight essentials in case luggage gets lost. Certainly money, travellers cheques, passport, valuables and make-up. Pack documents case where it can be reached easily.

Check the time you are due at airport, terminal or station. Book taxi accordingly.

Choose your reading for the journey: one of this frantic day's few pleasures. Apart from the quality of the literature consider: bulk (two slim volumes pack easier than one thick) and flexibility (means paperback). I favour one fiction, one non-fiction, one classic, one current rubbish. A family of four can't take four each!

If you reach the end of the day organized, reasonably untired and still excited — celebrate with a glass of something and go to bed early. Set the alarm.

If you're up late and frantic — take a sedative to make sure you at least get some relaxed sleep. Give the children a mild one too. Set the alarm clock AND ask for an alarm call. Sleep well, and start again at the beginning next year.

Pack this book.

I have written this checklist from a woman's point of view in the expectation that all of this will be done by the woman. I see no reason why it should be so, though I suspect in most families it is. In which case item 1 is: get your husband to read the countdown and ask him to share it out — or at least collaborate!


## Business travel countdown

This is an altogether crisper affair than the annual holiday jamboree. If you travel because of work then it's likely you already do it often — or aspire to. So the rules have a different set of priorities.

Readiness is all: being ready to go at a moment's summons. This means having everything prepared — from passports and jabs annually checked out to clean socks and hankies.

Luggage: depending on length of stay you will have a choice of a soft carry-on-the-plane case for a weekend or three days; a larger holdall or small suitcase from three to seven days; a full-scale suitcase for longer. You will know from experience what you can pack into each. It's a good idea to keep a typed checklist in each so you can pack hurriedly and casually without fear of forgetting something vital.

# Part 5

# Travellers with Special Needs

# Chapter 37
# Children

The guiding principle for babies and toddlers should be to disturb their natural routine as little as possible. To do this, there has to be a routine in the first place. So for the last few days before you travel keep life as regular and placid as possible. This is no time for anxious visits to the dentist, birthday parties, staying up late or last-minute health injections. Get all that out of the way earlier. Don't talk too much to toddlers of how thrilling and different the journey will be. At least appear to be taking it in your stride. The day before travelling keep toddlers off fried foods.

## Plan early

**Jabs** Start checking out all jabs necessary at least two months in advance. Babies under two years old do not need extra inoculations, but check that routine ones against diphtheria, whooping cough and tetanus (that's a three-in-one), polio and measles are complete. Jabs against smallpox are no longer a health-clinic routine; if you're expecting to travel a good deal you'll find that some countries require smallpox vaccination. The safest time is over twelve months of age.

**Passport** Even a tiny baby must be entered on a parent's passport (see page 171).

**Health** You may want to have the added security of fully comprehensive health insurance. If you're going on a package holiday for a journey booked through a travel agent, ask either the tour operator, or the agent to advise you. Otherwise, consult an insurance broker or an insurance company direct (see page 175).

**Medicines** Ask your doctor's advice. If your baby's having treatment, take the prescriptions with you. Wise stand-bys: a treatment for diarrhoea, travel-sickness pills and a liquid sedative. I've used a spoonful of the latter simply to induce sleep on night flights: the same would apply to long overnight drives.

## Where you go

You may have no choice. If, for example, work takes a parent abroad then it's up to the family to cope. But you're not the first and you're not alone. The Women's Corona Society was founded in 1950 to offer service and friendship between women in many lands. It holds free one-day briefing courses at which you meet someone from the country concerned. These deal mainly with tropical countries. Advice is given on running a home, health and child care. They also run a children's escort service — for members only— looking after children travelling to and from school in Britain. There are eight branches in Britain, and branches in thirty-two other countries. Details of activities and membership from the Executive Secretary, Women's Corona Society, Murray House, Vandon Street, London SW1H OAG; telephone 01-222 2251/2.

## Holidays

When planning a holiday with children, avoid countries with endemic diseases that would be dangerous to them. Leave North Africa and parts of the Middle East until they're older. Self-catering is probably the easiest. You simply transfer your own routines to another setting. Make especially sure that sanitation, tap-water, supplies and the local doctor are reliable: and that's more easily done in Britain. But they do have babies abroad! So the problems won't be unfamiliar. If you're self-catering, it's the journey itself and what you take that's the problem: once there it's easy.

### Hotels, guest-houses, farms, etc.

**In Britain** Many don't take small children. Some boast that they welcome children. Herald Advisory Services (see p. 128) lists opportunities, with phone numbers. Individual resort brochures will also have listings. The British Tourist Authority(see page 122)publishes a booklet, 15p, called *Children on Holiday*, which lists fifty-two hotels and inns in the U.K. with a resident day-time nanny, and eight baby-sitting organizations in London. But some hotels make only token provisions — a swing on the lawn, or early tea-time sittings — which in themselves aren't enough. If in doubt, telephone and talk things over. For a baby you will want to be able to sterilize feeds. Ask if you'll be given access to the kitchen to do that yourself. Personally I'd go for somewhere off a main road, with a front garden (if the toddler makes off, he doesn't get far), as near to sea as possible (check for gently shelving sandy beach) and preferably a small-scale establishment (big places have the hardware but not the personal interest).

**Abroad in Europe** The younger they are the cheaper they travel. A child under three goes free on cross-Channel ferries, and on domestic British flights if it is travelling on a parent's knee; there is a small charge if it occupies a seat. Some car ferries around Greece make a charge from the age of one. Children under two cost 10% of the adult fare on most international flights if they share the parent's seat. Tour operators give similar concessions. Some allow children under two free flights and hotel room, if, of course, the cot is in the parent's room. But they'll charge for food and the cot. If you're planning to take your own then ask whether you'll still have to pay. Shop around at several travel agents for different offers. If you go by ferry then check which can offer you a cabin if you need it.

Many holiday packages include a free baby patrol during the evening (someone who listens at the door every hour or so) and a children's supervisor to take care of the children during the day. Ask whether they are qualified nurses or nannies or merely baby-sitting girls earning their way to a summer in the sun. Do the rooms on upper floors have solid balcony walls, or merely metal bars? Ask what the hotel's facilities are for boiling water, heating baby foods, dealing with nappies. Do they have cots, high chairs, play-pens and push-chairs? If not, take your own. Are rooms air-conditioned? Hotel meals should be all right for toddlers but drink bottled water, just to be safe.

Contact the national tourist office of the country and get information about climate, availability of baby foods and toiletries, medical facilities and pharmacies, and odd risks like mosquitoes and tap-water.

Earlier means cheaper: children under school age can benefit from cheap holiday rates earlier in the year. It's a better time for them, the weather's cooler, and there's less chance of prickly heat and other hot weather risks. Midday heat in the Mediterranean can be too much.

**Further afield** Infants and babes in arms on flights to the U.S. usually go for 66$^1$/$_3$% of the adult fare, but airline concessions vary: so does the treatment. Anglo-Saxon personnel will be efficient and helpful. But on Eastern airlines you'll find they're actually pleased to see babies, will fuss over them and fetch and carry whatever you need. A friend of mine would fly her family Air Cambodia or Air Burma in preference to B.A. or Pan Am, simply for the delight they take in children.

Basically, wherever Western civilization has reached, and settled, you will find ranges of baby foods and products similar to those on sale in Europe and America. Products such as Gerber, Heinz, and Nestlé are distributed or made under licence in places all over the world. Keep to the range of products your child is used to. It's less safe to buy locally made baby foods.

If you're making a long and convoluted journey, ring the manufacturers first and ask in which countries you can buy their baby foods. Take tins with you for those where you can't; Robinson's do tins of dehydrated baby foods. But you can carry this to excess: I travelled to Italy with luggage overweight by four dozen Heinz tins, only to find plenty on sale when I arrived. Anyway Italian pasta is instant baby food!

*Hotels* Use your judgement. If Western standards of hygiene prevail, you can usually trust them to boil tap-water for fifteen minutes if you insist firmly. In the East, however, they aren't often as scrupulous. Try − it will be difficult − to get into the kitchen and do it for yourself. Otherwise, buy bottled water and use that, or use water-sterilizing tablets.

## Which way to travel

Babies and toddlers need to keep to their own routine; the longer the journey the more difficult that is to sustain. If you're going your own way − car, caravan − you can adjust accordingly. It's worth spending a little more for comfort, travelling with children: first instead of second class, train rather than bus.

**Bus** Long bus or coach journeys are probably the hardest on baby, toddler or mother. However, coach travel is often cheaper than rail and you may have to take it.

There'll be long stretches without stops, little space, no toilet or feeding facilities at all.

**Trains** You'll have more space and, if there's a buffet, a supply of boiling water and people who could help. Toilet facilities don't suit toddlers very easily − and in a crowded train other passengers might not like it if your children get too noisy or athletic. So, it's really worth travelling at off-peak times or going first class, if you can.

**Boat** For travelling any distance, many passenger ships have trained nursery staff. Ask the shipping company what facilities there are. Cross-Channel ferries have a few cabins. They book up quickly either in advance or as people come on board. But they're worth booking for the quiet and privacy if you want to breast-feed. Boats only have railings round the sides so toddlers should be well reined or held firmly for walks on deck. I was taken to South America at the age of five: my parents found the strain of keeping perpetual watch during the two-week journey almost ruined the pleasures of the crossing.

**Car** The disadvantages of time are offset by having greater control. You can stop every two hours, have as long a break as you like, load luggage in the boot and arrange the back seat for the children's convenience: but car travel calls for planning.

All children should travel in the back − *never* on the front passenger seat. Toddlers should travel in a child safety seat securely anchored to the car.

A baby should travel in a carrycot with a carrycot restraint. They sleep better, and are less inclined to travel sickness if they travel end on rather than sideways. For a useful survey of safety devices for children in cars, see *Motoring Which?*, April 1977.

**By air** The best way to go once you're on board. Before that you have all the problems of car, coach and airport delays. Again, if you can afford it, money will be well spent on a taxi direct to the airport.

Many airports have places where you can breast-feed and change a baby. There is often a nurse there to help. Find out before you travel if there is one and, on arrival, ask one of the airport staff to direct you.

Tell the airline in advance and they'll provide baby food, nappies and even a 'skycot'. You'll get more help on long hauls than short, because the staff aren't so busy.

If you take your own cot − maximum size 760 × 406 × 203 mm (30 × 16 × 8 inches) − then it, plus baby paraphernalia kept in it, should not weigh more than 12 kg (26$\frac{1}{2}$ lb) − the baby's weight is not included. If you're carrying your baby you're allowed up to 6 kg (13 lb) of baby things in the cabin and no further baggage allowance.

*Ears*: Adults know about popping ears as the plane changes height and they swallow and gulp accordingly. Babies don't and you can't explain. Crying will clear it automatically. Otherwise, give a bottle of boiled water. Toddlers can be given a sweet to suck: many airlines carry barley sugars.

## What to take for the journey

Each year there are new and improved baby products that make feeding, changing and comfort ever easier. Don't stint yourself on these but don't go loaded down like a chemist's shop.

## Essentials

Large canvas bag for all the baby's things − with pockets if possible. Pack it the same way each time. Don't rummage: it creates chaos later.

Transparent polythene bags: wrap each set of baby needs in a separate one. Take a roll of extras, for disposing of dirty nappies, discarded rusks, tissues and cotton wool.

Bottle for boiled water and separate teats in a separate screw-top jar.

Bottle of milk (unless breast-fed). Don't take more than one bottle ready made up.

Equipment for making up further feeds: two more bottles, bottle brush, measuring spoon, sterilizing bowl and tablets, dried milk and a vacuum flask of boiled water.

Washing things: a wet flannel, soap in a plastic box, a small towel and roll or box of tissues − either toilet roll, kitchen paper or face tissues will be O.K.

Change of clothing: for spills and sickness. Also a lighter or heavier set if there's going to be a change of climate.

Disposable nappies, two pairs of nappy pants.

Towelling nappies for night-time.

First-aid box: travel-sickness pills, diarrhoea mixture, baby aspirins, doctor's sedative. Also cotton wool, baby lotion, safety pins, plasters, a roll of dressing and a roll of tape. A crêpe bandage, T.C.P., cream for insect bites, thermometer.

## For toddlers

Tins of baby food, cereal, tin-opener, spoon.

Several bibs: paper and towel ones get soggy quicker (keep them in plastic bags).

Bottle of fruit juice, ready diluted.

Plastic cup with spout.

Either potty or toddler's lavatory seat.

Nappies: toddlers who are already trained may well lapse back into baby habits under the strain of travel and change. Don't protest about it, simply be prepared.

## Good-idea optionals for babies

A carrying sling − though it'll be too sticky to use in the tropics.

A small folding push-chair. You may need a sun canopy: some hotels have them.

Clothes line and pegs: you can buy tiny plastic packs.

Other disposables − things like nappy liners, bottom wipes. Browse round a big chemist's for helpful new ideas.

If you'll be beyond the reach of boiled water, take a small camping stove and small saucepan.

## For toddlers

A full range of toys and playthings.

A favourite piece of blanket, teddy or dummy.

## For you

Cotton cape if you're shy of breast feeding in strange places.

A stick of refresher cologne or solid scent for keeping baby smells under control.

Apron, lightweight and as capacious as you need, for coping on your knee.

A hip-flask of something strong for when things get you down.

## Feeding on the move

**Breast-feeding** Technically the easiest, socially the most awkward. Seek as much privacy as possible. On a coach ask the courier to sit you next to a woman. By car, find a secluded lane or lay-by. On a ferry, hire a cabin. At an airport, find a nursery. On a flight — ask the stewardess to help: they can seat you where a curtain can be pulled across. One way to retain some semblance of privacy is to wear a waist-length cape of cotton or nylon and feed your baby inside or under it.

You breast-feed because it's the natural thing to do: and in many countries they'll agree. You can happily breast-feed in countries like Spain, Italy and Greece, and it's always easier in rural areas.

**Bottle-feeding** There is no need to worry if made-up feed is cold. However, you can buy bottle muffs that will keep a freshly made feed from cooling for some time. Alternatively refrigerate a made-up feed before you leave; carry it in an insulated container and ask a stewardess, or waitress, to heat it up for you when you need it. If you're in a car, you can buy a bottle warmer that plugs into the cigarette lighter — or use a small camping stove. If you have to make up a bottle feed en route it's easiest at places where they have plenty of steaming water: galleys of airplanes, coffee bars, motorway cafés, airport restaurants. Otherwise, use the boiled water in your vacuum flask and renew it at the earliest opportunity.

**Toddlers** Can be very messy. Dress them in an all-round bib for a start, and provide some protection for surroundings. Spread newspaper or a plastic tablecloth on the car or aircraft seat; put a towel across your lap. Choose non-messy foods: sandwiches, cheese, slices of boiled egg, fruit, rather than jam, sticky buns, chocolate and lollies. Airflights are dehydrating so have plenty of fruit juice.

Keep a large bag for all rubbish, tissues, J-cloths and face flannel to hand.

## Boredom

Restless toddlers are the world's most difficult travellers. The moment you've left home they start asking how soon they'll be there. No time spent preparing how to keep them amused is ever wasted. You'll earn the silent thanks of fellow travellers, the admiration of travel staff and the envy of other mothers.

**Take with you** A box of small familiar toys — nothing too small, it could roll under the seat. For a baby choose a rattle with a gentle tone. Rings on a chain allow you to keep a grip on the toy while the child plays. Take one cuddly toy for going to sleep. On a train or ferry there will be a table: take crayons, felt tips, colouring books, rough paper. One new toy or book is a good idea. Children like taking out and putting in: a set of cups, a wrapped parcel or keys in an envelope will distract them for a while. Carry Plasticine or Play-doh in one polythene bag: pieces of Lego in another.

Older children will like to choose their own things. Make sure they include a small selection of books — picture ones to look at, story ones for you to read. Add puzzle and quiz books, and one or more of the I-Spy book series. They include: *I-Spy on a Car Journey*, *I-Spy on a Train*, *I-Spy at the Airport*, *I-Spy on the Motorway* and *I-Spy Buses and Coaches*.

**In trains and ferries** Expect them to play on the floor and get filthy. *Never* dress children up for travel.

**In the car** Here you can let rip without disturbing anyone. Sing songs, rounds, even hymns; you can be as noisy as you like. Try a nursery-rhyme competition seeing how many you can think of without repeating. Play I-Spy and spotting games: church spires, pubs. If your car has a cassette player or you have a portable one take along some children's stories. Johnny Morris has made some for small children (R.C.A.). On Argo, Glenda Jackson reads *The Secret Garden*, Nicol Williamson reads *The Hobbit* and Bing Crosby reads *Tom Sawyer*. Your local library may have these. Children love the same stories over and over again: how often depends on whether you can stand it. Otherwise, try story-telling yourself. Remember, that's how *Watership Down* began.

Pack a ball for when you stop. Give the kids a good chance to run around. It'll stop them being car-sick. Give them plenty of fresh air and exhaust them ready for sleep.

You'll find more ideas in: *Games to Play in the Car*, by Michael Harwood, 75p, published by Rapp & Whiting.

Plan to arrive no later than 16.00 or 16.30 so children have some non-travelling time before bed. Don't aim for long-distance records, choose hotels early and carefully if you're on tour.

**Travel-sickness** If you expect it, stick to very plain foods the day before and give pills an hour before setting out.

If he or she starts to complain in a car take immediate action. Stop and give them a chance to walk round; keep the car windows open, sit the child in the fresh air; keep them occupied and interested. Get a paper

T.C.T.—R

bag, plastic bag or tissues handy. Don't let them climb around. According to Dr. Spock salted biscuits are supposed to help.

On a plane there's usually a bag provided. Tell the stewardess.

## Once you're there

**Clothing** In a hot climate avoid nylon; prefer cotton. You may need a sun-hat or sun-shade. Dispense with socks and shoes. If a baby goes naked keep the direct sun off his skin. Keep the bedroom shaded and cool.

If toddlers want to splash in the sea, keep a couple of T-shirts for them to wear in the water.

In a cold climate, warm clothes are necessary. Some cold countries – e.g. Russia – have overwhelming central-heating systems, so don't keep a child heavily wrapped up indoors.

**Foods** If toddlers are not on tinned baby food, keep dishes as familiar as possible, especially for the first two days. Avoid strong, new tastes – they'll reject them anyway. If you're suspicious of local water, remember it's what's used for ice cubes and don't take any. If a child is suddenly food-faddy, let him be. Don't buy picnic foods that involve moist fillings, creamy salad-dressing. Also don't buy cold meats and pâtés that appear to have been on open display: flies and bacteria may have got at them. Hot food is safer. Only have fruit that you can peel: discard the skin of peaches, apples and pears. Keep a tin of prune purée for cases of constipation.

**Hotels** Have two plastic sheets: one to protect the mattress against bed-wetting (even a well trained toddler might lapse on holiday). The other to spread on the hotel-room carpet under the feed chair, or on the bed while the baby is changed.

Check on arrival that balconies, windows and french windows are safe. In Japan, traditional inn rooms are built with a drop at either end – one is where you leave your shoes, the other serves as a verandah. Both are hazards for a crawling baby.

Inspect the room for delicate objects and breakables and remove them to the top shelf of the wardrobe.

**Insects** There may be mosquitoes, so at night close all windows, spray with insecticide, and if you think that's not enough use an insect-repellent cream. Treat bites with T.C.P.

**Illness** If it's a mild tummy upset, no food for twenty-four hours. Put them to bed and allow only mineral water. For any illness in a baby or small toddler, get medical help.

**Thermometers** If you're used to the Fahrenheit scale take an English thermometer. At a glance you know that anything other than 98.4 °F is wrong. Continental thermometers use only the Celsius scale on which 36.9 °C is normal body temperature.

**Sunburn** Don't let it happen. Be meticulously careful the first few days. Let their skin become exposed for short sessions at a time. Avoid peak sunshine times: 11.00−16.00. Use a protective sun cream, but don't depend on it. Insist they play in the shade: hire a beach umbrella. If they do get burnt, apply calamine lotion or Boots After-Sun, and absolutely insist they keep out of the sun.

**Heat rash** Tiny spots in the body's moist places, and even all over. Treat with calamine lotion and keep the child in consistently cool places. For heat exhaustion put them to bed in a dark room with plenty to drink. If they don't recover after several hours, check with a doctor.

**Fans** In countries without air-conditioning the locals may use fans. They may be on sale as souvenirs. Put one to good use.

## Children on their own

### Travel

Most airlines make special arrangements for what they call 'unaccompanied minors'. Consult them in good time. If a young child is travelling by train, book him a seat, put him on board, and have a word with the guard. If you're worried about his food, mention it to the guard, or in the restaurant car. An appreciative tip would be appropriate.

For longer journeys alone consult the Embassy of the country involved, or the Women's Corona Society (see page 235).

### Holidays for unaccompanied children

These exist in Britain and elsewhere for groups and for singles. Look at two British Tourist Authority publications: *Children on Holiday*, which lists fifty-six separate U.K. organizations offering holidays, mostly residential, for unaccompanied children − some for as young as seven-year-olds; and *Britain: Youth Accommodation*, for young people in groups. This booklet is really for group organizers, but some places will take individual bookings.

### Y.H.A. Adventure Holidays

The Eagle Holiday Section offers walking tours for boys and girls aged eleven to fifteen in Switzerland, Luxembourg and on the Rhine (see Y.H.A. page 157).

### Colony Holidays

Founded in 1963 with the recognition of the Department of Education, as a non-profit-making educational trust. It runs community holidays with group activities, for British-born or British-educated children between eight and fifteen years old. Holidays are usually nine or twelve days long at one of thirty-four large guest-houses. Each colony takes between thirty-five and eighty children and has an overall director plus staff. Travel to and fro is organized by the Colony in collaboration with the National Bus Company. There are also Anglo-French Colony Holidays where equal numbers of French and British children live together. The trust also runs holidays on the Isle of Man and at Stornaway in the Outer Hebrides.

Some places are reserved for children from deprived homes, with finance from local authorities or other organizations.

For all details write to Colony Holidays, Lindon Manor, Upper Colwall, Malvern, Worcestershire WR13 6PP; telephone Colwall 40501 (S.T.D. code 0684).

# Chapter 38
# Young People

From the age of sixteen, young people will want to make their own holiday plans. Many can book and pay for holidays that are just like those which adults take. But organizations exist to help those who want holidays and visits designed specifically for them. The most comprehensive source of information is the Central Bureau for Educational Visits and Exchanges, 44 Baker Street, London W1M 2HJ; telephone 01-487 5961 or 01-486 5101; and 3 Bruntsfield Crescent, Edinburgh EH10 4HD; telephone 031 447 8024.

It's a long name for a rather crisp set-up that brings together heaps of international contacts and opportunities. It was founded in 1948 by the Ministry of Education and Unesco. It can help to arrange school exchanges (pupil and teacher), holidays for the disabled and the hard of hearing, sports and adventure visits, community work overseas, and many other things. If you have a special problem take it to them. Their booklets — jam-packed with suggestions — include:

*Study Holidays*: A full and detailed listing of study courses — anything from languages to sport — available in thirty-five countries including the

U.S.A., Russia, Poland, Mexico, Iceland and Turkey. It's impossible to summarize its abundance of facts — but read it slowly or you'll end up studying skiing in Finland when you wanted music in Austria.

*School Travel and Exchange*: Basically for teachers; or parent/ teacher associations. School travel to thirty-three countries including China and Albania.

*Sport and Adventure Holidays*: Even wider in scope: action holidays on offer by some 300 organizations (some charitable, some commercial) in over fifty countries. The choice includes overland safaris, three and a half weeks with a Sri Lanka family, or a fifteen-day botanical tour of Afghanistan. Some of these are for all ages, but many stop short around the mid-twenties.

Commercial organizations that are listed must have been in operation for two years and must supply references which are taken up. Any complaints are examined thoroughly: if found to be justified they are dropped from the listings.

*Volunteer Work Abroad*: This lists thirty-eight organizations that need volunteers for service overseas. Many are churches, or international organizations such as the Guides and Boys' Brigade. Each entry lists age limits, qualifications needed and a contact address.

## Students

Student Travel, N.U.S., was the largest travel agent in the world pro-liferating cheap student travel in all directions. Sadly it went into liqui-dation in November 1976. At the time it had some fifty offices in different universities: they closed down. Now the N.U.S. is picking up the pieces; offices are open again in major cities — Birmingham, Manchester, Leeds. Otherwise, student unions refer their members to the following address: Student Travel, 117 Euston Road, London NW1; telephone 01-387 9456 — the old address now offering a limited service. They have lists of cheap student flights available.

Student Travel Service (USIT) Ltd, 189 Wardour Street, London W1; telephone 01-437 1474. This is the Irish student organization — head office, Dublin — and it offers cheap charter flights, travel insurance and travel advice books. It also offers a full train service schedule at student rates.

There are other student travel agencies in London: the Dutch, German, Australian and Italian student bodies have offices here, with bargain travel deals. Further information can be obtained from national tourist offices.

## Student cards

The international student card currently costs £1 and runs out on 31 December of each year. To obtain it you need proof of registration from university, college or polytechnic, and photographs. This card will entitle you to cheap travel offers and reduced entrance fees all round the world. There are plenty of forgeries and, therefore, suspicious inspections. So provide as much evidence of authenticity as possible.

# Chapter 39
# The Disabled and Handicapped

If you cannot escape the confines of an illness, or a physical or mental handicap, at least you deserve the chance to escape from the regular, even monotonous, confines of your room, and routine way of life. With admirable thoroughness, both the Central Council for the Disabled, and the Disablement Income Group, have set about compiling bumper publications packed with useful information. I recommend them highly. This is a complex and specialist business, and there are plenty of organizations to consult for help.

*Holidays for the Physically Handicapped* — almost 600 pages for 65p from C.C.D., 34 Eccleston Square, London SW1V 1PE; telephone 01-821 1871. In this guide accommodation is classified to show the degree of disability that can be accommodated. Hotels and guest-houses are further classified into those providing special diets; those accepting epileptics; and those accepting incontinents. Door widths for wheelchairs are also given.

*An ABC of Services and Information for Disabled People* — by Barbara Macmorland: £1 from D.I.G., Attlee House, Toynbee Hall, 28 Commercial Street, London E1 6LR. This provides an extensively cross-referenced catalogue of all available advice, booklets and organizations, covering not just holidays and travel, but all handicapped needs.

## Other voluntary organizations that can help with holidays

*B.P. Scout Guild Holiday Homes Trust*: Baden Powell House, Queen's Gate London SW7 5JS.

*Break*: 20 Hooks Hill Road, Sheringham, Norfolk NR26 8N1. For disabled and/or deprived children.

*British Epilepsy Association*: 3/6 Alfred Place, London WC1E 7ED.

*British Polio Fellowship*: Bell Close, West End Road, Ruislip, Middlesex HA4 6LP.

*British Rheumatism and Arthritis Association*: 1 Devonshire Place, London W1N 2BD.

*British Sports Association for the Disabled*: Stoke Mandeville, Harvey Road, Aylesbury, Bucks HP21 8PP.

*Central Bureau for Educational Visits and Exchanges*: 44 Baker Street, London W1H 2HJ.

*The Chest, Heart and Stroke Association*: Tavistock House North, Tavistock Square, London WC1H 9JE.

*Church Army*: CSC House, North Circular Road, London NW10 7UG.

*Disabled Campers Club*: 28 Coote Road, Bexleyheath, Kent.

*The Disabled Drivers' Association*: Ashwellthorpe Hall, Ashwellthorpe, Norwich, Norfolk.

*The Elizabeth Fitzroy Homes*: The Coach House, Whitegates, Liss, Hants.

*Friends Service Council*: Friends' House, Euston Road, London NW1.

*'Holidays for the Disabled' Committee*: Caister Holiday Centre, Caister-on-Sea, Great Yarmouth, Norfolk.

*International Voluntary Service*: Cerelsole House, 53 Regent Road, Leicester.

*Inter-School Christian Fellowship*: 47 Marylebone Lane, London W1M 6AX.

*John Groom's Association for the Disabled*: 10 Gloucester Drive, Finsbury Park, London N4.

*Kids*: 17 Sedlescombe Road, London SW6 1RE.

*The Lady Hoare Trust for Thalidomide and Other Physically Disabled Children*: 7 North Street, Midhurst, West Sussex.

*The Multiple Sclerosis Society of Great Britain and Northern Ireland*: 4 Tachbrook Street, London SW2V 1SJ.

*National Association of Youth Clubs*: Devonshire Street House, 30 Devonshire Street, London W2N 2AP.

*Parkinson's Disease Society of U.K. Ltd.*: 81 Queen's Road, London SW19 8NR.

*PHAB*: 42 Devonshire Street, London W1N 2AP. It stands for Physically Handicapped and Able Bodied.

*Queen Elizabeth's Foundation for the Disabled*: Leatherhead, Surrey KT22 oBN.

*Riding for the Disabled Association*: Avenue 'R', National Agricultural Centre, Kenilworth, Warwicks.

*The Royal British Legion*: 49 Pall Mall, London SW1Y 5JY.

*St. Raphael Clubs*: 11 Thurlin Road, King's Lynn, Norfolk.

*The Scout Association*: Gilwell Park, Chingford, London E4 7QW.

*The Shaftesbury Society*: 112 Regency Street, Westminster, London SW1P 4AX.

*The Spastics Society*: 12 Park Crescent, London W1N 4EQ.

*Winged Fellowship Trust*: 79/80 Petty France, London SW1H 9HB.

*Young Disabled on Holiday*: Mrs. Valerie Garner, 11 Highfields, Forest Row, East Sussex RH18 5AJ.

*Youth Hostels Association*: Trevelyan House, 8 St. Stephens Hill, St. Albans, Herts AL1 2DY.

## Social service departments of Local Authorities

These often run holiday homes of their own. As a disabled person you should be registered with this department of your Local Authority. They will always try to help with travel and accommodation, if their budget allocations allow.

# Part 6

# Problems and Emergencies

# Chapter 40
# Sickness

## Adjusting to the heat

That gust of hot air that meets you as you step from the jet — somewhere near midnight — oh! the first delicious taste of being abroad! It can smell of exotic flowers, and strange flavours of foreign cooking or simply hot tar and dust. I love it, it's full of the excitement of a strange place and a new adventure beginning.

Next day, though, such romantic musings come to a sudden end. The sun is up early, metallic and hot, and stays there all day while you get used to walking, eating, working and travelling in the searing heat. Those who go to sunny places for holidays see them falsely. Those who go there to work, trade, decide, discuss and generally earn their living will have to take time to get used to it. Look how the summer of '76 had us gasping like fish out of water. Here are some pointers to make adjustment less painful.

**Slow down** You simply can't go nipping here and there as fast as you do in Britain. You'll get puffed, wet with sweat, red-faced and cross. To move more slowly and get the same amount done, you must be more methodical. Check you have all you need on setting out. Allow five minutes extra for short journeys. In some countries you can hire cars with air-conditioning. Make a study of shadows and always try to park in the shade — or where the shade is moving to. If you are late for an appointment, don't run. Phone and warn of the delay, and arrive in your own cool time.

**Sweating** This is one of the mechanisms by which the body adjusts to heat. You can expect your body to sweat more, to start sweating at a lower temperature than it usually does, and to go on sweating for longer periods. This means you are losing fluid from your body surface. Sweat is a salt-water solution. So you must make a point of keeping up sufficient intake of fluids and salt.

**Fluid intake** In every twenty-four hours you should drink one pint of fluid for every ten degrees Fahrenheit. That means if it's 90 °F you drink nine pints of fluid between 9 in the morning and 9 the next morning. Translated into litres and centigrade — this means something around four litres at 20 °C, five litres at 30 °C, and six litres at 40 °C in any twenty-four hours.

**Urine check** One simple principle is to keep the urine very nearly colourless. Once it becomes very yellow, it means you are dehydrated. Prolonged concentration of the urine can lead to kidney stones.

**Salt intake** The normal European diet contains about ten grammes of salt per twenty-four hours. In the tropics, depending on the heat and your physical exertion, you will need, on average, about twice as much. If you exercise vigorously while being short of salt you'll get intense muscle cramps. You can add extra salt to your cooking, or at the table. Or you can take salt tablets. These can be pills you swallow or a tablet that dissolves in water like an effervescent drink. It is preferable, however, to increase your salt intake through food. (I haven't ever tried but a little salt in water or fruit drinks tastes quite palatable in a hot climate.) You might find, as I do, that your appetite for salty things has increased. Hence the popularity of Spanish gazpacho. and all sorts of strong salamis. I once brought home from Majorca a particularly delicious kind of red sausage. It had tasted wonderful with hunks of baked bread and a jug of red wine under the Mediterranean sun. I fried them one London September morning: the family spat them out. They were too salty to be palatable. Yet they had tasted delicious just the week before.

As your body gets used to the heat your need for extra salt will decline. But your need for extra fluid continues.

*Warning*: don't increase your salt intake without increasing your fluid intake.

**Clothing** It must be able to absorb sweat.

*Wool* is the most absorbent, and strangely enough a fine wool dress, loosely cut, is not as inappropriate as you might think.

*Cotton*, however, is much the best. And cotton mixed with a small percentage of man-made fibre may keep its texture better. The fact is cotton keeps you cool, absorbs sweat, but can look like a limp rag after half a day. (See p. 225)

*Nylon* is impossible in the heat. Disastrous as nightwear. Wear cotton in bed — or nothing at all. I sometimes see Englishmen on holiday still wearing socks — often even sweaty nylon and Terylene socks! Don't! Bare feet and sandals will allow the feet to sweat healthily.

*Colours*: it's not by accident that people's preference is for light colours in the heat; white reflects heat, black absorbs it.

*Styles*: close-fitting and elegantly cut clothes that look well in London will feel very constricting in the heat. Try to maintain a layer of air between your clothes and your skin. It keeps you cool in the heat, and warm in the cold. String vests do the same. Cotton dresses should be loose, and fall freely. Tight belts and waistbands are bad styles for the heat. So are fitted shirts and figure-hugging trousers.

*Hats*: if the sunlight is direct and strong you will probably need a hat, at least initially. But if the weather is hot but overcast and humid, better to go without, to allow the head to sweat. Apparently it provides 25% of the body's sweating area. Men with a tendency to baldness need to watch they don't get sunburnt on the newly emerging patch. Men who've been bald for years will already know they need a hat.

## Heat afflictions

### Heat exhaustion

*Symptoms*: light-headedness, dizziness, mainly on moving around. Fainting after excessive activity. There may also be acute fatigue, nausea, yawning and blurring of vision.

*Treatment*: rest, fluid and salt.

### Heat stroke

This is more serious.

*Symptoms*: the temperature rises, the skin becomes dry and hot. You may lose consciousness. Heat exhaustion will usually precede it, so take warning at the first symptoms.

*Treatment*: send for the doctor. Until he comes wrap patient in a wet sheet to cool him or her down. Take the temperature regularly; when it drops to 39 °C (102 °F) stop the cooling.

### Prickly heat

*Symptoms*: an irritating skin rash of small red blisters on a pink skin. Body areas most likely to be affected are: the forearm, over the breastbone and collarbone, around the waist, under the arms and behind the knees.

*Treatment*: avoid wearing nylon fabric, or clothes that prevent the sweat evaporating or being absorbed. Bathe with a bland soap, one containing hexachlorophine, and dry well. Apply calamine lotion or dusting powder — an astringent lotion, such as a man's aftershave, could be just as effective.

## Sunburn

Only two weeks holiday and you desperately want a tan before you get back to the office. Somehow, to come back from a holiday pale suggests that the holiday was a failure. There is only one way to get a good even tan that doesn't go red and blister and peel — and that is slowly and methodically.

*Limit the time.* If you've arrived from a British summer to the Mediterranean sun, half an hour's full sunshine on the first day is enough. Half an hour each side that is — one hour in total.

If you come from an English winter, then fifteen minutes each side is enough. Increase it by half an hour each day.

Use good quality creams and lotions. Don't use so much that you fry. There are different types of cream for different needs.

Take care not to doze off in the sun. Watch others in your family don't do it either. A bad burn on the first day means you won't be able to sit in the sun again for at least three days, so you lose out anyway.

Auburn-haired people suffer the worst. Then fair-haired and fair-skinned people. People like me with a sallow complexion can usually push the limits a little more safely than the others. We pay for the privilege, by looking depressingly sallow all winter.

Tablet prevention: Sylvasun claims to reduce sunburn if you take two pills a day for two weeks. The statistical evidence is inconclusive, but many people feel they benefit.

Dress children in T-shirts and shorts — and let them go in the sea dressed. Then they can snorkel and swim all day with some protection, at least.

**Treatment for sunburn** Keep out of the sun — believe me you'll want to. Calamine lotion will soothe the skin. You may need a sedative to help you sleep — and heavy areas of painful sunburn can be very unromantic.

**Sun-sensitive people** They are the ones who can't sit in the sun at all without severe skin reaction. The only answer is a barrier cream. You won't tan, of course, but you can play on the beach with the children. Uvistat is a good one: the same firm also makes a lipscreen. Being more medical than cosmetic, you can get it on a N.H.S. prescription. Eversun (by Roche) grades its strength by UV (ultra-violet) numbers: No. 7 for the most sensitive. Spectraban is another, available at most chemists.

## Adjusting to altitude

Several great cities are particularly high: Nairobi, Johannesburg and Mexico City are at 1,800 metres (6,000 feet), Bogotá is at 7,750 metres (8,500 feet). You will find you have less wind: a flight of stairs will make you breathless. If you're a heavy smoker you might feel a tight pain across your chest. The body will adjust in about three weeks. If you remember, the British Olympic team for the Mexico Games went there four weeks before they began, so they would be thoroughly used to the altitude.

## Adapting to the cold

It's far easier for the body to stay warm than to rewarm itself once the cold has got at it. So — obviously — wrap up well.

**Body warmth** Hug it to you by layer upon layer of warm clothing rather than one huge thick garment. I know women who wear men's long johns, and men who wear women's tights. Both are snug. Women should go for long woollen-mix knickers, vest or waist-long spencers. Film crews in cold climes are issued with thermal underwear.

**Extremities** Any area of exposed flesh will leak body heat like mad. So close all gaps. That means wearing socks, scarves, hats and gloves. Russians go in for huge fur hats: no one goes out of doors without wearing one. You can buy them in Russia's tourist shops from about £35. Russian families pass them down through the generations. You'll find if you can keep fingers and toes warm, the body will stay warm too.

## Cold-weather ailments

**Chilblains** Dry red swellings, usually on fingers and feet, sometimes even noses and ears that itch intensely. Young women are especially prone. The cause is an exaggerated response of blood vessels to a lowering of the temperature. Don't allow the skin to learn to react this way. Prevent them by keeping warm and exercised when in the cold. Once there, chilblains won't go away until the climate's warmer.

**Snowblindness** This happens when the ultra-violet rays of the sun, reflected off snow (sand or sea too) burn the cornea. You get pain and swelling of the eyes. Prevent it by wearing dark glasses or goggles. If you get it, see a doctor. He will probably prescribe an ointment to go in the eyes, and dark glasses, even a bandage to shield the eyes — and a painkiller.

**Mountain hypothermia** This is when the central core of the body falls below 35 °C (95 °F). Exhaustion makes things worse. If you're on an expedition in a cold climate watch others and yourself for symptoms of apathy, stumbling or uncontrolled shivering. Stop at once and take shelter — in a hut, a lean-to, anything. Rewarm the sufferer by skin-to-skin contact. Use spare dry clothes and a sleeping-bag to wrap him up. A nip of alcohol or something hot from a thermos might help. If the condition doesn't improve, send for help. Once back at base, he should be rewarmed in a bath of water at 42−44 °C (108−111 °F).

**Over 3,600 metres (12,000 feet)** This is real explorers' territory. You face all the problems of high, thin, cold air. You need specialized advice. Dr. Peter Steele wrote a handy little booklet, *Expedition Travel and Your Health*, published by Bristol University.

## Traveller's diarrhoea

It's called by lots of funny names, some of them half affectionate as a cover for the embarrassment of it all. But we all know how awful it feels to have two or three days of the runs, possibly with vomiting and stomach pains. You feel right off your food. You even feel off the holiday. Or you may not be able to face business meetings and decisions.

**Prevention** It seems that people are most at risk in their first week abroad, that people from Northern Europe and North America seem more prone than others, that it's probably in a majority of cases an infective illness. Medical evidence at the moment seems to indicate that the best preventive medicine is a combination of streptomycin and sulphatriad. It's marketed as a tablet called Streptotriad. You can, if you want to be fanatically cautious, take it twice a day for a maximum of four weeks. Start the day you travel and if you return within four weeks, continue it for two days after you get home. But medical opinion is divided on the question of antibiotics as a preventive. Only use them if, for some special reason, you have to.

## Other diarrhoeas

Traveller's diarrhoea goes away after three days. If diarrhoea persists it may be one of a number of serious diseases caused by bad sanitation. These are:

*Typhoid fever, paratyphoid A and B*: These are increasingly common around the Mediterranean. Paratyphoid C is practically confined to Guyana. All are spread by milk and water contaminated by sewage, shellfish, tinned meat, uncooked and unwashed fruit, ice creams and the spread of infections from lavatories to kitchen. If you have had your T.A.B.T. jab you won't die from any of these diseases.

*Cholera*: Basically in India and Pakistan. Chronic diarrhoea is its first symptom.

*Bacillary dysentery*: Diarrhoea usually containing blood or mucus. Fever, colic, sometimes vomiting. *Consult a doctor*. If there isn't one around, take plenty of fluids and two tablets of Streptotriad three to four times a day for at least five days.

*Food poisoning*: Symptoms — nausea, vomiting and diarrhoea. Treatment: bed for twenty-four hours, hot-water bottle, sweet fruity drinks, sips of boiled milk. Kaolin mixture from doctor will check diarrhoea.

*Viral hepatitis*: Spread by faecally infected water.

*Brucellosis*: A milk-borne infection which sometimes occurs around the Mediterranean. Prolonged fever.

In all cases prevention is far better than cure. In his comprehensive book, *The Traveller's Health Guide*, Dr. Anthony Turner lists in full all the most rigorous precautionary steps you can take. Personally I take a good number of them: I don't always remember. I'm not always scrupulous enough. None of us are. However, in high-risk areas, for your own and your family's safety you would be wise to observe the following rules.

All drinking water should be boiled and, if kept, put in a refrigerator in clean, previously boiled bottles. All ice cubes must be made of this water only. Use boiled water or bottled water for cleaning your teeth. The filtering of water does not purify it. Water-purifying tablets are less effective than boiling, it takes longer and the water tastes of chlorine.

All milk should be boiled.

All cooked food should be well cooked. Cook food only once and eat soon afterwards. Do not eat food cooked previously and left out on show.

Be careful of shellfish: preferably see them alive first.

All fruit — including tomatoes — should be peeled.

Do not eat locally made ice cream. Go for one of the big proprietary firms which sell nationally. They'll be the ones with display cards in bars and cafés.

Fruit which cannot be peeled and green salad should be sterilized by chlorination. Salads are risky because the dressing might also be contaminated. Never eat watercress abroad.

Soft drinks like Coke and Pepsi are fine. So are the mineral waters made by the same firms. My advice is a bottle of plonk and a bottle of *acqua minerale* at a meal. Don't dilute it with water — it doesn't sterilize it.

Avoid fly-infested restaurants. Judge a place by its lavatories. If an establishment fails to keep them clean, what can you expect of the kitchens? Take your own toilet paper.

Take one tablet of Streptotriad, twice daily: this is Dr. Turner's suggestion. Lomotil (available on a doctor's prescription) is an adequate treatment once the illness strikes.

## Local infections

Don't swallow antibiotics at the first sign of something. You should ask a doctor first.

**Eyes** Sea-water or sun glare may make them inflamed. Wear sunglasses and use Brolene ointment.

**Ears** If you swim in dirty water you can get ear-ache and discharge. Drain the ear by leaning over on your side and shaking your head. Clean the ear with cotton wool (not a matchstick!) and keep it clean.

**Ear discharge** This can result from unhygienic swimming pools, even in the best-kept establishments. Antiseptic eardrops before and after swimming minimize the risk. Apply drops, then wipe out the ear.

**Teeth** If you get toothache through decay or a lost filling, make a small plug of rolled cotton wool, soak it in oil of cloves and jam it into the gap. Hot salt mouthwashes help clear out a dental abscess if it is discharging. Try to find a dentist.

**Throat** Gargle with salt or aspirin in warm water. One occasion in Tenerife I needed to recover my lost voice in order to film a holiday report. I gargled with port — it's an old actors' trick!

## Injuries

**Cuts and grazes** Wash with soap and water, or water with an antiseptic like Dettol or T.C.P. Antiseptic cream keeps the wound sticky and so delays the healing. So a dry dressing and plaster are best.

**Burns** If a burn is superficial leave it to the open air to form a crust and later peel off. Anything more serious needs a non-stick dressing and bandage.

**Blisters** Burst with a clean needle and drain off the fluid. Then put on a clean plaster. If a blister was caused by shoes rubbing, change shoes or wear a dressing or sock that prevents contact with the shoe at the blistered spot.

**Sprain** If the pain is truly excruciating and the swelling persists, check with a doctor that you've not broken it. Otherwise, bind it firmly with a crêpe bandage.

**Larger cuts** Clean thoroughly, and cover with gauze square. Pressure on the wound itself will stop most bleeding. Then apply a gauze wound dressing. Seek medical advice if in any doubt, or if you're not protected by a tetanus jab.

## Irritants

**Indigestion** Stop over-eating and take any mild indigestion tablet.

**Hangover** Try avoiding action, a glass of milk, cocoa or even alka seltzer before going on the town. Otherwise, sunglasses, lots of liquid and a darkened room.

Byron's remedy was hock and soda water. You can try the hair of the dog: it may just make you instantly drunk again. Some people put their faith in poisonous-tasting concoctions of which two — Fernet Branca and Undeborg — are both effective and a just punishment in themselves.

**Constipation** Eat plenty of fruit. Two peaches at once can often do the trick. Or take a Senokot late at night.

**Cystitis** Frequent passing of urine accompanied by pain. Drink gallons of water and if it doesn't go away see a doctor.

## Bites and stings

**Rabies** This is the dreadful disease that has so far been kept out of this country. But it occurs in most other parts of the world, including Europe. So travellers abroad may be at risk.

*Rabies vaccine* There is a vaccination to prevent rabies, but it is fairly toxic and is only given in special cases, for example to vets, or those working with vets, in high-risk areas, or if you've actually been bitten by a rabid animal. It is *extremely* rare for anyone who has developed rabies to recover. However, people who are bitten by rabid animals and then given the vaccine and serum at once, normally do not develop the illness. Only *immediate* vaccination before the disease has time to develop offers any hope of survival.

*Caution* When you are in an area where rabies is prevalent, don't go near animals. Don't stroke strays, for example, and advise children against fondling strange animals. This may seem hard-hearted to the animal-loving British. And foreign places often abound with whole packs of scrawny stray cats. But rabies is a truly appalling illness and leads to a horror-movie kind of death.

*If you are bitten or scratched* Wash the wound at once with soap and water, or detergent and water. At least flush the wound with clean water. If possible, apply alcohol to the wound.

Try to find the owner of the animal. Exchange names, addresses and telephone numbers with him and tell him to let you know at once if the animal develops any illness or dies within two weeks. Ask whether the animal has been vaccinated against rabies — where and when — and ask to see the certificate.

If you can't find the owner make a note of the date and place of the incident. Write down a description of the animal.

Report to the nearest doctor and hospital without delay. A course of vaccination may have to be started.

Report the incident to the nearest police station.

Report to your family doctor as soon as you get back to this country.

If this advice sounds excessively alarmist, remember — *rabies can kill*. You neglect it at your peril. You may feel foolish going through all the above routine and nothing develops. But think, if you didn't and it did!

**Insects** If in a malarial area see page 205. Otherwise, insect bites are *on the whole* merely irritants. Personally I react violently to mosquito bites and come over all lumpy and itchy. Prevention first: insect repellent on exposed skin each evening, closed windows and an aerosol spray each night before I go to sleep. Out of doors, say camping, bonfires will help. Cigarette smoke is good, but not worth taking it up again. Stixscreens fitted to windows with Velcro are good for camping and caravanning. If bitten, try hard not to scratch. Sometimes, the itch goes away. Otherwise calamine lotion takes away the irritation.

*Wasp stings* Apply vinegar.

*Bee stings* A solution of bicarbonate of soda applied on the sting helps.

*Chigoe flea* Found in Africa, the West Indies, and North and South America. It likes the sandy soil round beaches, though not the sea itself. It will burrow into the foot to lay its eggs. Use a sterilized needle to remove it. Apply antiseptic ointment.

**Snakes** They will not attack you unless they feel threatened. So make your presence felt in any area where you expect snakes. Use a long stick to stir the long grass ahead of you to give them a chance to escape. You'll be advised not to wear flip-flops or open thonged sandals. Holiday-makers often do: those who stay longer usually know better. Shine a torch ahead of you at night: snakes will slide away. Always shake your shoes in the morning, or whenever you come to put them on: small snakes or scorpions might lurk inside.

If you are bitten, call a doctor or get to one. Before he reaches you take these simple steps. Wipe the bite and cover it with a clean cloth. Do *not* cut into it. If the bite is on any limb, then apply a firm ligature or tourniquet just above the bite. It must be firm, not tight; you mustn't cut off the blood supply. Aspirin or alcohol in moderation can be taken against the pain. Don't try to kill the snake. But if it has already been killed take it with you for the doctor or hospital to identify. Otherwise, remember clearly the markings and colouring. You won't die. But you must take action to limit the scope of the poison.

**Scorpions** Common in Africa, Central and South America and the Caribbean. I have seen them in Italy. They look like a long beetle with a tail curving forward above the body: the sting is in the tail. Watch for them under stones, inside shoes. Don't walk around barefoot. They will only sting if disturbed, but it will feel like a very severe bee or wasp sting. Even worse for children: go to a doctor or hospital.

**Spiders** The redbacks of Australia and New Zealand are poisonous; so is the black widow of California. See a doctor.

*Tarantula spiders* A bite can kill. In areas where they exist, everyone is constantly wary. You can hear them coming: they make a clicking noise.

**Bilharzia** A parasite infection spread by a freshwater snail. It is widespread in Africa. So you must beware of swimming in lakes and pools. People in the area will know which waters are infected. Bilharzia is usually found where shrubs and growth overhang the water: you find them less often in flowing water. Watch where you bathe, swim or paddle and boil the drinking water.

**Jellyfish** More common in the Mediterranean and Indian Ocean than the North Sea or English Channel. However, the summer of '76 brought some of them round our shores. The Portuguese man-of-war is the nastiest. Jellyfish are usually shaped like a round flat plate of transparent jelly trailing strands underneath. These strands sting. Keep your eyes open. If you see one, expect more and come out of the water. You should never swim too far for someone to reach you if you are stung and shout out.

Take a jellyfish sting seriously. The pain will be harsh: apply calamine and take anti-histamine pills. If fever develops consult a doctor.

## Athlete's foot

A fungus infection picked up where ever the human race goes swimming together. Prevent its spread by drying feet whenever they become wet.

If you suspect you have athlete's foot, keep one towel isolated just for feet; don't share it. Wear cotton not nylon socks. Use foot powder dusted into socks. You can buy it without a prescription.

If athlete's foot develops you need an ointment or paint. The chemist can supply you in the U.K.

## Tuberculosis

Tuberculosis is widespread in some poor parts of the world. Holidaymakers and businessmen visiting for a short stay don't need to worry. People going abroad for a year or two — particularly if they are going to work among people in poor areas — should have a B.C.G. inoculation. Try to have it on an inconspicuous part of the body: it can leave a slight scar.

## Leprosy

Still exists in Equatorial Africa, and to some extent in India, Sudan, Ethiopia, Angola and the north of South America. It develops after long and close contact with leprous patients. Anyone staying no more than two or three years need not worry.

## Sexually transmitted diseases

Sexually transmitted (or venereal) diseases exist in all countries of the world, and are seriously on the increase in many places — including Britain. What's more, in many places some of the diseases have developed a resistance to all the usual antibiotics. There is one obvious way of avoiding it altogether, and it is 100% sure. You don't get V.D. from lavatory seats. Human nature being what it is, the disease is likely to continue.

*Symptoms*: across a wide range of sexually transmitted venereal diseases, the symptoms are variously a discharge, irritation, pain on urinating. If you suspect you are infected then seek treatment at once. There are special V.D. clinics attached to many British hospitals. You can go directly there without seeing your G.P. first. If abroad, go straight to a doctor.

### Rare but deadly

**Marburg virus disease** This was originally imported from Africa in a consignment of green monkeys used for medical research in the town of Marburg in Germany. (Hence the other name: Green Monkey disease.) The next occasion it was identified was in two people hitch-hiking through Zambia.

In October 1976 health controls at ports and airports in Britain were tightened. In the previous week several hundred deaths had occurred in Zaïre and the Sudan. The World Health Organization confirmed the illness as Marburg virus disease. All travellers arriving from certain areas of Sudan and all of Zaïre had to refer to their local medical officers for surveillance. Later in 1976 the disease seemed to have disappeared as suddenly as it came.

*Symptoms*: The onset of flu-like illness, diarrhoea, aches, pains and bleeding. There is a 90% mortality rate.

**Lassa fever** A fever spread in rats' urine — associated therefore with very primitive domestic conditions. Special care needed if tramping the bush in places where it exists: West Africa, Sierra Leone and North Nigeria.

*Symptoms*: Sore throat, puffiness of the face, bleeding, vomiting and passing blood.

**Ebola** The most recently diagnosed. It looks like Marburg virus but isn't. Prevalent in southern Sudan and northeast Zaïre.

## Stay alert

Travellers to tropical and subtropical countries should always remain
alert to news stories in the press and television that concern outbreaks of
little known but dangerous fevers in places they have or intend to visit.

## Homeopathy

You may prefer to treat all travel ailments with natural products rather
than the usual chemist's brands. If so write to A. Nelson & Co., 73 Duke
Street, London W1. They're homeopathic chemists and stock a leaflet
called *Homeopathy on Holiday*, and a holiday first-aid kit.

# Chapter 41
# Drink, Drugs and Sex

In different parts of the world, people's attitudes to some aspects of
human behaviour vary from permissiveness to condemnation. It's worth
making sure you know where you can't do whatever it is you like doing.

Always respect the customs in a strange country. It's a matter of courtesy
and not causing offence. The law is rarely involved but there are places
where it is. You can check out with the Foreign and Commonwealth
Office in London before you go. Here are some examples.

## Drink

Drinking alcohol is against the Muslim religion. But with increasing
trade and the influx of European businessmen into Arab states, the
system of total prohibition is under great strain. Basically the situation is
this: North African tourist-minded countries have never posed any
problem. Drink is on sale in cafés, shops and hotel bars. In Iran, too,
drink is available at a price. You get whisky and wine at the supermarkets. Only in the smaller towns − on the Iraq border, for example −
is it harder. You'll find fewer places where you can drink − perhaps one
or two restaurants after seven in the evening. In the United Arab
Emirates it is perfectly possible for travellers to buy drinks. Both Inter-
Continental Hotels at Dubai and Muscat have bars. The only Inter-
Continental that's dry is at Riyadh in Saudi Arabia.

Two of the strictest countries are Saudi Arabia and Qatar. In both, the

Wahabi sect of religious zealots are keen to insist on the ban. It leads to some cloak-and-dagger high-jinks. Better for a visitor not to meddle.

In Qatar, European residents are allowed, on production of a residence permit, a ration of some thirty bottles of spirit per month. They have to buy it from the bonded warehouse at roughly duty-free prices. But shortages push prices up and there is a black market. If you get desperate take the plane to Bahrain — it's only fifteen minutes away!

In Saudi Arabia even the airline is dry. Whisky costs anything from £20 a bottle on the black market. The record is rumoured to be over £90. Do not attempt to smuggle it in; they get very cross.

Libya is also very strict, and you can't take any in either.

The Yemen is strict, but they let you take in your own duty-frees. Buy them on the plane, they're cheaper than at Heathrow.

In Pakistan in April 1977 Mr Bhutto proceeded with what he called the 'Islamization' of Pakistan by imposing total prohibition. However, non-Muslims and foreigners are still allowed drink.

## Drugs

Cases of drug smuggling are the ones that give the British Consular Service its biggest headaches. Currently there's a British citizen under sentence of death in Tangiers for smuggling. The law was only introduced after he was sentenced, so risks aren't even confined to existing laws. Morocco is very heavy on drugs, so is Spain. There are some 100 Britons currently in Spanish prisons for drug offences. It can take a year before the case comes to trial; ten years is a medium sentence. Spanish jails are tough. The British consulate was so worried by the dangers, it issued 'Keep off the Grass' notices to be given out on passport inspection.

But smugglers keep at it: now the Amsterdam/Turkey route has been blown, they're showing interest in transit passengers through Moscow, in the belief people in transit aren't searched. They are.

*Avoid*: any offer of a quick profit. These are often made to families, with children, the more homely looking the better — again in the belief that they're less likely to be searched. They aren't. In many cases of discovered drug smuggling, the people protest that they didn't know. Don't take parcels to anywhere from strangers offering payment. Ignorance is no defence in law.

*If caught*: contact the British authorities. Ask the local police to do so.

## Nudity

Topless beaches are common in the Mediterranean, especially the South of France. It started at St. Tropez: now the 'mono-kini' is common on most beaches, but not in Monte Carlo. In Corsica nudity is permitted only on secluded beaches. On the Baltic and north coasts of West Germany nude bathing is legal: but they suggest one kind of bather shouldn't trespass into the other's area. Spain is not yet topless — but the habit's creeping in.

## Incorrect dress

Women must wear long skirts, almost to the floor, in Malawi, never trousers or miniskirts. Men with long hair will have it cut on landing at the airport. Miniskirts would be frowned on in Saudi Arabia, too.

In many countries the shoulders and upper arms of women should be covered: especially in Muslim countries, at Jewish shrines in Israel and in Catholic churches in Spain and Italy. However, some of the latter have become commercially minded tourist traps, with guided tours and postcard stalls, and in them I reckon I'm absolved from all obligations of piety. Similarly men with shorts are frowned on in certain sacred places. Warning notices usually abound: they don't have the force of law, but you might be asked to leave. Many such rulings concern buildings honouring the deity: you'd think He wouldn't be squeamish about the human body. But His missions often are. So respect their customs.

## Sexy magazines

You may enjoy girlie magazines such as *Penthouse* and *Playboy*. That's perfectly legal in most places. But some countries will object to you taking such printed matter across their frontiers. According to *Penthouse* they are not acceptable in the U.S.S.R. or in any African countries. North African countries are mostly Muslim and object on traditional grounds. The emerging nations of central and southern Africa disapprove on moral grounds, as does the Republic of South Africa.

## Homosexuality

This is a private matter for you — and should stay that way. It's the only guaranteed way for the traveller to avoid trouble. Homosexuality is now legally permitted in England, and a number of Western European countries, within certain limitations. But it is still illegal in many parts of the world.

For the complete global picture you need a copy of *Spartacus Gay Guide*, a remarkable publication which gives detailed country-by-country advice and information. Its symbols include: RT, rough types; OG, older gays; and GLM, gay and lesbian mixed. Its eighth edition comes out — if that's the phrase — in December 1977. You get it from P.O. Box 3496, Amster-

dam direct (they are also on the phone: Amsterdam 982508), or from *Gay
News*, 1A Normand Gardens, Greyhound Road, London W14 9SB,
£4.50.

# Chapter 42
# Emergencies

## Loss of passport

Precaution: before you travel, have a record of the number, date of issue
and place of issue, somewhere safe, like your diary or back pocket. Do not
surrender your passport to the police or leave it in a hotel room. If the
hotel reception ask to hold it overnight, retrieve it as soon as possible.
Once lost, contact the local police immediately. Then get in touch with
the nearest British embassy or consulate. They can issue emergency
travel documents.

## Loss of travellers cheques

You may have bought travellers cheques because you believe they will
save you trouble if you lose them, whereas if you carry cash and lose it,
it's gone and you're in a jam. This assumption is based on the belief that
if you lose travellers cheques you'll get an automatic on-the-spot refund;
this isn't by any means so. You may be refused a refund and be left
stranded until you can get money cabled to you from back home.

Because of the decline in sterling, British travellers try to hedge against
currency fluctuation by ordering through their own banks cheques
issued in major European currencies by Continental banks. This can
involve certain risks. The following findings — taken from *Business
Traveller*, No. 1, Winter 1976 — will give you some guidance:

**Germany:** certain major German banks guarantee immediate on-
the-spot refunds — up to DM 1000 — of their travellers cheques, if lost in
Germany itself.

**Switzerland:** leading banks there also offer immediate refunds on their
cheques lost in their country.

**Italy:** bank officials refuse to discuss the circumstances in which they
make refunds on their own lira cheques. Some Italian banks have been
known to refuse any refund at all — ever — even when none have been

fraudulently cashed. The only safety edge such cheques have over money is that thieves find them marginally harder to spend.

**America:** American banks which give on-the-spot refunds for their U.S. dollar cheques are: American Express, First National City Bank of New York (which claims 45,000 refund points around the world) and Bank of America.

**Britain:** the degree of protection offered by the big four British banks varies:

*Lloyds*: no on-the-spot refunds abroad. Until the branch that issued the cheques has received notification of their loss, you are still liable for any fraudulent conversions. Worth phoning to your Lloyds branch in Britain at once. The only circumstance in which you'll not be liable is if Lloyds can establish for you that the cashing bank was negligent — e.g. if the counter-signature varied from the original — in which case the claim is made against the foreign bank. Incidentally, Lloyds don't require foreign banks to demand and inspect passports when cashing their cheques.

*Midland*: no on-the-spot refunds abroad. In case of loss, contact the bank's International Division in London. The refund should be through in one week: if you're starving meanwhile contact the nearest British consulate. Provided you contact London as soon as possible, you are not held liable for cheques cashed by the thief.

*National Westminster*: yes, on-the-spot refund abroad in full for account holders once a Natwest branch or corresponding bank has telexed the issuing branch in the U.K. and confirmed your bonafides. Non-account holders must wait while investigations are made. Whether or not you are liable for cheques cashed by the thief in the time before notification is put through is up to the discretion of your branch manager. Usually, in practice a known customer is not held liable.

*Barclays*: yes, on-the-spot refunds in full the moment any branch or agent has been told of the loss by you and telexed the issuing branch in the U.K. for authorization. It'll probably take a few hours — but if you can give evidence of purchase (the note in the back of your passport) you'll be allowed up to the equivalent of £100 ($250 in Barclay's U.S. currency cheques) right away.

*Thomas Cook*: yes, on-the-spot refunds in full, once they have telexed, from any Cook branch or agent. You're not held liable for fraudulent cashing. Cook's issue their own cheques in U.S., Canadian, Australian and Hong Kong dollars, West German marks, French and Swiss francs, Spanish pesetas and Japanese yen — on the same terms.

*Your own bank*: ask your bank manager when you order cheques whether you can expect immediate on-the-spot replacement if you lose them. If not, find a bank that will do so. Ring ABTA, (01-580 8281) for the latest list of banks that offer that service. Otherwise, the Banking Information Service, 10 Lombard Street, London EC1 (01-626 8486) will tell you what the current practice of different banks is, but they don't make *Which?*-type comparisons.

Now you realize travellers cheques aren't the bundle of instant security you thought, consider the alternative. You could take cash and insure against its loss. Rates of insuring cash vary but are probably around 50p per £100. Banks usually charge 1% for issuing travellers cheques, i.e. £1 per £100. You also pay the cashing bank a percentage everytime you cash a travellers cheque. Belgian banks regularly make a minimum charge of £2.

## Loss of money

Report your loss to the local police, and to the local British consulate.

If you have reserves of money locally you're O.K. You may have friends or relations nearby who can help out. Otherwise, you will need to call on money from the U.K. Go to a local bank and ask them to phone, telex or cable your own U.K. bank and ask them to telegraph money to you. If your bank balance is low and your bank manager refuses you will have to ask friends to put money into your account. Cabling for money and getting it through takes about a couple of days. If banks, relations and friends can't or won't help then the British consulate staff can make you a loan but don't depend on it. You can't just drop in for an advance when passing. You have to be designated a D.B.S. — a distressed British subject — and have to sign an undertaking to repay the amount plus a £3 charge. You may have to yield your passport as a security for repayment; they can issue emergency travel documents. If they pay your fare home it must be by the cheapest route. They refuse to comment on how long you're allowed to pay; most people are grateful enough to do it on return. So far no one has ever been taken to court.

**Destitute** If you are penniless while waiting for money to come through, the British consulate will apply commonsense. If you're in the back of beyond, the consul might even invite you to stay with him. In a major city he would contact one of many organizations able to help, e.g. the Salvation Army or Commonwealth Club. Each case is treated on its merits: the book of rules is there, but on-the-spot commonsense carries as much weight.

**Students** I have heard from practitioners of the jeans-and-T-shirt-plus-knapsack way of seeing the world that some British consulates are brusque and dismissive in dealing with what they see as the 'hippie' tribe. The fact remains that if you have a British passport then you have a right to ask for help. It might be advisable to tidy up a bit first, not look too dishevelled and unkempt. If you feel such a concession threatens your integrity then ask all the same.

The Consular Service in London rejected such criticism: 'Nowadays many of the Consular Service are of that same generation. There's no longer any gap.'

## Loss of tickets

**Airline tickets** Once a booking has been made, the airline's computer will have a record of it. Go to their ticket office and explain: they will be able to check if the ticket was issued. You will be required to sign an indemnity saying that you are responsible up to the value of the misplaced ticket. They will then issue a duplicate. The indemnity is their guarantee against fraud. If your ticket has been stolen then two people might turn up for the flight. If it's an overseas flight, there will be a discrepancy between the name of the stolen ticket and the name in the imposter's passport, so all will be revealed.

**Cruise tickets** Any loss after embarkation doesn't matter. But again you will have to complete a letter of indemnity against a new ticket being issued. All tickets have passengers' names on them, so any imposter would be revealed by the different name on his passport.

**British Rail** If you arrive without one, they'll ask you to pay. Explain the loss and give name and address to the ticket collector. British Rail must sue if they don't believe you. For you to have a case you must have supporting evidence: someone with you when you bought the ticket. Credit-card sales voucher is the best.

## Loss of baggage

**Air travel** If your baggage doesn't turn up on the carousel or conveyor belt, go to the lost-baggage desk. Give descriptions, and the baggage tags which are usually stapled to your ticket. They will set about tracing it. If it doesn't turn up after a good search of the airport, it will be counted as 'a temporary loss'. You can claim an amount between £20 and £25 for basic immediate necessities. In certain circumstances it could be more. If you're a businessman arriving to sign an international contract, but travelling in jeans, you could claim the cost of a decent outfit. If the bag is subsequently found, you don't have to return the money. If it isn't, then any preliminary payment is deducted from the final claim. Compensation is made at the flat I.A.T.A. rate of £11.70 per kilo. Special valuables should be covered under personal insurance (see page 174).

## Political unrest

**Before you go** If you are unsure of the political stability of the country you're going to, consult the Foreign and Commonwealth Office in London (01-233 3000). They will give you the most up-to-date news and advice they have.

**On arrival** Contact the British embassy in the country. Give them the addresses where you will be staying, your travelling route, dates and phone number. Take the embassy's phone number wherever you go. If the situation gets sticky they will phone you and suggest you leave. This is how they handled the Lebanon and Cyprus crises. It could arise any moment in Uganda.

**Which countries?** Many countries dislike us politically but need our currency (even ours). In any country behind the Iron Curtain, or anywhere at all outside Europe that doesn't have a strong British presence or connection, register your name, address and phone number at the embassy in the first twenty-four hours. Some countries, of course, have 'troubles' even while they have tourists. Portugal's tourism, for example, suffered a slump while its political life was disturbed. In fact tourists were never in any danger there.

Similarly the Republic of South Africa has well over a million people with British citizenship. The Embassy couldn't phone them all if trouble became threatening. In such cases it's up to you to read newspapers, listen to the radio (B.B.C. World Service) and stay in touch with the many British contacts — airlines, travel agencies, Salvation Army — for information on latest developments.

In a politically explosive situation keep to cities or, if you must travel, main routes. Don't get nosey or start voicing opinions. Leave as soon as possible: only stay if you have to.

The B.B.C. World Service goes everywhere twenty-four hours a day. Its musical signature is 'Oranges and Lemons'. It provides news headlines every hour on the hour seventeen or eighteen hours a day. It will take plenty of knob-twiddling to find it. Or you might tune in to Voice of America, Radio Australia or Radio South Africa. All would carry news of what they considered serious international crises.

## Travellers' tips

James Cameron, in remote countries, always makes a point of calling on the consulate: 'Unless people occasionally do it, he hasn't got a job at all.' Businessmen and holiday-makers on their own should make contact in case of illness or accident.

In political upheavals, the greatest risk you run is the risk of being ignored. Count yourself lucky.

Jean Robertson (*Sunday Times*): 'As far as holidays are concerned, if tour operators are going in, you can reckon it's safe. But people on holiday cut themselves off, not reading papers or hearing news. If things are at all risky, keep yourself well briefed daily. And *don't* ignore the advice of tour operators or the F.C.O.'

In the 1974 Cyprus crisis some people adopted a 'we've paid so we're staying' attitude. Planes sent to fetch them came back empty. It could have been disastrous − and their own fault.

Jon Swain (*Sunday Times*), taken prisoner by gunmen in Ethiopia: 'Remember, when under extreme threat from others that you are living second by second, that even the slightest gesture of protest could provoke anger in an already excited situation. Behave, if you can, with calm and total absence of aggression.' He tells how, ordered at gunpoint from a bus by a highly volatile Ethiopian soldier he expected to be shot at any moment − in the hope of delay, he stepped slowly forward, held out his hand and introduced himself. He lived to tell the tale.

## Breaking local laws

Ignorance is no defence. But you may unwittingly break a country's driving, parking or other laws. Usually local police will be indulgent to foreigners and let you go with a caution.

If, however, you are arrested and charged then contact the British consul at once. It's a good idea to have his address and phone number with your travel documents. Otherwise it'll be listed in the telephone directory, or ask the police, a hotel reception desk, an airline office or tourist agency. The consul will put you in touch with a local lawyer. You will have to face the legal costs yourself, so ask him what are the financial implications for you of what he's doing.

All British embassies and consulates have a duty officer always on call throughout the weekend and overnight.

## Flight problems

**Flights diverted** The cost of accommodating passengers and arranging for them to reach their destinations must be met by the airline. If a flight to London is diverted to say, Manchester or Glasgow, the duty officer at the arrival airport will decide what to do. Passengers would most probably be given the railway fare to London but taxis onward from the London rail terminal would be at their own expense. If a passenger had left his car parked at Heathrow he could expect to be reimbursed for a taxi to the West London Air Terminal and the coach fare to Heathrow. If passengers take a meal on the train the cost of this could be claimed back. Usually, however, no petty cash changes hands. The claims for money spent must be sent to the airline concerned − e.g. B.A. Customer

Relations, West London Air Terminal, Cromwell Road, London SW7 4ED; telephone 01-370 4255.

**Those who are waiting for you** Announcements are made in airports if an aircraft is being diverted. It may also be possible to send a personal message from your aircraft to waiting relatives, colleagues, etc. If your message is urgent ask the stewardess to ask the captain if he can radio ahead. Obviously if even as few as 20% of the passengers on a Jumbo make the same request, it's impossible to cope with. So be very scrupulous about what you consider urgent. Once landed – at the wrong destination – messages can then be transmitted more easily and quickly.

**Flight delays** In recent years there have been crises in Gatwick, Malaga, Palma and such places because of aircraft delayed by industrial action. Sit tight. Turn to the tour operator's representative for advice. Most disputes are sorted out within twelve hours.

## Car breakdown

**Abroad** You have broken down in a mountain pass, where they don't speak English and there is no garage. Contact local people and ask for the police. The police will summon garage help. If they can't or don't, you can phone the British consulate for advice. Give fullest possible details. In an extreme case they will ring a garage for you, or contact the police and tell them what's happening.

**In Britain** In minor emergencies, call for the A.A. or R.A.C. if you belong. Otherwise, walk or thumb a lift to the nearest telephone or garage.

## Pestering

### Women – by men

A woman alone attracts predatory, greedy, even violent men. It's bad around the Mediterranean, in big lonely cities. It can be a persistent nuisance in some Muslim countries where their own women are kept private and inaccessible, so they regard western dress and freedom as an open invitation. You can either:

1 Avoid the situation: don't go out at night. Ask for a table facing the wall in a restaurant, and take a book with you.

2 Chum up with others: other itinerant women will have the same problem. You might spot a friendly family you could join for a drink or meal.

3 Swear loud and clear: in your own language or theirs. Public places best; takes nerve – usually effective.

4 Complain to the police – but they're male too.

5 Carry ammunition: they do in movies. Suggestions include hatpins and a drum of pepper.

## Rich – by poor

The world has its beggars: the worst areas are in Bombay – some 150,000 live and die on the pavement. Currently the State government are trying to clear up the problem with temporary housing.

And in Morocco you'll be pestered by flocks of children, many asking to be adopted. You'll be mobbed if you picnic in the country and you can't even expect enough privacy to spend a penny.

In response, make clear your attitude. Either refuse, or pay what small change you can and make it clear that's all. Any shilly-shallying and you'll never be left alone.

## Death

If someone dies abroad, the official world moves into action. The travel courier, hotel or police will contact the nearest British consul. He telexes or phones to the Foreign and Commonwealth Office in London. Whatever the hour of day or night the F.C.O. will inform the next-of-kin named in the deceased's passport. For dealing with the body there are specialist operators in the U.K. Kenyon Air Transport are *the* experts, 12 Chiltern Street, London; or Thomas Cook.

The Foreign and Commonwealth Office will set the machinery in motion, but they cannot fund any transaction. The U.K. undertakers will, therefore, set out their terms. Bringing a body back for burial is very costly. Spain to London costs from £970 to £1,020 as far as Heathrow. This money must be made immediately available in full. (The next stage of the journey – from Heathrow onwards – does not have to be funded in advance.)

Certain countries – for example, in Africa – insist on burial within a certain number of hours, to comply with local health laws. Decisions must, therefore, be made at once. Local undertakers are then instructed to prepare the body – usually embalmed in a hermetically sealed metallic container – and all documentation for the airfreight flight home. Cost goes by weight. Some routes, e.g. the North Atlantic, have a 100% surcharge on dead bodies, and a 200% surcharge on cremated remains. Out of suffering comes forth profit. Nevertheless, airfreight can still be cheaper than surface. If the U.K. undertaker suggests the body *must* be landed at Heathrow and then trucked onwards – you're being done. It's possible to fly a body to other U.K. destinations. 90% of bereaved want the remains brought home. It's very costly.

## Local burial

The alternative is local burial. Kenyons will organize this from London.

They will be able to negotiate with foreign undertakers and keep costs within bounds. For this they charge a service fee. In any area that has a Christian community, a Christian service can be arranged; in Europe and North America this is obviously quite simple. But in some countries the final resting place might not be yours for ever — for example, in Switzerland and Spain, space for the coffin is rented and when the rental expires the bones are moved to a communal charnel-house. Check. Burial is not so easy along the African coast of the Mediterranean: but Muslim cemeteries where they exist, treat the Christian tradition with respect. Kenyons have even organized a funeral in Kabul, and arranged for a memorial to be sent out and set up.

## Cremation

This is much less common in Roman Catholic countries: Spain has only one crematorium; Portugal still has none. It's unheard of in Muslim countries. In China and Japan it's more common than burial. In India it's practised but arrangements can be a little primitive. Ashes can be either scattered locally or airfreighted home. It's obviously cheaper than bringing a body.

Personally, I rather fancy some corner of a foreign field; perhaps the Anglican cemetery in Rome along with Shelley and Keats.

## Burial at sea

If someone dies on a sea voyage, the ship can deal with it. They have all the gear; the captain has the authority to conduct a burial. Funerals are usually conducted in the middle of the night. The ship stops, the engines turn off, until the ceremony is completed. There's an eery stillness until it's over and the journey is resumed.

## Personal crisis or tragedy

The Salvation Army will give you practical help and, if required, spiritual support. They operate in the following eighty-two countries; their number will be in the local phone book:

| | | | |
|---|---|---|---|
| Antigua | Chile | Guyana | Malaysia |
| Argentina | Congo | Haiti | Malta |
| Australia | Costa Rica | Hong Kong | Mexico |
| Austria | Cuba | Iceland | Mozambique |
| Bahamas | Curaçao | India | Netherlands |
| Bangladesh | Denmark | Indonesia | New Zealand |
| Barbados | Eire | Ireland | Nigeria |
| Belgium | Faroe Islands | Italy | Norway |
| Belize | Fiji | Jamaica | Pakistan |
| Bermuda | Finland | Japan | Panama |
| Bolivia | France | Kenya | Papua New Guinea |
| Brazil | Germany | Korea | Paraguay |
| Burma | Ghana | Lesotho | Perú |
| Canada | Grenada | Malawi | Philippines |

T.C.T.—T

| Portugal | South Africa | Tanzania | United States of |
| Puerto Rico | Spain | Trinidad and | America |
| Rhodesia | Sri Lanka | Tobago | Uruguay |
| St. Helena | Surinam | Uganda | Venezuela |
| St. Kitts | Swaziland | United Kingdom: | Virgin Islands |
| St. Lucia | Sweden | England, | (U.S.A.) |
| St. Vincent | Switzerland | Scotland, Wales, | Zaïre |
| Singapore | Taiwan | N. Ireland | Zambia |

# Chapter 43
# Rights and Wrongs

The law provides a system for the redressing of grievances. The grievances that may afflict the traveller can vary in seriousness from a poor meal where a good one was expected, to the burning down of a foreign hotel involving loss of property, personal injury, inconvenience, delay and general large-scale distress. In all cases, redress will depend on the legal relationship between yourself and those against whom you have a grievance. In most consumer problems the relationship will be in the nature of a contract: whenever you buy anything — goods or services — the relationship between buyer and seller is that of a contract.

What you want to know when something goes wrong is who is legally to blame. The answer is: whoever broke the contract. But in the travel business there may be problems in establishing who broke the contract.

## The independent traveller abroad

If you buy travel service abroad, independently of any tour operator, you have a separate contract with each hotelier, restaurateur, local transport company, car-hire firm, taxi owner, etc. Therefore, you depend entirely on the laws of the country in which you made the contract for redress of any grievance. U.K. law offers you a strong case against a hotel that promised you first-class accommodation and turned out to be fly-blown and filthy — but you would be reckless to take to court a one-star hotel in downtown Delhi because there wasn't hot and cold water when you expected it. You would be operating in a legal system not highly keyed to consumer protection and the finer points of product satisfaction. The most you could do would be to complain strongly at the time, and try to insist the hotel supplied the services it claimed to, or move.

The degree to which local laws offer you redress varies from country to country. On the whole the more developed a country, the more legal protection it will offer its citizens and visitors. You won't know what your legal rights are. Basically it is better abroad to resolve a grievance by other than legal means if possible: e.g. change hotels, hire cars, etc. But if you have a very strong grievance – e.g. personal injury – then consult either the local office of a British or American travel agent, or the nearest British consulate. They will tell you if it is worth hiring a local lawyer to fight a case for you. It may, and probably will, cost you a tidy sum, and there's no holiday insurance to cover that! Worst of all there will not be enough time before you move on to pursue a grievance. So the outfit responsible can snap its fingers at you and there's little you can really do about it.

## Package tours

When you buy a package holiday, whether one generally on offer in a brochure, or one specifically tailored to your needs, you enter into a contract with the tour operator. The deal is: you pay him a lump sum, he arranges all the components of the package. If something goes wrong, the sole person with whom you have the contract is the tour operator. It is him you should pursue.

Tour operators, however, have devised various ways of restricting total liability. These are enshrined in the booking conditions, by which a tour operator limits – he would say 'defines' – his liability.

Some operators – not all – declare in their booking conditions that they act *merely as agents* for hotels, airlines, etc. This means that your contract is not with the operator but with each provider of part of the holiday individually. The operator will insist, therefore, that any grievance of yours against, for example, a hotel should be taken up with it directly. This complicates the matter of who you can legally blame. It is very doubtful whether this works legally – so generally you are best advised to hold the tour operator liable.

However, many tour operators do not include this clause and it has never been tested in law. The Consumers' Association believes that if your package holiday went wrong, and you sought redress in court, the tour operator could not shrug off his obligations by having such a clause in the booking conditions.

The Association of British Travel Agents has drawn up a Code of Conduct, agreed with the Office of Fair Trading, giving guidance to A.B.T.A.'s members. A code of practice merely offers guidelines to the trade; it does not have the force of law. However, it states that booking conditions shall not exclude 'the tour operator's contractual duty to exercise diligence in making arrangements for his clients'. Thus he is obliged 'to exercise diligence in making arrangements' — but what if all his diligence comes to nought and the arrangements for which you paid still fall through? Such an issue has not been tested in court.

## Doctrine of fundamental breach

This is your great defence. If the package for which you pay is *substantially* different from what you thought you were buying then there has been a fundamental breach of contract. This is likely to outweigh all protests of diligence from the tour operator. The fact is you purchased A, and were given B. In cases of significant failure to provide what was promised it is likely that any court would uphold such a complaint.

A law, only recently come into effect, tightens up your legal rights: it's called the *Unfair Contract Terms Act (1977)*. In time this will supercede the doctrine of fundamental breach in consumer cases. Basically the Act says that a company or trader cannot in satisfaction of a contract provide something *quite different* from what it offered or promised. This will cover matters such as car hire, caravan rental, the changing of resorts on package tours, etc. It also says that the trade can never exclude liability for causing death or personal injury by negligence, and any other exclusion clause is only effective if proved to be fair and reasonable.

## Restrictive Trade Practices Act

Since September 1976 this has applied to services as well as goods. The Office of Fair Trading is implementing the provisions that outlaw restrictive practices. In the travel trade it was once the case that A.B.T.A. laid down certain rules which travel agents agreed to observe — e.g. no one discounted the brochure prices of holidays, and A.B.T.A. laid down a scale of cancellation payments. These are now considered restrictive practices, and so have ceased to operate. The travel business as a consequence, has become far more competitive. Cut-price packages sprouted during summer 1976 and it will go on. The previously agreed A.B.T.A. scale of cancellation charges can now be challenged. The amount of deposit required is now up to the individual trader. It is open to negotiation.

## Railways in the U.K.

When you buy a ticket you are legally entering into a contract. The contractual obligations of B.R. are set out in its bylaws. Any railway station should be able to show you a copy on request. The bylaws set out what B.R. are obliged to do — and all the things they are not obliged to do. They're under no obligation to get you to your ticket's destination by a certain time, or to guarantee you a seat. There's no obligation to feed you, warm you or protect you, and so on.

If you feel you have a legitimate grievance check it out with the bylaws, because they are the legal conditions you unwittingly accepted when you bought a ticket. Again the consumer's defence would be the doctrine of the fundamental breach or the Unfair Contract Terms Act.

## Airlines

Members of I.A.T.A. meet from time to time as necessary to discuss fares and ticket conditions. Their recommendations are sent to government for approval. If and when approval is obtained these fares and conditions become official.

**Accidents** The liability of airlines in case of accidents is determined by the Warsaw Convention, which sets out the top limit of any claim, both for passengers and baggage.

U.S. law does not acknowledge the Warsaw Convention. In claims made by passengers to and from America, in American courts, the limits of liability are higher. The claimants in the 1974 DC10 disaster are circumventing all liability through contract between passenger and operator and are suing the manufacturer of the plane for negligent design. Unlike in the U.K., the idea that a manufacturer is responsible for his products after they have been sold is a legal doctrine in the U.S.A.

**Other claims** Ticket conditions set out in small print, the legal obligation the airline entered into when it sold the ticket. This will cover baggage, delays, diversions, etc.

## Loss of travel tickets

Basically all operators — railways, airlines etc. — are only liable to transport those who have a ticket. If you *can prove satisfactorily* that you had one, they will issue a substitute. They may charge for the administration, or ask for an indemnity in case two passengers turn up (see page 268).

## Eating out

The catering trade in the U.K. is controlled by the 1955 Food and Drugs Act. Certain conditions are laid down that must be met by any establishment selling food to the public: these regulations cover such things as distance of lavatories from food area, no smoking where food is prepared, facilities for washing hands etc.

If you feel you have a complaint go first to the Environmental Health Officer of the district (see local phone book, or local authority; they will direct you), who should take up the complaint for you.

## Consumer ploy

The holiday, catering and travel trade are in business to sell goods and services that give satisfaction and bring them a reasonable return. They are happiest when there are no complaints. But in the interest of their industry they often group themselves into organizations such as A.B.T.A.

The single protesting consumer can feel outmatched before he starts. After all, the sellers of travel write the booking conditions. What chance has the common man?

Read booking conditions carefully. If you disagree, question them. For example when hiring a car, you are often required to sign, saying the car was in perfect order: but you don't know. Amend the clause to read, 'On first inspection it appears to be in good order'.

Join the Consumers' Association (publishers of *Which?*), 1 Caxton Hill, Hertford SG13 7LZ; telephone Hertford 57773.

Try the ploy of 'reasonable deduction'. This applies in situations where you have not yet paid for services which have been seriously below the standard you were entitled to expect. Here you can take the initiative. You stay in what claims to be a slap-up hotel and have had truly awful service. But you haven't paid. The ball is in your court. Calculate a reasonable deduction and explain to the manager why you will not pay in full. They will be amazed at first, then bewildered, then furious; they will assume you are a crook or a nut. You must remain polite, calm and firm. Put your case in writing (keep a copy), then and there, if they insist. Invite them to sue you.

Have your luggage already locked away in your car and outside the hotel, otherwise they may attempt to detain it until you pay (that's their legal right). If they do, pay under protest, retaining the right to claim back later by legal proceedings.

*Be reasonable*: your complaint must be specific. And the service supplied must be *significantly worse* than you might reasonably expect. It would be grotesque and unreasonable to deduct from a restaurant bill because the chef had an off night and the food was a little below par. But if you were served food that was unquestionably 'off' you should not pay. But you shouldn't eat it either!

## Pity the poor trader

Providers of goods and services sometimes complain that consumerism has got out of hand. Certainly sometimes people 'try it on' — complaining unreasonably, creating grievances in the hope of getting money back. Some purchasers of package tours have been known to drop cigarette butts under the bed on arrival, in order to complain they were still there at the end of the stay. Others diligently photograph every crack in the plaster, fly on the wall or piece of fluff on the floor. Tour operators aren't fools. You may do it once, and successfully. But if you've really taken them for a ride once, they'll be inclined to remember your name! So lay off — you're queering the pitch for legitimate and reasonable complaints.

## How to make a claim

Look up 'Courts' in the phone book. You should bring a case in the County Court that serves the district in which the person you're claiming against operates, or where the booking was made, whichever you prefer.

Ask for the free booklet, *Small Claims in the County Court* (they'll ask for an s.a.e.) and for a Request Form.

With the help of the booklet fill in the Request Form. Write out in your own words what happened and what amount you claim. Don't try to be legalistic or argumentative: simple facts only. There must be three copies. Take them and a fee (usually 10% of what you're claiming — you get it back if you win) to the County Court. They will serve the claim to the other side for you. There is a good chance that the other side will make a fair offer as soon as they get the summons. If not, they have to put in their defence. There will then be a pre-trial review. Ultimately the case will probably go to arbitration under the small claims procedure in the County Court.

# Part 7

# Coming Home

# Chapter 44
# How to Handle British Customs

## Start before you arrive

Pass the time on train, plane or ferry listing all the things you've bought abroad.

Pack the articles so they are accessible. You may have to show them. Customs are not responsible for loss or damage to baggage at the time of customs examination or afterwards. And they don't have to repack the cases: you have to!

Look out the receipts you should be carrying for new-looking watches, cameras, binoculars and furs which you actually purchased in Britain, or receipts from previous payments of customs charges on goods you are carrying.

Check over the list of goods you're allowed to take in without paying U.K. excise or import duty or V.A.T.: duty and tax-free/paid allowances (known simply as duty-frees to most of us). There are two separate lists of these allowances. The first covers goods bought in a shop in an E.E.C. country on which you have paid V.A.T. and/or duty to that country. The second covers goods bought anywhere else.

## Duty and tax-free/paid allowances Group I: from the E.E.C.

To remind you, the nine E.E.C. countries are: Belgium, Denmark, France, German Federal Republic, Irish Republic, Italy, Luxembourg, the Netherlands and the U.K. *Note*: the Channel Islands are regarded as being outside the E.E.C. You are allowed to bring in *more* duty-frees from the E.E.C. than from outside it, *but* only if you bought them in an ordinary shop (not an airport duty-free shop or on a ship or aircraft) and paid local V.A.T. and/or duty on them (some goods may have a zero rate of duty but be liable for V.A.T.).

*Tobacco*: 300 cigarettes *or* 150 cigarillos *or* 75 cigars *or* 400g (14 oz) of tobacco.

*Alcohol*:       EITHER   1¹/2 litres (52.8 U.K. fl oz) over 38.8° proof (22.2% alcohol) (whisky, gin, rum, brandy, vodka and most liqueurs will be over 38.8°. But advocaat, cassis, fraise and suze may be less. The label on the bottle should tell you.

OR   3 litres of fortified wine under 38.8° proof (this covers port, sherry, vermouth, madeira and aperitifs)

OR   3 litres of sparkling wine (such as champagne and spumante)

*N.B.* These 3 litres are *alternatives* to the spirits, *not in addition*.

PLUS   3 litres of still table wine (claret, sauternes, graves and chianti, Burgundy, hock and Moselle are usually still — some are sparkling and in that case would be *alternatives* to the spirit allowance)

*Persons under seventeen*: don't have a tobacco and drinks allowance.

*Perfume*: 75g (3 fl oz or 99 cc).

*Toilet water*: 375 cc (13 fl oz).

*Other goods*: up to a value of £50: yes, even a camera or a watch may be imported duty and tax-free as long as the receipt says it cost less than £50.

## Duty and tax-free/paid allowances Group II: from outside the E.E.C.

This means the rest of the world, including Gibraltar, Malta, Hong Kong, the Channel Islands, everywhere.

*Tobacco*:       *British residents*: 200 cigarettes *or* 100 cigarillos *or* 50 cigars *or* 250g (9 oz) tobacco.

*If you live outside Europe and are entering Britain*: 400 cigarettes *or* 200 cigarillos *or* 100 cigars *or* 500g (18 oz) tobacco.

*Alcohol*:       EITHER   1 litre (35 U.K. fl oz or 1³/4 pints) over 38.8° proof (22.2% alcohol)

OR   2 litres of fortified wine, under 38.8° proof

OR   2 litres of sparkling wine

PLUS   2 litres of still table wine

*Perfume*: 50g (2 fl oz or 60 cc).

*Toilet water*: 250 cc (9 fl oz)

*Other goods*: up to a value of £10.

*Note*: within the alcohol and tobacco categories you can mix the goods: e.g. 150 cigarettes plus 75 cigarillos.

*Reductions*: there are reduced allowances for certain people crossing the Irish land boundary, to seamen and aircrew members! It might pay to have friends!

*Visitors* to the U.K. for less than six months are allowed to bring in all their personal effects, including their car, as long as they intend to take them out again.

## You can't bring in

### Controlled drugs

This means such drugs as opium, heroin, morphine, cocaine, cannabis, amphetamines (including benzedrine) and L.S.D. Anonymous parcels carried for friends are also your responsibility if they turn out to be full of dope.

### Horror comics, indecent and obscene books, magazines, films and other articles

You may call it indoor sport or psychotherapy but if the customs officer thinks it contravenes Section 42 of the Customs Consolidation Act 1876, i.e. if it appears to be an indecent and obscene article, he has the right to seize it (it is on the basis of previous decisions by courts that he may consider an article indecent or obscene). If he does seize it, you have, as with any other article seized by a customs officer, thirty days in which to claim that your goods are not liable to seizure. H.M. Customs and Excise *must* then take proceedings in court to have the article condemned as indecent and obscene. The hearing is by a magistrates' court whose decision is final. You *cannot* ask for a jury trial and bring witnesses to testify to the merit of the work concerned.

### Counterfeit coins

### Flick-knives

### Explosives, including fireworks

### Gas pistols and aerosol tear-gas sprays

## You can bring in – on conditions

Plants and bulbs; firearms and ammunition; radio transmitters, including walkie-talkie sets; most live animals and birds; items derived from rare species of animals; uncooked and partially cooked meat and poultry; gold coins.

### Flower people

If your hobby is your garden and you like to bring plants back from places you visit you must observe certain regulations. All cut, dried or pressed flowers, and all flower seeds can be brought through customs with no problems. But different rules apply for wild and cultivated plants.

**Wild flowers and plants:** write to the Plant Health Branch of the Ministry of Agriculture, Fisheries and Food, Great Westminster House, Horseferry Road, London SW1P 2AE. Apply for a licence saying where and when you will be bringing in wild flowers. The Plant Health Branch will then issue a licence requiring that you notify them when you are back and hold the plants for at least twenty-one days for inspection. Only spot checks are made, so you may hear nothing more from them. If they do inspect, there is no charge.

Additionally, certain species of wild plants also need to be imported under a licence issued by the Department of the Environment. The granting of such a licence does not obviate the necessity of obtaining a licence from the Plant Health Branch where this is required.

**Cultivated plants:** you may want to buy bulbs on a trip to Holland. In such a case the plant must be inspected by a plant health officer in the country of purchase. You'll find them through the local nursery or the country's ministry of agriculture. They will issue a Phyto-Sanitary Certificate which you hand to customs on arrival. Many vegetables will also require a Phyto-Sanitary Certificate issued by the country of origin.

## Firearms and ammunition

Anyone can buy a gun in America. But you couldn't bring it through customs unless you could offer proof that you already had a licence to hold firearms. Incidentally, if you are a genuine collector, declare so at once. Any guns that come to light in airport searches will be held. So will you. I once saw a child's plastic machine-gun confiscated.

## Walkie-talkie sets

There are import prohibitions on walkie-talkies (including radio microphones and microbugs) operating on frequencies between 26.1 and 29.7 MHz and 88 and 108 MHz. These are not allowed in unless Home Office authority to import, and licence to operate, is obtained.

## Live animals

You can take your pet with you on holiday. It wouldn't be worth it for two weeks, but for a much longer stay or tour you might want to.

You'll need an export licence to take your pet out of the country, and most countries require a veterinary health certificate before allowing an animal in; get one, if necessary, before you apply for an export licence and send it in with your application. Make your application to either The

Secretary, Ministry of Agriculture, Fisheries and Food, Government Buildings, Hook Rise South, Tolworth, Surbiton, Surrey KT6 7NF; telephone 01-337 6611, or to The Secretary, Department of Agriculture and Fisheries for Scotland, Chesser House, 500 Gorgie Road, Edinburgh EH11 3AW; telephone 031-443 4020, if you live in Scotland.

You should also take steps before setting out that will make quarantine arrangements on return run smoothly. If you are coming into the country by air you'll need a red 'rabies control' label and boarding document; if you are coming by sea, you'll only need the boarding document. Write to M.A.F.F. in Tolworth, or to the Department of Agriculture and Fisheries for Scotland in Edinburgh if the animal is to be quarantined in Scotland, and they will send you the necessary forms and a list of quarantine stations in the U.K. These are private establishments licensed by the Ministry as being up to required quarantine standards. There are some sixty in all. Choose one that suits you for price and location and arrange with them to have someone to collect your animal at point of entry. You can't take the animal to quarantine yourself, there must be an 'authorized carrier'. This authorized person takes the animal to the quarantine station where it stays for six months. Costs vary with size; small cats and dogs about £5 a week, big dogs around £10.

There are only six ports and eight airports at present authorized as landing points for rabies susceptible animals. These are:

*Ports*: Dover; Eastern Docks, Harwich; Navy Yard Wharf, Hull; Liverpool; International Hoverport (Pegwell Bay), Ramsgate; and Southampton.

*Airports*: Birmingham; Edinburgh; Gatwick; Glasgow; Heathrow; Leeds; Manchester; and Prestwick.

Slightly different systems apply to mice, rabbits, parrots, etc; contact either of the above addresses for information.

*Warning*: It is very unwise to buy birds abroad; they may carry psittacosis (ornithosis). It can kill — you *and* them.

The penalties for landing an animal in Great Britain without a licence are severe and at the moment (1977) the maximum penalty is an unlimited fine and/or up to one year's imprisonment. There are *no* exceptions to the rules.

If you are applying to bring in an animal from abroad allow plenty of time — at least six weeks.

All this is only necessary if you're going, or coming in from, outside the British Isles; there is free movement of animals within the U.K., including N. Ireland, the Republic of Ireland, the Channel Islands, Isle of Man, etc.

## Items derived from rare animals

Certain items, including fur skins (and garments made from fur skins) and plumage are subject to conservation restrictions. Check with Customs and Excise, Kings Beam House, Mark Lane, London EC3; telephone 01-626 1515, if you think you might contravene the restrictions.

## Uncooked or partially cooked meat and poultry

These are subject to import licensing. If you are thinking of bringing any in, contact Customs and Excise (address and number above) for details as to what restrictions apply to imports from which countries.

## Gold coins

If you're bringing in one or two gold coins as souvenirs declare them on entry as personal effects (go through the red channel). Whether or not they will be allowed into this country is up to the customs officer's discretion.

# Gazetteer

# Gazetteer

*Population*: the figures given are estimates of population in July 1975 — the latest date for which a worldwide comparison was available.

*Visas*: the information under this heading relates only to citizens of the U.K. and Commonwealth. Nationals of other countries may find that they need to have a visa where U.K. citizens do not, and vice versa. If you are not a U.K. citizen, contact the Consulate or Consular Section of the Embassy of the country you want to visit and find out what they require.

*Jabs*: requirements for vaccinations change very little but occasionally there are outbreaks of infection (usually cholera) in countries that were previously clear. Airlines, travel agents and tour operators always have up to the minute information on vaccination requirements.

*Time*: the approximate period during which Daylight Saving Time is used is given for countries which adopted it in 1977. Precise starting and finishing dates vary from year to year. They are given at the beginning of volume 1 of the *A.B.C. World Airways Guide*.

*Reference books*: for convenience the standard guide books to individual countries and regions of the world are all listed in the bibliography. A few particularly interesting books on specific countries are mentioned in the Gazetteer.

## Afghanistan

*Area:* About 647,000 km² (about 250,000 square miles).
*Capital:* Kabul.
*Population:* 19,280,000. 50% Pathans, several nomadic minorities.
*Occupation:* Agriculture, animal husbandry.
*Climate:* Varied. Kabul (at 1,830 m, 6,000 feet) minimum −25 °C (13 °F). July/August maximum 32 °C (90 °F). Summer temperatures in lowlands reach a maximum of 50 °C (122 °F). Generally dry, rainy season March to May. Occasional snow December to March. Extreme mountain areas uninhabitable.
*Measures:* Metric.
*Electricity:* 220 V a.c. Plugs: Continental two-pin. Electricity not reliable in rural areas.
*Transport:* One airport: Kabul. One direct flight a week from London by Ariana Afghan Airlines. Alternatively connections at Beirut, Tehran, Moscow. No railways. Buses connect principal towns. Petrol stations rare. Cars: third-party insurance compulsory − get it at the border. Bicycles can be hired from Kabul hotels.
*Currency:* Afghani = 100 puls. Not more than 500 Afghanis may be taken in or out.
*Religion:* Muslim.
*Visa:* Yes. Tourist visa for thirty days issued at London embassy or at Kabul or Kandahar airports for U.S. $5. Can be extended but you then need an exit permit. Embassy at 31 Prince's Gate London SW7 1QQ; telephone 01-589 8891.
*Jabs:* Smallpox, cholera, typhoid. Take anti-malaria precautions. Boil drinking water; wash fruit.
*Language:* Dari (a dialect of Persian) or Pushtu. Most educated Afghans speak English, French or German. Interpreters from Afghan Tourist Organization.
*Time:* G.M.T. + 4½.
*Hotels:* Top-flight hotel: Kabul Inter-Continental. Carvan hotel in Shar-i-Nao area of Kabul does six to a room − a money-saver for young people. Cheapish hotels in downtown Kabul: hippie clientele.
*Shop hours:* 08.00 to 18.00 Saturday to Thursday. No business Thursday afternoon or all Friday.
*British Embassy:* Karte Parwan, Kabul; telephone 30511/12/13.
*Tourist Office:* Afghan Tourist Organization, 3 Carlisle Avenue, London EC3; telephone 01-480 6524.

## Albania

*Area:* 28,748 km² (11,100 square miles).
*Capital:* Tirana.
*Population:* 2,482,000.
*Occupation:* Predominantly agricultural, but increasing industrialism with aid from China. Exports: petroleum, ores, wood products, tobacco, mostly to China.
*Climate:* Temperatures from −4 to 34 °C (25 to 93 °F). Worst time: January and February. Frequent cyclones in winter.
*Measures:* Metric.
*Transport:* Airlines: Matév (Hungarian) or Jugoslavenski Aerotransport from Belgrade. Rinas Airport. No internal flights. Many shipping lines. New, modern railways (302 km) linking main towns and many branch lines. Very few cars (end 1976), mostly official. Bicycles and mules. Roads not very good as yet, city links O.K.
*Currency:* lek = 100 quintars. Local currency may not be imported or exported.
*Religion:* 70% Muslim. Others: R.C. and Greek Orthodox.
*Visa:* Yes: only issued for groups of ten or more. People of unkempt appearance refused entry.
*Jabs:* Smallpox.
*Language:* Albanian. The Tosk dialect is the official standard. Geg dialect spoken in north.
*Time:* G.M.T. + 1 (+ 2 May to September).
*British Embassy:* U.K. has not had diplomatic relations with Albania since 1946.
*Tourist Office:* Albturist, Bld. Dëshmorët e Kombit 8, Tirana.

## Algeria

*Area:* 2,381,741 km² (919,594 square miles). Mainly desert and mountains. 80-km (50-mile) wide fertile belt along coast.
*Capital:* Algiers.
*Population:* 16,776,000.
*Occupation:* Agriculture and cattle. Oil and natural-gas production, food processing.
*Climate:* Coast: June to September warm and humid: 27 to 32 °C (81 to 90 °F). Otherwise 13 to 24 °C (55 to 71°F). Southern desert: maximum in summer 43 °C (109 °F) (day), minimum 10 °C (50 °F) (night). Rain: October to May, heaviest November to February.
*Measures:* Metric.
*Electricity:* 127 or 220 V a.c.
*Transport:* Main airport Algiers. Air Algeria flights from London three times a week. Also Air France. Rail connection with Morocco and Tunisia. Railways link main towns. Good state-run bus service. Motorists would do well if in

desert to fit special 'Sahara' tyres and
an oil filter.
*Currency:* Algerian dinar = 100 centimes.
You may take 50 dinars in or out.
*Religion:* Islam. Also some Christians and
Jews.
*Visa:* No.
*Jabs:* Smallpox recommended. Yellow
fever and/or cholera if arriving from
infected areas. Don't drink tap-water.
*Language:* Official: Arabic. Business:
French.
*Time:* G.M.T. until 1 October 1977. Then
G.M.T. + 1 (+ 2 May to September).
*Hotels:* European-style in resorts and big
cities.
*Bank Hours:* Winter: 07.45 to 11.50 and
14.15 to 17.00 Monday to Friday.
Summer: 07.15 to 11.00 and 15.00 to
17.30 Monday to Friday.
*British Embassy:* Résidence Cassiopée,
Bâtiment B, 7 chemin des Glycines,
(B.P.43), Algiers; telephone 605601/4.
*Reference Book:* Booklet from Algerian
National Tourist Office, with map.
*Tourist Office:* Algerian National Tourist
Office, 35 St. James's Street, London
SW1; telephone 01-839 5315/8.

## Andorra

*Area:* 453 km² (175 square miles).
*Capital:* Andorra la Vella.
*Population:* 27,000.
*Occupation:* Tourism, agriculture (tobacco,
potatoes).
*Climate:* Alpine: cold winters with a lot of
snow; warm summers.
*Measures:* Metric.
*Transport:* Good road connects French
and Spanish frontiers. Bus service
from Andorra la Vella to Barcelona and
to Perpignan.
*Currency:* French and Spanish.
Restrictions as for France and Spain as
appropriate.
*Religion:* Roman Catholic.
*Visa:* No.
*Jabs:* No.
*Language:* Catalan. French and Spanish
also widely spoken.
*Time:* G.M.T. + 1 (+ 2 April to
September).
*British Consulate-General:* Edificio Torre
de Barcelona, Avenida Generalisimo
Franco 477, (P.O. Box 12111),
Barcelona 11, Spain; telephone
2591601/2391300.
*Tourist Office:* Sindicat d'Initiativa de les
valls d'Andorra, 63 Westover Road,
London SW18 2RF.

## Angola

*Area:* 1,246,700 km² (481,353 square
miles). Low coastal belt rising to
interior plateau up to 1,800 m (6,000
feet).
*Capital:* Luanda.

*Population:* 6,761,000.
*Occupation:* Coffee production, iron and
diamond exports, increasing petroleum
production; also livestock, tobacco,
cotton, sugar, cocoa.
*Climate:* Tropical in north, temperate and
dry in south. Luanda: December to
April hot and humid. June to August,
hot with cool evenings. Rainfall:
torrential in northern mountains.
*Electricity:* 220 V a.c. Plugs: two round
pins.
*Transport:* One major international airport:
Luanda. No direct flights from London.
Airlines: T.A.P., Alitalia, U.T.A.,
Aeroflot. Railways connect main
towns. Extensive all-weather roads,
only limited number are ashphalted.
*Currency:* Kwanza = 100 centavos. Local
currency may not be taken in or out.
*Religion:* Christianity and traditional.
*Visa:* Yes (very difficult to obtain).
*Jabs:* Smallpox, yellow fever.
*Language:* Portuguese, Spanish, French,
very little English.
*Time:* G.M.T. + 1.
*Hotels:* Now only one in Luanda, the
Panorama.
*Bank Hours:* Banking services not
operating in mid-1977.
*British Consulate-General:* Luanda:
telephone 22487 or 34583. There is
only a local employee there at present
(mid-1977) as diplomatic relations have
not yet been established.

## Argentina

*Area:* 2,766,889 km² (1,068,300 square
miles). The eighth largest country in
the world. 4,000 km (2,500 miles) of
coastline. 3,700 km (2,300 miles) from
north to south. 1,450 km (900 miles)
wide.
*Capital:* Buenos Aires.
*Population:* 25,383,000. 75% urban. Large
European population.
*Occupation:* Producing vegetable and
animal products, and livestock.
*Climate:* Great variations. Buenos Aires
reaches 37 °C (98 °F) in summer
(December to February). Subtropical in
north. Temperate centre. Sub-antarctic
in south. Rain in central populous area
throughout the year.
*Measures:* Metric.
*Electricity:* 220 V a.c.
*Transport:* Main airport, Ezeiza, 22 miles
from Buenos Aires by motorway.
Airlines: British Caledonian and
Aerolineas Argentinas direct from
London. Airport tax on departing
international flights. Domestic flights
from Jorge Newbury airport (usually
called 'Aeroparque'). Rail network
covers interior. Bus services between
Buenos Aires and most towns in
interior. 43,000 km railways being
reorganized. 140,000 km roads: 25,000

km excellent, 25,000 km O.K., rest not
so good. Drive on right.
*Currency:* Peso = 100 centavos. Old and
new currencies both circulate. 10 old
pesos = 10 new centavos. No
restrictions on import or export.
*Religion:* 95% R.C.
*Visa:* No.
*Jabs:* Smallpox.
*Language:* Spanish: interpreters through
hotels and newspapers. Little official
English.
*Time:* G.M.T. − 3.
*Hotels:* Large European and American
chains — 5 star. Cheaper hostelries:
hotels 1, 2 and 3 star. Youth hostels
(spartan) as in Britain.
*Shop Hours:* 09.00 to 19.00.
*Bank Hours:* 10.00 to 16.00.
*British Embassy:* Luis Agote 2412, (Casilla
de Coreo 2050), Buenos Aires;
telephone 807071/9.

## Australia

*Area:* 7,686,848 km² (2,967,903 square
miles). Mountains on eastern
seaboard. Desert plateau interior.
*Capital:* Canberra.
*Population:* 13,502,000. 99% European.
Increasing at 1.2% per annum. Over
60% in New South Wales and Victoria.
Sydney 2.7 million. Melbourne 2.4
million.
*Occupation:* Mining, meat and animal
products, coal, sugar, machinery,
chemicals, fruit, wheat.
*Climate:* Great variation. Perth, Adelaide,
Canberra up to 38 °C (100 °F) in
summer (December to February). Dry.
Sydney and Brisbane have humid
subtropical summers. Interior: very
hot, very dry, Can fall below freezing at
night. Rainfall: generally light. Heaviest
in south and east.
*Measures:* Metric. Australian clothing
sizes: English or American system.
Socks, stockings, gloves, shoes, hats —
the same as English. All others metric.
*Electricity:* 220/240 V a.c. 50 Hz. Outlets for
110 V also supplied in leading hotels.
Plugs: flat three-pin of unique design.
Two-point pins set at 43° angle. Move
to get new plugs.
*Transport:* Five international airports. B.A.
and Qantas make daily flights to and
from London. Rail links between all
major cities, but rail travel is slow:
Perth to Adelaide 45 hours. Interstate
air travel more convenient. Regular
air-conditioned coach services between
major cities.
*Currency:* Australian dollar = 100 cents.
You may take out 250 dollars.
*Religion:* All denominations represented.
*Visa:* Yes. Can't work on a tourist visa. If
staying over six months, need Reserve
Bank of Australia authority to take

money out. Immigrants must be of
sound health and able to support
themselves.
*Jabs:* Smallpox. If travelling via Asia,
cholera. Check on others.
*Language:* English: 'Strine'.
*Time:* Western Australia G.M.T. + 8;
South Australia and Northern Territory
G.M.T. + 9½; remainder G.M.T. + 10.
But from November to March the
following states adopt Daylight Saving
Time: South Australia (G.M.T. + 10½),
New South Wales, Victoria and
Tasmania (all G.M.T. + 11).
*Hotels:* Modern hotels and motels, and
small private hotels. Always book
ahead for Sydney — also for Adelaide
during Arts Festival (March),
Melbourne during November races,
Perth late September and October.
*Shop Hours:* 09.00 to 17.00, Monday to
Friday. 09.00 to 12.00 Saturday. One
late night (Thursday or Friday) to 21.00
in major cities. Post offices shut at
weekend.
*Bank Hours:* 10.00 to 15.00 Monday to
Thursday. 10.00 to 17.00 Friday.
*British High Commission:* Commonwealth
Avenue, Canberra; telephone 730422.
There are British consulates-general at
Adelaide, Brisbane, Melbourne, Perth
and Sydney (see local telephone
directories).
*Reference Book:* Comprehensive book
from Australian Tourist Commission.
*Australia for Everyone* (Melbourne:
Wren, 1974).
*Tourist Office:* Australian Tourist
Commission, 4th Floor, 49 Old Bond
Street, London W1X 4PL; telephone
01-499 2247/8.

## Austria

*Area:* 83,849 km² (32,374 square miles).
Landlocked. Mountainous.
*Capital:* Vienna.
*Population:* 7,523,000.
*Occupation:* Mining metals, coal, timber,
tourism.
*Climate:* Temperate: range from −14 to 32
°C (7 to 90 °F). Snow January to March.
*Measures:* Metric.
*Electricity:* 220 V a.c.
*Transport:* Schwechat: Vienna airport. B.A.
and Austrian Airlines offer frequent
flights direct to and from London.
Railway: from London, via Ostend or
Paris. State system, 400 miles track.
Motoring: seat belts and first-aid kit
compulsory. U.K. licence accepted.
Maximum speed on overland roads
100 k.p.h. (63 m.p.h.) and on
motorways 130 k.p.h. (80 m.p.h.).
Built-up areas 55 k.p.h. (35 m.p.h.).
Drunken driving severely penalized:
AS 5,000 fine and confiscation of
licence.

*Currency:* Austrian Schilling = 100 Groschen. You may take out 15,000 Schillings.

*Religion:* Mainly R.C. Some Lutheran.

*Visa:* No. Up to six months on normal passport.

*Jabs:* None: unless from infected area.

*Language:* German. Interpreters through Vienna University.

*Time:* G.M.T. + 1.

*Hotels:* International standards of hotels: high in all major cities. Tourist Board classification A1, A, B, C. Highly geared to year-round tourist industry, in cities and mountains. Farm holidays with choice of 4,000 addresses. Youth hostels in many places for members of International Y.H.A. — book in advance. Intensive camping facilities. No carnet needed for caravans. Discount rates for members of F.I.C.C., the A.I.T. and F.I.A. In Alps: 700 mountain refuges, open from spring till autumn. Total of 10,000 beds and mattress, accommodation for 20,000 more.

*Shop Hours:* Monday to Friday 08.00 to 18.00. Saturday 08.00 to 12.00.

*Bank Hours:* 08.00 to 12.30, 13.30 to 15.30 Monday to Friday. Later on Thursday.

*British Embassy:* Reisnerstrasse 40, A-1030 Vienna 3; telephone 731575/9. Consulate at Wallnerstrasse 8, A-1010 Vienna.

*Tourist Office:* Austrian National Tourist Office, 30 St. George Street, London W1R 9FA; telephone 01-629 0461.

## Bahamas

*Area:* 13,935 km² (5,380 square miles). Some 700 islands in an 800-km (500-mile) long chain. (Bimini 80 km (50 miles) off Florida to Inagua closest to Haiti.)

*Capital:* Nassau.

*Population:* 204,000. Twenty-two islands inhabited. 85% Bahamian.

*Occupation:* Tourism and banking.

*Climate:* Ideal all year round. November to May — air temperature 21 °C (70 °F). June to September — air temperature 29 °C (85 °F). 80% humidity in summer. Heaviest rain in June, July and October.

*Measures:* Imperial, except for petroleum products where U.S. gallon is customary.

*Electricity:* Standard North America. 120/208 V, three-phase, four-wire, 60 Hz; or 120 V, single-phase, three-wire, 60 Hz. Plugs: two or three flat pins.

*Transport:* Nassau International Airport. Airlines: British Airways, Lufthansa International, Air Bahama, Eastern, Delta, Air Canada, Air Jamaica, Ecuatoriana, Bahamasair. Ports: Nassau and Freeport. No railways. Roads: visitors can drive up to three months on U.K. or international licence. Drive on left. Petrol: measured in U.S. gallons. In Nassau and Freeport, cars, scooters and bicycles for hire. Private flying popular.

*Currency:* Bahamian dollar (B$) = 100 cents. At par with U.S. dollar. No more than 70 dollars may be taken out.

*Religion:* Church of England, Baptist, Greek Orthodox, Presbyterian, Roman Catholic, Methodist and Seventh Day Adventist.

*Visa:* No. Visitors can stay up to eight months if they have means of support and on-going ticket. Residence permits require application to the Chief Immigration Officer. These should be accompanied by evidence of character and financial standing.

*Jabs:* Smallpox, yellow fever and cholera if travelling from an infected area.

*Language:* English.

*Time:* G.M.T. − 5 (− 4 April to October).

*Hotels:* No standard classification. Thirty-six in Nassau and eighteen in Freeport. Camping in public areas prohibited. For places to stay licensed by Bahamian Government get 'Accommodations' leaflets from Tourist Board.

*Shop Hours:* 09.00 to 17.00 Monday to Saturday. Supermarkets stay open later. Some shops close at noon on Friday, some on Thursday.

*Bank Hours:* 09.30 to 15.00 Monday to Thursday. 09.30 to 17.00 Friday.

*British High Commission:* Bitco Building, Third Floor (P.O. Box N 7516), East Street, Nassau; telephone area code 809 325-7471/3/4/5.

*Tourist Office:* Bahamas Ministry of Tourism, 23 Old Bond Street, London W1X 4PQ; telephone 01-629 5238.

## Bahrain

*Area:* 622 km² (240 square miles). Islands 29 km (18 miles) off Arabian coast in Persian Gulf.

*Capital:* Manama.

*Population:* 256,000.

*Occupation:* Petroleum production and refining. Also pearls, aluminium smelting, shrimps.

*Climate:* Summer: hot and humid, up to 44 °C (111 °F), humidity 85%. Winter: mild, 10–20 °C (50–65 °F). Rain: 75 mm (3 inches) annually.

*Measures:* Imperial, local and metric. Are now attempting to change to metric.

*Electricity:* 230 V a.c. Plugs: three flat pins.

*Transport:* International airport: Manama. B.A., Qantas, Gulf Air, Singapore International, Air India, Middle East — all direct from London. Taxis at airport. No railways. Roads: drive on right; international driving permit.

*Currency:* Bahrain dinar (BD) = 1000 fils. No restrictions on import or export.

*Religion:* Muslim.
*Visa:* Not for British subject born or
resident in U.K. May need second
passport if existing one carries Israel
stamp.
*Jabs:* Smallpox. Also yellow fever and
cholera if travelling from infected area.
Health: take precautions against
enteritis and prickly heat.
*Language:* Official: Arabic. English used in
business.
*Time:* G.M.T. + 3.
*Hotels:* Best to reserve well in advance.
Hilton and Western-style.
*Shopping:* 08.00 to 12.00 and 15.30 to
18.30 Saturday to Thursday. Closed
Friday.
*Bank Hours:* 07.30 to 12.00 Saturday to
Wednesday. 07.30 to 11.00 Thursday.
*British Embassy:* Al Mathaf Square,
Manama (P.O. Box 114); telephone
54002.

## Bangladesh

*Area:* 143,998 km² (55,598 square miles).
Flat with many waterways. Mountains
in northeast and southeast.
*Capital:* Dacca.
*Population:* 76,815,000, increasing 3% a
year.
*Occupation:* Agriculture: jute, rice, sugar
cane, wheat, tea.
*Climate:* Tropical. Temperatures from 6 °C
(42 °F) in January to 37 °C (98 °F) in
June. Rain: average 2540 mm (100
inches) a year. Rainy season: April to
October.
*Measures:* Metric.
*Electricity:* 220 or 240 V a.c. (expect
fluctuations and power cuts). Plugs: 13
A, three flat pins, or 15A, three round
pins.
*Transport:* International airport: Dacca. Air
India. Countrywide railway network,
slow and subject to delays. Terminals:
Dacca and Chittagong. Roads: drive on
left and expect many ferry crossings.
*Currency:* Taka = 100 paise. You may take
20 takas in or out.
*Religion:* Muslim majority, Hindu minority.
*Visas:* Yes. You must present three
photos. There is no charge. Consulate
at 28 Queensgate, London SW7 5JA;
telephone 01-584 0081.
*Jabs:* Smallpox, typhoid and cholera.
Yellow fever if arriving from areas
where endemic. Take anti-malarial
tablets and safeguards against tummy
upsets.
*Language:* Official: Bengali.
*Time:* G.M.T. + 6.
*Hotels:* Inter-Continental. Bills must be
paid in hard currency or travellers
cheques. Provincial towns have
Government-run rest-houses. Must
book in advance.
*Shop Hours:* 09.00 to 21.00 Monday to
Friday. 09.00 to 14.00 Saturday.

*Bank Hours:* 09.30 to 13.30 Monday to
Thursday. 09.00 to 11.00 Friday and
Saturday.
*British High Commission:* P.O. Box 90,
D.I.T. Building Annexe, Dilkusha, Dacca
2; telephone 243251/3.
*Reference Book:* L. F. Rushbrook Williams,
*A Handbook for Travellers in India,
Pakistan, Nepal, Bangladesh and Sri
Lanka (Ceylon),* 22nd edition (London:
John Murray, 1975).

## Barbados

*Area:* 431 km² (166 square miles). Island
east of the Windward Islands. 65%
cultivated, mostly sugar cane. Slightly
larger than Isle of Wight. Known in the
Caribbean as 'Little England' because
of its peculiarly English air.
*Capital:* Bridgetown.
*Population:* 245,000. 90% African
descendants. 6% European.
*Occupation:* Production of sugar, rum,
molasses, cotton. Tourism. Light
industry.
*Climate:* Subtropical. Temperature range
24–30 °C (75–85 °F). Humidity 74%.
Sunsets sudden, around 18 00. Healthy
and pleasant climate. Cooled by
northeast trade winds. Rainfall: June
to November — heavy showers.
*Measures:* Imperial; metrication in
progress.
*Electricity:* 110 V a.c. 50 Hz. Plugs:
American, two flat pins.
*Transport:* One international airport:
Grantley Adams, near Bridgetown (11
miles). Airlines direct from Britain:
British West Indian, Pan Am, B.A.
Airport charge on departure. No
railways. Mini-Mokes, scooters,
bicycles. Interesting but erratic bus
service (25¢ flat rate). U.K. or
international driving licence, which
must be registered with police on
arrival. Drive on left.
*Currency:* Barbados dollar = 100 cents
(called the BAJAN dollar) = 50¢ U.S.
You may take in an unlimited amount
of local currency but you can only take
out what you imported and declared.
*Religion:* Predominantly Christian. Jewish,
Hindu, Muslim minorities.
*Visa:* No.
*Jabs:* Smallpox except for those travelling
direct from U.S.A. or Canada.
*Language:* English.
*Time:* G.M.T. – 4.
*Hotels:* Hilton, Holiday Inn. Plenty in the
same class. Higher rates from
December to April. 10% service
charge, 8% government tax.
*Shop Hours:* 08.00 to 16.00 Monday to
Friday. 08.00 to 12.00 Saturday.
*Bank Hours:* 08.00 to 13.00 Monday to
Thursday. 08.00 to 13.00 and 15.00 to
17.50 Friday.
*British High Commission:* 147/9 Roebuck

Street, (P.O. Box 676C), Bridgetown; telephone 63525.

*Reference Books:* F. A. Hoyos, *Barbados, Our Island Home* (London: Macmillan, 1960). Ronald Tree, *A History of Barbados* (London: Hart-Davis, 1972).

*Tourist Office:* 6 Upper Belgrave Street, London SW1X 8AZ; telephone 01-235 2449.

## Belgium

*Area:* 30,513 km² (11,781 square miles). Largely flat. Ardennes mountains in the east.

*Capital:* Brussels.

*Population:* 9,796,000 (including 780,000 foreigners). 86% urban.

*Occupation:* Coal, manufacturing, agriculture.

*Climate:* Temperatures from 4 °C (39 °F) in winter to 23 °C (74 °F) in summer. Coldest December to February: average 4–9 °C (39–48 °F). Rain: 815 mm (32 inches) a year. Wettest early winter. Snow: December to March.

*Measures:* Metric.

*Electricity:* Usually 220 V a.c., occasionally 110/115 or 130. Two-pin round plugs.

*Transport:* Three international airports: Brussels, Antwerp, Ostend. Airlines: B.A., Sabena, Air France, Alitalia, K.L.M., Lufthansa, Pan Am, Luxair. Dense railway network, good bus and train services. Car ferries from Dover, Felixstowe, Folkestone, Hull, Southend.

*Currency:* Belgian franc = 100 centimes. No restrictions on import or export.

*Religion:* Predominantly R.C.

*Visa:* No. If staying more than three months, or intending to work, apply to the consulate.

*Jabs:* None.

*Language:* Bilingual: French and Dutch. German on the frontier. English spoken.

*Time:* G.M.T. + 1 (+ 2 April to September).

*Hotels:* First-class hotels in all major cities.

*Shop Hours:* Department stores 09.15 to 18.00 Monday to Saturday, Friday until 21.00. Supermarkets: 09.00 to 20.00 Monday to Thursday and Saturday. Friday 09.00 to 21.00.

*Bank Hours:* 09.00 to 12.00 and 13.30 to 16.30. Some open all day in summer.

*British Embassy:* Brittania House, rue Joseph II, B-1040 Brussels; telephone (02)2191165. Consulates at Antwerp, Ghent, Liège and Ostend.

*Tourist Office:* Belgian National Tourist Office, 66 Haymarket, London SW1Y 4RB; telephone 01-930 9618.

## Belize

*Area:* 22,965 km² (8,867 square miles).

*Capital:* Belmopan.

*Population:* 140,000.

*Occupation:* Agriculture, sugar, bananas,

citrus, forestry, fishing. Dyewood trade killed by advent of synthetic dyes.

*Climate:* Subtropical. Temperature range: 21–35 °C (70–95 °F). Very humid. Rain frequent and heavy September to October.

*Measures:* Imperial. But petrol sold by U.S. gallon.

*Electricity:* 110/220 V 60 Hz.

*Transport:* International airport: Belize. No direct flight from U.K. — go via Miami. Embarkation tax. No passenger trains. Road surfaces poor, especially in wet weather. Drive on right. International and foreign driving licence.

*Currency:* Belize dollar = 100 cents. No restrictions on import or export.

*Religion:* Predominantly Christian.

*Visa:* None required for British or Commonwealth citizens.

*Jabs:* Smallpox, T.A.B.T. and yellow fever recommended. Take anti-malarial pills.

*Language:* English, Spanish.

*Time:* G.M.T. – 6.

*Hotels:* No official rating. Few top-class hotels. Belize City has numerous second-class hotels and motels. There are camping sites in outlying areas.

*Shop Hours:* Close at 12.00 on Wednesday. Some open evenings until 21.00.

*Bank Hours:* Half-day closing Wednesday and Saturday.

*British Embassy:* Refer to Governor's Office, Belize House, Belmopan; telephone 2146.

*Tourist Office:* West Indies Committee, 18 Grosvenor Street, London W1X 0HP; telephone 01-629 6353.

## Benin (formerly Dahomey)

*Area:* 112,622 km² (43,484 square miles) on West African coast.

*Capital:* Porto Novo. Government centre: Cotonou.

*Population:* 3,112,000. Forty-five tribes. 14% urban.

*Occupation:* Agriculture, mainly palm products.

*Climate:* High humidity. Tropical in north: temperature range 20–34 °C (68–93 °F). Rain: July to October. Equatorial in south with two rainy seasons, March to July and September to November.

*Measures:* Metric.

*Electricity:* 220 V a.c. 50 Hz. Plugs: two round or square pins.

*Transport:* International airport: Cotonou. No direct flights from London. Go British Caledonian Airways or Nigerian Airways to Lagos, then overland, or via Paris by Air Afrique or U.T.A. to Cotonou. Embarkation tax. Railway link from Cotonou to Parakou. Mostly east-west on south coast. Roads: drive on right. International driving permit. Coach services along main roads.

*Currency:* C.F.A. franc. No restrictions on import or export.
*Religion:* Mainly traditional. Christian and Muslim minorities.
*Visa:* Yes. It costs £4 and you must present two photos. Consulate at 125-129 High Street, Edgware, Middlesex HA8 7HS; telephone 01-951 1234.
*Jabs:* Smallpox, yellow fever and cholera. (Typhoid recommended.) Take anti-malaria precautions.
*Language:* Official: French.
*Time:* G.M.T. + 1.
*Hotels:* No official categories. A few in Cotonou, Parakou and Abomey.
*Shop Hours:* 09.30 to 13.00 and 16.00 to 19.00 Monday to Friday, 15.30 to 19.30 Saturday.
*Bank Hours:* 08.00 to 11.30 and 14.30 to 15.30 Monday to Friday.
*British Embassy:* c/o British High Commission, Eleke Crescent, Victoria Island, Lagos, Nigeria.

## Bermuda

*Area:* 53 km² (20.5 square miles). About 150 coral stone islands in west Atlantic. Ten largest are linked.
*Capital:* Hamilton.
*Population:* 56,000. Highly concentrated on twenty islands.
*Occupation:* Tourism.
*Climate:* Subtropical. April to November maximum: 27 °C (80 °F). November to April minimum: 10 °C (50 °F). Rain: 1,438 mm (56.6 inches) a year.
*Measures:* Metric, imperial and American.
*Electricity:* 115 V — lights. 115/230 V — power. All a.c. 60 Hz. Plugs: two or three flat pins.
*Transport:* One international airport: Hamilton. Airlines: B.A., Pan Am, Qantas. No railways. Bus and ferry system, motor-assisted cycles. Left-hand drive at 20 m.p.h. (32 k.p.h.). Visitors may *not* hire cars.
*Currency:* Bermuda dollar (BD) = 100 cents. Canadian and U.S. currencies accepted. You may take in up to BD 250 but you can only take out what you imported and declared.
*Religion:* Christian. C. of E. established.
*Visa:* No.
*Jabs:* Smallpox if arriving from an infected area.
*Language:* English.
*Time:* G.M.T. − 4 (− 3 April to October).
*Hotels:* Plenty of first-class hotels: book in advance. 4% government tax payable on leaving.
*Shop Hours:* 09.00 to 17.00 Monday to Saturday.
*Bank Hours:* 09.30 to 15.00 Monday to Thursday. 09.30 to 15.00 and 16.30 to 18.00 Friday.
*British Governor:* Government House, Hamilton; telephone 2-3600.

*Tourist Office:* Bermuda Department of Tourism, 84 Baker Street, London W1M 1DL; telephone 01-487 4391.

## Bolivia

*Area:* 1,098,581 km² (424,164 square miles). Straddling the Andes. The centre point of South America: comprises mountains, plateau, semi-tropical and fertile plains.
*Capital:* Sucre (official). La Paz (de facto).
*Population:* Estimates vary from 4,688,000 in September 1976 to 5,634,000 in mid-1975. 66% Indian. 33% urban.
*Occupation:* Mining, agriculture.
*Climate:* Four zones: lowlands, average temperature 29 °C (84 °F); low valleys north of La Paz, average temperature 24 °C (75 °F); high valleys, gouged by the rivers of the Cordillera Central, average temperature 19 °C (66 °F); Altiplano, average temperature 10 °C (50 °F).
*Measures:* Metric.
*Electricity:* La Paz: 110 V a.c., 220 V. Other places 220 V. Plugs: two flat or round pins.
*Transport:* Two international airports at La Paz and Santa Cruz. Airport tax on departure. Air is the only way to reach many parts. Railways: three main routes link La Paz, Cochabamba, Sucre, Potosí and Oruro. Also a railway from Santa Cruz to Argentina and Brazil. Roads: not first class; deteriorate in rainy season. Bus service: erratic, but worth trying.
*Currency:* Bolivian peso = 100 centavos. No restrictions on import or export.
*Religion:* Christian: mainly R.C.
*Visa:* No.
*Jabs:* Smallpox. Typhoid probably wise. Injections against hepatitis and yellow fever recommended. Take time to adjust to altitude.
*Language:* Official Spanish. Also Aymara and Quechua.
*Time:* G.M.T. − 4.
*Hotels:* First-class hotels in La Paz. Adequate hotels in Santa Cruz and Cochabamba. Local taxes vary.
*Shop Hours:* 09.00 to 12.00 and 14.00 to 18.00 Monday to Friday. 09.00 to 12.00 Saturday.
*Bank Hours:* 09.00 to 12.00 and 14.00 to 16.30 Monday to Friday.
*British Embassy:* Avenida Arce 2732-2754, Casilla 694, La Paz; telephone 51400 and 29401/2/3/4.
*Tourist Office:* Dirección Nacional de Turismo, Avenida Camacho Esqina Loayza 1614, La Paz, Bolivia.

## Botswana

*Area:* 600,372 km² (231,804 square miles), situated in the centre of Southern Africa, bordered by Republic of South

Africa, Namibia and Rhodesia.
Southwest area is Kalahari Desert,
swamp and farmland in north, plains
in east.
*Capital:* Gaborone.
*Population:* 691,000. Major towns: Lobatse,
Francistown.
*Occupation:* Cattle raising, tourism, mining
(also 10,000 'Bushmen' live by hunting).
*Climate:* Up to 600 mm (24 inches) a year
rainfall in the north, very low in south
(Kalahari Desert).
*Transport:* Airport at Gaborone. Flights
from Johannesburg by South African
Airways and from Lusaka by Zambia
Airways. No public road transport.
*Currency:* South African currency is used
in Botswana. Restrictions as for South
Africa.
*Visa:* Not for Commonwealth citizens.
*Jabs:* Smallpox.
*Measures:* Metric.
*Electricity:* 240 V.
*Religion:* Christianity. Traditional.
*Language:* English, Setswana.
*Time:* G.M.T. + 2.
*Hotels:* Three in Gaborone (including
Holiday Inn), two in Lobatse, two in
Francistown.
*British High Commission:* Queens Road
(Private Bag 23), Gaborone; telephone
2483.

## Brazil

*Area:* 8,511,965 km² (3,286,482 square
miles) — almost half of South America.
Fifth largest country in the world and
has the eighth largest population.
*Capital:* Brasília.
*Population:* 107,145,000. (Half the
population of South America. Half of
all Brazilians are under twenty-five.)
62% European, mainly Portuguese.
54% urban.
*Occupation:* Cotton, coffee, minerals,
cattle, sugar, soya.
*Measures:* Metric, occasionally imperial.
*Electricity:* Brasília: 220/240 V 60 Hz a.c.
São Paulo and Rio: 110 V 60 Hz a.c.
Plugs: two round pins.
*Warning:* outside cities and hotels take
care using showers — they are
electrically operated by water pressure
and the earthing is often faulty.
*Climate:* Amazon valley, steamy heat.
Southern plateau, temperate. Winter in
Rio (May to October) like summer in
Europe. Summer everywhere
(November to April) tropical, maximum
38 °C (100 °F). Rainfall: tropical. North:
January to April; Northeast: April to
July.
*Transport:* Main international airports at
Rio, São Paulo and Recife. Airlines:
British Caledonian, Varig, Air France,
Aerolineas Argentinas, Swissair,
Lufthansa and others. Air travel best
for long distances internally. Railways:

good service Rio to São Paulo. Express
bus services throughout the country.
Driving is frenetic and dangerous.
*Currency:* Cruziero = 100 centavos. No
restrictions on import or export.
*Religion:* Christian: mainly R.C.
*Visa:* Not required by British passport
holders unless stay exceeds three
months.
*Jabs:* Smallpox. Typhoid and yellow fever
advisable.
*Language:* Portuguese. Interpreters not
easy to find, particularly outside the
major cities.
*Time:* East (including all coast and
Brasília): G.M.T. − 3. West: G.M.T. − 4.
State of Acre: G.M.T. − 5.
*Hotels:* Lavish hotels in major cities. In
Rio: camping on beach. For camping
in Brasília contact Detur tourist office.
*Shop Hours:* Usually 09.00 to 17.00
Monday to Friday. Saturday morning.
Some open late.
*Bank Hours:* 10.00 to 16.00 Monday to
Friday.
*British Embassy:* Avenida das Vacões,
Lote 8, Brasília; telephone 25 2710.
Consulate-General: Rio, Praia do
Flamingo 322; telephone 225 7387.
Consulate-General: São Paulo, Avenida
Paulista 1938; telephone 287 7722.
*Tourist Office:* Brazilian Tourist Office, 35
Dover Street, London W1X 3RA;
telephone 01-493 9819.

## Brunei

*Area:* 5,765 km² (2,226 square miles) on
north of Borneo.
*Capital:* Bandar Seri Begawan.
*Population:* 147,000. Two-thirds Malay,
with Chinese and other minorities.
*Occupation:* Oil.
*Measures:* Imperial and local measures —
ganyang (gallon), tahil (1⅓ oz), kati
(1⅓ lb).
*Electricity:* 240 V a.c.
*Climate:* Tropical. Average temperatures
24−35 °C (75−95 °F). High humidity.
Worst October to January. Rainfall:
monsoon from April to August. Buy an
Asian paper brolly against the heat.
*Transport:* One airport: Bandar Seri
Begawan. Airlines: B.A. direct from
Britain, Singapore Airlines from
Singapore, Royal Brunei Airlines. No
public railways: Shell has small 13-km
(8-mile) line between Seria and Badas.
Bus connections between large towns.
370 km roads and 720 km dirt tracks.
*Currency:* Brunei dollar = 100 cents.
Singapore or Malaysian currency also
accepted. Not more than 1,000 dollars
may be taken in or out.
*Religion:* Muslim.
*Visa:* No.
*Jabs:* Cholera, smallpox, typhoid.
*Language:* Malay, Chinese dialects, Tamil,
some English.

*Time:* G.M.T. + 8.
*Hotels:* Three first-class in Bandar Seri
Begawan.
*Bank Hours:* 09.00 to 12.00 and 14.00 to
15.15 Monday to Friday. 09.00 to 11.00
Saturday.
*British High Commission:* Jalan Residency;
telephone 22231 and 23121. Also
above Hongkong Bank; telephone
26001.

## Bulgaria

*Area:* 110,912 km² (42,823 square miles).
Balkan country, bordering Black Sea.
*Capital:* Sofia.
*Population:* 8,722,000. 58% urban.
*Occupation:* Farming, manufacturing and
chemical industry, increasing tourism
including skiing.
*Measures:* Metric.
*Electricity:* 220 V a.c. 50 Hz. Plugs: two
round pins, Continental.
*Climate:* Considerable variation. Sofia —
temperatures range from −17 °C to
36 °C (2 °F to 96 °F). Winters: cold with
snow. Rain: 635 mm (25 inches) a
year.
*Transport:* International airport: Sofia.
Airlines from London: B.A., Balkan
Bulgarian Airlines. Railways: Sofia
terminal for international links. Service
connects all main towns. Roads: drive
on right. Speed limit: 50 k.p.h. (30
m.p.h.) in towns; 100 k.p.h. (62 m.p.h.)
outside. Some road hazards go
unmarked. Driving at night is tricky.
Petrol stations do not do repairs: this
is done at service centres. No spares
for Western cars. Very serious to drink
and drive. Petrol coupons (discount
rate) for special visitors can be bought
at border. When booking through
Balkantourist and Shipka get from 50
litres of petrol free!
*Currency:* Lev = 100 stotinki. No
restrictions on import or export.
*Religion:* Eastern Orthodox. Muslim
minorities. Observance discouraged.
*Visa:* No, for tourists up to two months.
Check with embassy, 12 Queens Gate
Gardens, London SW7 5NA; telephone
01-584 9400.
*Jabs:* None — unless travelling from area
of smallpox or cholera.
*Language:* Bulgarian. Guides speak
English.
*Time:* G.M.T. + 2.
*Hotels:* Government classifications: de
luxe, first, second and third class. No
Western chains. Large hotels in Sofia,
Plovdiv and Varna. Balkan Tourist
Office arranges booking and meal
vouchers. Can also book into private
lodgings of varying standards. Motels
situated near tourist attractions.
Camping sites: many facilities free.
*Shop Hours:* 08.00 to 13.00 and 16.00 to
19.00 Monday to Saturday.

*Bank Hours:* 08.00 to 12.00 Monday to
Friday. 08.00 to 11.00 Saturday.
*British Embassy:* Boulevard Marshal
Tolbukhin 65-67, Sofia; telephone
885361.
*Reference Books:Bulgaria Today,
Balkantourist News.* Alan Ryalls,
*Bulgaria for Tourists* (Havant: Kenneth
Mason, 1972).
*Tourist Office:* Bulgarian National Tourist
Office, 126 Regent Street, London W1R
3FE; telephone 01-437 2611.

## Burma

*Area:* 676,552 km² (261,218 square miles).
Lush river valleys, ringed by
mountains.
*Capital:* Rangoon.
*Population:* 31,240,000 (2·2% growth rate).
Mainly rural, in river valley.
*Occupation:* 69% agriculture.
*Climate:* Monsoonal. Temperature in
Rangoon October to February 21 °C (70
°F); February to May 32 °C (90 °F). May
to October very wet. Rain: 5080−6350
mm (200−250 inches) a year on coast;
760−2540 mm (30−100 inches) a year
inland.
*Measures:* Imperial, metric and local.
*Electricity:* 230 V a.c. 50 Hz.
*Transport:* One international airport:
Rangoon. Airlines: B.A., Burma
Airlines, India, Air France, K.L.M.,
Aeroflot, Thai International, Pan Am.
Railway links between major towns;
best is Rangoon to Mandalay. The road
to Mandalay is actually the river trip
through the gorges, Bhario to
Mandalay on to Pagan. Remote areas
in north difficult to visit for security
reasons. Trucks converted to Buses,
rough and cheap. Also, see Burma by
boat.
*Currency:* Burmese kyat (pronounced
'chat') = 100 pyas. 100,000 kyats = 1
lakh. 10,000,000 kyats = 1 crore. No
restrictions on import or export.
*Religion:* Buddhist, Christian, Hindu.
*Visa:* Yes. Transit visa valid for
twenty-four hours, tourist visa for
seven days. Others up to three
months. Visa costs £2·65. You must
present four photos and your smallpox
and cholera vaccination certificates.
Legal action if you arrive without a
visa. If you stay over three months,
you must register. Declare jewellery
and foreign-made valuables on entry.
Keep documents to avoid paying duty
when you leave. Embassy at 19A
Charles Street, London W1X 8ER;
telephone 01-499 8841.
*Jabs:* Cholera, smallpox, yellow fever.
Typhoid recommended. Take
anti-malaria precautions.
*Language:* Burmese.
*Time:* G.M.T. + 6½.

*Hotels:* Up-market European-style hotels in Rangoon. Some hotels require payment in foreign currency. Small, local hotels run by Chinese: charge for one room same for one as for two people.
*Shops:* 09.30 to 16.00 Monday to Saturday. Markets later.
*Banks:* 10.00 to 14.00 Monday to Friday. 10.00 to 12.00 Saturday.
*British Embassy:* 80 Strand Road, (P.O. Box 638), Rangoon; telephone 15700.
*Tourist Office:* Department of Tourism, Government of the Union of Burma, Secretariat, Rangoon.

## Burundi

*Area:* 27,834 km² (10,747 square miles).
*Capital:* Bujumbura.
*Population:* 3,763,000.
*Occupation:* Subsistence agriculture. Burundi is one of the poorest countries in the world.
*Climate:* Tropical but mild with moderate humidity. Average temperature in plateau region is 20 °C (68 °F) and average rainfall is 1190 mm (47 inches) a year.
*Measures:* Metric.
*Electricity:* 220 V a.c. 50 Hz.
*Transport:* International airport at Bujumbura. No direct flight from London. Go via Brussels on Sabena. No railways. Dense road network but only 80 km have asphalt surface.
*Currency:* Burundi franc. No limit on imports. Export limited to 2,000 Burundi francs.
*Religion:* Half R.C., the rest traditional.
*Visa:* Yes: it costs 350 Belgian francs and takes four days to issue. You need three photos and your smallpox vaccination certificate. Embassy at Square Marie Louise 46, B-1040 Brussels, Belgium; telephone 7335592.
*Jabs:* Smallpox and yellow fever. Cholera and T.A.B.T. recommended. Take anti-malaria precautions.
*Language:* French.
*Time:* G.M.T. + 2.
*British Consulate:* Honorary Consul at B.P. 1344 Bujumbura; telephone 3206.
*Tourist Office:* Office National du Tourisme, Bujumbura.

## Cambodia

*Area:* 181,035 km² (69,898 square miles). Three-quarters forested, flat delta of Mekong River.
*Capital:* Pnompenh (also spelt Phnom-Penh).
*Population:* 8,110,000.
*Occupation:* Agriculture, fishing, forestry.
*Climate:* Tropical monsoon. November to March: dry and cool. April to July: hottest. Rain: heaviest July to September.
*Measures:* Metric.
*Electricity:* 220 V a.c. (Pnompenh); 110 V a.c. (Siem Reap).
*Transport:* The frontiers are closed. There is one flight a fortnight from Peking by the Chinese Civil Aviation service.
*Currency:* Riel.
*Religion:* Buddhism.
*Visa:* Yes.
*Jabs:* Smallpox, cholera. Typhoid recommended. Take anti-malaria precautions.
*Language:* Cambodian, French widely spoken. English was taught as main foreign language.
*Time:* G.M.T. + 7.
*British Embassy:* Staff withdrawn.

## Cameroon, United Republic of

*Area:* 475,442 km² (183,569 square miles). Three areas: plains, equatorial forests, uninhabited uplands.
*Capital:* Yaoundé.
*Population:* 6,500,000. 200 tribes.
*Occupation:* 80% agriculture.
*Climate:* Yaoundé 17–31 °C (63–88 °F). Hottest December to March, coolest July to September. Rain: Yaoundé heaviest September to May. Dry seasons very dusty.
*Measures:* Metric.
*Electricity:* 110/220 V a.c. 50 Hz. Plugs: two round pins.
*Transport:* Airlines: connections at Paris via U.T.A. or Cameroon Airlines, connections at Ghana or Nigeria via British Caledonian. Air best for internal travel. Rail terminals: Douala and Yaoundé with links to three other towns, slow but cheap. Roads poor, especially in rainy season. Frequent and cheap buses, local.
*Currency:* C.F.A. franc. Up to 20,000 francs may be taken in or out.
*Religion:* Christian, Muslim and traditional.
*Visa:* Yes. Need a second passport if also visiting Portuguese territory, South Africa or Rhodesia. Embassy at 84 Holland Park, London W11 3SB; telephone 01-727 0771.
*Jabs:* Smallpox, yellow fever (if staying over eighteen days), and cholera. Take anti-malaria tablets.
*Language:* Officially bilingual: French and English.
*Time:* G.M.T. + 1.
*Hotels:* In cities, European-style hotels. Book in advance.
*Bank Hours:* East: 08.00 to 11.30 and 14.30 to 15.30 Monday to Friday. West: 08.00 to 13.30 Monday to Friday.
*British Consulate:* Soppo Priso Building, rue Alfred Saker, (B.P. 1016), Douala; telephone 422177.
*British Embassy:* Le Concorde, avenue J. F. Kennedy, (B.P. 547), Yaoundé; telephone 220545/220796.

*Tourist Office:* Commissariat Général au Tourisme, (B.P. 266), Yaoundé.

## Canada

*Area:* 9,976,139 km² (3,851,802 square miles). Second largest country in the world. 777,000 km² (0.3 million square miles) of fresh water.
Divided into five regions:
*Atlantic Canada:* New Brunswick, Prince Edward Island, Nova Scotia, Newfoundland. (Bond of history, sea, Scottishness and French Acadian background.)
*Midwest:* Manitoba, Saskatchewan and part of Alberta. 'The wide open spaces'. 'Big sky' country.
*The North:* Yukon and Northwest Territories. 'Mysterious', 'last frontier', trail of '88.
*Ontario/Quebec:* Where Canada's two cultures meet. St. Lawrence land.
*Western:* West Alberta and the Rockies, British Columbia. 'Wondrous West'.
*Capital:* Ottawa.
*Population:* 22,831,000, distributed in a belt 160 km (100 miles) wide along the U.S./Canadian border. The provinces of Ontario and Quebec are the most heavily populated.
*Occupation:* Fishing along coasts. Agriculture and livestock in the central prairies. Minerals in north. Widespread manufacturing industries and forestry.
*Climate:* Varied: summers hotter, winters colder than Europe. Temperatures: Vancouver, January 3 °C (37 °F), July 18 °C (64 °F); Montreal, January −9 °C (16 °F), July 21 °C (70 °F); Winnipeg, January −18 °C (0 °F), July 20 °C (68 °F).
*Measures:* Imperial, but ton = 2,000 pounds.
*Electricity:* Mostly 110 V; therefore European gadgets need a transformer if they are not provided with a voltage-selection switch.
*Transport:* International airports in all main cities. British flights mainly to Toronto, Montreal and Vancouver. Railways: Canadian Pacific and Canadian National. Most passengers go C.N. Coast to coast takes four days: sleeper advisable. Buses: good cross-country. Local service fairly cheap. Drive on the right. Members of the A.A. are entitled to similar service from Canadian A.A.
*Currency:* Canadian dollar = 100 cents. No limits on import or export.
*Religion:* Most Christian denominations: French-Canadian areas mainly R.C.
*Visa:* Not for a stay of up to three months. U.S. visa needed to cross border.
*Jabs:* No. Insect repellent needed for some areas in summer. Take out medical insurance: treatment is costly.

*Language:* English and French — bilingual. You'll need French in Quebec.
*Time:* Six time zones from G.M.T. − 3½ to G.M.T. − 8. From April to October clocks are advanced 1 hour except in Yukon Territory.
*Hotels:* First-class hotels in major cities. Standards less high around train and bus terminals.
*Shop Hours:* Usually open until 17.30 or 18.00. Fridays until 21.00. Many shopping centres open longer hours.
*Bank Hours:* 10.00 to 15.00 or 16.30 Monday to Thursday. 10.00 to 18.00 Friday. Late opening in some suburban shopping centres.
*Police:* Carry guns. Attitude to drugs enlightened if no obvious abuse. Hitch-hiking technically illegal in many areas but frequently seen.
*British Government Offices:* Ottawa: 613-237-1530. Halifax: 902-422-7488. Montreal: 514-866-5863. Edmonton: 403-428-0375. Toronto: 416-864-1290. Quebec: 418-525-5187. Vancouver: 604-683-4421. Winnipeg: 204-942-3151.
*Reference Book: Touring Canada,* with road maps. From Canadian Government Office of Tourism. *Canada* (Ottawa: Information Canada, annual).
*Tourist Office:* Canadian Government Office of Tourism, Canada House, Trafalgar Square, London SW1Y 5BJ; telephone 01-930 0731.

## Cape Verde

*Area:* 4,033² (1,557 square miles). Fifteen islands 450 km (280 miles) west of Dakar.
*Capital:* Praia on São Tiago.
*Population:* 294,000; mainly descendants of Portuguese settlers and African slaves.
*Occupation:* Agriculture (bananas, sugar cane, coffee, etc.) but very unsuccessful because of lack of expertise, machinery and good weather. Economic situation dire.
*Climate:* High temperatures and chronic shortage of rainfall.
*Measures:* Metric.
*Electricity:* 220 V a.c.
*Transport:* Airport on Ilha do Sal served by South African Airways and T.A.P. Inter-island air transport by Transportes Aéreos de Cabo Verde.
*Currency:* Cape Verde escudo = 100 centavos. You may take 1,000 escudos in or out.
*Religion:* R.C.
*Visa:* Yes, available on arrival.
*Jabs:* Smallpox and yellow fever. Cholera recommended.
*Language:* Portuguese, local creole called Crioulo.
*Time:* G.M.T. − 2 (− 1 in summer).
*British Embassy:* None. Nearest representative is at Dakar, Senegal.

*Tourist Office:* Centro de Informação e Turismo, (Caixa Postal 118), Praia, São Tiago.

## Cayman Islands

*Area:* 259 km² (100 square miles). Three islands south of Cuba.

*Capital:* George Town on Grand Cayman Island.

*Population:* 11,000. 80% on Grand Cayman.

*Occupation:* Finance, tourism.

*Climate:* Hot: May to October 24—34 °C (75—93 °F). Cool: November to April 18—27 °C (65—85 °F). Rain: 1420 mm (56 inches) a year. Heaviest May to October.

*Measures:* Imperial.

*Electricity:* 110 V a.c. 60 Hz (same as the U.S.A.).

*Transport:* Two airports on Grand Cayman. No direct route from U.K.; go via Florida or Jamaica on Cayman Airways from Miami or Kingston. Bus services: infrequent. Drive on the left (some one-way streets in George Town).

*Currency:* Cayman Islands dollar (CI$) = 100 cents. No limit on amount you can take in but you can only take out CI$50.

*Religion:* Various: R.C., Protestant and Evangelical.

*Visa:* No. Remember to keep CI$2.40 for travel tax on departure.

*Jabs:* No.

*Language:* English, with local accent.

*Time:* G.M.T. — 5.

*Hotels:* Mostly small but comfortable. Holiday Inn and others. Rates are high. Residential clubs. Most hotels are 'oriented to provide the ultimate in casual beach living'.

*Bank Hours:* 08.30 to 13.00 Monday to Thursday. 08.30 to 13.00 and 16.30 to 18.00 Friday.

*British Governor:* Government House, George Town, Grand Cayman; telephone 2290.

*Tourist Office:* West India Committee, 18 Grosvenor Street, London W1X 0HP; telephone 01-629 6353.

## Central African Empire

*Area:* 622,984 km² (240,535 square miles). Landlocked rocky plateau at very centre of Africa.

*Capital:* Bangui.

*Population:* Estimates of population vary from 1,637,000 in 1971 to 2,370,000 in 1970. Eighty ethnic groups.

*Occupation:* Agriculture, livestock, diamond export.

*Climate:* Tropical, hot, humid. Temperature range: 14—38 °C (58—100 °F). Humidity 93%. Rain: heavy May to November; dry December to April.

*Measures:* Metric.

*Electricity:* 220 V a.c. 50 Hz. Plugs: three round pins.

*Transport:* One international airport at Bangui. Fly U.T.A. or Air Afrique from Paris. Railways: none. Roads: only fair. Trans-African Highway will go through Bangui.

*Currency:* C.F.A. franc. 75,000 francs may be taken in or out.

*Religion:* 60% traditional. Christian and Muslim minorities.

*Visa:* Yes. It costs £1.80 and you must present three photos. Apply to French Consulate General at 24 Rutland Gate, London SW7; telephone 01-584 9628.

*Jabs:* Smallpox, cholera, yellow fever. Typhoid recommended. Take anti-malaria precautions.

*Language:* Official: French.

*Time:* G.M.T. + 1.

*Hotels:* Three small hotels of reasonable standard in Bangui.

*Shop Hours:* 07.00 or 08.00 to 18.30 or 19.00 with long lunch.

*Bank Hours:* 07.00 to 12.00 Monday to Saturday.

*British Consulate:* Refer to Douala in Cameroon.

## Chad

*Area:* 1,284,000 km² (495,754 square miles) in central North Africa. Semi-desert, but includes vast Lake Chad.

*Capital:* N'Djamena.

*Population:* 4,030,000.

*Occupation:* Agriculture: cotton and food crops.

*Climate:* Generally desert. Average temperature at N'Djamena 29 °C (85 °F) but can drop to freezing at night. Rain: June to October.

*Measures:* Metric.

*Electricity:* 220 V a.c. 50 Hz. Plugs: two round pins.

*Transport:* One airport: N'Djamena. Fly U.T.A. or Air Afrique from Paris. Internal air network. No railways. Road travel can be dangerous outside N'Djamena because of rebels, landmines, etc. South is cut off from east and north for four months during summer rain.

*Currency:* C.F.A. franc. No limit on the amount you can take in but you may only take out 10,000 francs.

*Religion:* Muslim in north, Christian or traditional in south.

*Visa:* Yes. It costs £1.80 and you need two photos. Apply to French Consulate General at 24 Rutland Gate, London SW7; telephone 01-584 9628.

*Jabs:* Yellow fever, smallpox, cholera. Typhoid recommended. Take anti-malaria precautions.

*Language:* Official: French. Little English.

*Time:* G.M.T. + 1.

*Hotels:* One class of hotel only — the top class. One or two in N'Djamena.
*Shop Hours:* 07.00 or 08.00 to 18.30 or 19.00 Tuesday to Saturday with long lunch.
*Bank Hours:* 07.00 to 12.00 Monday to Saturday.
*British Consulate:* Socopao du Tehad (B.P. 751), N'Djamena; telephone 2932.

## Chile

*Area:* 756,945 km² (292,258 square miles).
*Capital:* Santiago.
*Population:* 10,253,000. 70% Spanish/Indian.
*Occupation:* Agriculture, mining.
*Climate:* Very varied. Santiago: 10 °C (50 °F) in July to 28 °C (82 °F) in January. Warm and dry in the north. Central area: rain from May to August. South: one of the world's wettest regions.
*Measures:* Metric, but also measure of 100 pounds called quintal.
*Electricity:* 220 V a.c. 50 Hz. Two-pin plugs.
*Transport:* One international airport: Santiago. Direct from Britain: British Caledonian. Airport tax: 10% of the air fare. Railways: cities connected by fast diesel/electric service. Buses: good long-distance coach service. Roads: British or international licence valid. Hitch-hiking officially prohibited, but possible at service stations.
*Currency:* Peso. No restrictions on import or export.
*Religion:* R.C. Some Evangelical and Anglican.
*Visa:* Not for a stay of up to ninety days. Complete a tourist card on arrival. A visit can be extended for one further ninety-day period.
*Jabs:* Smallpox.
*Language:* Official: Spanish.
*Time:* G.M.T. − 4 (− 3 October to February).
*Hotels:* Sheraton and others in Santiago and Valparaiso.
*Shop Hours:* 10.00 to 19.00 Monday to Friday. 09.00 to 13.00 Saturday.
*Bank Hours:* 09.00 to 14.00 Monday to Friday.
*British Embassy:* La Concepcion 177, Providencia. Santiago; telephone 239166.
*Tourist Office:* 31 Portland Place, London W1; telephone 01-636 9939.

## China, People's Republic of

*Area:* 9,596,961 km² (3,705,401 square miles) divided by Yellow River and Yangtze River in North, Centre and South.
*Capital:* Peking.
*Population:* 822,653,000. 80% rural.
*Occupation:* Agriculture: rice, cotton, tea, hemp, jute, flax. Industry.

*Climate:* Very varied. Peking: dry and dusty. Temperatures from − 7 to 37 °C (19−98 °F), highest in July. Average humidity 91%. South and Shanghai: subtropical, hot until October. Rain: heaviest July and August.
*Measures:* Metric, but old Chinese weights still used.
*Electricity:* 220 V a.c. 50 Hz. Plugs: usually two or three flat pins.
*Transport:* Three main international airports: Kwangchow, Shanghai and Peking. Airlines: B.A. to Hong Kong, C.A.A.C. (Chinese Airlines) from Paris to Shanghai. Railways link major cities, but distances are huge. Good idea to carry towel and toilet paper on trains.
*Currency:* Renmimbi yuan = 100 fen. No restrictions on import or export.
*Religion:* No organized, but Confucianism, Buddhism and Taoism exist.
*Visa:* Yes. It costs £2.40 and takes two weeks to issue. Register ports of entry and movements within country. Evidence of visits to Taiwan may cause difficulties. Consulate at 31 Portland Place, London W1N 3AG; telephone 01-636 5637.
*Jabs:* Smallpox, typhoid. Cholera recommended. Take anti-malaria pills.
*Language:* Chinese.
*Time:* G.M.T. + 8.
*Shop Hours:* 09.00 to 19.00 including Sundays.
*British Embassy:* 11 Kuang Hua Lu, Chien Kuo Men Wai, Peking; telephone 521961/4.
*Reference Books:* China International Travel Service, *Tourist Guide to China* (Peking: Foreign Languages Press, 1974).
*Tourist Office:* Luxingshe, China International Travel Service, Hsi-tan Building, Peking.

## Colombia

*Area:* 1,138,914 km² (439,736 square miles). Fourth largest country in South America.
*Capital:* Bogotá.
*Population:* 23,542,000. 58% urban. European, negro and Indian descent.
*Occupation:* Coffee growing and export.
*Climate:* Mostly hot and damp. Humidity up to 88%. But Bogotá and outer areas cooler. Bogotá: 8−18 °C (47−65 °F). Rainfall: heaviest June to September.
*Measures:* Metric, but traditional measures still used for land areas.
*Electricity:* 110/120 V a.c. 60 Hz. Plugs: American, two flat pins.
*Transport:* Four airports: Bogotá, Barranquilla, Cali and Medellín. Sixteen hours from U.K. Airlines direct from Britain: B.A. and V.I.A.S.A. Airport tax. Cheap internal flights (eighteen lines). Railways: link main towns, but no international connections. Subject to

delays. Buses better. Roads: often no
signposts. Preferable to drive in
daylight because sometimes unpaved.
Fuel is very cheap.
*Currency:* Peso = 100 centavos. No limit
on amount you may take in but you
may only take out 500 pesos.
*Religion:* R.C. mainly. Also Protestant
churches.
*Visa:* No. You can stay up to ninety days,
but you must have tickets for a return
or onward journey.
*Jabs:* Smallpox. Also yellow fever if from
infected area. Have gamma globulin
injection against hepatitis. May need
time to get used to higher altitude.
There is a risk of malaria outside urban
areas and at altitudes below 1,000 m
(Bogotá is at 2,610 m).
*Language:* Official: Spanish.
*Time:* G.M.T. − 5.
*Hotels:* Hilton, Inter-Continental and
others. Outside main cities hotels
include meals in charges.
*Shop Hours:* 09.00 to 16.30 Monday to
Saturday. Closed for lunch for two
hours.
*Bank Hours:* 09.00 to 15.00 Monday to
Friday.
*British Embassy:* Calle 38, No. 13−35,
Pisos 9−11, Bogotá; telephone 698100.
Consulates at Cali, Medellín and
Barranquilla.
*WARNING:* Colombia is on a major
drug-smuggling route: don't accept
unidentified parcels from others.

## Comoro Islands

*Area:* 2,171 km² (838 square miles).
Volcanic islands in Madagascar
archipelago.
*Capital:* Moroni.
*Population:* 306,000. Arab, African and
East Indian descendants.
*Occupation:* Agriculture, distillation of
perfume.
*Climate:* Coolest and driest May to
October. Coast areas very hot in
summer (December to March).
Rainfall: mainly in summer.
*Transport:* International airport: Moroni.
Regular air services from Madagascar.
Most travel is by boat. Only 750 km
roads, only 400 km are all-weather.
*Currency:* C.F.A. franc.
*Religion:* Muslim.
*Jabs:* Smallpox. Yellow fever and cholera
recommended. Take precautions
against malaria. Medical facilities
scarce.
*Language:* Swahili, French, Arabic and
Malagasy.
*Time:* G.M.T. + 3.
*Hotels:* Several on Grande Comore.
*British Embassy:* None.
*Note:* Although claimed by the Comoro
government as part of its territory, the
island of Mayotee (area 375 km² (145

square miles), population 38,000) is
administered by France. French
currency is used there.

## Congo, People's Republic of

*Area:* 342,000 km² (132,047 square miles).
*Capital:* Brazzaville.
*Population:* 1,345,000, primarily Bantu.
After 1970, there was a mass exodus
from country areas. 75% now live
around Brazzaville and Pointe Noire.
*Occupation:* Agriculture, livestock,
forestry, fishing.
*Climate:* Hot and humid. Average
temperatures 21−27 °C (70−80 °F).
Rain: 1420 mm (56 inches) a year.
Rainy season October to December
and April to May. Occasional storms in
dry season January to March.
*Measures:* Metric.
*Electricity:* 220 V a.c.
*Transport:* International airport:
Brazzaville. Airlines: U.T.A., Air
Afrique. Main railway link —
Brazzaville and Pointe Noire. Roads:
243 km of tarred roads, others by Land
Rover only. Boat service up and down
Congo (Zaïre) river — erratic.
*Currency:* C.F.A. franc. No limit on amount
you may take in but you may only take
out 25,000 francs.
*Religion:* Some R.C., also traditional.
*Visa:* Yes. It costs 50 French francs and
takes three weeks to issue. You must
present two photos and your smallpox
and yellow fever vaccination
certificates. Apply to Embassy at 57 bis
rue Scheffer, Paris 16, France;
telephone Paris 7277709.
*Jabs:* Yellow fever, smallpox, cholera.
Take anti-malaria precautions.
*Language:* French, little English.
*Time:* G.M.T. + 1.
*Hotels:* No major chains. Hotels in
Brazzaville and Pointe Noire.
*Shop Hours:* 08.00 to 18.30 Tuesday to
Sunday. Close two hours for lunch.
*Bank Hours:* 07.00 to 12.00 Monday to
Saturday.
*British Embassy:* Refer to Kinshasa, Zaïre.

## Costa Rica

*Area:* 50,700 km² (19,575 square miles).
*Capital:* San José.
*Population:* 1,968,000, mostly of Spanish
descent. 34% urban.
*Occupation:* Agriculture: coffee, bananas,
sugar cane, rice and livestock.
*Climate:* Coastal lowland tropical:
maximum 35 °C (95 °F). Interior plateau
temperate: maximum 26 °C (79 °F). San
José: 15−26 °C (59−70 °F). Rain: June
to November. In central plateau 1955
mm (77 inches) a year.
*Measures:* Metric.
*Electricity:* 110 V a.c. 60 Hz. Plugs:
two-point knife-edge.

*Transport:* One international airport — San José. No direct flights from London. Connect at Miami with Pan Am and L.A.C.S.A. Railways connect main towns. Roads: insurance stamps compulsory. Regular-grade petrol only. High-compression engines need adjusting. Foreign driving licence not accepted. Get a temporary permit from the traffic authorities.
*Currency:* Colon = 100 centimos. No restrictions on import or export.
*Religion:* R.C., some Protestant.
*Visa:* No: U.K. citizens usually permitted to stay ninety days. Exit visa is required if stay is more than thirty days. People of unkempt appearance refused entry.
*Jabs:* Smallpox. There is a risk of malaria outside urban areas at altitudes below 500 m.
*Language:* Spanish.
*Time:* G.M.T. − 6.
*Shop Hours:* 08.00 to 12.00 and 14.00 to 18.00 Monday to Saturday.
*Bank Hours:* 08.00 to 11.00 and 13.30 to 15.00 Monday to Friday. 08.00 to 11.00 Saturday.
*British Consulate:* Paseo Colon 3202, Apartado 10056, San José; telephone 215816.
*Tourist Office:* Instituto Costarricense de Turismo, P.O. Box 777, San José.

## Cuba

*Area:* 114,524 km² (44,218 square miles).
*Capital:* Havana (La Habana).
*Population:* 9,194,000 (mid-1974).
*Occupation:* Sugar dominates the economy; and meat. Production of molasses, rum, brandy, tobacco, nickel.
*Climate:* Subtropical. Havana: 19−30 °C (66−86 °F). Humidity 63−86%. Rain: often torrential. Heaviest summer and autumn (May to October).Cooler, dry season November to April. Most public places air-conditioned and very chilly.
*Measures:* Metric, but American and old Spanish measures still used.
*Electricity:* 110 V a.c. 60 Hz.
*Transport:* Havana International Airport. No direct flights from London. Go via Madrid or Mexico on Iberia or Cubana de Aviación. B.A. flies to Mexico weekly. Unitours (Canada) run package tours to Cuba. 18,115 km of railways and 20,000 km of roads. New eight-lane highway being built to link Pinar del Río and Santiago de Cuba. Buses link main cities. Very little scope for private travel.
*Currency:* Peso = 100 centavos. No restrictions on import or export.
*Religion:* Mainly R.C.
*Visa:* Yes. It costs £3.14 and takes three weeks to issue. You need three photos. It is best if you apply through a package-tour agency or with sponsorship from an official Cuban

organization. Those holding Cuban visas will find visas for entry into certain Central American countries invalidated, e.g. a visit to Cuba puts a five-day time-limit on subsequent visit to Mexico. So visit Cuba last! All visitors must have tickets for onward journey. Embassy at 57 Kensington Court, London W8 5DQ; telephone 01-937 8226
*Jabs:* Smallpox. Typhoid advisable.
*Language:* Dialect of Spanish, and Spanish. Some English.
*Time:* G.M.T. − 5 (− 4 April to September).
*Hotels:* State classified as de luxe, first and second class. Few with complete service. Meal service is often very slow. Must book through government agency. Hotel guest's visitor not allowed above ground floor. National Tourist Office in Havana will book anywhere!
*Shop Hours:* 12.30 to 19.30 Monday to Saturday. Many things unobtainable: take razor blades, pharmaceuticals, books, paper, etc. with you.
*Bank Hours:* 08.00 to 12.00 and 14.15 to 16.15 Monday to Friday. 08.00 to 12.00 Saturday.
*British Embassy:* Edificio Bolívar, 8° Piso, Capdevila 101−103, (Apartado 1069), Havana; telephone 615681.
*Tourist Office:* Instituto Nacional de la Industria Turistica de Cuba, Malecon y G. Vedado, Havana.

## Cyprus

*Area:* 9,251 km² (3,572 square miles). Island.
*Capital:* Nicosia.
*Population:* 639,000: 78% Greek, 20% Turkish Cypriots, at loggerheads.
*Occupation:* Agriculture and tourism.
*Climate:* Summers hot and dry; winters cool and wet. From 12 to 38 °C (53 to 100 °F). Rain: average 510 mm (20 inches) a year, mainly November to March. Snow on hills January to February.
*Measures:* Metric, imperial and local.
*Electricity:* 240 V a.c. 50 Hz. Plugs: 5A, three round pins or 13A, three flat pins.
*Transport:* International airport: Nicosia. Departure tax. Airlines: B.A., Cyprus Airlines, Olympic. Roads: drive on left, international or foreign driving licence must be presented to Registrar of Automobiles. Bus services limited, but do occur, only no night buses. Village buses only early morning for markets.
*Currency:* Cyprus pound = 1,000 mils. 10 pounds may be taken in or out.
*Religion:* Greek Orthodox and Muslim.
*Visa:* No.
*Jabs:* None — unless travelling from infected area. Typhoid jab advisable.

T.C.T.—W

*Language:* Greek and Turkish.
*Time:* G.M.T. + 2.
*Hotels:* Classified five star to one star by
Tourist Organization. New ones being
built in Greek Cyprus. Famagusta still
(1977) a ghost town.
*Shop Hours:* Vary. Typically 08.00 or 09.00
to 12.00 and 15.00 to 18.00 or 19.00
Monday to Saturday.
*Bank Hours:* 08.30 to 12.00 Monday to
Saturday.
*British High Commission:* Alexander Pallis
Street, (P.O. Box 1978), Nicosia;
telephone 73131/7.
*Reference Book:* Paul Watkins, *See Cyprus*
(London; Format Books, 1972).
*Tourist Office:* Cyprus Tourism
Organization, 213 Regent Street,
London W1R 8DA; telephone 01-734
9822.
*Note:* In 1975 Turkish forces invaded
Cyprus and moved Greek Cypriots
from the north of the island, setting up
there a 'Turkish-Cypriot Federated
State'. There is bitter animosity
between the Turkish and Greek
communities.

## Czechoslovakia

*Area:* 127,869 km² (49,370 square miles).
34.8% forest; 45,000 species of fauna,
3,000 of flora.
*Capital:* Prague (Praha).
*Population:* 14,802,000. 65% Czechs, 30%
Slovaks.
*Occupation:* Engineering, machine tools,
glass, ceramics, textiles, footwear.
*Climate:* Warm summer, colder winter.
Prague: from − 16 to 33 °C (3 to 91 °F).
Worst November to February. Colder
in eastern areas. Rain: thunderstorms
in summer, snow in winter.
*Measures:* Metric.
*Electricity:* 220 V a.c. 50 Hz. Sockets
unique: need local plugs.
*Transport:* International airport: Prague.
Direct flights from London: B.A. and
Czechoslovakian Airlines. Railways link
Prague to all main cities. Also Prague–
London connection possible. Roads:
U.K. licence valid. Drive on right, signs
in kilometres. City speed limits 40−60
k.p.h. (25−37 m.p.h.). Car hire in
Prague, Bratislava and Brno. Buy petrol
coupons at entry point to
Czechoslovakia or at Zivnostenska
Bank, 104−106 Leadenhall Street,
London EC3 (50p postage). Don't mix
local with foreign lubricating oil. Public
transport tickets bought in advance
from tobacconist shops or ticket kiosks.
Tram system in Prague.
*Currency:* Koruna = 100 halers. Local
currency may not be taken in or out.
Tourists granted 75% bonus over
official rate of exchange.
*Religion:* Tolerated. Mainly R.C.

*Visa:* Yes: it costs £3 and you need two
photos. Foreigners must register entry
and change of address. People with
dual Czech/U.K. citizenship not
protected by U.K. in Czechoslovakia.
Embassy at 28 Kensington Palace
Gardens, London W8 4QY; telephone
01-727 3966.
*Jabs:* No.
*Language:* Czech and Slovak: some
German and French. Interpreters
through official tourist bureau.
*Time:* G.M.T. + 1.
*Hotels:* Ministry of Trade classification: A
de luxe, A plus, B plus, B and C. Book
through national tourist agency.
Caravan sites available: some 15 May
to 30 September; most 15 June to 15
September. Only camp on sites −
heaven help you if you cause a forest
fire. Purchase CEDOK currency voucher
(in London at CEDOK or at border into
country). You *can't* book.
*Shop Hours:* 08.00 to 12.00 and 14.00 to
18.00 Monday to Friday.
*Bank Hours:* 08.00 to 14.00 Monday to
Friday.
*British Embassy:* Thunovska 14, Prague 1;
telephone 533347.
*Tourist Office:* Czechoslovak Tourist
Board. 17−18 Old Bond Street, London
W1; telephone 01-629 6058.

## Denmark

*Area:* 43,069 km² (16,629 square miles)
including 500 islands. Kingdom of
Denmark also includes the Faeroe
Islands (area 1,399 km²; 540 square
miles) and Greenland (area 2,175,600
km²; 839,771 square miles).
*Capital:* Copenhagen (København).
*Population:* 5,059,000. 45.6% urban.
*Occupation:* Small farms or light industry.
*Climate:* As in Scotland with longer and
colder winters. Temperatures range
from − 12 to 28 °C (11 to 83 °F). Up to
84% humidity. High summer June to
the end of August.
*Measures:* Metric.
*Electricity:* 220/380 V a.c. 50 Hz. Plugs:
two-pin round.
*Transport:* One international airport:
Copenhagen. Airlines: S.A.S., B.A.,
K.L.M., Aer Lingus, Austrian Airlines,
Alitalia, Air France, Lufthansa, Pan Am,
Sabena, Swissair. Extensive, efficient
rail network. Main islands linked by rail
and car ferries. Road: drive on the
right. Seat belts compulsory. Travel on
buses in metropolitan areas for flat
rate up to one hour. Good bicycle
tracks beside all main roads.
*Currency:* Krone = 100 øre. No restriction
on amount you can take in but you can
only take out what you imported and
declared.
*Religion:* 95% Evangelical–Lutheran. Also
other denominations.

*Visa:* No.
*Jabs:* No.
*Language:* Danish: English widely spoken. Very little German; less French.
*Time:* G.M.T. + 1.
*Hotels:* No official categories. Many first-class hotels. Hostels: information from the Use-It Youth Centre in Copehagen. Some theft in large hostel sites. Danish inns plentiful everywhere. Camping sites by the hundred.
*Shop Hours:* 08.00 to 17.30 with late shopping Friday. Open Saturday morning.
*Bank Hours:* 09.30 to 16.00 Monday to Friday; late closing Thursday.
*British Embassy:* Kastelsvej 38-40, DK-2100 Copenhagen Ø; telephone (01) 144600.
*Tourist Office:* Danish Tourist Board, Sceptre House, 169-173 Regent Street, London W1R 8PY; telephone 01-734 2637.

## Djibouti

*Area:* 22,000 km² (8,494 square miles).
*Capital:* Djibouti.
*Population: 106,000.*
*Occupation:* Import/export. Shipping on coast. Nomadic herding inland.
*Climate:* June to August hot (up to 45 °C (113 °F) and dry. May and September hot and damp. Average rainfall: Djibouti 125 mm (5 inches) a year, mostly November and March.
*Measures:* Metric.
*Electricity:* 220/380 V a.c. 50 Hz.
*Transport:* Airport at Djibouti. Fly from U.K. via Addis Ababa by Air Djibouti and Ethiopian Airlines. Departure tax. Trains between Djibouti, Dire Dawa and Addis Ababa — sleepers.
*Currency:* Djibouti franc.
*Religion:* Islam. Also Christian churches in Djibouti.
*Visa:* No.
*Jabs:* Smallpox, cholera (yellow fever if from infected area). Take care against prickly heat.
*Language:* Official French. Local Arabic. English understood.
*Time:* G.M.T. + 3.
*Hotels:* European style in Djibouti. Water should be boiled.
*Shop Hours:* 08.00 to 12.00 and 16.00 to 20.00 Monday to Saturday.
*Bank Hours:* 07.00 to 12.00 Monday to Saturday.
*British Embassy:* None. Refer to British Embassy, Addis Ababa, Ethiopia.

## Dominican Republic

*Area:* 48,734 km² (18,816 square miles).
*Capital:* Santo Domingo.
*Population:* 4,697,000. 60% rural.
*Occupation:* Agriculture: sugar, coffee, tobacco, cocoa.

*Climate:* Tropical. June to October 34–37 °C (93–98 °F), high humidity. November to April 27–29 °C (80–85 °F), dry with cool nights. June to November: hurricane season.
*Measures:* Metric and U.S.
*Electricity:* 115 V a.c. 60 Hz. Plugs: two flat pins.
*Transport:* International airport near Santo Domingo. Fly via New York, Miami or Madrid. Embarkation tax. No passenger rail service. Roads rough. Quite good buses travel between towns, but capital's bus service limited.
*Currency:* Peso oro = 100 centavos. No restrictions on import or export.
*Religion:* R.C. Also Protestant churches.
*Visa:* No.
*Jabs:* Smallpox. T.A.B. recommended.
*Language:* Spanish. Interpreters available through hotels.
*Time:* G.M.T. – 5 (– 4 in summer).
*Hotels:* No official rating. Loews, Gulf + Western, Sheraton and others.
*Shop Hours:* 08.00 to 12.00 and 14.00 to 18.00 Monday to Friday. 08.00 to 12.00 Saturday.
*Bank Hours:* 08.00 to 12.30 Monday to Friday. Some open Saturday morning.
*British Embassy:* Avenida Independencia 506, Santo Domingo; telephone 682.3128/9.

## Ecuador

*Area:* 283,561 km² (109,483 square miles).
*Capital:* Quito.
*Population:* 6,733,000. 40% Indian, 10% European, 40% mixed.
*Occupation:* Agriculture. Increasing development of petroleum.
*Climate:* Temperate in Quito: temperatures 3–27 °C (37–80 °F); average 16 °C (60 °F). Guayaquil on coast: tropical, humidity up to 94%. Rain: December to April on coast.
*Measures:* Metric, imperial and Spanish measures and weights.
*Electricity:* 110 V a.c. 60 Hz. Plugs: two-pin flat.
*Transport:* Two international airports: Quito and Guayaquil. Fly, via Miami or Paris, by B.A. or Air France. Also K.L.M., Iberia, Lufthansa. Railways link three main cities. Roads: main trunk roads busy with lorries and buses travelling at 30–40 m.p.h. — resist the temptation to overtake without being able to see ahead: it could send you over the edge! Petrol — cheap but poor quality. Hitch-hiking not difficult — but cold in mountains.
*Currency:* Sucre = 100 centavos. U.S.$ travellers cheques preferred to sterling. No restrictions on import or export of local currency.
*Religion:* R.C. Protestant and Jewish minorities.

*Visa:* No: but you must get an embarkation/disembarkation card from an Ecuador consulate; you have to buy a tourist stamp for 50 sucres at the airport and put it on your card before you leave. You must have onward or return tickets. Consulate at Flat 3B, 3 Hans Crescent, Knightsbridge, London SW1X 0LS; telephone 01-584 2648.
*Jabs:* Smallpox. Cholera and yellow fever if from infected area. Take precautions against stomach upsets and hepatitis. There is a risk of malaria in Esmeraldas, Napo and Pastaza provinces.
*Language:* Spanish.
*Time:* G.M.T. − 5.
*Hotels:* No official rating. Inter-Continental and others of high standard.
*Shop Hours:* 08.30 to 18.30 (closed for lunch for two hours) Monday to Friday.
*Bank Hours:* 09.00 to 12.00 and 15.00 to 16.30 Monday to Friday.
*British Embassy:* Gonzalez Suarez 111, (Casilla 314), Quito; telephone 230070/3.
*Tourist Office:* Dirección Nacional de Turismo, Santa Prisca 106, P.O. Box 2454, Quito.

## Egypt, Arab Republic of

*Area:* 1,001,449 km² (386,661 square miles). The Sinai Peninsula has been occupied by Israel since the Six-Day War.
*Capital:* Cairo.
*Population:* 37,233,000. Fellahin, Bedouin and Nubian races.
*Occupation:* Cotton, fruit growing, petroleum.
*Climate:* Sometimes very hot. Temperatures from 18−38 °C (65−100 °F). Rainfall: minimal.
*Measures:* Metric
*Electricity:* 220 V a.c. 50 Hz. 110 V in some places.
*Transport:* International airports: Cairo and Alexandria. Airlines: B.A., United Arab Airlines. Roads: drive on right. Petrol stations few and far between. Spares difficult. Pedestrians should watch for vehicles in cities. Railways: nationalized, connecting all major points. Cheap, good service with sleepers. Student reductions. Public transport usually overcrowded. Car hire difficult, try small ads in the press.
*Currency:* Egyptian pound = 100 piastres. Local currency may not be taken out. Only 20 pounds may be taken in.
*Religion:* Muslim, Coptic Christian minority.
*Visa:* Yes. It costs £2.45. You need one photo. Consular Affairs Office of Embassy at 19 Kensington Palace Gardens, London W8; telephone 01-229 8818. Travellers must register name and address with passport

authorities within forty-eight hours — usually your hotel will do it, but check.
*Jabs:* Smallpox. Yellow fever and cholera if from infected area. Take precautions against sunburn, headaches, dysentery. Typhoid jab recommended.
*Language:* Arabic. Also French, English, Greek.
*Time:* G.M.T. + 2.
*Hotels:* Government-classified from five to one star. Many boarding-houses and inexpensive hotels.
*Shop Hours:* 08.30 to 13.30 and 16.30 to 19.00 Monday to Thursday and Saturday.
*Bank Hours:* 08.30 to 12.30 Monday to Thursday and Saturday. 10.00 to 12.00 Sunday.
*British Consulate:* Ahmed Raghal Street, Garden City, Cairo; telephone 20850/9.
*Tourist Office:* Egyptian State Tourist Office, 62A Piccadilly, London W1; telephone 01-493 5282.

## El Salvador

*Area:* 21,393 km² (8,260 square miles) on Pacific coast of Central America.
*Capital:* San Salvador.
*Population:* 4,007,000.
*Occupation:* Agriculture: coffee, cotton, sugar. Coffee is the basis of the country's prosperity.
*Climate:* Varies with altitude: average temperature in San Salvador 22 °C (72 °F) with only 3° variation. Best: November to January. Rain: 1830 mm (72 inches) a year.
*Measures:* Metric and local weights and measures.
*Electricity:* 110/220 V a.c. 60 Hz. Plugs: American two-pin.
*Transport:* International airport: San Salvador. Fly via New York, Miami or Jamaica. Airlines include Pan Am and Iberia. Two main railways: San Salvador to Santa Ana and into Guatemala. Roads: you must show proof of ownership and register if you take a car in. Need El Salvador plates after sixty days. Good bus service round country.
*Currency:* Colon = 100 centavos. No restrictions on import or export.
*Religion:* R.C. with some Protestant churches.
*Visa:* No. But use a separate passport if visiting Cuba first. Tourist cards valid for ninety days are issued by the carrier taking you in.
*Jabs:* Smallpox. Take precautions against typhoid, malaria.
*Language:* Spanish.
*Time:* G.M.T. − 6.
*Hotels:* Classified: de luxe, first, second class etc. Sheraton, and others. Hostels: camping north of San Salvador and at Lake Ilopango and at El Chorro (14½ km south from San

Salvador and 16 km north from San
Salvador respectively).
*Shop Hours:* 08.00 to 12.00 and 14.00 to
18.00 Monday to Friday. Saturday
morning.
*Bank Hours:* 08.30 to 11.30 and 14.30 to
17.00 Monday to Friday.
*British Embassy:* 11A Avenida Norte Bis,
No. 611, Colonia Dueñas, (Apartado
2350), San Salvador; telephone
219106/220590/223945.

## Equatorial Guinea

*Area:* 28,051 km² (10,831 square miles).
Coastal area and islands bounded by
Cameroon and Gabon.
*Capital:* Malabo.
*Population:* 310,000.
*Climate:* Average temperatures 21–34 °C
(70–93 °F). Rain: heaviest October to
December, January to May.
*Measures:* Metric.
*Electricity:* 220 V a.c. 50 Hz.
*Transport:* Airport: Malabo. Fly Iberia from
Madrid. Embarkation tax.
*Currency:* Ekuele = 100 céntimos. Spanish
pesetas and C.F.A. francs generally
negotiable. No restrictions on import
or export of local currency.
*Religion:* Nominally R.C., but recently
systematic persecution of Christians.
*Visa:* Yes: from embassy at Alonso Cano
27, Madrid. It is advisable to apply two
months in advance. Tourism is not
encouraged.
*Jabs:* Smallpox, yellow fever, cholera.
Take anti-malaria precautions.
*Language:* Spanish and numerous African.
*Time:* G.M.T. + 1.
*Hotels:* Reasonable and air-conditioned in
Malabo and Bata.
*Bank Hours:* 09.00 to 12.00 Monday to
Saturday.
*British Consulate:* Refer to Douala,
Cameroon.

## Ethiopia

*Area:* 1,221,900 km² (471,777 square
miles).
*Capital:* Addis Ababa.
*Population:* 27,946,000. Mainly Hamitic
and Semitic, but Arab, Indian and
Greek minorities.
*Occupation:* Farming: subsistence, coffee,
livestock.
*Climate:* Lowlands, hot and humid. Hill
country, warm. Uplands, cool. Addis
Ababa: 2–29 °C (35–85 °F). Rainy
season: February to March and July to
September. The Danakil Depression,
near the Red Sea, is the hottest place
on earth — 60 °C (140 °F).
*Measures:* Metric and local.
*Electricity:* 220 V. Plugs: two-pin
Continental.
*Transport:* Two international airports:
Addis Ababa and Asmara. Direct from
London: B.A. and Ethiopian Airlines.

Embarkation tax. Railway: Djibouti to
Addis Ababa line. Enjoyable method of
travel when political situation is calm.
Roads: drive on right. Repairs and
refuelling limited outside cities.
Frontiers sometimes closed without
warning. Never travel in one car —
always in convoy of two, in case one
breaks down. If you have a breakdown
stay with the car, lie under it to keep
cool, drink radiator water if no other.
Do not go exploring.
*Currency:* Birr = 100 cents. Up to 100 birr
may be taken in or out.
*Religion:* Coptic Christianity, Muslim and
traditional.
*Visa:* Yes. They cost £3.50. You must
present your smallpox and yellow
fever vaccination certificates and two
photos. Embassy at 17 Prince's Gate,
London SW7 1PZ; telephone
01-589 7212.
*Jabs:* Cholera, smallpox, yellow fever.
Typhoid, tetanus also advisable. Take
precautions against malaria and
mosquitoes. High altitude might have
effects.
*Language:* Amharic. English taught in
schools.
*Time:* G.M.T. + 3.
*Hotels:* No official rating. Hilton and others
in Addis Ababa.
*Shop Hours:* 08.00 to 20.00, with two- or
three-hour lunch, Monday to Friday.
*Bank Hours:* 09.00 to 17.00 Monday to
Friday. Three-hour lunch.
*British Consulate:* Papassinos Building, 4th
Floor, Ras Desta Demtew Avenue,
Addis Ababa; telephone 151305.
Consult them before leaving Addis
Ababa for any other part of Ethiopia.
*Tourist Organization:* Ethiopian Tourist
Organization, Ras Makonnen Avenue,
P.O. Box 2183, Addis Ababa; telephone
447470.
*Note:* There has been considerable
political upheaval since the overthrow
of Haile Selassie. Rebel groups operate
in some areas and the Eritrean
secessionist movement has been
fighting for its cause since 1962.
Recently Europeans have got caught
up in these fights with very unpleasant
consequences.

## Fiji

*Area:* 18,272 km² (7,055 square miles).
Over 300 islands, about 100 inhabited.
*Capital:* Suva.
*Population:* 573,000.
*Occupation:* Agriculture, sugar cane,
copra, tourism, gold mining.
*Climate:* Tropical and steaming.
Temperatures: 18–32 °C (65–90 °F).
Heavy rain December to April. Rainfall:
1780–3050 mm (70–120 inches) a
year. High humidity. Possible tropical
cyclones.

*Measures:* Imperial.
*Electricity:* 240 V a.c. 50 Hz. Plugs: special three-pin.
*Transport:* International airport: Nadi. Fly from U.K. by B.A. and Air New Zealand. Also Qantas, Pan Am, U.T.A., C.P. Air. No railways: small boats between islands. Roads: not good. Drive on left. International and U.K. driving licence. Buses: very overcrowded. Coaches are used for travelling around the island of Viti Levu.
*Currency:* Fijian dollar = 100 cents. You may take in any amount of local currency but you may only take out 100 dollars.
*Religion:* Christian, Hindu, Muslim.
*Visa:* No. A visitor's permit for one month is issued on entry, and may be extended for up to six months, but must have return ticket and proof of adequate means.
*Jabs:* Smallpox. Cholera and yellow fever if from infected areas.
*Language:* English, Fijian, Hindi, Cantonese.
*Time:* G.M.T. + 12.
*Hotels:* No official rating. First class in Suva, Lautoka and Nadi. Book in advance.
*Shop Hours:* 08.00 to 17.00. Late night Friday.
*Bank Hours:* 10.00 to 15.00 Monday to Friday.
*British High Commission:* Civic Centre, Stinson Parade, (P.O. Box 1355), Suva; telephone 311033 or 23280.
*Tourist Office:* Fiji High Commission, 34 Hyde Park Gate, London SW7 5DN; telephone 01-584 3661.

## Finland

*Area:* 337,009 km² (130,120 square miles). Over three-quarters is forests and lakes.
*Capital:* Helsinki.
*Population:* 4,707,000.
*Occupation:* Paper and pulp, forestry and agriculture.
*Climate:* Very cold winters, warm summers. Temperature range from − 24 to 28 °C (− 11 to 82 °F). Humidity up to 85%. Snow: January to March in south and central Finland, November to April in the north. About 22 hours of daylight in Helsinki in the summer.
*Measures:* Metric.
*Electricity:* 220 V a.c. 50 Hz.
*Transport:* International airport: Helsinki. Fly from U.K. by B.A. or Finnair. Railways: Helsinki linked to all main points and connections to Sweden and U.S.S.R. Book in advance. If you intend to do a lot of travel by rail get a Finnrail Pass from railway stations and authorized agencies (on production of passport). Roads: drive on right. Strict

drinking/driving rules. Flat-rate fare on urban buses and trams.
*Currency:* Markka = 100 pennia. You may take in any amount of local currency but you may only take out 3,000 markkaa.
*Religion:* Mainly Lutheran.
*Visa:* No.
*Jabs:* No: take precautions against mosquitoes in June in Lapland.
*Language:* Finnish or Swedish. Some English. Interpreters can be found through travel agencies.
*Time:* G.M.T. + 2.
*Hotels:* No official rating: first-class hotels in all main towns. Often crowded. Book well in advance. Motels on main highways. About 120 youth hostels, 200 holiday villages, 350 camping sites: most open from 10 June to 15 August.
*Shop Hours:* 08.30 to 17.00 Monday to Friday. Close earlier Saturday. Helsinki Railway Station Shops: 10.00 to 22.00; Sundays and holidays 12.00 to 22.00.
*Bank Hours:* 09.15 to 16.15 Monday to Friday.
*British Embassy:* Undenmaankatu 16−20, SF-00120 Helsinki 12; telephone 12574.
*Tourist Office:* Finnish Tourist Board, Finland House, 56 Haymarket, London SW1Y 4RN; telephone 01-839 4048.

## France

*Area:* 547,026 km² (211,208 square miles). Divided into ninety-five départements.
*Capital:* Paris.
*Population:* 52,913,000. 63% urban.
*Occupation:* Broadly industry in north and east, agriculture in south and west.
*Climate:* Temperate in the north. Mediterranean in the south. Paris 4−18 °C (40−65 °F) in winter, summer up to 27 °C (80 °F).
*Measures:* Metric.
*Electricity:* 220 V a.c. 50 Hz — usually. Plugs: two-pin round, standard European.
*Transport:* Airports: three in Paris, also all main cities. All international airlines including B.A., British Caledonian, Air France. Railways link all main cities. Driving: visitors' cars go in duty- and tax-free for six months. Toll charge on major highways. Buy metro tickets (first or second class) in Paris by the book for cheap travel. They are valid for buses as well. Over 500 miles of navigable rivers and canals.
*Currency:* Franc = 100 centimes. You may not take more than 5,000 francs out of the Franc Zone. No restriction on amount you may take in.
*Religion:* Predominantly R.C.
*Visa:* No.
*Jabs:* No.
*Language:* French.

*Time:* G.M.T. + 1 (+ 2 April to
September).
*Hotels:* Every type in plenty. Booking in
advance — even if only twenty-four
hours — advisable.
*Shop Hours:* 09.30 to 18.00 with local
variations. In provincial towns, all
shops shut between 12.00 and 14.00.
*Bank Hours:* 09.00 to 16.00 Monday to
Friday. Travellers cheques cashed from
07.30 to midnight at Le Bourget and at
Invalides air terminal.
*British Embassy:* 35 rue Faubourg
St-Honoré, 75008 Paris; telephone
2669142. Also consulates in Bordeaux,
Lyon, Lille, Marseille, and Strasbourg.
*Reference Books: Logis de France et
Auberges Rurales,* published by La
Fédération Nationale de Logis de
France, 25 rue Jean Mermoz, F-75008
Paris. J. Herson McCartney, *French
Farm and Village Holiday Guide,*
published by BHAM Books, 12-14
Whitfield Street, London W1; covers
1,000 moderately priced holiday
houses in France. *Relais de Campagne
et Châteaux,* published by the French
government, available from French
Tourist Offices. Covers a de luxe
selection of hotels where you can
expect attractive locations, lavish
facilities, superb food and top prices.
*Camping and Caravanning in France,*
published annually by Michelin.
*Tourist Office:* French Government Tourist
Office, 178 Piccadilly, London W1V
0AL; telephone 01-493 3171.

## French Guiana

*Area:* 91,000 km² (35,135 square miles).
*Capital:* Cayenne.
*Population:* 60,000.
*Occupation:* Mining, forestry. Also French
space station at Kourou. Bauxite.
*Climate:* Tropical. Average temperature at
sea level: 27 °C (80 °F). Rainy seasons:
April to August, November to January.
One rainy season in south: April to
September. Rainfall 3,555 mm (140
inches) a year on the coast.
*Measures:* Metric.
*Electricity:* 127/220 V a.c. 50 Hz.
*Transport:* One international airport:
Cayenne. Travel from Paris on Air
France. Taxis only to get into town:
bargain the price. No railways: interior
most accessible by boat. Roads: good
around Cayenne. Drive on right.
International licence required.
*Currency:* French franc = 100 centimes.
Restrictions as for France.
*Religion:* Predominantly R.C.
*Visa:* No: but ticket for onward travel
required.
*Jabs:* Yellow fever if staying for more than
two weeks or if arriving from an
infected area. Smallpox if arriving from
an infected area. Sleep under net in

non-air-conditioned rooms. Risk of
malaria January to March.
*Language:* French. Also a Creole dialect.
Some English.
*Time:* G.M.T. − 3.
*Hotels:* One main hotel in Cayenne and
Kourou. No official rating. Expensive
by comparison with Guyana and
Surinam.
*Bank Hours:* 07.00 to 11.30 and 14.00 to
16.00 Monday to Friday. Saturday
morning. If in extreme need Air France
Office, place des Palmistes.
*British Consulate:* 22 rue l'Alouette, (P.O.
Box 664), Cayenne; telephone 1034.
*Note:* If you wish to visit an Amerindian
village you must get permission from
the Prefecture in Cayenne before
arriving in French Guiana.

## French Polynesia

*Area:* About 4,000 km² (1,544 square
miles), comprising 130 islands in South
Pacific.
*Capital:* Papeete on Tahiti.
*Population:* 128,000. More than half on
Tahiti.
*Occupation:* Exports phosphates, copra,
vanilla.
*Climate:* Subtropical. Cooled by ocean
breezes. December to February: warm
and moist, 22−32 °C (72−90 °F). March
to November: cool and dry, 18−22 °C
(64−72 °F).
*Currency:* C.F.P. franc = 100 centimes.
You may not take more than the
equivalent of 5,000 French francs out
of the Franc Zone. Import unrestricted.
*Visa:* Not for a day of less than thirty days
if onward travel tickets are held.
*Jabs:* Smallpox. Yellow fever if arriving
from an infected area.
*Measures:* Metric.
*Electricity:* 110/220 V a.c.
*Language:* French, English.
*Time:* G.M.T. − 10.
*British Embassy:* None.
*Tourist Office:* Tahiti Tourist Board, Box
65, Papeete, Tahiti.
*Note:* All baggage of passengers coming
from Fiji or Samoa is collected on
arrival at Papeete for compulsory
disinfection.

## French West Indies

*Area:* Guadeloupe: 1,779 km² (687 square
miles). Martinique: 1,102 km² (425
square miles).
*Capitals:* Guadeloupe: Basse-Terre.
Martinique: Fort-de-France.
*Population:* Guadeloupe: 354,000.
Martinique: 363,000.
*Occupation:* Agriculture: sugar cane.
*Climate:* Tropical but varied. High
humidity, especially during rainy
season (May to November). Average
temperature 28 °C (83 °F).

*Measures:* Metric.
*Electricity:* Generally 220 V a.c. 50 Hz but some of Martinique and all of St. Martin is 110 V.
*Transport:* International airport at Pointe-à-Pitre, Guadeloupe. No railways. International driving permit.
*Currency:* French currency. Import and export restrictions as for France. U.S. currency widely used on St. Martin.
*Religion:* R.C.
*Visa:* No.
*Jabs:* Smallpox and yellow fever if from infected areas.
*Language:* French.
*Time:* G.M.T. − 4.
*Bank Hours:* 08.00 to 12.00 and 14.30 to 16.00 Monday to Friday.
*Shop Hours:* 08.00 to 12.00 and 15.00 to 18.00 Monday to Saturday.
*British Vice-Consulate:* c/o De Verteuil & Boyd S.A.R.L., B.P. 20, Pointe-à-Pitre, Guadeloupe.

## Gabon

*Area:* 267,667 km² (103,347 square miles).
*Capital:* Libreville.
*Population:* Estimates vary from 950,000 in 1970 to 526,000 in 1975.
*Occupation:* Mining, petroleum and timber.
*Climate:* Tropical. Temperatures from 21−32 °C (70−90 °F). Rainy: October to mid-May. Dry: May to September. Monsoon throughout wet season. Trade winds in dry season. Very high humidity.
*Measures:* Metric.
*Electricity:* 220 V 50 Hz. Plugs: two round pins.
*Transport:* One international airport: Libreville. Travel via Paris on U.T.A./Air Afrique. Trans-Gabon railway should be finished by early 80s. Roads often impassable. International driving permit. River Ogooué is a main transport route.
*Currency:* C.F.A. franc. No limit on import. Export limited to 75,000 francs.
*Religion:* Christian and traditional with Muslim minority.
*Visa:* Yes. It costs £6.00 and takes fifteen days to issue. You need three photos. Embassy at 66 Drayton Gardens, London SW10 9SB; telephone 01-370 6441.
*Jabs:* Yellow fever, smallpox, cholera. Take anti-malaria precautions.
*Language:* French.
*Time:* G.M.T. + 1.
*Hotels:* No official rating. Inter-Continental in Libreville.
*Shop Hours:* Closed Monday. 08.00 to 18.30 Tuesday to Saturday with long lunch closing.
*Bank Hours:* 07.00 to 12.00 Monday to Friday. Best to take French franc travellers cheques.

*British Consulate:* Refer to Douala, Cameroon.

## Gambia

*Area:* 11,295 km² (4,361 square miles). Only 24−48 km (15−30 miles) wide.
*Capital:* Banjul.
*Population:* 524,000.
*Occupation:* Farming (groundnuts).
*Climate:* Subtropical. Temperature range: 9−40 °C (49−104 °F). Rainy season: May/June to October, 1,015 mm (40 inches) a year. Average humidity: 85%.
*Measures:* Imperial.
*Electricity:* 230 V a.c. 50 Hz. Plugs: 15 A, three round pins or 13 A, three square pins.
*Transport:* One international airport: Banjul. Direct from London: British Caledonian, Sierra Leone Airways. No railways. Roads: those off the main tracks difficult from July to November. UK or international driving licence. Government steamer travels 480 km (300 miles) up Gambia river. Trans-Gambia highway links to Senegal. Big road-building programme. No part of country more than 24 km (15 miles) from navigable inland waterway.
*Currency:* Dalasi = 100 batuts. No limit on import. Export limited to 75 dalasi.
*Religion:* 90% Muslim, with Christian minority.
*Visa:* No: must have tickets for onward travel. Temporary visas granted on arrival.
*Jabs:* Smallpox, cholera and yellow fever, and enteric innoculation recommended. Take anti-malaria precautions.
*Language:* English and French.
*Time:* G.M.T.
*Hotels:* No official rating. Some first class in Banjul.
*Shop Hours:* 08.00 to 17.00 Monday to Friday. Closed for two to three hours for lunch. 08.00 to 12.00 Saturday.
*Bank Hours:* 08.00 to 13.00 Monday to Friday. 08.00 to 11.00 Saturday.
*British High Commission:* 78B Wellington Street, (P.O. Box 507), Banjul; telephone 244.

## German Democratic Republic

*Area:* 108,178 km² (41,768 square miles).
*Capital:* Berlin.
*Population:* 16,850,000.
*Occupation:* Industry: metal manufacture, chemicals, electronics. Agriculture.
*Measures:* Metric.
*Electricity:* 220 V three-phase a.c. 50 Hz. Plugs: Continental two-pin.
*Climate:* Temperate: warm summers, May to September, maximum 33 °C (91 °F); quite cold winters, November to February, minimum − 16 °C (3 °F).

GHANA

*Transport:* Three international airports: Leipzig, Berlin-Schoenefeld, Dresden. Direct from London on B.A. or L.O.T. (Polish). Railways: good service between East Berlin and main cities. Supplement on faster trains. Government travel agency: the Reiseburo. Roads: surfaces in small towns sometimes cobbled. Tourists can take their cars. International driving permit. Very widespread bus service.
*Currency:* Mark = 100 pfennigs. Local currency may not be imported or (apart from special commemmorative coins) exported. Visitors over the age of sixteen must buy at least 13 marks a day with foreign currency while staying in the G.D.R.
*Religion:* Evangelical 50%. 10% R.C. (Nominally atheist.)
*Visa:* Yes. It costs £3.30. Embassy at 34 Belgrave Square, London SW1X 8QB; telephone 01-235 4465. Transit visas can be got at Berlin-Schoenefeld Airport if travelling to West Berlin. A visa is necessary for a day trip from West to East Berlin and may be obtained at the sector crossing points.
*Jabs:* No. Cholera if arriving from infected area. Free medical treatment for British visitors except for car accidents.
*Language:* German. Interpreters through Intertext.
*Time:* G.M.T. + 1.
*Hotels:* Government classified de luxe, first and second class. State-run Interhotel Group. Youth hostels for foreign students. There is a shortage of hotel accommodation so book in advance.
*Shop Hours:* 10.00 to 19.00 Monday to Friday. Five-day week is legal requirement, so most closed Saturday and Sunday.
*Bank Hours:* 09.00 to 17.00 Monday to Friday.
*British Embassy:* 108 Berlin, Unter den Linden 32-34; telephone 220 2431.
*Tourist Office:* Berolina Travel Ltd., 19 Dover Street, London W1X 3PB; telephone 01-629 1664.

## Germany, Federal Republic of

*Area:* 248,577 km² (95,976 square miles).
*Capital:* Bonn.
*Population:* 61,832,000.
*Occupation:* Steel, mining, shipbuilding, chemical, engineering and automotive industries, oil refining.
*Climate:* Temperate. Similar to the U.K.
*Measures:* Metric.
*Electricity:* General supply 220–250 V a.c. 50 Hz, except in remote places where electricity is d.c. Private generating plants. Two-pin plugs earthed at side.
*Transport:* Airports at all main cities. Berlin has two, of which Tegel is the most modern. Airlines include B.A., Pan Am and Lufthansa. Trains: reliable service linking all main cities. D.B. tourist card allows nine to sixteen days unlimited travel, including buses, coaches and Rhine steamers. Ferry connection to London. Customs inspection carried out on T.E.E.s. Roads: urban speed limit 50–60 k.p.h. (31–37 m.p.h.). Autobahns 105–130 k.p.h. (65–80 m.p.h.) recommended limit, but traffic frequently exceeds this. International or foreign driving licence. British licence valid for one year. Drive on right. Traffic too fast to stop for hitch-hikers on Autobahns.
*Currency:* Deutschemark = 100 pfennigs. No restrictions on import or export.
*Religion:* Both Protestant and R.C.
*Visa:* No. (Smallpox if arriving from an infected area.)
*Jabs:* No.
*Language:* German. English widely spoken.
*Time:* G.M.T. + 1.
*Hotels:* Large selection in all main towns. All hotels serve rolls, meat, cheese and coffee breakfasts. 800 youth hostels. Also, camping sites.
*Shop Hours:* 09.00 to 18.00 Monday to Friday. Saturday morning. Vary around the country slightly: check.
*Bank Hours:* Vary: check on arrival. Usually 08.30 to 13.00 and 14.00 to 16.00 (18.00 Thursday). Shut Saturdays, Sundays.
*British Embassy:* D-5300 Bonn, Friedrich-Ebert Allee 77; telephone 234061. Consulates in all major cities.
*Tourist Office:* German National Tourist Office, 61 Conduit Street, London W1R 0EN; telephone 01-734 2600.

## Ghana

*Area:* 238,537 km² (92,099 square miles).
*Capital:* Accra.
*Population:* 9,610,000.
*Occupation:* Agriculture (cocoa), mining (gold).
*Climate:* Tropical. Hot and dry in north, hot and humid in forests of Ashanti and southwest plains. Warm and dry on coast. Humidity high except in north. Rainy seasons: April to July, September to October.
*Measures:* Imperial.
*Electricity:* 230/250 V a.c. 50 Hz. Plugs: three round or flat pins.
*Transport:* International airport: Accra. Direct from U.K. on British Caledonian, Ghana Airways. Railway from Accra to Takoradi and Kumasi. Slow. Roads: drive on the right. Transport includes State-run buses, mini buses and taxis. International driving permit endorsed by Police Licensing Officer.
*Currency:* Cedi = 100 pesawas. Not more than 20 cedis may be taken in or out.

*Religion:* 42% Christian. Muslim minority in north.
*Visa:* Yes. It costs 25p. Commonwealth citizens need entry permits. Holders of Rhodesian passports and white nationals of Portugal refused entry. Consular Section of High Commission at 38 Queen's Gate, London SW7 5HT; telephone 01-584 6311.
*Jabs:* Smallpox, yellow fever. Cholera if arriving from infected area. T.A.B.T. recommended. Take anti-malaria precautions.
*Langauge:* Official: English. Many local languages.
*Time:* G.M.T.
*Hotels:* No official rating. State Hotels Group generally of a high class.
*Shop Hours:* 08.00 to 12.00 and 14.00 to 17.30. Half-day closing Wednesday and Saturday.
*Bank Hours:* 08.30 to 14.00 Monday to Thursday. 08.30 to 15.00 Friday.
*British High Commission:* 3rd Floor, Barclays Bank Building, High Street, (P.O. Box 296), Accra; telephone 64651.

## Gibraltar

*Area:* 6 km² (2.3 square miles). A rocky peninsula, 4 km (2½ miles) long and 1.2 km (¾ mile) wide.
*Population:* Estimates vary from 27,000 in mid-1975 to 29,000 in mid-1974.
*Occupation:* Naval base.
*Climate:* Mediterranean. Temperature: 7–29 °C (45–85 °F). Rain: September to May. During summer months, humidity can be very high, due to Levanter (warm, moist, easterly breeze).
*Measures:* Imperial.
*Electricity:* 240 V a.c. 50 Hz. Plugs: three flat pins.
*Transport:* One airport. Airlines: B.A., Gibair, British Caledonian. Drive on right. International or U.K. driving licence. Third-party insurance required. No railways. Popular port for yachts: good marina.
*Currency:* Pound = 100 pence. You may take in any amount of local currency but you may only take out 25 pounds.
*Religion:* Mainly R.C. Jewish and Hindu minorities.
*Visa:* No.
*Jabs:* No, unless from infected area. If sick, hospitals treat G.B. patients at very small charge, covered by British social security.
*Language:* English, Spanish.
*Time:* G.M.T. + 1.
*Hotels:* No official rating. Holiday Inn and others of like standard.
*Shop Hours:* 09.00 to 13.00 and 15.00 to 19.00 Monday to Friday. 09.00 to 13.00 Saturday. When cruise liners are in, shops are allowed extra hours and open on Sundays and public holidays.

*Bank Hours:* 09.00 to 15.30 Monday to Friday. Re-open 16.30 to 18.00 Friday.
*British Governor:* The Convent, Gibraltar; telephone 5908/5933.
*Reference Book:* Handbook from Gibraltar Tourist Office.
*Tourist Office:* Gibraltar Tourist Office, 2 Grand Buildings, Trafalgar Square, London WC2; telephone 01-930 2284.

## Greece

*Area:* 131,944 km² (50,944 square miles).
*Capital:* Athens.
*Population:* 9,046,000. 52% urban.
*Occupation:* Agriculture: grain, cotton, tobacco, olives, fruit. Tourism. Mining. Industry, especially in Athens and Salonika.
*Climate:* Mediterranean: temperatures down to 0 °C (32 °F) in winter, up to 38 °C (100 °F) in summer. Rain: mainly November to March.
*Measures:* Metric.
*Electricity:* 220 V a.c. Plugs various: two or three pins, round, flat or square.
*Transport:* One international airport: Athens. Airlines from London: B.A., Olympic. Extensive railway network. Possible to go from London to Athens by train. 50% rebate to students on railways on production of passport and proof of current academic activity. International or foreign driving licence. Tourists may get petrol at cut price, with coupons obtained at entry points to country, branches of the National Bank of Greece, and N.T.O.G. (Tourist Office). Drive on right. Two toll roads: great trunk road to North and West to Peloponnese. Very extensive bus service in cities, towns and long distance. Some of the roads are calamitous. Extensive network of ferries to the larger islands from Piraeus and other ports.
*Currency:* Drachma = 100 lepta. Not more than 750 drachmas may be taken in or out.
*Religion:* 97% Greek Orthodox.
*Visa:* No.
*Jabs:* Only if arriving from infected area.
*Language:* Modern Greek. English spoken in cities and in popular tourist areas.
*Time:* G.M.T. + 2 (+ 3 April to September).
*Hotels:* All classes in most towns. Greek Tourist Board classifications: de luxe, A, B, C and D. Overbooking crisis in 1976: so get confirmation. Possible to combine flight and vouchers for cheap accommodation in pensions. Camping restricted to proper camping sites. Y.M.C.A. and Y.W.C.A. youth hostels.
*Shop Hours:* flexible.
*Bank Hours:* 08.00 to 13.00 Monday to Saturday.
*British Embassy:* 1 Ploutarchou, Athens 139; telephone 736211.

*Reference Book:* A most magnificent book called *Greece* from the National Tourist Organization of Greece. The most beautiful pictures in any of the books I've seen!

*Tourist Office:* National Tourist Organization of Greece, 195–197 Regent Street, London W1R 8DL; telephone 01-734 5997.

## Guatemala

*Area:* 108,889 km² (42,042 square miles).
*Capital:* Guatemala City.
*Population:* 5,540,000 (mid-1973). 45% Amerindian.
*Occupation:* Agriculture: coffee, cotton, bananas, sugar cane, maize, beans. Light industry.
*Climate:* Varies. Coast: hot and humid. Highlands: dry and cool. Guatemala City temperatures: November to January 28–30 °C (82–86 °F), but 4–6 °C (39–42 °F) at night; March to May 37 °C (98 °F), down to 7 °C (45 °F) at night. Rainy season: May to October.
*Measures:* Metric and Spanish.
*Electricity:* 110 V a.c. 60 Hz. Plugs: two square pins.
*Transport:* International airport: Guatemala City. No direct flight from London. Airlines include Pan Am, T.A.C.A., Air Panama, Aviateca, S.A.H.S.A., K.L.M., Iberia. Railways: Guatemala City linked to main cities. Possible to go to Mexico City by train, changing at border. Roads: compulsory to stop at army checkpoints. Don't park on the streets at night: risks of break-ins. International driving permit. Bus service to Mexico and rest of Central America.
*Currency:* Quetzal = 100 centavos. No restrictions on import or export.
*Religion:* R.C. predominant.
*Visa:* Yes — from a consulate in Europe or en route in the U.S.A. or Mexico.
*Jabs:* Smallpox if coming from an infected area. Avoid over-exertion in high altitudes. Take mosquito repellent. Risk of malaria exists outside urban areas in some departments at altitudes below 1,000 m.
*Language:* Spanish. English understood in business circles.
*Time:* G.M.T. – 6.
*Hotels:* No official rating. First class in Guatemala City. In the Chichicastenango, a village in the highlands of Maya-Quiche, is the Mayan hotel, one of the best in the country.
*Shop Hours:* 08.00 to 18.00 Monday to Friday. Two-hour lunch-break. Saturday morning.
*Bank Hours:* 09.00 to 15.00 Monday to Friday.

*British Consulate:* Edificio Maya, Via 5, No. 4–50, 8° Piso, Zone 4, Guatemala City; telephone 61329.

## Guinea

*Area:* 245,857 km² (94,926 square miles).
*Capital:* Conakry.
*Population:* 4,416,000.
*Occupation:* Agriculture, iron ore, alumina.
*Climate:* Tropical and humid. Temperatures 18–34 °C (64–94 °F). Humidity very high — 89%. Rain: average 4,290 mm (169 inches) a year, mostly May to October.
*Transport:* One international airport: Conakry. No direct flight from London. Go via Paris and Amsterdam on Air France, K.L.M. Also Ghana Airways, Air Afrique or Air Guinee. Railway: Conakry to Kindia and Kankan. Roads: impassable in rainy season.
*Measures:* Metric.
*Electricity:* 220 V a.c. 50 Hz.
*Currency:* Sily = 100 cauris. Old currency 1 sily = 10 Guinea francs. Both currencies still quoted. Local currency may not be taken in or out.
*Religion:* Muslim majority. Christian minority.
*Visa:* Yes. It costs 48 French francs and takes seven days to issue. You must present your smallpox vaccination certificate and two photos. Tourists not welcome. Journalists forbidden unless at invitation of Government.
*Jabs:* Smallpox, yellow fever. T.A.B.T. recommended. Take anti-malaria precautions. Take supplies of toiletries with you.
*Language:* Official: French.
*Time:* G.M.T.
*Hotels:* Some reasonable. Not all do food.
*Shop Hours:* 07.30 to 18.30 with two-hour break for lunch.
*Bank Hours:* Mornings only Monday to Saturday.
*British Consulate:* La Torréfaction Guinéenne, (B.P.158), Conakry; telephone 43705 (office); 62165 (home).

## Guinea-Bissau

*Area:* 36,125 km² (13,948 square miles).
*Population:* 525,000.
*Occupation:* Agriculture (rice, groundnuts, coconuts), herding. Large bauxite deposits have been located.
*Climate:* Tropical, hot and wet.
*Measures:* Metric.
*Electricity:* 220 V a.c.
*Transport:* Airport at Bissau served by T.A.P.
*Currency:* Guinea peso = 100 centavos.
*Religion:* Muslim and traditional.
*Visa:* Yes: available on arrival.
*Jabs:* Smallpox and yellow fever. Cholera recommended. Take anti-malaria precautions.

*Language:* Portuguese.
*Time:* G.M.T.
*British Embassy:* Refer to Dakar, Senegal.
*Tourist Office:* Centro de Informacão e Turismo, (Caixa Postal 294), Bissau.

## Guyana

*Area:* About 215,000 km² (about 83,000 square miles).
*Capital:* Georgetown.
*Population:* 791,000. 50% Eastern India descent.
*Occupation:* Agriculture: sugar, rice. Mining: bauxite. Fishing.
*Climate:* Tropical. Temperature range 22–31 °C (72–88 °F). Rain: 2,030–2,795 mm (80–110 inches) a year. Rainy seasons April to August and November to January. One rainy season in south: April to September.
*Measures:* Imperial.
*Electricity:* 110 V a.c. 50 Hz, changing by 1978 to 60 Hz. Wide variety of plugs.
*Transport:* International airport: Georgetown. Airlines: B.A., S.L.M./A.L.M., British West Indian Airways. Embarkation tax. No railways — main interior links by river.
*Currency:* Guyana dollar = 100 cents. Local currency may not be taken in or out.
*Religion:* Hindu, Muslim and Christian.
*Visa:* No.
*Jabs:* Smallpox. Cholera and yellow fever if arriving from infected area. There is a risk of malaria in some non-urban areas.
*Language:* Official: English.
*Time:* G.M.T. − 3.
*Hotels:* No official ratings. Good hotels in Georgetown.
*Shop Hours:* 08.00 to 16.00 daily with lunch closing. Saturday: morning only.
*Bank Hours:* Mornings, Monday to Saturday.
*British High Commission:* 44 Main Street, (P.O. Box 625), Georgetown; telephone 65881.

## Haiti

*Area:* 27,750 km² (10,714 square miles). One-third of island of Hispaniola.
*Capital:* Port-au-Prince.
*Population:* 4,584,000. 90% African origins.
*Occupation:* Agriculture: coffee, sugar, fruit. Light industry. Tourism. Bauxite.
*Climate:* Subtropical. Temperatures from 24 to 35 °C (75–95 °F). Cooler in mountains. Rainy season: April to June, September to November.
*Measures:* U.S. weights and measures.
*Electricity:* 110 V a.c. 60 Hz.
*Transport:* International airport: Port-au-Prince. No direct flight from London. Airlines: Pan Am, Air France. Airport to city by shared taxi. Must give driver your full address as he is responsible to police to see you go there. Railways: used only for goods. Roads: an asphalt road from Port-au-Prince to Pétionville (10 km). An asphalt road from Pétionville to Kenscoff (16 km).Buses (*camionnettes*) run between these towns: otherwise taxis called *'publiques'* and lorries.
*Currency:* Gourde = 100 centimes. No restrictions on import or export.
*Religion:* Predominantly R.C. Voodoo practised.
*Visa:* Not for a visit of thirty days or less but you must have tickets for onward travel.
*Jabs:* Smallpox. Cholera and yellow fever if from infected area. T.A.B.T. advisable. Prophylaxis against malaria essential.
*Language:* French: official. Creole. Many speak English — conscious of importance of tourist trade.
*Time:* G.M.T. − 5.
*Hotels:* No official rating. Several first class in Port-au-Prince.
*Bank Hours:* 09.00 to 13.00 Monday to Friday.
*British Consulate:* Shell Building, rue Pavée, Port-au-Prince; telephone 21227.
*Tourist Office:* Departement du Tourisme, Port-au-Prince.

## Honduras

*Area:* 112,088 km² (43,277 square miles). Part of the old Mayan Empire. Now one of the seven countries of the land bridge between North and South America.
*Capital:* Tegucigalpa.
*Population:* 3,037,000.
*Occupation:* Agriculture: bananas, coffee, meat. Forestry.
*Climate:* Tropical. Hot and humid on coast, cooler in hills. Rain frequent on Atlantic coast throughout the year. Heavy September to February. Average temperature in Tegucigalpa: 23 °C (74 °F). Hurricane territory.
*Measures:* Metric and old Spanish.
*Electricity:* 110/220 V a.c. 60 Hz. Plugs: two-pin.
*Transport:* International airports: Tegucigalpa, San Pedro Sula. Served by Honduras Airlines. No direct flights from London. Railways for crop transport only. Five good main roads: North Highway, Pan American Highway, Southern Highway, North Coast Highway, Western Highway. Foreign or international driving licence. Travel often by ox-cart and mule.
*Currency:* Lempira (also known as peso) = 100 centavos. No restrictions on import or export.
*Religion:* Predominantly R.C.
*Visa:* Not for a stay of up to ninety days.

*Jabs:* Smallpox. T.A.B.T. recommended.
Take anti-malaria precautions. Use a
mosquito net.
*Language:* Spanish.
*Time:* G.M.T. − 6.
*Hotels:* No official rating. First class in
Tegucigalpa and San Pedro Sula.
*Shop Hours:* 08.00 to 18.00 Monday to
Friday. Lunch closing. Saturday
morning.
*Bank Hours:* 08.30 to 16.30 Monday to
Friday. Lunch closing.
*British Consuls:* The Embassy closed in
November 1975 (Honduras claims
neighbouring Belize). There are
honorary consuls at Tegucigalpa
(telephone 220069) and San Pedro Sula
(telephone 04522140).

## Hong Kong

*Area:* 1,045 km² (403 square miles):
mainland area and numerous islands.
*Capital:* Victoria.
*Population:* 4,367,000. 98% Chinese.
*Occupation:* Tourism, manufacturing.
*Climate:* Subtropical. Temperature range:
February 16 °C (60 °F) to July 28 °C
(82 °F). Spring (March to May) —
temperature rises and humidity is high.
Rain in summer (late May to
mid-September) — humid. Rainfall:
2,160 mm (85 inches) a year.
Occasional tropical storms. Best
season autumn, late September to
early December. December to February
chilly.
*Measures:* Imperial, changing to metric.
*Electricity:* 200 V a.c. 50 Hz. Plugs vary.
*Transport:* International airport: Hong
Kong. Airlines: B.A., Pan Am, K.L.M.,
Lufthansa, Swissair. Plenty of taxis.
Limousine and airport coach service to
major hotels. Railway: within Hong
Kong to Sheung Shui. Kowloon to
Canton in China nineteen times daily.
33.5 km (20.8 miles) long — get out at
Lo Wu for Canton, walk across frontier
and get on Chinese National Railway.
Ferries: major links around islands.
Possible to hire motor boats called
*Walla-walla.* Cross Harbour Tunnel
(three years old) 1¼ miles long.
Roads: all visitors with valid overseas
licence can drive for twelve months; if
a new arrival wants to stay, Hong
Kong driving licence from Transport
Building, 2 Murray Road. Buses and
minibuses plentiful; trams on Hong
Kong Island.
*Currency:* Hong Kong dollar = 100 cents.
No restrictions on import or export.
*Religion:* Mostly Buddhist and Taoist:
many minorities.
*Visa:* No.
*Jabs:* Smallpox and cholera advisable.
Many hospitals have resident doctors:
reasonably priced hospital treatment
available. Passengers are

recommended to hold a valid
international certificate for cholera if
arriving from infected local areas.
*Language:* English and Cantonese
Chinese.
*Time:* G.M.T. + 8.
*Hotels:* No official rating. Some of the
most de luxe in the world. Several
major chains. Cheaper hotels in
Wanchai area and near ferry terminal,
Kowloon. Y.M.C.A. in Hong Kong and
Kowloon.
*Shop Hours:* Central 09.00 to 18.00;
Queens Road 10.00 to 20.00; Kowloon
commercial 10.00 to 22.00. Many open
late seven days a week. Bargaining still
possible on roadside stalls, bazaars
and 'local' shops.
*Bank Hours:* 10.00 to 15.00 Monday to
Friday. 09.30 to 12.00 Saturday.
*British Governor:* Government House,
Victoria; telephone 232031.
*Reference Book:* Facts and information
available from Hong Kong Tourist
Association, including booklet, *The
Stop and Shop* bargain guide to Hong
Kong.
*Tourist Office:* Hong Kong Tourist
Association, 14−16 Cockspur Street,
London SW1Y 5DP; telephone
01-930 4775.

## Hungary

*Area:* 93,030 km² (35,919 square miles).
*Capital:* Budapest.
*Population:* 10,540,000.
*Occupation:* Agriculture (wheat and
maize). Considerable industrialization
in recent years.
*Climate:* Hot summers, cold winters.
Budapest: January − 13 °C (8 °F), July
32 °C (90 °F). Rain: 840 mm (33 inches)
a year, mostly in winter.
*Measures:* Metric.
*Electricity:* 220 V a.c. 50 Hz. Plugs: two
round pins.
*Transport:* International airport: Budapest.
Airlines from U.K.: B.A., Malév.
Embarkation tax. Railways: link all
major cities. Road: drive on right.
International permit and insurance
required. Third-party insurance
compulsory. No speed limit on
highways with one or two exceptions.
City transport: buy tickets in advance
at kiosks or tobacconists. Budapest
Metro: coin-operated barriers.
*Currency:* Forint = 100 fillers. After arrival,
visitors must change the equivalent of
U.S.$7.40 daily into forint, throughout
stay. Not more than 400 forints may be
taken in or out in local currency.
*Religion:* R.C. Protestant minority.
*Visa:* Yes. It costs £3. Issued by Consulate
abroad or at road border points and
airport. Visitors must register with
police. Hotels do it automatically.
Consular Section of Embassy at 35B

Eaton Place, London SW1; telephone
01-235 2664.
*Jabs:* None.
*Language:* Hungarian (Magyar); German
also widely spoken. Interpreters
through State Tourist Office.
*Time:* G.M.T. + 1.
*Hotels:* Government rating system: de
luxe, A1, A2, B and C. Some State-run:
some indefinite, e.g. Inter-Continental.
Small hotels and rooms. Camping
possible. Always book everywhere.
*Shop Hours:* 09.00 to 18.00 Monday to
Friday. 09.00 to 15.00 Saturday.
*Bank Hours:* 09.00 to 13.00 Monday to
Friday. 09.00 to 11.00 Saturday.
*British Embassy:* Harmincad Utca 6,
Budapest V; telephone 182880.
*Tourist Office:* Danube Travel, 6 Conduit
Street, London W1R 9TG; telephone
01-493 0263.

## Iceland

*Area:* About 103,000 km² (about 40,000
square miles). Volcanic. 80%
uninhabitable.
*Capital:* Reykjavík.
*Population:* 218,000.
*Occupation:* Agriculture, fishing.
*Measures:* Metric.
*Electricity:* 220 V a.c. 50 Hz. Plugs: two
round pins, local variety.
*Climate:* Warmer than you might think.
Average temperature in Reykjavík in
January — 1 °C (30 °F), in July 11 °C
(52 °F). Strong winds and severe gales
in winter. Rain: 835 mm (34 inches) a
year, heavier in summer. In summer,
only three hours darkness at night.
*Transport:* International airport: Reykjavík.
Served by Flugleidir from U.K. No
railways. Roads in country often
unpaved, drive on right. International
driving permit. Specially built buses all
over the island and air services cover
the whole area.
*Currency:* Krona = 100 aurar. Not more
than IKr 1,500 may be taken in or out.
*Religion:* Evangelical Lutheran with
minorities.
*Visa:* No.
*Jabs:* No.
*Language:* Icelandic. English widely
spoken.
*Time:* G.M.T.
*Hotels:* No official rating. Camping
available everywhere.
*Shop Hours:* 09.00 to 18.00 Monday to
Thursday. 09.00 to 22.00 Friday.
Saturday morning.
*Bank Hours:* 09.30 to 15.30 Monday to
Friday.
*British Embassy:* Laufasvegur 49 (P.O.
Box 230), Reykjavík; telephone 15883.
*Reference Book: Iceland in a Nutshell* from
Iceland Tourist Association, Öldugata
3, Reykjavík.

*Tourist Office:* Iceland Tourist Information
Bureau, 73 Grosvenor Street, London
W1X 9DD; telephone 01-499 9971.

## India

*Area:* 3,287,590 km² (1,269,343 square
miles) (including Indian-held part of
Jammu and Kashmir).
*Capital:* New Delhi.
*Population:* 598,097,000. Increasing at one
million per month.
*Occupation:* Agriculture: tea, jute, cotton,
sugar. Manufacturing: animal
foodstuffs, iron and steel, textiles,
chemicals.
*Climate:* There are four distinct seasons:
the cold season (December to March);
the hot season (April to May); the
rainy season (June to September); and
the pleasant season (October to
November). Mean temperatures: Delhi
7—35 °C (45—95 °F), Calcutta 18—32 °C
(65—90 °F) humid, Bombay 16—32 °C
(60—90 °F) humid, Madras 21—32 °C
(70—90 °F) humid. Maximum
temperatures of about 41 °C (105 °F)
and 44 °C (112 °F) are reached during
May in Madras and Delhi respectively.
*Measures:* Metric.
*Electricity:* 220 V a.c. 50 Hz. (In some areas
d.c.). Plugs: round two- or three-pin.
*Transport:* Main international airports:
Delhi, Bombay, Calcutta, Madras.
Airlines from U.K.: B.A., Air India,
Qantas, Pan Am, J.A.L. Embarkation
tax Rs 20. Railways: built largely in
nineteenth century — still link most
major towns. Some carriages are
air-conditioned. Book in advance
always. Local trains: people travel free
by hanging on outside. Roads: 30
m.p.h. in cities. Drive on left.
International driving permit.
Third-party insurance compulsory.
*Currency:* Rupee = 100 paisa. Local
currency may not be taken in or out.
*Religion:* Largely Hindu, also Muslim,
Sikh, Jain, Buddhist, Parsee and
Christian.
*Visa:* No: unless of Asian descent with
passport prefixed C or D.
*Jabs:* Smallpox and cholera
recommended. Yellow fever if from
infected area.
*Language:* Hindu (official). English. Many
local languages. A few words of Urdu
are useful.
*Time:* G.M.T. + 5½.
*Hotels:* Not too many although the
position is improving rapidly. Book.
Classified by Government Department
of Tourism: de luxe, five star to one
star. Also, traveller bungalows (*dak*),
cheap but take own bedding:
sleeping-bag, pillow, blankets, etc.
*Shop Hours:* Hours vary but generally they
do not open until 10.00. Two hours
lunch closing.

*Bank Hours:* Generally 10.00 to 14.00 Monday to Friday. Saturday morning in some cities.
*British High Commission:* telephone Delhi: 690371. Bombay: 274874. Calcutta: 445171. Madras: 83136.
*Reference Books:* L. F. Rushbrook Williams, *A Handbook for Travellers in India, Pakistan, Nepal, Bangladesh and Sri Lanka (Ceylon),* 22nd edition (London: John Murray, 1975). L. F. Rushbrook Williams, *Handbook to India, Burma, Ceylon and Pakistan* (London: John Murray, 1975).
*Tourist Office:* Government of India Tourist Office, 21 New Bond Street, London W1Y 0DY; telephone 01-493 0769.

## Indonesia

*Area:* 1,919,270 km² (741,033 square miles) (including West Irian and East Timor).
*Capital:* Djakarta.
*Population:* 136,716,000. Malays.
*Occupation:* Petroleum products, copra, coffee, rubber, sugar, spices.
*Climate:* Always hot. Average temperature 27 °C (80 °F). Cooler in the hills. High humidity. Air-conditioning necessary for comfort. Rain: monsoon October to April.
*Measures:* Metric.
*Electricity:* 220 V a.c.
*Transport:* International airport: Djakarta. From U.K.: B.A. to Singapore, then transfer for Djakarta on Cathay Pacific, Indonesian Airlines, Singapore Airlines. Islands linked by planes and boats (State-run and private). Railways in Java and Sumatra. Railway link from Djakarta to Surabaja and Banjuwangi (for ferry to Bali). Roads: international driving permit. Roads o.k. in Java, but not much anywhere else. Bicycle rickshaw, *betjak,* shared with other passengers.
*Currency:* Rupiah = 100 sen. Not more than 2,500 rupiahs may be taken in or out.
*Religion:* Mostly Muslim (94%). Christian and Hindu minorities.
*Visa:* Yes. It costs £1.20 and takes four days to issue. You need two photos. Embassy at 38 Grosvenor Square, London W1X 9AD; telephone 01-499 7661. Special permission necessary to visit West Irian.
*Jabs:* Smallpox, cholera, T.A.B.T. and yellow fever recommended. Take anti-malaria precautions. Insect repellent. Expect tummy upsets.
*Language:* Indonesian.
*Time:* West (Java, Sumatra, Bali) G.M.T. + 7; Central (Borneo, Celebes, Timor) G.M.T. + 8; East (Moluccas, West Irian) G.M.T. + 9.
*Hotels:* Tourist Board classification: de luxe, first, standard. Good number of top-class hotels. Boarding-houses called *losmen.*
*British Embassy:* Jalan M. H. Thamrin 75, Djakarta; telephone 41098.
*Tourist Office:* Indonesian Council for Tourism, Djalan Diponegoro 25, Djakarta.

## Iran

*Area:* 1,648,000 km² (636,295 square miles).
*Capital:* Tehran.
*Population:* 33,019,000.
*Occupation:* Petroleum production and refining, cotton, agriculture, textiles, mining. Large merchant class — dealing in banking and insurance.
*Climate:* Varies. Tehran: January 3 °C (38 °F), July 29 °C (84 °F), rain heaviest in March. Caspian coast: regular rainfall, fresh breezes. Gulf coast: hot and humid, dust storms.
*Measures:* Metric.
*Electricity:* 220 V a.c. 50 Hz. Plugs: two round pins.
*Transport:* International airlines: Tehran and Abadan. Direct from UK: B.A. and Iranair. Embarkation tax. Railways: one train a week to Europe. Tehran linked to main cities. Good railway services, but not many. Roads: international driving permit — may need two photos. Make sure you are insured. Driving customs are very dodgy and the foreigner is always in the wrong. Inform consulate if you have an accident and do not sign anything. Buses are the most popular way to travel — they go everywhere.
*Currency:* Rial. You may take in any amount of local currency but may not take out more than 3,000 rials.
*Religion:* Islam, mainly Shia sect.
*Visa:* No.
*Jabs:* Smallpox. T.A.B.T. recommended. Cholera and yellow fever if from infected area.
*Language:* Farsi (Persian). Translators through Ministry of Justice.
*Time:* G.M.T. + 3½ (+ 4½ March to September).
*Hotels:* Tourist office classifications: de luxe, four star, three star etc. Major international chains. Schools used as hostels in summer.
*Shop Hours:* Closed afternoons in summer, open evenings.
*Bank Hours:* 08.00 to 13.00 Saturday to Thursday. Also 16.00 to 18.00 Saturday to Wednesday. Friday closing.
*British Embassy:* Avenue Ferdowsi, (P.O. Box 1513), Tehran; telephone 45011.
*Tourist Office:* Iran Information and Tourist Centre, 17–25 Sloane Street, London SW1X 9NE; telephone 01-235 4441.

## Iraq

*Area:* 434,924 km² (167,925 square miles).
*Capital:* Baghdad.
*Population:* 11,124,000.
*Occupation:* Mainly agriculture: grain, rice, tobacco, barley, dates, cotton, liquorice. Cement. Petroleum.
*Climate:* Subtropical. Summers, May to September, very hot and dry, except round Basra which is humid. Winters cold. Little rain. Flooding April to May caused by melting of the mountain snows.
*Measures:* Metric.
*Electricity:* 220 V a.c. 50 Hz. Plugs: two- and three-pin Continental.
*Transport:* International airport: Baghdad. Direct from U.K.: B.A. and Iraqi Airways. Railways link Baghdad with Basra and Kirkuli. Regular service. Special arrangements can be made for stops to see archaeological sites. From Mosul, the line goes to Syria, Turkey and Europe. Roads: metalled roads link major towns. Large development programme under way. International driving permit — two photos required.
*Currency:* Iraqi dinar = 1000 fils. You may not take in more than 25 dinars or take out more than 5 dinars.
*Religion:* Islam with large Christian minority.
*Visa:* Yes. It costs £2.80 and takes six weeks to issue. Also, different passport if visiting Israel. Embassy at 21-22 Queen's Gate, London SW7 5JG; telephone 01-584 7141.
*Jabs:* Smallpox. T.A.B.T. and cholera recommended.
*Language:* Arabic, some Turkish, Kurdish and English.
*Time:* G.M.T. + 3.
*Hotels:* None of top class by international standards. First, second and third class rating by Tourist Board. There are guest-houses, but only one Youth Hostel (Y.H.A.). Book well in advance — generally full.
*Shop Hours:* Open mornings and early evenings. Closed Friday.
*Bank Hours:* Mornings only Saturday to Thursday. Closed Friday.
*British Embassy:* Sharia Salah ud-Din, Karkh, Baghdad; telephone 32121.

## Ireland, Republic of

*Area:* 70,283 km² (27,136 square miles).
*Capital:* Dublin.
*Population:* 3,127,000.
*Occupation:* Agriculture, industry.
*Climate:* Temperate. Slightly milder than U.K. Famous for fine, soft rain and mists.
*Measures:* Imperial, going metric.
*Electricity:* 220 V a.c.
*Transport:* International airports: Dublin, Cork, Shannon. Airlines: Aer Lingus,

B.A. Railways: connect main towns. Roads: foreign or international driving licence. Network of minor roads across the country. Watch for horsedrawn vehicles!
*Currency:* U.K. currency legal tender, alongside Republic notes of same value. Not more than Ir£25 may be taken out. No restrictions on amount that may be taken in.
*Religion:* Largely R.C.
*Visa:* No. U.K. citizens do not need a passport.
*Jabs:* No.
*Language:* English, Irish.
*Time:* G.M.T. (+ 1 March to October).
*Hotels:* Tourist Board classifications: A*, A, B*, B, C and D. Also possible to stay in Irish Country Houses: see Guide. Farm holidays and cottage holidays (self-catering) — list from Irish Tourist Board.
*Shop Hours:* 09.00 to 13.00 and 14.00 to 18.00 Monday to Friday. Some close Saturday afternoon.
*Bank Hours:* 10.00 to 15.00 Monday to Friday. One late night a week.
*British Embassy:* 33 Merrion Road, Dublin 4; telephone 695211.
*Tourist Office:* Irish Tourist Office, Ireland House, 150 New Bond Street, London W1Y DAQ; telephone 01-493 3201.

## Israel

*Area:* Originally 20,700 km² (7,992 square miles) but now over 77,700 km² (30,000 square miles) including territory occupied after Six-Day War.
*Capital:* Jerusalem.
*Population:* 3,371,000. 85% Jews, 15% Arabs.
*Occupation:* Agriculture for home and export. High-technology industries.
*Climate:* Warm and dry in hills and south. Humid coastal plain. Long, hot summers April to November. Cool, wet winters.
*Measures:* Metric. Some Israeli land measures.
*Electricity:* 220 V a.c. 50 Hz.
*Transport:* International airport: Tel Aviv. Direct from U.K.: B.A., El Al. Security very tight, so add an hour to all flight times. Avoid travelling during the week of Passover: no in-flight food or booze. Railways: link all main cities. Buses too, but often crowded. Public transport basically good and cheap but not always convenient. Also can be hot and overcrowded. For tourism it is useful to hire a car. Roads: 50 k.p.h. (31 m.p.h.) speed-limit in towns, 90 k.p.h. (56 m.p.h.) on highways; but rarely enforced. Drive on right. Seat belts compulsory outside towns. Israelis drive aggressively: be prepared to hold your own. If police catch you, you must pay. U.K. and international

driving licence. Parking a nightmare; fined if towed away. On Yom Kippur — the most religious day — Jews are not supposed to drive cars. This custom is also observed by non-Jews in Jewish areas.
Sherut: shared taxis from town centres. Cheaper than taxis: cost a little more than buses. Ideal way to get around. Find them near town bus stations. Do not tip.
*Currency:* Israeli pound (or *lira*, plural *lirot*) = 100 agorot. Not more than 200 pounds may be taken in or out. Not more than 180 pounds may be converted into foreign currency on leaving.
*Religion:* Judaism. Also important Muslim and Christian minorities.
*Visa:* No. If passport stamped on entry to Israel, you will need a second to get into Arab states.
*Jabs:* No. T.A.B.T. recommended.
*Language:* Hebrew and Arabic are official languages. Majority of signs in both Hebrew and English. English widely spoken, together with French, German and other European languages.
*Time:* G.M.T. + 2.
*Hotels:* Tourist Ministry grades hotels from five star to one star. Service often casual: don't get angry, it's just their style. Plenty of international-style hotels. Excellent hostels, good camping sites. You can also stay on a kibbutz and work for keep. No pubs: social meeting places are cafés for tea and coffee, though alcohol may also be served. Israelis traditionally do not drink alcohol much. A 28% surcharge is added if you pay in local currency.
*Shop Hours:* Open morning and evening: closed Friday evening and all Saturday.
*Bank Hours:* 08.30 to 12.00 Sunday to Friday. 16.00 to 17.00 Sunday, Monday, Tuesday, Thursday.
*British Embassy:* 192 Rehov Hayarkon Street, Tel Aviv 63405; telephone (03) 249171/5. British Consulate at Beit Sahar, 23 Ben Yehuda Street, Tel Aviv; telephone (03) 54514/5. British Consulate-General at Sheikh Jarrah, East Jerusalem; telephone (02) 282481; and Tower House, Station Road, West Jerusalem; telephone (02) 37619/37724.
*Tourist Office:* Israel Government Tourist Office, 59 St. James's Street, London SW1A 1LL; telephone 01-493 2431.

## Italy

*Area:* 301,225 km² (116,303 square miles).
*Capital:* Rome.
*Population:* 55,810,000.
*Occupation:* Industry in north: steel, cars, machinery. Agriculture in south.
*Climate:* Mediterranean: summers always warm, hot in south. Winters cold and wet, more extreme in north.

*Measures:* Metric.
*Electricity:* 110/220 V a.c. 50 Hz. Plugs: Continental two round pins.
*Transport:* International airports: Rome, Milan. Embarkation tax. Direct from U.K.: B.A. and Alitalia. Rail links between all main towns. Roads: drive on right. Foreign driving licence valid if it has an official translation (in England, obtained from A.A.). Italians drive fast and furiously with much sounding of horns. Do not be intimidated.
*Currency:* Lira: paper units of large denominations. Often stamps or sweets given as small change. Not more than 35,000 lira may be taken in or out.
*Religion:* R.C.
*Visa:* No: register with police on arrival. Hotels do it for you.
*Jabs:* No.
*Language:* Italian. They like you to have a go! Many hoteliers speak English.
*Time:* G.M.T. + 1 (+ 2 May to September).
*Hotels:* Tourist Board classifications: de luxe, four star, three star, etc. Smaller hotels often satisfactory. Clean with good food. Italy affiliated to Y.H.A. Also many camping sites.
*Shop Hours:* 09.00 to 13.00 and 16.00 to 19.00 or 19.30. Small self-owned shops all hours. (Various regional differences.)
*Bank Hours:* 08.30 to 13.30 Monday to Friday. Some later into afternoon, depending on area.
*British Embassy:* Via XX Septembre 80A, I-00187 Rome; telephone 4755551. Consulates in all main cities.
*Tourist Office:* Italian State Tourist Office, 201 Regent Street, London W1R 8AY; telephone 01-439 2311.

## Ivory Coast

*Area:* 322,463 km² (124,503 square miles).
*Capital:* Abidjan.
*Population:* Estimates vary from 4,885,000 to 6,673,000. Eighty tribes.
*Occupation:* Agriculture, coffee, cocoa, timber, bananas, fishing.
*Climate:* Tropical: equatorial rain forests in south, drier savannah in north. High humidity on coast. Rainy: May to July, October to November. Avoid travelling in rainy seasons.
*Measures:* Metric.
*Electricity:* 230 V a.c.
*Transport:* International airport: Abidjan. No direct flight from U.K. (British Caledonian intend to operate from 1978.) Connections in Ghana and Nigeria. Railway: one main line from Abidjan to Upper Volta. Roads: good network. Small, private bus services operate in addition to state bus company.

*Currency:* C.F.A. franc. No limit on import but not more than 10,000 francs may be taken out.
*Religion:* Traditional. Muslim and Christian minorities.
*Visa:* No.
*Jabs:* Smallpox, yellow fever. Take anti-malaria and tummy-upset precautions.
*Language:* French.
*Time:* G.M.T.
*Hotels:* No official rating. Several firstclass in Abidjan. Otherwise, cheaper and o.k. in suburb of Treichville. Book in advance. Club Mediterranée Village at Assinie.
*Shop Hours:* 08.00 to 12.00 and 14.30 to 18.30 Monday to Friday. Earlier closing: 17.30 Saturday.
*Bank Hours:* 08.00 to 11.30 and 14.30 to 16.30 Monday to Friday.
*British Embassy:* 5th Floor, Immeuble Shell, Ave. Lamblin, (B.P. 2581), Abidjan; telephone 226615.

## Jamaica

*Area:* 10,926 km² (4,232 square miles).
*Capital:* Kingston.
*Population:* 2,029,000. 90% African and mixed stock.
*Occupation:* Agriculture: sugar, bananas, citrus. Mining of bauxite. Fishing. Tourism.
*Climate:* Tropical. Temperature range 4–27 °C (40–80 °F). Humidity — up to 87%. July to October is hurricane season. June to August can be oppressively hot. Best months December to April. Rain intermittent from May — daily tropical showers in September, October and November.
*Measures:* Imperial, American and metric.
*Electricity:* 110 V a.c. 50 Hz.
*Transport:* Two international airports: Kingston and Montego Bay. Direct from U.K.: B.A. and Air Jamaica. Railways: Kingston to Montego Bay and Port Antonio. Roads: drive on right, international driving permit.
*Currency:* Jamaican dollar = 100 cents. Local currency may not be taken in or out.
*Religion:* 75% Protestant.
*Visa:* No.
*Jabs:* Smallpox. Cholera and yellow fever if coming from infected areas.
*Language:* English.
*Time:* G.M.T. − 5 (− 4 April to October).
*Hotels:* No official rating. Many large luxury hotels, especially round Montego Bay. Also lavish villas for rental to the rich. The Friend's Society have a hostel in Kingston.
*Shop Hours:* Half-day closing Wednesday in Kingston.
*Bank Hours:* 09.00 to 13.00 Monday to Thursday. Late opening Friday.

*British High Commission:* 58 Duke Street, (P.O. Box 628), Kingston; telephone 932 1930.
*Tourist Office:* Jamaica Tourist Board, 6–10 Bruton Street, London W1X 8HN; telephone 01-493 3647.

## Japan

*Area:* 372,313 km² (143,751 square miles).
*Capital:* Tokyo.
*Population:* 110,953,000. Over 70% urban.
*Occupation:* Heavy industry, cars, ships, electronics. ¬
*Climate:* Temperatures in Tokyo from − 1 °C (30 °F) in January to 32 °C (90 °F) in summer. November to March dry, cold and bright. March to August wet, humid. September: lovely bright autumns — risk of typhoons.
*Measures:* Metric.
*Electricity:* 110 V. Plugs: two flat pins.
*Transport:* International airport: Tokyo. Air direct from U.K.: B.A., Japan Air Lines. Railways: fast, punctual and extremely good service. Roads: drive on left. International driving permit. Driving styles hazardous. Hitch-hiking rare.
*Currency:* Yen. No limit on import but no more than 30,000 yen may be taken out.
*Religion:* Shinto, Buddhism, Japanese-speaking Christian churches in sizeable towns.
*Visa:* No.
*Jabs:* Smallpox. Cholera and typhoid if coming from infected areas.
*Language:* Japanese: some railway station signs in Western script.
*Time:* G.M.T. + 9.
*Hotels:* Western-style hotels in main cities. Traditional inns beautiful but you need to speak the language. Japan Travel Bureau: best of internal travel accommodation. Japan also has 'short stop hotels' — two hours for £15! Youth hostels public and private — book. I.Y.H.A. Members.
*Shop Hours:* Excellent dept. stores: Isetan, Takashimaya, Daimaru, Mitsu Koshi. Open 10.00 to 18.00, closed one day a week.
*Bank Hours:* 09.00 to 15.00 Monday to Friday and Saturday morning. U.K. bank branches in Tokyo and Osaka. Major cities only for travellers cheques.
*British Embassy:* 1 Ichiban-cho, Chiyado-Ku, Tokyo 102; telephone 265-5511.
*Reference Books:* Japanese Tourist Board leaflet — excellent. W. Duncan, *A Guide to Japan* (London: Ward Lock, 1976).
*Tourist Office:* Japan National Tourist Organization, 167 Regent Street, London W1R 7FD; telephone 01-734 9638.

## Jordan

*Area:* 97,740 km² (37,738 square miles).
About 6,300 km² (2,435 square miles)
occupied by Israel since Six-Day War.
*Capital:* Amman.
*Population:* 2,702,000.
*Occupation:* Agriculture, peasant
smallholdings, phosphate mining.
*Climate:* Arid. May to September hot and
dry, cool evenings. Temperäte in hills.
Very hot in Jordan valley. Rain
showers December to May.
*Measures:* Metric.
*Electricity:* 220 V a.c. 50 Hz. Plugs: various.
*Transport:* International airport: Amman.
Direct from London by Royal
Jordanian Airlines and B.A.
good main roads − south from
Amman through the desert. Road tax
on entry. International driving permit
valid for six months only for those
who enter with own car. Otherwise,
need Jordanian licence.
*Currency:* Dinar = 1000 fils. Not more than
100 dinars may be taken in and not
more than 25 dinars may be taken out.
*Religion:* Muslim. Christian minority.
*Visa:* Yes. If your passport has visa for
Israel, you will not be allowed in. Use
a second passport.
*Jabs:* Smallpox and cholera if from
infected area.
*Language:* Arabic. English widely spoken.
*Time:* G.M.T. + 2.
*Hotels:* Ministry of Tourism classification:
five star (i.e. de luxe) to one star. Good
rest-houses: spare but cheap. Youth
hostel at Jabal Weibdeh near
Department of Arts and Culture. No
official camping sites but possible to
camp on outskirts of towns.
*Shop Hours:* 08.00 to 18.00 Saturday to
Thursday. Lunch closing.
*Bank Hours:* 08.00 to 12.30 Saturday to
Thursday.
*British Embassy:* Third Circle, Jebel
Amman, (P.O. Box 87); telephone
37374/5.
*Tourist Office:* Jordan Tourist Board, 211
Regent Street, London W1; telephone
01-437 9465.
*Note:* Tourists in Jordan can visit the
Israeli-occupied West Bank of the
Jordan River. Get a permit from a
travel agent when you have been in
the country for forty-eight hours.

## Kenya

*Area:* 582,646 km² (224,960 square miles).
*Capital:* Nairobi.
*Population:* 13,399,000.
*Occupation:* Agriculture: tea, coffee,
cereals, cotton, sisal, pyrethrum. Food
processing.
*Climate:* Tropical along coast. Hot and dry
in north. Temperate in highlands.

Rainy seasons in Nairobi: April, June,
October to November.
*Measures:* Metric.
*Electricity:* 240 V a.c. 50 Hz. Plugs: two
round or three square pins.
*Transport:* International airport: Nairobi.
Direct flight from London by B.A.
Embarkation tax. Railways between
main cities. Main railway crosses
country east to west. Good roads
between major towns. Drive on left.
U.K. licence endorsed by Kenya good
for ninety days. (In game reserves
elephants have right of way!) Good but
busy bus services. Air charter
common.
*Currency:* Kenya shilling = 100 cents.
Local currency may not be taken in or
out.
*Religion:* Traditional African, Christian,
Muslim.
*Visa:* No. Visitor's pass issued on arrival.
But Asian holders of British passports
need visa and at least Shs. 4,000 in
foreign currency.
*Jabs:* Smallpox required. Yellow fever
recommended. Cholera required only if
arriving from an infected area. T.A.B.T.
recommended. There is a risk of
malaria varying from province to
province and depending on time of
year: seek advice.
*Language:* Swahili, English.
*Time:* G.M.T. + 3.
*Hotels:* No official rating. Of international
standard in Nairobi and Mombasa.
Lavish holiday hotels at coast resorts,
especially Malíndi.
*Shop Hours:* 09.00 to 13.00 and 14.00 to
18.00 Monday to Saturday. 09.00 to
12.00 Sunday.
*Bank Hours:* 09.00 to 13.00 Monday to
Friday. Saturday morning.
*British High Commission:* 13th Floor,
Bruce House, Standard Street, (P.O.
Box 30465), Nairobi; telephone 335944.
*Reference Book:* Kenya Tourist Office
Booklet.
*Tourist Office:* 318 Grand Buildings,
Trafalgar Square, London WC2N 5HB;
telephone 01-839 4477.

## Korea, Republic of (South Korea)

*Area:* 98,484 km² (38,025 square miles).
*Capital:* Seoul.
*Population:* 34,663,000.
*Occupation:* Manufacturing, clothes,
textiles, electricals, farming, fishing.
*Climate:* Summers, hot and humid July to
August; winters, dry and cold December
to February. Rainy season: July.
*Measures:* Metric and imperial.
*Electricity:* 110/220 V a.c. 60 Hz.
*Transport:* International airport: Seoul. No
direct flights from U.K.: go via Hong
Kong or Tokyo. Main towns linked by
rail and bus. International driving
permit.

*Currency:* Won. Local currency may not be taken in or out.
*Religion:* Several: Buddhism, Confucianism, Christianity, Shamanism.
*Visa:* No, up to sixty days.
*Jabs:* Smallpox. Cholera advisable.
*Language:* Korean. Some English and Japanese.
*Time:* G.M.T. + 9.
*Hotels:* Ministry of Tourism classification: de luxe, first, second and third class. International standards in Seoul.
*Bank Hours:* 09.30 to 16.00 Monday to Friday. Saturday morning.
*British Embassy:* 4 Chung Dong, Sudaimon-Ku, Seoul; telephone 75 7341.
*Tourist Office:* Bureau of Tourism, Ministry of Transportation, Seoul.

## Korea, Democratic People's Republic of (North Korea)

*Area:* 120,538 km² (46,540 square miles).
*Capital:* Pyongyang.
*Population:* 15,852,000.
*Occupation:* Agriculture: rice, barley, cotton, tobacco, hemp, ginseng. Mining: gold, copper, iron, tungsten. Industry.
*Climate:* Dry, cold winters. Hot, humid summers (July to August). Rain in July.
*Measures:* Metric.
*Transport:* International airport at Pyongyang. Flights by Aeroflot from Moscow. 10,500 km of railways. River and coastal navigation important for passenger and freight transport.
*Currency:* Won = 100 chon (or jun).
*Religion:* Buddhism, Confucianism, Taoism.
*Language:* Korean. (North and South Korea use different systems for writing Korean in the Latin alphabet.)
*Time:* G.M.T. + 9.
*British Embassy:* The U.K. has never recognized the Democratic People's Republic of Korea which it regards as having been set up by Soviet occupying forces in defiance of a United Nations resolution.
*Tourist Office:* Korean International Tourist Bureau, 'Ryuhaingsa', Pyongyang.

## Kuwait

*Area:* 17,818 km² (6,880 square miles).
*Capital:* Kuwait City.
*Population:* 996,000.
*Occupation:* Petroleum is basis of economy.
*Climate:* Extreme heat in summer. May to October 38 °C (100 °F) in the shade, worse July to August. Winters fairly cold. Rain November to January, 165 mm (6½ inches) a year. Sandstorms.

Little vegetation, small oases. Afforestation scheme.
*Measures:* Metric.
*Electricity:* 240 V a.c. 50 or 60 Hz. Plugs: three flat pins, or two- or three-pin Continental.
*Transport:* International airport: Kuwait City. Direct from London: B.A., Kuwait Airlines, Air India, Pakistan International. No railways. Roads: U.K. or international licence not accepted, but car-hire firms will arrange Kuwaiti licence. Speed limit 45 k.p.h. (28 m.p.h.) in Kuwait City, 70 k.p.h. (43 m.p.h.) outside.
*Currency:* Kuwaiti dinar = 1,000 fils. No restrictions on import or export.
*Religion:* Muslim.
*Visa:* No. Must have a No Objection Certificate, obtainable from Kuwaiti Consulates abroad. Passports with visa to Israel refused.
*Jabs:* Smallpox. T.A.B.T. advisable. Cholera and yellow fever if from infected area. Take salt tablets.
*Language:* Arabic. English second language.
*Time:* G.M.T. + 3.
*Hotels:* Ministry of Tourism classification: de luxe, four star, three star, etc. Hilton and Sheraton in an expanding hotel-building programme. At moment, about twenty hotels listed.
*Shop Hours:* Saturday to Thursday until 20.30 and Friday morning.
*Bank Hours:* Generally mornings only but some branches open some afternoons.
*British Embassy:* Al-Khaleej Street, P.O. Box 2, Safat; telephone 432046/9.

## Laos

*Area:* 236,800 km² (91,429 square miles).
*Capital:* Vientiane.
*Population:* 3,303,000.
*Occupation:* Agriculture: rice, tobacco, cotton and opium.
*Climate:* Subtropical: temperatures vary with altitude. Vientiane 13−38 °C (55−100 °F). Southwest monsoon: May to October. Best time to visit in dry, cool season from mid-November to February.
*Measures:* Metric.
*Electricity:* 220 V a.c. 50 Hz. Plugs: two-pin.
*Transport:* International airport: Vientiane. No direct flight from U.K. Go via Bangkok on Thai Airways. No railways. Roads: international driving permit. Travel limited by security. Mekong River used as highway. Road or train from Bangkok to Nong Khai, in northeast Thailand, then ferry or taxi to Vientiane.
*Currency:* Kip = 100 at.
*Religion:* Buddhist, R.C. minority.
*Visa:* Yes. Exit permit also necessary. Issue of visas suspended. Check with Embassy at 5 Palace Green, London W8 4QA; telephone 01-937 9510.

*Jabs:* Smallpox and cholera. Take
anti-malaria precautions.
*Language:* Laotian, Chinese, Thai,
Vietnamese, French and English.
*Time:* G.M.T. + 7.
*Hotels:* Lang Xang Hotel (U.S. dollars
only) is the leading hotel in Vientiane,
Government run. Also cheap and
primitive boarding-houses.
*British Embassy:* Pandit J Nehru Street,
(P.O. Box 224), Phone Xay Quarter,
Vientiane; telephone 2333.

## Lebanon

*Area:* 10,400 km² (4,015 square miles).
*Capital:* Beirut.
*Population:* 2,869,000.
*Occupation:* Port work, transport, food
industries, cement, tobacco, furniture
and leather goods. Buying and selling
(trading) — one of the chief banking
and taxation refuges in the world.
Banks may not reveal names of
customers or balances.
*Climate:* Mediterranean. Long, hot, dry
summers. Warm, wet winters. Rainfall:
can be heavy November to February.
Snow in mountains.
*Measures:* Metric.
*Electricity:* 110/220 V a.c. 50 Hz.
*Transport:* International airport: Beirut.
Direct flight from London: B.A., Middle
East Airlines. Embarkation tax varies.
Roads: above average for Middle East.
Make sure you carry good maps as the
signposting is minimal. International
driving permit. Petrol is cheap. The
two railway lines are reserved for
goods traffic. Buses are very cheap but
unreliable. Taxis and shared (service)
taxis are normally used.
*Currency:* Lebanese pound = 100 piastres.
No restrictions on import or export.
*Religion:* Half Muslim, half Christian,
encompassing a large number of sects.
*Visa:* Yes. Obtainable on arrival. Passports
with Israeli visa refused.
*Jabs:* Smallpox. Yellow fever if from
infected area. Mild dysentery not
unusual — curable by liquid diet of tea
without milk and separate dish of
curdled milk.
*Language:* Arabic; some English and
French.
*Time:* G.M.T. + 2.
*Hotels:* Tourist Board classifications: 4 star
A, 4 star B, 4 star C, 3 star A, 3 star B,
3 star C etc. International standards in
Beirut. Camping is free — there is a list
of sites issued by Tourist Board.
Tourist Board for Young People very
helpful and cheap hostels.
*Shop Hours:* Vary. Stay open late in
winter.
*Bank Hours:* Mornings only Monday to
Saturday.
*British Embassy:* Ave de Paris, RasBeirut,
Beirut; telephone 362500.

*Reference Book:* Jean Morineau, *Lebanon
Today* (Editions Jeunes Afriques,
1976).
*Tourist Office:* Lebanese Tourist and
Information Office, 90 Piccadilly,
London W1; telephone 01-409 2031.
*Note:* The country is attempting to recover
from a recent devastating civil war.
Ceasefire has been imposed by Syrian
forces.

## Leeward Islands

*Area:* Anguilla: 91 km² (35 square miles).
Antigua: 442 km² (171 square miles).
Montserrat: 98 km² (38 square miles).
St. Kitts–Nevis: 266 km² (103 square
miles). For other islands in the
Leeward chain see French West Indies,
Virgin Islands and Netherlands Antilles.
*Capitals:* Antigua: St. Johns. Montserrat:
Plymouth. St. Kitts–Nevis: Basseterre.
*Population:* Anguilla: 6,000. Antigua:
74,000. Montserrat: 12,000. St.
Kitts–Nevis: 59,000.
*Occupation:* Tourism, sugar, cotton.
*Climate:* Subtropical. April to December
average temperatures: 28–29 °C
(82–84 °F). January to March average
temperature: 24 °C (75 °F). Rainfall:
occasionally stormy June to October.
*Measures:* Imperial.
*Electricity:* Antigua: 110 V a.c. 60 Hz. Other
islands: 240 V a.c. 50 Hz.
*Transport:* International airport: St. Johns,
Antigua. Direct from U.K. by B.A. No
railways. Roads: international driving
permit.
*Currency:* East Caribbean dollar = 100
cents. No limit on import but you may
only take out what you brought in and
declared.
*Religion:* Predominantly Anglican.
*Visa:* No.
*Jabs:* Smallpox unless arriving direct from
the U.S.A. Cholera and yellow fever if
arriving from infected areas.
*Language:* English.
*Time:* G.M.T. − 4.
*Hotels:* No official rating. Several
first-class holiday hotels on Antigua,
Nevis and St. Kitts.
*Shop Hours:* 08.00 to 16.00 Monday to
Saturday. Early closing Thursday.
*Bank Hours:* Antigua and Montserrat:
08.30 to 12.00 Monday to Friday and
also 15.00 to 17.00 Friday. St.
Kitts–Nevis and Anguilla: 08.00 to
12.00 Monday to Saturday, except
Thursday. 08.00 to 11.00 Thursday.
*British Commissioner:* Anguilla: The
Valley; telephone 451.
*Deputy British Government
Representative:* Antigua: 38 St. Mary's
Street (P.O. Box 483), St. Johns;
telephone 20342. St. Kitts–Nevis: refer
to St. Lucia.
*British Governor:* Montserrat: Government
House, Plymouth; telephone 2409.

326

LESOTHO

*Tourist Office:* Eastern Caribbean Tourist Association, Room 222, 200 Buckingham Palace Road, London SW1 9TJ; telephone 01-730 6221/2.

## Lesotho

*Area:* 30,355 km² (11,720 square miles). Completely surrounded by Republic of South Africa.
*Capital:* Maseru.
*Population:* 1,039,000 plus about 125,000 absentee workers.
*Occupation:* Subsistence agriculture. 'Tourism' (Lesotho offers entertainments — films, books, etc. — that are banned in the Republic of South Africa). Economy depends on earnings of men who go to work in the Republic.
*Climate:* Rainy season October to March. Temperatures below freezing in winter.
*Measures:* Metric.
*Electricity:* 220 V a.c.
*Transport:* International airport at Maseru. Flights by South African Airways from Johannesburg. Short railway line from Maseru to Bloemfontein–Natal railway line. Roads mainly in western lowlands. International driving permit.
*Currency:* South African. Restrictions as for South Africa.
*Religion:* 75% Christian. Rest traditional.
*Visa:* No.
*Jabs:* Smallpox. Cholera and yellow fever if arriving from an infected area.
*Language:* English and Sesotho.
*Time:* G.M.T. + 2.
*Hotels:* Two in Maseru: Holiday Inn and Victoria.
*British High Commission:* P.O. Box 521, Maseru; telephone 3961.
*Tourist Office:* Lesotho Tourism Office, P.O. Box 527, Maseru.

## Liberia

*Area:* 111,369 km² (43,000 square miles).
*Capital:* Monrovia.
*Population:* 1,708,000.
*Occupation:* Subsistence agriculture.
*Climate:* Tropical. Temperatures from 21 to 32 °C (70 to 90 °F). Rainy season May to November, 3,810 mm (150 inches) a year on coast. Very high humidity.
*Measures:* Imperial, some U.S.
*Electricity:* 110/120 V a.c. 60 Hz. (220 V for air-conditioners). Plugs: two round or square pins.
*Transport:* International airport: Monrovia. Direct from U.K. by British Caledonian. Embarkation tax. Internal air links between main towns. No railways. Roads difficult in wet season. U.K. and international driving licence valid for thirty days after inspection. Drive on right.

*Currency:* Liberian dollar = 100 cents (L$1 = US$1). No restrictions on import or export.
*Religion:* Mostly traditional.
*Visa:* Yes: it costs £2.29. You need two photos and your smallpox and yellow fever vaccination certificates. Take spare photos for exit visa. Embassy at 21 Prince's Gate, London SW7 1QB; telephone 01-589 9405.
*Jabs:* Smallpox and yellow fever. Cholera if from infected area. Take anti-malaria precautions.
*Language:* English official.
*Time:* G.M.T.
*Hotels:* No official rating. Inter-Continental in Monrovia.
*Shop Hours:* 07.30 to 16.00, closed for lunch. Smaller shops open longer hours.
*Bank Hours:* 08.00 to 12.00 and 14.00 to 16.00 Monday to Friday.
*British Embassy:* Mamba Point, (P.O. Box 120), Monrovia; telephone 21055.

## Libyan Arab Republic

*Area:* 1,759,540 km² (679,361 square miles).
*Capital:* Tripoli.
*Population:* 2,444,000 of which 90% live on coastal strip.
*Occupation:* Agriculture, herding, oilfields and oil processing.
*Climate:* Mediterranean on coast. Desert, dry and arid interior. Can reach 38 °C (100 °F) June to August. High humidity. Rainfall: irregular, October to March.
*Measures:* Metric.
*Electricity:* West: 125 V a.c. 50 Hz. East: 220 V a.c. 50 Hz. Plugs: Continental, two round pins.
*Transport:* International airport: Ben Gashir, 19 km (12 miles) from Tripoli. Direct from U.K. on British Caledonian, B.A. and Libyan Arab Airlines. Embarkation tax. No railways. Roads: international driving permit. U.K. passport holders may not be able to drive across frontier into Egypt.
*Currency:* Libyan dinar = 1000 dirhams. Not more than 20 dinars may be taken in or out.
*Religion:* Muslim (Sunni).
*Visa:* Yes: it costs £2.90. You must present your smallpox vaccination certificate and two photos. Transit visas necessary for less than twenty-four hours. Exit permit necessary. Passport with visa to Israel refused. Passport details must be in Arabic: British passport office has a stamp for this. Must register on arrival. Embassy at 58 Prince's Gate, London SW7 2PW; telephone 01-589 5235.
*Jabs:* Smallpox. Yellow fever if from infected area. Certificates must include an Arabic translation. Climate can aggravate asthma and bad chests.

**Language:** Arabic.
**Time:** G.M.T. + 2.
**Hotels:** Department of Tourism classification: de luxe, first class, second class etc. International standards in Tripoli and Benghazi.
**Shop Hours:** Friday closing.
**Bank Hours:** Mornings only in winter. Also 16.00 to 17.00 in summer.
**British Embassy:** 30 Sharia Gamal Abdul Nasser, Tripoli; telephone 31191.
**Tourist Office:** Embassy of the Libyan Arab Republic, 58 Prince's Gate, London SW7 2PW; telephone 01-589 5235.

## Liechtenstein

**Area:** 157 km² (61 square miles).
**Capital:** Vaduz.
**Population:** 24,000.
**Occupation:** Metal manufacturing. Large artificial teeth factory. Liechtenstein is a popular tax-haven.
**Climate:** Mild.
**Measures:** Metric.
**Transport:** The railway line from Feldkirch (Austria) to Buchs (Switzerland) has 18.5 km of track and three stations in Liechtenstein. It is operated by Austrian Federal Railways. Good bus service. Modern roads.
**Currency:** Swiss (but centimes called Rappen and francs called Franken). No limits on import or export.
**Visa:** No.
**Jabs:** No.
**Language:** German (local dialect is called Alemannish).
**Time:** G.M.T. + 1.
**British Consulate-General:** Dufourstrasse 56, CH-8008 Zurich, Switzerland.
**Tourist Office:** National Tourist Office, Postfach, FL-9490 Vaduz.

## Luxembourg

**Area:** 2,586 km² (998 square miles).
**Capital:** Luxembourg City.
**Population:** 357,000.
**Occupation:** Steel, chemicals, plastics, rubber, agriculture, vine growing.
**Climate:** Temperate: summers cool, winters mild and wet.
**Measures:** Metric.
**Electricity:** 220 V a.c. Plugs: two round or flat pins.
**Transport:** International airport: Luxembourg City. Fly direct by B.A., Luxair. Embarkation tax varies with destination. Rail links between main towns. Good bus services. Roads: U.K. or international driving licence. Fines for traffic offences are collected on the spot.
**Currency:** Luxembourg franc = 100 centimes. No limits on import or export.

**Religion:** Largely R.C. Protestant and Jewish communities in large towns.
**Visa:** No.
**Jabs:** No.
**Language:** Official French, but main commercial language is German. Chamber of Commerce, Luxembourg, may be able to recommend translators.
**Time:** G.M.T. + 1 (+ 2 April to September).
**Hotels:** No official rating. Many of international standard. Holiday Inn at Common Market Centre. Y.H.A. overnight tax of 5% levied in Luxembourg City is included on bill.
**Shop Hours:** 08.00 to 12.00 and 14.00 to 18.00 Tuesday to Saturday. 14.00 to 18.00 Monday.
**Bank Hours:** 09.00 to 12.00 and 13.30 to 16.30 Monday to Friday.
**British Embassy:** 28 boulevard Royal, Luxembourg; telephone 29864.
**Tourist Office:** Luxembourg National Trade and Tourist Office, 66 Haymarket, London SW1Y 4RF; telephone 01-930 8906.

## Macao

**Area:** 16 km² (6 square miles) including two small islands at mouth of Canton River.
**Population:** 271,000 (mostly Chinese).
**Occupation:** Tourism — gambling casinos the big attraction. Growing industries.
**Climate:** Tropical. Wettest April to August. Temperature range: 16–28 °C (60–82 °F).
**Measures:** Metric.
**Electricity:** 110/220 V a.c. 50 Hz.
**Transport:** Fly to Hong Kong and take the ferry or hydrofoil (75 minutes). Taxis. Bicycles for hire.
**Currency:** Macao dollar = 100 cents. Hong Kong currency accepted (HK$1 = M$1.07). No limits on import or export of local currency.
**Religion:** Buddhist and R.C.
**Visa:** Yes: unless staying less than seven days. Obtainable from Portuguese Consulate-General, 3 Pedder Street, Hong Kong. Everyone must have a valid passport, unless Brazilian or Portuguese.
**Jabs:** Smallpox. Yellow fever if from infected area.
**Language:** Portuguese, Cantonese, English.
**Time:** G.M.T. + 8.
**Hotels:** No official rating. Not grand — usually small, clean and comfortable. Majority are air-conditioned.
**Shop Hours:** 09.00 to 17.30 Monday to Saturday.
**Bank Hours:** 10.00 to 15.00 Monday to Friday. Saturday morning.
**British Consulate:** British Trade Commission, 9th Floor, Gammon

House, 12 Harcourt Road (P.O. Box 528), Hong Kong; telephone 5-230176.
*Tourist Office:* Macao Tourist Information Bureau (represented by Marketing Services (Travel and Tourism) Ltd.), 52 High Holborn, London WC1V 6RL; telephone 01-242 3131.

## Madagascar

*Area:* 587,041 km² (226,657 square miles). Island off Mozambique.
*Capital:* Antananarivo.
*Population:* 8½ million. Originally came from Indonesia.
*Occupation:* Agriculture: coffee, vanilla, rice, spices, sugar cane, cattle.
*Climate:* Central highlands: cool subtropical, nights can be chilly. Coast: hot or very hot. Dry season April to October. Rain November to March.
*Measures:* Metric.
*Electricity:* 110/220 V a.c. 50 Hz.
*Transport:* International airport: Antananarivo. Direct from U.K. by B.A., Air France. Embarkation tax varies. Railway links between Antananarivo and Tamatave. Air Madagascar links all main towns. Roads: northern roads inferior, secondary roads impassable after rain.
*Currency:* Malagasy franc. Not more than 5,000 francs may be taken in or out.
*Religion:* Ancestor cult. Half of population also Christian.
*Visa:* Yes. Apply early. Costs 30 French francs. You have to supply two photos. Embassy at 1 boulevard Suchet, Paris 16; telephone 5041816.
*Jabs:* Smallpox, cholera and yellow fever if from infected areas. T.A.B.T. advisable. Take anti-malaria precautions.
*Language:* French and Malagasy.
*Time:* G.M.T. + 3.
*Hotels:* No official rating. Few first class in Antananarivo and Tamatave
*Shop Hours:* 08.00 to 12.00 and 14.00 to 18.00 Monday to Saturday.
*Bank Hours:* 08.00 to 11.00 and 14.00 to 16.00 Monday to Friday.
*British Consulate:* 5 rue Robert Ducrocq, Behoririka, Antananarivo, P.O. Box 167.
*Note:* Women must wear skirts with hemline below the knee. Penalty for contravention: 10 days in prison.

## Malawi

*Area:* 118,484 km² (45,747 square miles).
*Capital:* Lilongwe.
*Population:* 5,044,000. 95% rural.
*Occupation:* Subsistence farming.
*Climate:* Tropical. Temperature range from 24 to 33 °C (75 to 91 °F) depending on altitude. Hottest in October and November. Rainfall mostly December to March, falls in heavy showers or

thunderstorms. At any time: chiperoni, a cold wind from the southeast.
*Measureş:* Imperial, except for pharmaceuticals and petrol.
*Electricity:* 230–240 V. Plugꞩ three square pins.
*Transport:* International airport: Blantyre. Direct from U.K. by B.A. or Air Malawi. Two main railways link Malawi to Mozambique coast. Roads: main tourist routes have bituminized or first-class gravel surface. U.K. driving licence. Motor cruiser with nine berths provides week-long return cruises up and down Lake Malawi, calling at ten ports.
*Currency:* Kwacha = 100 tambala. Local currency may not be taken out and not more than 20 kwachas may be taken in.
*Religion:* Christian, Muslim.
*Visa:* No.
*Jabs:* Smallpox. Cholera and yellow fever if from infected area. Take anti-malaria precautions. Some pools and rivers unsafe because of bilharzia, but Lake Malawi is safe.
*Language:* English and Chichewa and other local languages.
*Time:* G.M.T. + 2.
*Hotels:* No official rating. Some of international standard in Blantyre.
*Shop Hours:* 08.00 to 16.00 Monday to Friday.
*Bank Hours:* Mornings only Monday to Saturday. Commercial Bank opens 16.30 to 18.00 on Friday.
*British High Commission:* Lingadzi House, (P.O. Box 30042), Lilongwe 3; telephone 31544.
*Tourist Office:* Marketing Services (Travel and Tourism) Ltd., 52 High Holborn, London WC1V 6RL; telephone 01-242 3131.
*Note:* Women must wear skirts which cover the knees. Women must not wear trousers, although this rule is relaxed in game parks. Short dresses or trousers are allowed inside some international hotels. 'Hippy' appearance (particularly men's hair below the collar-line) is not allowed.

## Malaysia

*Area:* 329,749 km² (127,317 square miles).
*Capital:* Kuala Lumpur.
*Population:* 11,900,000.
*Occupation:* Agriculture, rubber, palm oil, forestry, tin mining.
*Climate:* Tropical with little variation. Hot and humid, cooler in the hills. Rain all year: 3,050 mm (120 inches) a year.
*Measures:* Local, often Imperial.
*Electricity:* 230 V a.c. 50 Hz. Plugs: three square pins.
*Transport:* International airports: Penang (West), Kota Kinabalu (East). Direct flight from U.K.: B.A. Embarkation tax.

Good internal airway system. Railway: from Kuala Lumpur to Singapore and from Bangkok. Good trains everywhere but Borneo. Roads: U.K. or international driving licence. Straits Steamship Co., Singapore to Borneo. Luxury coaches connect cities. Good way to see all sights is a guided coach tour.
*Currency:* Malaysian dollar = 100 cents. Currency no longer interchangeable with Brunei. Not more than 1,000 Malaysian dollars may be taken in or out.
*Religion:* Muslim, Buddhist, Confucian, Taoist, Christian.
*Visa:* No. Persons of unkempt ('hippie') appearance refused entry.
*Jabs:* Smallpox. Yellow fever and cholera if from infected areas. Take anti-malaria precautions.
*Language:* Malay (now being universally taught), Tamil, Chinese, English (actually the main, common language).
*Time:* West: G.M.T. + 7½. East: G.M.T. + 8.
*Hotels:* Tourist Board classification: de luxe, first and tourist class. Air-conditioned in most large towns. Holiday Inns etc. Small and inexpensive Chinese hotels — clean and adequate. Government rest-houses.
*Shop Hours:* 09.00 to 18.00 Monday to Friday. Saturday morning. In Muslim areas, close Thursday afternoon and all Friday.
*Bank Hours:* Often very early in Sabah area.
*British High Commission:* 13th floor, Wisma Damansara, Jalan Semantan, (P.O. Box 1030), Kuala Lumpur 23–03; telephone 28179.
*Tourist Office:* Tourist Development Corporation of Malaysia, 17 Curzon Street, London W1Y 7FE; telephone 01-409 0400.

## Mali

*Area:* 1,240,000 km² (478,766 square miles).
*Capital:* Bamako.
*Population:* 5,697,000.
*Occupation:* Agriculture: rice, grain, peanuts, cotton, rubber.
*Climate:* Tropical: varies with region. Three seasons: November to February warm, February to May very hot, June to October rainy. Sahara always hot and dry.
*Measures:* Metric.
*Electricity:* 220 V a.c. 50 Hz.
*Transport:* International airport: Bamako. No direct flight from U.K. Railway from Bamako to Kayes and on to Dakar, Senegal. Roads: international driving permit. Trans-Saharan road from Algeria little used and very hazardous.

Bus services from Niger, Upper Volta and Guinea.
*Currency:* Mali franc. Local currency may not be taken out but there are no restrictions on taking it in to Mali.
*Religion:* Muslim.
*Visa:* Yes: it costs 50 French francs. Two photos.
*Jabs:* Smallpox, yellow fever and cholera. Take anti-malaria precautions.
*Language:* French and local languages.
*Time:* G.M.T.
*Hotels:* Two main hotels in Bamako.
*Shop Hours:* 09.00 to 12.00 and 15.00 to 18.00 Monday to Friday. Saturday morning.
*British Embassy:* Refer to Dakar, Senegal.

## Malta

*Area:* 316 km² (122 square miles).
*Capital:* Valletta.
*Population:* 300,000.
*Occupation:* Once British Services base; now ship-repairing, agriculture, tourism, light industry.
*Climate:* Mediterranean: cool winters, hot summers. July to September, average 32 °C (89 °F). October to May, average 23 °C (73 °F).
*Measures:* Metric and Maltese.
*Electricity:* 240 V a.c. 50 Hz.
*Transport:* International airport: Luqa. Embarkation tax. Direct from U.K. B.A., Air Malta. Passenger and car ferry to Gozo. No railways. Car ferry from Italy. Roads: drive on left. U.K. driving licence. *Karrozzin* — horsedrawn cabs.
*Currency:* Maltese pound = 100 cents. No restrictions on import but no more than 25 pounds may be taken out.
*Religion:* Strongly R.C. There are churches of other denominations.
*Visa:* No.
*Jabs:* Smallpox, yellow fever and cholera, only if from infected area.
*Language:* Maltese and English.
*Time:* G.M.T. + 1 (+ 2 April to September).
*Hotels:* Hotels Board categories: de luxe, 1A, 1B, 2A, 2B, 3, 4. Plenty of big holiday hotels, also guest-houses. Heavily booked in summer. Camping — no organized sites: nor for caravans.
*Shop Hours:* 09.00 to 12.30 and 16.00 to 19.00 Monday to Friday. 09.00 to 12.30 and 16.00 to 18.00 Saturday.
*Bank Hours:* Morning only Monday to Saturday.
*British High Commission:* 7 St. Anne Street, Floriana; telephone 21285/23651.
*Tourist Office:* Malta Government Tourist Office, 24 Haymarket, London SW1; telephone 01-930 9851.

## Mauritania

*Area:* 1,030,700 km² (397,955 square miles).

*Capital:* Nouakchott.
*Population:* 1,318,000.
*Occupation:* Agriculture: dates, grain, livestock. Some mining and fishing.
*Climate:* Tropical. Dry and arid in desert of north. Atlantic winds cool the coast. Warm October to May, hot and humid June to November. Storms likely.
*Measures:* Metric.
*Electricity:* 220 V a.c.
*Transport:* International airport: Nouakchott. Airlines: Air Afrique, U.T.A. Railways: one, primarily for freight. Roads: many sand tracks needing cross-country vehicles, spares kit and convoy travel. International driving permit.
*Currency:* Ouguiya = 5 khoums. No restriction on import but no more than 1,000 ouguiyas may be taken out.
*Religion:* Muslim.
*Visa:* Yes. A seven-day visa costs 40 French francs. A three-month visa is 100 French francs. Two photos needed.
*Jabs:* Smallpox. Yellow fever recommended. Cholera if from infected area. Take anti-malaria precautions.
*Language:* French, Arabic.
*Time:* G.M.T.
*Hotels:* No official rating. At least one international hotel in Nouakchott.
*Bank Hours:* 08.00 to 11.15 and 14.30 to 16.30 Monday to Friday.
*British Embassy:* Refer to Dakar, Senegal. Honorary Consul is W. Brown, Boîte Postale 629, Nouakchott; telephone 52839.

## Mauritius

*Area:* 2,045 km² (790 square miles).
*Capital:* Port Louis.
*Population:* 899,000.
*Occupation:* Sugar, tea, growing and processing. Increasing tourism. Light industries.
*Climate:* Tropical maritime. No extremes. Very humid on coast in summer. Occasional cyclones October to March.
*Measures:* Metric.
*Electricity:* 220 V a.c. Plugs: three flat pins.
*Transport:* International airport: Plaisance on southeast coast. Direct from U.K. by B.A., Air Mauritius. No railways. Roads: drive on left. International or U.K. driving licence. Over 1,000 km (600 miles) of second-class roads, scenic drives. Bus services link main towns, villages and resorts.
*Currency:* Mauritius rupee = 100 cents. Not more than 700 rupees may be taken in and not more than 350 rupees taken out.
*Religion:* Christian, Hindu, Muslim, Buddhism.
*Visas:* No. Onward tickets necessary.
*Jabs:* Smallpox. Yellow fever and cholera if from infected area.

*Language:* French, English, Hindi, Creole, Chinese.
*Time:* G.M.T. + 4.
*Hotels:* No official rating.
*Shop Hours:* 08.00 to 19.00 Monday to Saturday.
*Bank Hours:* 10.00 to 14.00 Monday to Friday. Saturday morning.
*British High Commission:* P.O. Box 586, Cerné House, Chaussée Street, Port Louis; telephone 20201.
*Reference Book:* D. Alexander, *Holiday in Mauritius: A Guide to the Island* (Cape Town/London: Purnell, 1973).
*Tourist Office:* Mauritius Tourist Office, 32 Shaftesbury Avenue, London W1; telephone 01-437 6394.

## Mexico

*Area:* 1,972,547 km² (761,603 square miles).
*Capital:* Mexico City.
*Population:* 60,145,000.
*Occupation:* Agriculture: coffee, maize, beans, sugar cane, sorghum, sisal, rice. Mining: silver, gold, coal, iron. Industry: iron, steel, chemicals, petroleum.
*Climate:* Varies with altitude from tropical lowlands to snowy mountains. Mexico City (2,300 m; 7,500 feet) warm: 19 °C (67 °F) year-round average. Rainy season: Mexico City, June to September.
*Measures:* Metric.
*Electricity:* Mexico City: 125 V a.c. 60 Hz. Elsewhere: 110–120 V a.c. 60 Hz.
*Transport:* International airport: Mexico City. Direct from U.K.: B.A. Embarkation tax. Rail links between Mexico City and all principal cities. Buses: book ahead and try to start at beginning of route. Roads: U.K. driving licence. Mexican insurance needed. Underground in Mexico City.
*Currency:* Peso = 100 centavos. Save 20-centavo coins, for use in some telephones. No restrictions on import or export of local currency.
*Religion:* Mainly R.C.
*Visa:* No: but a tourist card is needed (supplied by airline). Card F.M.8 allows stay of up to thirty days. Card F.M.5 up to 180 days. Need evidence of onward travel and sufficient funds.
*Jabs:* Smallpox. There is a risk of malaria outside urban areas in some states.
*Language:* Spanish. Some English.
*Time:* General: G.M.T. − 6. Baja California Sur and North Pacific Coast: G.M.T. − 7. Baja California: G.M.T. − 8 (− 7 April to October).
*Hotels:* No official rating. Good international hotels in main cities. Book in advance. Also many motels.
*Shop Hours:* Usually 10.00 to 19.00 Monday, Tuesday, Thursday and Friday.

Bank Hours: 09.00 to 13.30 Monday to Friday. Sterling travellers cheques not easily negotiable.
British Embassy: Lerma 71, Guautemoc, (P.O. Box 96 bis), Mexico 5, D.F.; telephone 5 114800.
Tourist Office: Mexican National Tourist Council, 52 Grosvenor Gardens, London SW1X OAX; telephone 01-730 0128.

## Monaco

Area: 1.49 km² (368 acres), lying at the foot of the Southern Alps.
Capital: Monte Carlo. Built on a narrow strip of coastline.
Population: 25,000 of whom 4,500 are Monegasque.
Occupation: Running the Casino; tourism; manufacturing luxury goods; precision instruments, publishing.
Climate: Mild in winter, rising from 8 °C (47 °F) in January and February to 16 °C (80 °F) in summer (mean average 27 °C (61 °F) ). 2,583 hours sun per year.
Measures: Metric.
Transport: Nice, Côte d'Azur Airport is 22 km away. Connection by taxi (F80) or by special bus (F20). From Monte Carlo Railway station there is an extensive train service from and to all towns on the Côte d'Azur from Cannes to Menton. Buses every 12 minutes round the principality. Connections to surrounding areas 06.00 to 01.00 every half hour on a seaside route. Middle Corniche route and long distance to Menton, La Turline, Roquebrune Village, Italy. Helicopters link Nice Airport and golf clubs. Drive on right. Rules of the road as in France.
Currency: French franc: some small-value Monegasque coins. Restrictions as for France.
Religion: Mainly R.C. But churches of Anglican, Jewish, Protestant and Baha'i faiths.
Visa: No.
Jabs: No.
Language: French: a lot speak English.
Time: G.M.T. + 1 (+ 2 April to September).
Hotels: Big chain hotels, Holiday Inn, Loew's etc. All Government approved and under the star system (1–4 star de luxe), not forgetting the Mecca of all gourmets, the Hotel Mirabeau. Small hotels are good too. Prices include tax and service.
Shop Hours: 08.30 to 13.00.
Bank Hours: 09.00 to 12.00 and 14.00 to 16.00 every day except Saturday and Sunday and public holidays.
British Consulate: 24 avenue du Prado, 13006 Marseille; telephone 534332.
Tourist Office: Service du Tourisme, 2A boulevard des Moulins, Monte Carlo.

## Mongolia

Area: 1,565,000 km² (604,249 square miles).
Capital: Ulan Bator.
Population: 1,444,000.
Occupation: Herding sheep, goats, horses, cows, camels. Large proportion of population is nomadic.
Climate: Extreme. Winter temperatures well below freezing. Little rainfall.
Measures: Metric.
Transport: Airport at Ulan Bator: flights by Aeroflot from Moscow. Internal air services provided by Mongolian Civil Air Transport. 1,500 km of roads. 1,397 km of railways.
Currency: Tögrög (or tughrik) = 100 möngö.
Religion: Little religious activity. Once centre of Lamaism.
Visa: Yes: it costs £2 and takes two weeks to issue. Embassy at 7 Kensington Court, London W8 5DL; telephone 01-937 0150.
Jabs: Smallpox.
Language: Mongolian.
Time: G.M.T. + 8.
British Embassy: 30 Enkh Taivny Cudamzh, (P.O. Box 703), Ulan Bator; telephone 51033/4.
Tourist Office: Foreign Tourist Service Bureau, Juulchin, Ulan Bator.

## Morocco

Area: 446,550 km² (172,414 square miles).
Capital: Rabat.
Population: 17,305,000.
Occupation: Agriculture: cereals, citrus, vegetables. Increasing tourism.
Climate: Mediterranean on coast. Average 23 °C (73 °F) in summer, 16 °C (60 °F) in winter. Interior: more extreme. Rain: slight November to March.
Measures: Metric.
Electricity: 110/220 V a.c. 50 Hz.
Transport: International airports: Tangier and Casablanca. Direct from U.K.: B.A., British Caledonian, Royal Air Maroc. Embarkation tax. Rail links between main towns, but trains infrequent. Car ferries from Spain and Gibraltar. Roads: U.K. driving licence. Drive on right. Good roads in south. Tourists can get special rate on petrol with coupons. Purchase must be made in foreign currency from Banque Marocaine du Commerce Extérieure and they can be cashed in at end of stay.
Currency: Moroccan dirham = 100 'centimes' (coins actually old Moroccan francs). Local currency may not be taken in or out.
Religion: Muslim. Jewish and Christian minorities.

*Visa:* No. Passport with Israel visa refused. Hippie appearance disliked, can be refused entry.
*Jabs:* Smallpox if arriving from infected area or certain African countries. T.A.B.T. advised. Coast may affect those with asthma or sinus trouble.
*Language:* Arabic, French, Spanish, some English.
*Time:* G.M.T.
*Hotels:* Ministry of Tourism classifications: five to one star. International hotels in all big cities, small hotels further south; attractive and clean. Youth hostels (I.H.Y.A.).
*Shop Hours:* Stores: 08.30 to 12.00 and 14.30 to 19.00. Close 19.00 Saturday and open again Monday morning.
*Bank Hours:* 08.30 to 16.30 Monday to Friday.
*British Embassy:* 28 bis avenue Alla ben Abdallah, (B.P. 45), Rabat; telephone 20905/6. Also, Consulates at Casablanca, telephone 261440; and Tangier, telephone 35895.
*Tourist Office:* Moroccan National Tourist Office, 174 Regent Street, London W1R 6HB; telephone 01-437 0073.

## Mozambique

*Area:* 783,030 km² (302,329 square miles).
*Capital:* Maputo.
*Population:* 9,239,000.
*Occupation:* Agriculture: sugar, cotton, rice, nuts, tea, sisal, fruit, vegetable oil. Copra, timber, fishing, some coal-mining, oil-refining, light industry.
*Climate:* Tropical. Two seasons: April to September warm and dry, October to March hot and wet.
*Measures:* Metric.
*Electricity:* 220 V a.c. 50 Hz. Various plugs.
*Transport:* International airport: Maputo. No direct flight from U.K.: go via Johannesburg or Lisbon and Angola. Internal airlines between main towns. Railway: Beira to Tete and lines from Mozambique and Nacala to inland towns. Roads: largely unpaved, 37,106 km of road, only 3,849 km first class. International driving permit.
*Currency:* Mozambique escudo = 100 centavos. Local currency may not be taken in or out.
*Religion:* Largely R.C.
*Visa:* Yes. It costs 200 escudos and you have to apply to the Ministry of Foreign Affairs, Maputo.
*Jabs:* Smallpox. Cholera recommended. Yellow fever if arriving from endemic area or staying more than two weeks. Take anti-malaria precautions. Private medical practice illegal.
*Language:* Portuguese.
*Time:* G.M.T. + 2.
*Hotels:* Tourist Board classifications: 5 star–1 star. International standards in Beira and Maputo.

*British Embassy:* 310 avenida Vladimir I. Lenine, Maputo; telephone 26011.

## Namibia (South-West Africa)

*Area:* 824,292 km² (318,250 square miles).
*Capital:* Windhoek, Swakopmund (summer).
*Population:* 883,000.
*Occupation:* Mining (diamonds, copper), fishing, agriculture (beef and dairy farming).
*Climate:* Characterized by alternate periods of severe drought and excessive rainfall, though 75% of territory has less than 406 mm (16 inches) of rain a year.
*Transport:* Airport: Strydom, twenty-five minutes from central Windhoek.
*Currency:* South African currency is used in Namibia. Restrictions as for Republic of South Africa.
*Visa:* As for the Republic of South Africa.
*Jabs:* Smallpox. Yellow fever if arriving from endemic area.
*Measures:* Metric.
*Electricity:* 220/230 V a.c.
*Religion:* African traditional beliefs and Protestant.
*Language:* English, Afrikaans, German.
*Time:* G.M.T. + 2.
*Hotels:* Several first class in Windhoek.

## Nepal

*Area:* 140,797 km² (54,362 square miles).
*Capital:* Katmandu.
*Population:* 12,572,000. 85% rural.
*Occupation:* Agriculture: rice, grain, maize and wheat, jute, animal products. Tourism.
*Climate:* Varies with altitude. Tropical, hot and humid in south; subtropical in centre. Alpine in north. Southwest monsoon second week of June to first week of October — all rain falls then.
*Measures:* Metric.
*Electricity:* 220 V a.c. 50 Hz. Still d.c. in a few places.
*Transport:* International airport: Katmandu. Airlines: Royal Nepal, Thai, Burma, Bangladesh, Indian. Railways: narrow-gauge Government Railway from Jayangar (India) to Janakpur pilgrimage centre. Buses from and to Katmandu (book), check details locally. Travel within Katmandu good: elsewhere roads poor. Drive on left. International driving permit. Scheduled inland air service Royal Nepal Airlines to nineteen airports.
*Currency:* Nepalese rupee = 100 paisa. Local currency may not be taken in or out.
*Religion:* Hinduism, Buddhism.
*Visa:* Yes. Seven-day tourist visa available at Katmandu Airport for US$5. Extension requires permission from

Dept. of Immigration, Putali Sadak, Katmandu.
*Jabs:* Smallpox and cholera. Yellow fever if arriving from endemic area. T.A.B.T. recommended. Risk of malaria outside Katmandu at altitudes below 1,200 m.
*Language:* Nepali. English taught.
*Time:* G.M.T. + 5 hours 40 minutes.
*Hotels:* Government classifications: five, four, three stars. Best hotels expensive; those with lower standards are cheap. Projected Inter-Continental not ready. Katmandu is end of hippie trail. Service charge 10%, Government tax 5%. Tea-houses on some trails and roads, take all your own bedding; very cheap.
*British Embassy:* Lainchaur, (P.O. Box 106), Katmandu; telephone 11588.
*Reference Book:* L. F. Rushbrook Williams, *A Handbook for Travellers in India, Pakistan, Nepal, Bangladesh and Sri Lanka (Ceylon),* 22nd edition (Murray, London 1975). Stan Armington, *Introduction to Nepal* (Trail Finders Ltd., London 1975) a book of information and advice for overland travel, available only from Trail Finders whose address is 48 Earl's Court Road, London W8.
*Tourist Office:* Department of Tourism, Ministry of Industry and Commerce, Ram Shah Path, Katmandu.

## Netherlands

*Area:* 40,844 km² (15,770 square miles).
*Capital:* The Hague ('s Gravenhage, usually abbreviated to Den Haag).
*Population:* 13,653,000.
*Occupation:* Industry, heavy engineering, electric, oil etc. Agriculture, including flower growing.
*Climate:* As U.K. Winters − 3 °C (26 °F), summers 27 °C (80 °F). January to March, canals freeze.
*Measures:* Metric.
*Electricity:* 220 V two-phase a.c. 50 Hz. Plugs: two round pins.
*Transport:* International airports: Amsterdam and Rotterdam. Direct flights: B.A., British Caledonian, K.L.M. Excellent rail links between all main towns. Car ferries from U.K. Roads: drive on right. International or U.K. driving licence. Motor-launch canal tours. Buses excellent — in many towns you can buy books of tickets which offer a great saving. A horde of cyclists everywhere in Holland.
*Currency:* Guilder = 100 cents. No restrictions on import or export.
*Religion:* R.C. and Protestant equally.
*Visa:* No.
*Jabs:* No.
*Language:* Dutch. English widely spoken.
*Time:* G.M.T. + 1 (+ 2 April to September).

*Hotels:* Classifications by Tourist Office, Dutch Automobile Club (five to one star), the Hotel and Catering Trade Organization (one down to five). Confusing! N.R.C. (National Reservation Centre) has a large selection of rooms in every price range — telephone 020/211/211; telex 15754 Holland. Small hotels spotless — excellent value. Cleanest hotels in Europe.
*Shop Hours:* Some close Monday morning or Wednesday afternoon. Late shopping Thursday and/or Friday. Usual hours: 08.30 or 09.00 to 17.30 or 18.00 Monday to Friday. 08.30 or 09.00 to 16.00 Saturday.
*Bank Hours:* 09.00 to 15.00 Monday to Friday.
*British Embassy:* Lange Voorhout 10, The Hague; telephone 645800. Consulates-General at Amsterdam (telephone 736128) and Rotterdam (telephone 361555).
*Tourist Office:* Netherlands National Tourist Office, Savory & Moore House, 2nd Floor, 143 New Bond Street, London W1Y OQS; telephone 01-499 9367.

## Netherlands Antilles

*Area:* 961 km² (371 square miles). Three islands (Aruba, Curaçao and Bonaire) off the coast of Venezuela and two and a half islands (Saba, St. Eustatius and south half of St. Martin) at the north end of the Leeward Islands.
*Capital:* Willemstad on Curaçao.
*Population:* 242,000.
*Occupation:* Tourism, Shell Oil.
*Climate:* Tropical: uncomfortably hot. Average temperatures: 24−32 °C (75−90 °F). Hottest August to November. Rain: average 610 mm (24 inches) a year. Heaviest November to December.
*Measures:* Metric.
*Electricity:* Southern islands: 127/220 V a.c. 50 Hz. Leeward Islands: 110 V a.c. 50 Hz. Plugs: two-pin, Continental and American.
*Transport:* International airport: Willemstad. Airline: K.L.M. Embarkation tax. Taxis and buses available. Petrol cheap. No railways.
*Currency:* Netherlands Antilles florin or guilder = 100 cents. Not more than 100 Netherlands Antilles florins may be taken in or out. The import of Dutch or Surinam silver coins is prohibited.
*Religion:* R.C. Protestant and Jewish minorities.
*Visa:* No.
*Jabs:* No. Mosquito nets useful, also insect spray.
*Language:* Official: Dutch. English and Spanish. Also Papiamente in southern

islands (mixture of Portuguese, Dutch, English and French).
*Time:* G.M.T. − 4.
*Hotels:* Major leading chains and others.
*Shop Hours:* 08.00 to 12.00 and 14.00 to 18.00 Monday to Saturday.
*Bank Hours:* 08.30 to 11.00 and 14.00 to 16.00 Monday to Friday.
*British Consulate:* Edificio La Estancia, Piso 12, Avenida La Estancia No. 10, Ciudad Comercial Tamanaco, (Apartado 1246), Caracas, Venezuela; telephone 911091/911477.

# New Caledonia

*Area:* 19,058 km² (7,358 square miles). A group of islands in the Pacific about 1,795 km (1,115 miles) east of Australia and the same distance northwest of New Zealand. Largest island is New Caledonia. Others are Loyalty Islands, Isle of Pines, Huon Islands and Chesterfield Islands.
*Capital:* Nouméa.
*Population:* 125,000.
*Occupation:* Mining (world's third largest nickel producer), agriculture (coffee, copra, cotton, tobacco, fruit).
*Climate:* Warm December to April, fine May to November. Rain can be very heavy December to April.
*Transport:* Nouméa Airport. Airlines: Air New Zealand, Qantas, U.T.A. Roads: only 300 km are bitumen-surfaced. Only allowed to drive if you are over twenty-five. U.K. or international licence.
*Currency:* C.F.P. franc. No restrictions on import but not more than 60,000 francs may be taken out.
*Visa:* No.
*Jabs:* Smallpox. Typhoid recommended.
*Measures:* Metric.
*Electricity:* 220 V a.c. 50 Hz.
*Religion:* R.C. and Protestant.
*Language:* French and English.
*Time:* G.M.T. + 11.
*Tourist Office:* Office du Tourisme, P.O. Box 688, Nouméa.

# New Hebrides

*Area:* 14,763 km² (5,700 square miles). Ten main islands, sixty-nine islets.
*Capital:* Port Vila, on Efate Island.
*Population:* 90,000 (mainly Melanesian).
*Occupation:* Agriculture: cocoa, coffee, cattle, fishing, copra.
*Measures:* Metric.
*Electricity:* 220−250 V a.c.
*Climate:* Hottest October to April, average temperature 30 °C (86 °F). Most rain falls in summer. Cyclones may occur November to April. Cool season May to September.
*Transport:* International airports: Bauer Field, Efate (for Vila) and Pekoa, on Espiritu Santo Island (for Santo Town).

No railways. Roads: some built by Allied forces during Second World War. Land is steeply mountainous, covered by forests, festooned with liana, tropical climbing plants.
*Currency:* Australian currency and New Hebrides francs ($A1 = FNH 100). New Hebrides francs may not be taken in or out.
*Visa:* A visitor's permit for a stay of up to four months is issued on arrival. Onward tickets are required.
*Jabs:* Take precautions against malaria.
*Language:* Many local languages. English and French for government.
*Time:* G.M.T. + 11.
*Hotels:* Two international-style hotels. Several smaller but good. Motels.
*British Resident Commissioner:* British Residency, Vila; telephone Vila 252.
*Reference Books:* A. Coates, *Western Pacific Islands* (London: H.M.S.O., 1971). *Pacific Islands Yearbook and Who's Who* (Sydney: Pacific Publications, annual).

# New Zealand

*Area:* 286,676 km² (110,686 square miles).
*Capital:* Wellington.
*Population:* 3,087,000. Large Maori minority. 81% urban.
*Occupation:* Agriculture: wool, meat, dairy produce. Commerce.
*Climate:* Temperate with no extremes. Temperature range 16−28 °C (60−83 °F), warmer in north. Summer September to February. Summers mostly dry. Wellington is probably the world's windiest city: daily average wind speed is 29 k.p.h. (force 4).
*Measures:* Imperial and metric.
*Electricity:* 230 V a.c. 50 Hz. Plugs: three flat pins; special design peculiar to New Zealand.
*Transport:* International airports: Wellington, Christchurch and Auckland. Direct from U.K.: B.A. Railways: express trains throughout both islands; they have no bars. Roads: current U.K. driving licence valid up to one year.
*Currency:* New Zealand dollar = 100 cents. Only coins or 1, 2 or 5 dollar notes may be taken in or out. Not more than 50 dollars may be taken out but there is no limit on import.
*Religion:* Christian denominations.
*Visa:* No.
*Jabs:* Smallpox.
*Language:* English. Maori also.
*Time:* G.M.T. + 12 (+ 13 November to March).
*Hotels:* No official rating. Many of international standards. Prices quoted usually for room only. Plenty of hotels. Youth hostels (Y.H.A.). Wide range of motels.
*Shop Hours:* 09.00 to 17.30 Monday to Friday.

*Bank Hours:* 10.00 to 16.00 Monday to Friday.
*British High Commission:* Reserve Bank of New Zealand Building, 9th Floor, 2 The Terrace, Wellington 1 (P.O. Box 1812); telephone 726049. Auckland Office: 9th Floor, Norwich Union Building, Queen Street, Auckland 1; telephone 32973.
*Reference Book:* M. Shadbolt, *The Shell Guide to New Zealand,* 3rd edition (London: Michael Joseph, 1976).
*Tourist Office:* New Zealand Tourist and Publicity Department, New Zealand House, Haymarket, London SW1Y 4TQ; telephone 01-930 8422.

## Nicaragua

*Area:* 130,000 km² (50,193 square miles).
*Capital:* Managua.
*Population:* 2,155,000.
*Occupation:* Agriculture: cotton, coffee, sugar, cocoa; stock raising; fishing.
*Climate:* One of the hottest in Latin America: temperatures from 30 to 42 °C (86–107 °F). Dry season November to May. Very high humidity. Severe earthquake 1972.
*Measures:* Metric and U.S.
*Electricity:* 110 V a.c. 60 Hz. Plugs: American, two flat pins.
*Transport:* International airport: Managua. No flight direct from U.K.: go via Miami, Mexico City or Panama. Embarkation tax. One railway (diesel and fast) running north and south of Managua. Roads: Pan American highway down west coast, Honduran border to Costa Rica 2,060 km; all O.K. U.K. driving licence O.K. for thirty days.
*Currency:* Córdoba = 100 centavos. No restrictions on import or export.
*Religion:* Mainly R.C.
*Visa:* No.
*Jabs:* Smallpox. Cholera if from infected area. T.A.B.T. advisable. Take anti-malaria precautions.
*Language:* Spanish. English widely understood.
*Time:* G.M.T. – 6.
*Hotels:* Tourist Board rating: five star to one star. Inter-Continental, the only one of international standing.
*Shop Hours:* 08.00 to 17.30 Monday to Saturday. Longish lunch.
*Bank Hours:* 08.30 to 12.00 and 14.00 to 16.00 Monday to Friday. 08.30 to 11.30 Saturday.
*British Consulate:* Viajes Griffith (Apt. 949), No. C8 Centro Comercial San Francisco, Carretera A. Masaya, Managua; telephone 8785.

## Niger

*Area:* 1,267,000 km² (489,191 square miles).
*Capital:* Niamey.

*Population:* 4,600,000. 50% Hausa. Many nomads.
*Occupation:* Nomadic herding in north, farming in south.
*Climate:* Hot desert. Temperatures 24–34 °C (75–93 °F). Highest April to October. Pleasant in winter. Heaviest rain in August.
*Measures:* Metric.
*Electricity:* 220 V a.c. 50 Hz.
*Transport:* International airport: Niamey. No direct flight from U.K. Go via Paris. Hotel vehicles into town. No railways. Paved roads. International driving permit.
*Currency:* C.F.A. franc. No restriction on import but not more than 25,000 francs may be taken out.
*Religion:* Muslim.
*Visa:* No.
*Jabs:* Smallpox, yellow fever and cholera. Take anti-malaria and stomach-upset precautions.
*Language:* French official.
*Time:* G.M.T. + 1.
*Hotels:* No official rating. One or two good ones in Niamey.
*Shop Hours:* 08.00 to 12.00 and 15.00 to 18.30 Monday to Friday. 08.00 to 12.00 Saturday.
*Bank Hours:* Closed in afternoon.
*British Embassy:* Refer to Ivory Coast.

## Nigeria

*Area:* 923,768 km² (356,668 square miles).
*Capital:* Lagos.
*Population:* 62,925,000. 250 tribal groups.
*Occupation:* Agriculture.
*Climate:* Tropical: temperatures range from 19 to 35 °C (67 to 95 °F). North: hot and dry. South: hot and wet. Rainy in North: April to September. Rainy in South: March to November. Wind: the harmattan from the desert — December to March.
*Measures:* Metric.
*Electricity:* 230 V a.c. 50 Hz. Plugs: various.
*Transport:* International airport: Lagos. Direct route from U.K.: British Caledonian, Nigerian Airways. 3,500 km of railways: Lagos–Kano–Port Harcourt. Roads: international driving permit with two photos. Congested traffic in Lagos. Many roads in bad repair. Privately owned, cheap bus services. An attempt to allow only cars with even numbers on roads one day, those beginning with odd numbers the next.
*Currency:* Naire = 100 kobo. No more than 20 nairas may be taken in or out.
*Religion:* Mainly tribal. Some Muslim, some Christian.
*Visa:* Yes. You must get a visa before you leave for Nigeria. Consular Section of Embassy at 178–202 Great Portland Street, London W1; telephone 01-580 8611.

*Jabs:* Smallpox, yellow fever, cholera.
T.A.B.T. recommended.
*Language:* English official. Also Hausa,
Yoruba, Ibo and Fulani.
*Time:* G.M.T. + 1.
*Hotels:* No official rating. International
standard in Lagos. Accommodation in
short supply. Book in advance.
*Shop Hours:* 08.30 to 12.00 and 14.30 to
16.30 (or up to 18.00) Monday to
Friday. 08.00 to 13.00 Saturday.
*Bank Hours:* 08.00 to 13.00 Monday to
Thursday 08.00 to 15.00 Friday.
*British High Commission:* Kajola House,
62–64 Campbell Street, (P.M.B. 12136),
Lagos; telephone 51630. Deputy High
Commissions at Ibadan (telephone
21551) and Kaduna (telephone 22573).
*Tourist Office:* Nigeria Office, 9
Northumberland Avenue, London
WC2; telephone 01-839 1244.

# Norway

*Area:* 324,219 km² (125,181 square miles)
(excluding Svalbard and Jan Mayen in the
Arctic).
*Capital:* Oslo.
*Population:* 4,007,000.
*Occupation:* Petroleum, fishing, small
industrial businesses, commerce,
forestry, paper and pulp.
*Climate:* Summers cool, winters cold.
Snow: November to March. Oslo:
– 18 °C (0 °F) in winter, 29 °C (84 °F) in
summer.
*Measures:* Metric.
*Electricity:* 220–230 V a.c. 50 Hz.
*Transport:* International airport: Oslo.
Direct from U.K.: B.A., S.A.S. Railways:
five main routes radiate from Oslo.
Book in advance. Roads: drive on
right. International or U.K. driving
licence. Urban parking difficulties
because of meters. Ferry services are a
part of road network, often the only
link between fjord villages. Ferries to
U.K. Buses supplement the rail service
where no railway exists.
*Currency:* Krone = 100 øre. Only coins
and notes of denomination NKr 100 or
smaller may be taken in or out. No
limit on import but no more than NKr
800 may be taken out.
*Religion:* Evangelical Lutheran.
*Visa:* No.
*Jabs:* No.
*Language:* Norwegian. English widely
spoken.
*Time:* G.M.T. + 1.
*Hotels:* No official rating. Good range in
all main towns. Camping available all
over. Hostel accommodation in schools
and farms. Tourist huts for those on
walking tours. Youth hostels good,
some have private bathrooms, some
communal showers.
*Shop Hours:* 08.30 to 17.00 Monday to
Friday. Saturday morning.

*Bank Hours:* 08.45 to 16.15 Monday to
Friday. Late opening Thursday.
*British Embassy:* Thomas Heftyesgate 8,
Oslo 2; telephone 563890.
*Tourist Office:* Norwegian National Tourist
Office, 20 Pall Mall, London SW1Y
5NE; telephone 01-839 6255.

# Oman

*Area:* 212,457 km² (82,030 square miles).
Lies at extreme northeast of Arabian
Peninsula.
*Capital:* Muscat.
*Population:* 766,000.
*Occupation:* Economy based on oil
production. Cereals, dates, limes,
pomegranates, fishing.
*Climate:* May to October, hot and humid
— up to 44 °C (111 °F). December to
March, mild and pleasant. Rain 75 mm
(3 inches) a year.
*Measures:* Various.
*Electricity:* 220 V a.c. 50 Hz. Various plugs.
*Transport:* International airport: Saab, 42
km (26 miles) from Muscat. Airlines:
B.A., Gulf Air, Iran Air, Kuwait etc.
Most towns have a military airstrip. No
railways. Roads: there is a network of
tarmac main roads and numerous
graded tracks. Rural bus service good.
Travel outside capital may need official
permission. Drive on right.
*Currency:* Rial Omani = 1,000 baiza. No
restrictions on import or export.
*Religion:* Muslim.
*Visa:* Yes.
*Jabs:* Smallpox and cholera. Yellow fever
if from infected area. T.A.B.T.
advisable. Take remedies for tummy
upsets and anti-malaria precautions.
*Language:* Arabic. Some English in
business and government circles.
*Time:* G.M.T. + 4.
*Hotels:* Four of international standard.
*British Embassy:* P.O. Box 300, Muscat;
telephone 722/411.

# Pakistan

*Area:* 803,940 km² (310,402 square miles).
Also 83,807 km² (32,358 square miles)
of Jammu and Kashmir held by
Pakistan.
*Capital:* Islamabad.
*Population:* 70,260,000.
*Occupation:* Cotton, rice, sugar cane.
*Climate:* Tropical in southern plains.
Temperate in northern hills. Karachi —
average temperature 27–38 °C
(80–100 °F). Winter: December to
March. Summer: April to June. Rainy
season: July to September. Storms
can be violent.
*Measures:* U.K. and local, going metric.
*Electricity:* 220/240 V a.c. Plugs: 5A two
round pins; 15A three round pins.
*Transport:* International airports: Karachi
and Islamabad. Direct from U.K.:

Pakistan International and B.A.
Railways: between all major cities.
Air-conditioned cars available. Roads:
drive on left. International driving
permit with two photos. Driving
difficult in Lahore. Carry food and extra
fuel for long rural trips. Can drive over
the Khyber Pass to Afghanistan.
*Currency:* Rupee = 100 paisa. No more
than 20 rupees may be taken in or out.
*Religion:* Muslim. Parsee minority.
*Visa:* No.
*Jabs:* Smallpox. Cholera and T.A.B.T.
strongly recommended. Yellow fever if
from infected area. Take anti-malaria
precautions and mosquito repellent.
*Language:* Urdu and English.
*Time:* G.M.T. + 5.
*Hotels:* Ministry of Tourism classification:
five star, four, three, two, etc.
Numerous of international standard in
cities. Rest-houses in rural areas.
Y.W.C.A. and others in main towns.
Book in advance.
*Shop Hours:* 09.30 to 13.00 and 15.00 to
20.00 Monday to Saturday.
*Bank Hours:* 09.00 to 13.00 Monday to
Thursday. Saturday: 09.00 to 10.30
rural; 09.00 to 11.30 in main cities.
*British Embassy:* Diplomatic Enclave,
Ramna 5, (P.O. Box 1122), Islamabad;
telephone 22131/5. Consulate-General
at York Place, Runnymeade Lane, Port
Trust Estate, Clifton, Karachi;
telephone 532041/6.
*Reference Books:* L. F. Rushbrook
Williams, *A Handbook for Travellers in
India, Pakistan, Nepal, Bangladesh and
Sri Lanka (Ceylon),* 22nd edition
(London: John Murray, 1975). L. F.
Rushbrook Williams, *Handbook to
India, Burma, Ceylon and Pakistan*
(London: John Murray, 1975).
*Tourist Office:* Embassy of Pakistan, Trade
Division, Tourist Branch, 39 Lowndes
Square, London SW1X 9JN; telephone
01-235 2044.

## Panama

*Area:* 75,650 km² (29,209 square miles).
*Capital:* Panama City.
*Population:* 1,668,000.
*Occupation:* Agriculture: bananas, sugar.
Petroleum refining, shrimp fishing.
*Climate:* Hot and humid all year. Cooler
inland in mountains. Temperature:
19–34 °C (67–94 °F). Heavy rain
October to November. High humidity.
*Measures:* Metric and U.S.
*Electricity:* 110 V three-phase a.c. 60 Hz.
Plugs: American, two flat pins.
*Transport:* International airport: Panama
City (Tocumen). Direct from U.K. by
B.A. Embarkation tax. Railway links
Panama to Colón. Good highways
including Trans Isthmian. The Pan
American Highway goes as far south

as Chepo. Bus service in cities good;
long distance services to north.
*Currency:* Balboa = 100 centésimos. U.S.
currency circulates (there are no
Panamanian banknotes, only coins). 1
balboa = US$1. No restrictions on
import or export.
*Religion:* R.C.
*Visa:* No: unless coming on business.
*Jabs:* Yellow fever and anti-malaria tablets
advisable if travelling into jungle.
*Language:* Spanish. English widely
understood.
*Time:* G.M.T. – 5.
*Hotels:* Tourist Board classification: de
luxe (five star) to three star, etc.
Accommodation scarce during tourist
season (December to March). Book. No
hostels.
*Shop Hours:* 08.00 to 18.00 Monday to
Saturday with long lunch.
*Bank Hours:* 08.00 to 13.00 Monday to
Friday. Closed Saturday.
*British Embassy:* Via España 120, Panama
City; telephone 230451.
*Note:* Canal Zone is permanently leased to
the U.S.A. although the arrangements
are under discussion. Area of Canal
Zone is 1,432 km² (553 square miles)
and its administrative centre is Balboa
Heights. Population 44,000. U.S.
currency is the legal tender and
Panamanian coins also circulate.

## Papua New Guinea

*Area:* 461,691 km² (178,260 square miles).
Eastern half of the island of New
Guinea, north of Australia; also about
600 nearby islands — including
Admiralty Islands, New Britain, New
Ireland and Bougainville.
*Capital:* Port Moresby.
*Population:* 2,756,000.
*Occupation:* Subsistence agriculture,
mining, increasing tourism.
*Climate:* Tropical with high temperatures
and high humidity all year round.
Rainfall exceeds 2,030 mm (80 inches a
year) (up to 3,555 mm (140 inches) in
Papua Gulf).
*Transport:* Airport: Port Moresby. No
direct flight from U.K. Fly by B.A. to
Hong Kong and then by Air Niugini to
Port Moresby. Good internal air
service. Charter aircraft also available.
Roads: in most towns are sealed but
not in the country.
*Currency:* Kina = 100 toea. Australian
currency also circulates. 1 kina = $A1.
No restrictions on import or export.
*Religion:* United Church, R.C., Seventh
Day Adventist, Protestant, Lutheran
and Jehovah's Witness.
*Visa:* Yes. Apply to Australia House,
Strand, London WC2B 4LA; telephone
01-836 2435.
*Jabs:* Smallpox and cholera. Typhoid

recommended. Take anti-malaria
precautions.
*Language:* Pidgin English is lingua franca,
over 600 languages are spoken
including English.
*Time:* G.M.T. + 10.
*Bank Hours:* 09.00 to 14.00 Monday to
Friday. 08.30 to 10.00 Saturday.
*British High Commission:* United Church
Building (3rd Floor), Douglas Street,
(P.O. Box 739), Port Moresby;
telephone 212500.
*Reference Book:* Judy Tudor, *Papua New
Guinea Handbook,* 7th edition (Sydney:
Pacific Publications, 1974).
*Tourist Office:* P.N.G. Office of Tourism,
P.O. Box 73, Port Moresby, Papua New
Guinea.

## Paraguay

*Area:* 406,752 km² (157,048 square miles).
*Capital:* Asunción.
*Population:* 2,647,000.
*Occupation:* Agriculture: cattle, corn,
wheat, cotton, beans, tobacco, fruit.
*Climate:* Subtropical. Always warm. Hot in
summer. Temperatures: 2–41 °C
(35–105 °F). Rainy season October to
April.
*Measures:* Metric.
*Electricity:* 220 V a.c. 50 Hz. Plugs: two
round pins.
*Transport:* International airport: Asunción.
No direct flight from U.K. Fly via
Frankfurt, Madrid or by B.A. or British
Caledonian to other South American
connections. Luggage is inspected at
the airport. A tax is payable. Irregular
and slow railway service from
Asunción to Encarnación. But internal
travel usually by excellent bus service.
Roads: international 'carnet de
passages en douanes', car registration
and driver's licence.
*Currency:* Guaraní. No restrictions on
import or export.
*Religion:* R.C.
*Visa:* No, if just a tourist. Must have a
tourist card, price US$1 from carrier.
Passport with Cuban visa refused.
Hippie-looking people disapproved.
*Jabs:* Smallpox. T.A.B.T. advisable. Yellow
fever if from infected area. Medical
care good but expensive.
*Language:* Spanish and Guaraní.
*Time:* G.M.T. – 4 (– 3 October to
February).
*Hotels:* No official rating. Good ones in
Asunción. Often fully booked July to
August. Cheaper, smaller hotels hard
to find.
*Shop Hours:* Open early: 07.00. Long
lunch.
*Bank Hours:* 07.30 to 11.00 Monday to
Friday.
*British Embassy:* 25 de Mayo 171, (P.O.
Box 404), Asunción; telephone 49146.

## Peru

*Area:* 1,285,216 km² (496,224 square
miles).
*Capital:* Lima.
*Population:* 15,615,000.
*Occupation:* Agriculture: cotton, coffee,
sugar, rice. Mining.
*Climate:* Jungle: tropical with heavy rain
all year. Mountains: temperate, rain
October to April.
*Measures:* Metric.
*Electricity:* In Lima: 220 V a.c. 60 Hz.
*Transport:* International airport: Lima.
Direct from U.K.: British Caledonian.
Embarkation tax. Central and southern
railway systems — latter connects with
boats on Lake Titicaca. Trains can fill
up two hours before departure. Roads:
watch out for uneven surfaces.
International driving permit. Pan
American highway runs north-south
along coast. Lorries or buses on main
highways create hazardous clouds of
dust: beware overtaking! City driving
often erratic in style. Hitch-hiking easy
on coast, but in mountains and jungle
it's usual to pay the driver.
*Currency:* Sol. Not more than 1,000 sols
may be taken in. If you take out local
currency you must show by receipts
that it was obtained at authorized
exchange offices.
*Religion:* R.C.
*Visa:* Not if tourist, but get a tourist card
('cédula C') from carrier (free).
*Jabs:* Smallpox. Yellow fever if from
infected area. High Andes altitude may
cause discomfort — and may affect
those with heart trouble.
*Language:* Spanish and Quechua. English
understood. Interpreters through
agencies or some hotels.
*Time:* G.M.T. – 5.
*Hotels:* Tourist Board classification: five
star, four, three, etc. State Tourist
Hotels acceptable (food fair).
*Shop Hours:* January to March: 10.45 to
20.00. Rest of the year: 09.00 to 12.30
and 15.30 to 20.00. Some closed
Saturday. Many close later.
*Bank Hours:* 08.30 to 11.30 Monday to
Friday. Open longer April to December
(09.15 to 12.45).
*British Embassy:* Edificio 'El Pacífico
Washington', Plaza Washington,
Avenida Arequipa, (P.O. Box 854),
Lima; telephone 283830.
*Tourist Office:* Touring y Automovil Club
del Peru, César Vallejo 699 Lince,
Casilla 2219, Lima.

## Philippines

*Area:* 300,000 km² (115,830 square miles).
*Capital:* Manila.
*Population:* 42,513,000.
*Occupation:* Agriculture (sugar, copra,
vegetables), mining.

*Climate:* Tropical. March to June hot, dusty and humid. July to October wet, with occasional typhoons. November to February cool.
*Measures:* Metric.
*Electricity:* 220/110 V a.c. 60 Hz. Plugs: various.
*Transport:* International airport: Manila. No direct flight from U.K. Go B.A. or Qantas to Hong Kong or Bangkok. No railways: inter-island sea services. Roads: mainly along coasts. Drive on right. Local licence issued on showing U.K. licence. Or, international driving permit. Hire a car to see all the islands.
*Currency:* Peso = 100 centavos. No more than 500 pesos may be taken in or out. No more than 5 pesos in coins may be taken out.
*Religion:* Largest Christian community in Asia. 80% R.C. Muslim minority.
*Visa:* No: up to twenty-one days. After twenty-one days, you need passport, visa and ticket to next place in your travels. Visa issued by Philippine Consul required. After fifty-nine days, register with Board of Immigration — the temporary visa is for one year.
*Jabs:* Smallpox. Cholera and yellow fever if from infected area. There is a risk of malaria in some areas (not in Manila) at altitudes below 600 m.
*Language:* Pilipino, English, Spanish, and numerous local languages.
*Time:* G.M.T. + 8 (+ 9 March to June).
*Hotels:* No official rating. Lots of new hotels scheduled to open in 1977. Major international chains. Hostels with air-conditioning. Youth hostel in Manila and now all over the area — Y.H.A. of the Philippines. Rooms cheap and air-conditioned.
*Shop Hours:* Usually 09.00 to 17.30 Monday to Saturday.
*Bank Hours:* 09.00 to 20.00 Monday to Friday. Some open Saturday morning.
*British Embassy:* Electra House, 115−117 Esteban Street, Legaspi Village, Makati, Rizal; telephone 89 1051.
*Tourist Office:* Department of Tourism, P.O. Box 3451, Manila.

## Poland

*Area:* 312,677 km² (120,725 square miles).
*Capital:* Warsaw (Warszawa).
*Population:* 34,020,000.
*Occupation:* State-run industry: coal, shipping, metal manufacture. Agriculture: part state, part privately owned.
*Climate:* Temperate: hot summers, cold winters. Mountain area most extreme. Snow in winter: November to February.
*Measures:* Metric.
*Electricity:* 220 V a.c. Plugs: two-pin.
*Transport:* International airport: Warsaw. Fly from U.K.: B.A., L.O.T. Railways

link all main towns. Roads: international driving permit. Drive on right. Urban speed limit 50 k.p.h. (31 m.p.h.). No limit outside cities. Do not sound horns in towns. Watch out for cyclists and horse drawn vehicles.
*Currency:* złoty = 100 groszy. Local currency may not be taken in or out.
*Religion:* R.C.
*Visa:* Yes.
*Jabs:* Not if arriving from Europe.
*Language:* Polish. Interpreters through State travel office.
*Time:* G.M.T. + 1 (+ 2 April to September).
*Hotels:* Department of Tourism classification: A, B, C, D and E. First-class hotels scarce — book in advance. Most do not include breakfast. Government guest-houses and pensions — also hostels through ORBIS (Government travel agency). If no accommodation booked, apply to local 'Reception Centres' who will find a room. The Nieborov Palace near Warsaw is a State Museum that offers cheap, but baroque accommodation to artists, writers and those approved by its curator, Professor Loremy.
*Shop Hours:* 07.00 to 18.00 daily. Everything closes one Saturday per month.
*Bank Hours:* 09.00 to 13.00.
*British Embassy:* Aleja Róż 1, Warsaw; telephone 281001.
*Tourist Office:* Polish Tourist Information Centre, 'Orbis', 313 Regent Street, London W1R 7PE; telephone 01-580 8028.

## Portugal

*Area:* 92,082 km² (35,553 square miles).
*Capital:* Lisbon (Lisboa).
*Population:* 8,762,000.
*Occupation:* Agriculture, fruit, mines, fishing, tourism.
*Climate:* No extremes. Temperature range: 8 to 37 °C (46 to 98 °F). South: long, hot summers, little rain. North: longer winters, more rain. Algarve: very hot in summer.
*Measures:* Metric.
*Electricity:* 220 V a.c. 50 Hz (110 V in some areas). Plugs: two round pins.
*Transport:* International airport: Lisbon. Direct from U.K.: B.A. and T.A.P. Railways between main cities. Book in advance. Roads: drive on right, U.K. or international licence. Underground in Lisbon.
*Currency:* Escudo = 100 centavos. Not more than 1,000 escudos may be taken in or out.
*Religion:* R.C.
*Visa:* No.
*Jabs:* Smallpox and yellow fever if arriving from infected area.
*Language:* Portuguese.

*Time:* Continental Portugal: G.M.T. (+ 1 March to September). Madeira: G.M.T. Azores: G.M.T. − 1.
*Hotels:* Tourist Office classification: five star to one star. First class in Lisbon, Oporto and sea resorts. Posadas and estelegars are Government-controlled: excellent for touring, but book in advance — list from National Tourist Office. Youth hostels, camping sites. Villa developments good, but building frozen since Revolution.
*Shop Hours:* Mostly 09.00 to 13.00 and 15.00 to 19.00 Monday to Friday. Saturday morning.
*Bank Hours:* 09.30 to 12.00 and 14.00 to 16.00 Monday to Friday. 09.30 to 11.30 Saturday.
*British Embassy:* Rua de S. Domingos à Lapa 35−39, Lisbon 3; telephone 661191.
*Tourist Office:* Portuguese National Tourist Office, 20 Lower Regent Street, London SW1; telephone 01-930 2455.

## Puerto Rico

*Area:* 8,897 km² (3,435 square miles). Island in Greater Antilles, Caribbean, with Atlantic to the north.
*Capital:* San Juan.
*Population:* 3,087,000, mainly in the coastal plain.
*Occupation:* Tourism, light manufacturing, agriculture (livestock, coffee, sugar, tobacco). Many people go to the U.S.A.
*Measures:* American.
*Electricity:* 110−115 V a.c. 60 Hz. Plugs: two-pin flat.
*Climate:* Temperature range: 23−28 °C (73−82 °F).
*Transport:* Airlines include B.W.I.A., Iberia, Avianca, Air France. All local airlines have offices at airport of San Juan. (Antilles Air Boats as well land in harbour and so save taxi fare!) No. 17 bus to San Juan from airport, but you must have exact fare. Only a narrow-gauge railway between Fajardo and El Yunque on Sunday. It's a very small island. International driving permit. Drive on right. Hertz hire cars at airport. Buses plentiful. Fixed-charge fares. In San Juan, buses go against traffic in specially marked lane — yellow lines.
*Currency:* U.S. currency. No restrictions on import or export.
*Religion:* Mainly R.C., but most Protestant religions represented and a Jewish community.
*Visa:* Yes. Entry requirements as for U.S.A.
*Jabs:* No.
*Language:* Spanish: a lot speak English.
*Time:* G.M.T. − 4.
*Hotels:* Major hotel chains: Hilton, Holiday Inn, Sheraton, Inter-Continental. Lots of small hotels.

*British Consulate:* Room 1014, Banco Popular Center, Hato Rey; telephone (809) 767 4435.
*Tourist Office:* Puerto Rico Tourism Development Co., P.O. Box BN, San Juan, Puerto Rico 00936.

## Qatar

*Area:* 11,000 km² (4,247 square miles). A peninsula on west coast of Arabian Gulf.
*Capital:* Doha.
*Population:* Estimates vary from 92,000 in 1975 to 100,000 in 1969.
*Occupation:* Fishing, horticulture, petroleum.
*Climate:* Very hot and humid in summer, up to 52 °C (125 °F). Mild winters, 16−27 °C (60−80 °F). Rainfall: 75 mm (3 inches) a year.
*Measures:* Metric and Imperial.
*Electricity:* 220−240 V a.c. 50 Hz. Plugs: three flat pins.
*Transport:* International airport: Doha. Direct from U.K.: B.A., Gulf Air. Taxis into town. No railways, but helicopter and internal small plane hire common. Roads: international driving permit. Metalled roads link Doha and oil centres of Dukhan and Umm Said and also Salwa. Main road to Saudi Arabia excellent. Drive on right.
*Currency:* Qatar riyal = 100 dirhams. No restrictions on import or export.
*Religion:* Muslim (strict).
*Visa:* No.
*Jabs:* Smallpox. Cholera if from infected area. T.A.B.T. and polio recommended. Health service comprehensive and free (oil money).
*Language:* Arabic. English spoken, especially in towns.
*Time:* G.M.T. + 3.
*Hotels:* No official ratings. Three main hotels in Doha.
*Shop Hours:* Friday closed: open all other days dawn to noon and 15.30 to dusk.
*Bank Hours:* 07.30 to 11.30 Saturday to Thursday.
*British Embassy:* P.O. Box 3, Doha; telephone 321991.

## Reunion

*Area:* 2,510 km² (969 square miles). Volcanic island in Indian Ocean, east of Madagascar and South African coast.
*Capital:* St. Denis.
*Population:* 501,000 (increasing rapidly).
*Occupation:* Sugar production.
*Climate:* Tropical/subtropical. Summer November to April. High humidity. Otherwise, no extremes of temperature at any time of year. Rainfall: high, distributed throughout year. Also cyclones; driest September to November.

*Transport:* No direct flight from U.K., go
Air France from Paris. One
international airport. No railway.
*Currency:* French franc = 100 centimes.
Restrictions as for France.
*Visa:* No.
*Jabs:* Smallpox. Cholera recommended.
*Measures:* Metric.
*Religion:* R.C.
*Language:* French.
*Time:* G.M.T. + 4.
*Shop Hours:* 08.00 to 12.00 and 14.00 to
18.00.
*British Embassy:* None.

## Rhodesia

*Area:* 390,580 km² (150,804 square miles).
*Capital:* Salisbury.
*Population:* 6,310,000. 94% African.
*Occupation:* Farming, tobacco, mining
(gold, copper, coal), citrus fruit.
*Climate:* Temperate. Temperature range:
16−27 °C (60−80 °F). Rarely humid.
Rainy season November to March.
*Measures:* Metric.
*Electricity:* 220 V a.c. 50 Hz.
*Transport:* International airport: Salisbury.
Fly from London on South African
Airways or T.A.P. from Lisbon. Roads:
drive on left, major roads link main
towns; a few secondary roads, rest are
pretty grim. Railways: very little track;
just main lines, to big towns like
Bulawayo, Fort Victoria, Umratu and
Bulawayo to Wankie. Most whites
drive cars; most Africans use the very
good and frequent bus services.
*Currency:* Rhodesian dollar = 100 cents.
Local currency may not be taken in or
out.
*Religion:* 15% Christian. Rest traditional
African beliefs.
*Visa:* No. Visitors must have onward travel
tickets and sufficient means to support
themselves during their stay.
*Jabs:* Smallpox. Cholera and yellow fever
if from infected area.
*Language:* English.
*Time:* G.M.T. + 2.
*Hotels:* Tourist Board grading: five to one
star. Several hotels of top international
standard, hunting lodges, safari
lodges, etc. Widespread caravan and
camping facilities.
*Shop Hours:* 08.00 to 17.00.
*Bank Hours:* 08.30 to 14.00 Monday to
Friday, except Wednesday (08.30 to
12.00). 08.30 to 11.00 Saturday.
*British Embassy:* There has been no
British representative in Rhodesia since
its unilateral declaration of
independence in 1965.
*Reference Book:* Booklets from Rhodesian
National Tourist Board, Kingstons Ltd.

## Romania

*Area:* 237,500 km² (91,699 square miles).
*Capital:* Bucharest (Bucureşti).

*Population:* 21,245,000.
*Occupation:* Manufacturing of production
machinery, oil, chemicals, agriculture
(maize, wheat, sunflowers, grapes,
intensive livestock units).
*Climate:* Hot summers; long, cold winters;
pleasant springs and autumns.
Average temperatures: January −2 °C
(28 °F) to July 24 °C (75 °F). Bucharest
from −17 to 37 °C (2 to 98 °F).
*Measures:* Metric.
*Electricity:* 110 V a.c. 50 Hz. 220 V in new
buildings. Plugs: Continental, two
round pins.
*Transport:* International airport: Bucharest.
Direct from U.K.: B.A. or Tarom. Rail
links: between all towns. Roads: U.K.
or international driving licence. Speed
limit in towns 60 k.p.h. (37 m.p.h.), in
the country 100 k.p.h. (62 m.p.h.).
*Currency:* Leu = 100 bani. (Plural of leu is
lei.) Local currency may not be taken in
or out.
*Religion:* Romanian Orthodox.
*Visa:* Yes. It costs £2.50. Embassy at 4
Palace Green, London W8 4QD;
telephone 01-937 9666/8. When you
check into accommodation, you must
register and must surrender your
passport — returned later. When
leaving, you have to fill in a form
declaring purchases and value.
*Jabs:* No: but smallpox and T.A.B.T.
advisable.
*Language:* Romanian. Also German,
French and Hungarian. English spoken
in main hotels and tourist areas and by
younger people.
*Time:* G.M.T. + 2.
*Hotels:* Government classification: de luxe,
first A, first B. Several in the de luxe
class in Bucharest.
*Shop Hours:* 09.00 to 15.00 Monday to
Friday. 09.00 to 13.00 Saturday
(variable). Many food shops open till
22.00 every day.
*Bank Hours:* 08.00 to 11.00 Monday to
Saturday.
*British Embassy:* 24 Strada Jules Michelet,
Bucharest; telephone 11.16.35.
*Tourist Office:* Romanian National Tourist
Office, 98/99 Jermyn Street, London
SW1Y 6EE; telephone 01-930 8812.

## Rwanda

*Area:* 26,338 km² (10,169 square miles) in
east central Africa, bounded on north
by Uganda, east by Tanzania, west by
Zaïre, south by Burundi.
*Capital:* Kigali.
*Population:* 4,198,000. Population includes
pygmies. One of the most densely
populated African countries.
*Occupation:* Coffee and tea growing,
hunting and subsistence farming.
Minerals.
*Climate:* Average temperature 23 °C
(73 °F). Tropical, but high altitude

keeps average temperature down.
*Transport:* One international airport: 12
km (7½ miles) from Kigali. Departure
tax. From U.K. go via Brussels by
Sabena.
*Currency:* Rwanda franc = 100 centimes.
Local currency may not be taken out.
*Visa:* Yes. Costs 250 Belgian francs. Takes
three days to issue. Two photos and a
'certificate of moral conduct' required.
Embassy at 101 boulevard Saint
Michel, B-1040 Brussels, Belgium;
telephone Brussels 734 1763.
*Jabs:* Smallpox, yellow fever (cholera and
T.A.B.T. recommended). Take
anti-malaria precautions.
*Measures:* Metric.
*Electricity:* 220 V a.c.
*Religion:* About half traditional religion,
half Christian — mainly R.C.
*Language:* French, Kinyarwanda, Kiswahili.
*Time:* G.M.T. + 2.
*British Consulate:* avenue Paul VI, (B.P.
356), Kigali; telephone 5905.
*Reference Book:* Tourist Guide issued by
Rwanda Tourist Office.
*Tourist Office:* Office Rwandais du
Tourisme et des Parcs Nationaux,
Kigali.

## San Marino

*Area:* 61 km² (24 square miles) built on
Mount Titano in the Appenines, north
central Italy. One of the world's
smallest countries.
*Capital:* San Marino City.
*Population:* 20,000.
*Occupation:* Tourism, agriculture (wheat,
wine), printing, postage stamps (in
demand all over the world),
manufacturing, textiles, leather,
wrought iron, cement.
*Measures:* Metric.
*Electricity:* 220 V a.c. 50 Hz.
*Climate:* Variable. Average 5–29 °C
(41–84 °F). Coolest October to April,
hottest June, July, August. May 23 °C
(73 °F) approximately.
*Transport:* No railways. No cars allowed
inside the ramparts. Connected with
Rimini and the Adriatic coast by
funicular to Borgo Maggiore, thence
helicopter to Rimini. There is a bus
service and a new highway down to
Rimini 7 km away. Any driving in the
area on right. International or national
driving licence (must be translated into
Italian — A.A. do it). Nearest airport:
Rimini.
*Currency:* Italian. San Marino issues its
own coins.
*Religion:* Devoutly R.C.
*Visa:* No.
*Jabs:* None.
*Language:* Italian.
*Time:* G.M.T. + 1 (+ 2 May to September).
*Hotels:* Twenty-seven hotels and fifty
restaurants. Not categorized. Of

different sizes from luxury to
'pensione'.
*Shop Hours:* 09.00 to 13.00 and 16.00 to
20.00.
*Bank Hours:* 08.30 to 13.30 Monday to
Friday. Not Saturdays.
*British Consulate-General:* Palazzo
Castelbarco, 2 Lungarno Corsini,
I-50123 Florence, Italy; telephone
272594.
*Tourist Office:* Ente Governativo per il
Turismo, Sport e Spettacolo, Palazzo
del Turismo, San Marino.

## São Tomé and Príncipe

*Area:* 964 km² (372 square miles). Two
islands off West Africa.
*Capital:* São Tomé.
*Population:* 80,000, mostly descendants of
African slaves.
*Occupation:* 90% of cultivatable land in
the hands of thirty agricultural
companies, the rest 11,000 small
proprietors. Export: cocoa and coffee.
*Measures:* Metric.
*Climate:* Equatorial. Heavy rainfall, mainly
June to mid September. Average
temperature 25 °C (77 °F).
*Transport:* International airport: São
Tomé. Airlines: T.A.P., Air Gabon.
*Currency:* Escudo = 100 centavos.
*Religion:* R.C.
*Visa:* Yes.
*Jabs:* Smallpox. Yellow fever
recommended. Take anti-malaria
precautions.
*Language:* Portuguese. Some English.
*Time:* G.M.T.
*British Embassy:* None.

## Saudi Arabia

*Area:* 2,149,690 km² (829,998 square
miles).
*Capital:* Riyadh.
*Population:* 8,966,000.
*Occupation:* Agriculture, herding, oil
production, trade.
*Climate:* Desert: up to 49 °C (120 °F) in the
shade. Red Sea areas hot and humid
all year. Riyadh: cold in winter,
occasional rain November to February.
Gulf Coast: dust storms May to
September.
*Measures:* Metric.
*Electricity:* According to area 100–120 V
60 Hz or 220 V 50 Hz. Erratic: do not
use razor or hair drier, voltages vary
and are often not marked.
*Transport:* International airport: Jedda and
Dhahran. Direct from U.K. by B.A. Also,
Riyadh. Railway: Riyadh to Dhahran,
slow. Good roads between main
centres. U.K. licence valid for three
months. International driving permit
not valid. Avoid November to
December, time of pilgrimage to
Mecca, very crowded.

*Currency:* Riyal = 100 halalah. No restrictions on import or export.
*Religion:* Only Muslim allowed.
*Visa:* Yes. Must have it before you arrive. Free to tourists. Takes two days. One photo required. Passports with Israeli visa refused. Christian priests need special permission to enter, obtained via British consul in Jedda.
*Jabs:* Smallpox (you'll need the certificate to get a visa). Cholera and yellow fever if from infected area. Take salt tablets and remedy for tummy upset.
*Language:* Arabic. English widely spoken.
*Time:* G.M.T. + 3. In some areas, sun time (set your timepiece at 12.00 at sunset).
*Hotels:* No official rating. First class in Jedda and Riyadh, including the Inter-Continental. Many chain hotels going to be built. Otherwise, standards low.
*Shop Hours:* Hours vary. Closed Friday. Open nights during Ramadan.
*Bank Hours:* 07.00 or 08.00 to 14.30. Money-changing booths open all the time (subject to religious requirements), all over the place.
*British Embassy:* Kilo 5, Medina Road, (P.O. Box 393), Jedda; telephone 52544.
*Note:* Saudi Arabia is a very strictly Muslim country. Women should not wear short skirts or trousers and should keep arms covered. Mecca and Medina are closed to non-Muslims. Because of security-consciousness, always ask before taking photographs at airports or of bridges, etc.

## Senegal

*Area:* 196,192 km² (75,750 square miles).
*Capital:* Dakar.
*Population:* 4,136,000.
*Occupation:* Agriculture and stock raising.
*Climate:* Tropical. Coast, hot and humid. Interior, hot and dry. Rain: July to October. Frequent thunderstorms.
*Measures:* Metric.
*Electricity:* 127/220 V a.c. 50 Hz. Plugs: two round pins.
*Transport:* International airport: Dakar. Direct from U.K.: British Caledonian. Railways radiate from Dakar, not into south. Roads: good along coast and between main towns. Interior roads bad. International driving permit.
*Currency:* C.F.A. franc. No restrictions on import or export.
*Religion:* 80% Muslim.
*Visa:* Yes: it costs £2.50. Two photos and your smallpox vaccination certificate needed. Embassy at 11 Phillimore Gardens, London W8 7QG; telephone 01-937 0925/6. If staying over three months, must deposit money as repatriation guarantee. Group visas for charter tourists.

*Jabs:* Smallpox and yellow fever. T.A.B.T. recommended. Cholera if from infected area. Take anti-malaria precautions. Medical expenses high.
*Language:* French official. Tribal languages. Little English.
*Time:* G.M.T.
*Hotels:* Tourist Board classification: four star to one star. Difficult to book at short notice: take letter confirming booking with you.
*Shop Hours:* 08.00 to 12.00 and 14.30 to 18.00. Longer lunch and open later June to November.
*Bank Hours:* 08.00 to 11.15 and 14.30 to 16.30. Monday to Friday.
*British Embassy:* 20 rue du Docteur Guillet, (B.P. 6025), Dakar; telephone 22383.

## Seychelles

*Area:* 376 km² (145 square miles). Group of islands. Main one is Mahé.
*Capital:* Victoria.
*Population:* 58,000, mixed French and African descent.
*Occupation:* Agriculture (coconut, copra products), fishing (frozen for export), cinnamon (oil and bark), guano, tourism.
*Climate:* Equable 24–29 °C (79–85 °F); coolest June to November, hottest December to May. Rain: December and January.
*Measures:* Metric.
*Electricity:* 220 V a.c. 50 Hz.
*Transport:* Airport: Mahé. B.A., British Caledonian, East Africa Airlines, Air France, Air Malawi, South Africa Airlines. No railroads. Praslin has 4 miles of tarmac and 20 miles of earth roads; Mahé has 67 miles of tarmac and 9 miles of earth roads; La Digue has 8 miles of earth roads. U.K. or international driving licence. Local Air Mahé operates Islander aircraft.
*Currency:* Seychelles rupee = 100 cents. No limit on import but not more than 100 rupees may be taken out.
*Religion:* Mainly R.C.
*Visa:* No. Visitor's pass for one month issued on arrival.
*Jabs:* Smallpox, cholera and yellow fever.
*Language:* English or Creole (French patois). Business bilingual French and English.
*Time:* G.M.T. + 4.
*Hotels:* No official rating. Now several luxury tourist hotels. Fisherman's Cove the most famous. A large building programme planned (advice — go now before it's ruined).
*Bank Hours:* 08.30 to 12.30 Monday to Friday. 08.30 to 11.30 Saturday.
*Shop Hours:* 08.00 to 17.00 Monday to Friday.
*British High Commission:* Victoria House, Victoria.

*Tourist Office:* Seychelles Tourist Information Office (represented by Intercommunications (P.R.) Ltd.), P.O. Box 4NH, London W1A 4NH; telephone 01-580 7765.

## Sierra Leone

*Area:* 71,740 km² (27,699 square miles).
*Capital:* Freetown.
*Population:* 2,729,000 (December 1974).
*Occupation:* Subsistence farming, diamond mining.
*Climate:* Tropical and humid. Temperatures: 21−34 °C (69−93 °F). Very wet: 3,300 mm (130 inches). Rainy season April to November.
*Measures:* Imperial.
*Electricity:* 230/240 V a.c. 50 Hz. Plugs: two round or three square pins.
*Transport:* International airport: Freetown. Journey to town centre by road and ferry takes up to two hours. Buses provided. Direct from U.K.: British Caledonian. Rail links from Freetown inland. Roads: international driving permit. Better to fly than drive up country.
*Currency:* Leone = 100 cents. Not more than 20 leones may be taken in or out.
*Religion:* Muslim.
*Visa:* No, but entry permit necessary. High Commission at 33 Portland Place, London W1N 3AG; telephone 01-636 6483/6.
*Jabs:* Smallpox and yellow fever. Cholera recommended. Take anti-malaria precautions.
*Language:* English and local languages. Also Pidgin English called Krio.
*Time:* G.M.T.
*Hotels:* No official ratings. Limited in number: three first class in Freetown.
*Bank Hours:* 08.00 to 13.00 Monday to Friday. 08.00 to 11.00 Saturday.
*British High Commission:* 3rd Floor, Standard Bank Building, Wallace Johnson Street, Freetown; telephone 23961.

## Singapore

*Area:* 581 km² (224 square miles).
*Population:* 2,250,000: 60% under twenty-five years old.
*Occupation:* Commerce, banking, tourism.
*Climate:* Tropical: sunshine all year. Temperatures: 21−32 °C (70−90 °F). High humidity. Rain: 2,310 mm (91 inches) a year. Heaviest October to March.
*Measures:* Imperial and local, changing to metric.
*Electricity:* 230 V a.c. 50 Hz. Plugs: three square pins.
*Transport:* International airport: Singapore. Direct from U.K. by B.A., Qantas, Singapore Airlines. Airport tax varies with destination. Minimal

railway. Roads: international driving permit will get you a Singapore licence. Also, sampans, Chinese junks, rickshaws.
*Currency:* Singapore dollar = 100 cents. Not more than 1,000 dollars may be taken in or out.
*Religion:* Traditional Chinese religions. Also Muslim and Christian.
*Visa:* No. Visit pass issued on entry.
*Jabs:* Smallpox. Cholera and yellow fever if from infected area. Take anti-malaria precautions.
*Language:* English, Malay, Tamil and Chinese.
*Time:* G.M.T. + 7½.
*Hotels:* No official rating. Major hotel chains. Also, small Chinese hotels and youth hostels.
*Shop Hours:* 09.00 to 18.00 Monday to Saturday. Plenty of markets and shops open at night.
*Bank Hours:* 10.00 to 15.00 Monday to Friday. 09.30 to 11.30 Saturday.
*British High Commission:* Tanglin Circus, Tanglin Road, Singapore 10; telephone 639333.
*Reference Book: Papineau's Guide to Singapore* (Tunbridge Wells: Abacus-Kent, frequently revised).
*Tourist Office:* Singapore Tourist Promotion Board, 33 Heddon Street, London W1R 7LB; telephone 01-437 0033.

## Solomon Islands

*Area:* 28,446 km² (10,983 square miles). Double chain of mountainous islands off northeast Australia.
*Capital:* Honiara on Guadalcanal.
*Population:* 190,000. Mostly Melanesian and Polynesian.
*Occupation:* Fishing, handicrafts, export of copra and timber.
*Measures:* Imperial, giving way to metric.
*Electricity:* 240 V a.c.
*Climate:* Warm, pleasant throughout the year. Lowest temperature 19 °C (66 °F). Rainfall: heavy November to April. Occasional squalls and cyclones.
*Transport:* Four aerodromes. Airlines: Air Ningini (for Qantas), Air Pacific, Air Nauru.
*Currency:* Australian.
*Religion:* Christian churches: R.C., Anglican, Evangelical.
*Visa:* No.
*Jabs:* Smallpox. Take anti-malaria precautions.
*Language:* Forty languages and forty dialects. Common language: Pidgin English.
*Time:* G.M.T. + 11.
*British Governor:* Government House, Honiara; telephone 222.

## Somalia

*Area:* 637,657 km² (246,200 square miles).
*Capital:* Mogadishu.
*Population:* 3,170,000.
*Occupation:* Herding.
*Climate:* Tropical. Hot, dry and arid in north, hot and fairly humid in south. Temperature range 27–32 °C (80–90 °F). Rain: hardly any.
*Measures:* Metric and Imperial.
*Electricity:* 220 V a.c. 50 Hz.
*Transport:* International airport: Mogadishu. Airlines: Alitalia or Somali Airlines from Rome. No railways. Roads poor. Drive on right. International driving permit, but test must be taken. Notify authorities if travelling outside Mogadishu.
*Currency:* Somali shilling = 100 centesimi. Not more than 150 shillings may be taken in and not more than 100 shillings taken out.
*Religion:* Mostly Muslim.
*Visa:* Yes: it costs £4 and takes three weeks to issue. You have to supply four photos. Embassy at 60 Portland Place, London W1N 3DG; telephone 01-580 7148.
*Jabs:* Smallpox, yellow fever and cholera. T.A.B.T. recommended. Take anti-malaria precautions.
*Language:* Somali, Arabic, some English.
*Time:* G.M.T. + 3.
*Hotels:* No official rating. Best operated by Ministry of Tourism.
*Bank Hours:* 08.00 to 11.30 Saturday to Thursday.
*British Embassy:* Waddada Xasan, Geeddi Abtoow 7–8, (P.O. Box 1036), Mogadishu; telephone 2288.

## South Africa, Republic of

*Area:* 1,221,037 km² (471,444 square miles).
*Capital:* Pretoria.
*Population:* 25,471,000. 68% Bantu.
*Occupation:* Mining, fishing, agriculture, manufacturing.
*Climate:* Pleasantly hot: varies from temperate to subtropical. Johannesburg: hot summers (October to March), cool winters. Durban: hot summers, warm winters. Cape Province: Mediterranean. Rain: in Johannesburg and Pretoria torrential storms frequent.
*Measures:* Metric.
*Electricity:* Pretoria and Port Elizabeth: 250 V. Elsewhere: 220 V a.c. 50 Hz.
*Transport:* International airport: Johannesburg — also Bloemfontein and Durban. Direct from U.K. by B.A. and South African Airways. Good railways link most towns. Roads: drive on left. International driving permit. Speed limit in towns 60 k.p.h. (37 m.p.h.), elsewhere 80 k.p.h. (50 m.p.h.).

*Currency:* Rand = 100 cents. Not more than 50 rand may be taken in and not more than 20 rand taken out.
*Religion:* Dutch Reformed Church dominates the culture: about 30% of whites belong to it. 13% of whites are Anglican. 1 million Methodists among blacks.
*Visa:* Not if of 'pure European descent'. You will need a different passport if also visiting Algeria, Cameroon, Guinea or Sudan.
*Jabs:* Smallpox. Yellow fever and cholera if from infected area.
*Language:* English, Afrikaans. Also, African languages, including Zulu and Xhosa.
*Time:* G.M.T. + 2.
*Hotels:* South African Tourist Corporation categories: five star to one star. Plenty of international standard in all main towns. Y.M.C.A., Y.W.C.A.; Y.H.A. — which double for accommodation for motorized travellers over vast distances. Motels too.
*Shop Hours:* Usually 08.30 to 17.00 Monday to Friday. Saturday morning.
*Bank Hours:* 09.00 to 15.30 Monday, Tuesday, Thursday and Friday. 08.30 to 11.00 Saturday. 09.00 to 13.00 Wednesday.
*British Embassy:* 6 Hill Street, Pretoria; telephone 743121. Consulates-General at Johannesburg (telephone 834-6411), Cape Town (telephone 43.7266), and Durban (telephone 313131). Consulates at Port Elizabeth (telephone 2-2319) and East London (telephone 2-1971).
*Tourist Office:* South African Tourist Corporation, 13 Lower Regent Street, London SW1Y 4LR; telephone 01-839 7462.

## Spain

*Area:* 504,782 km² (194,897 square miles).
*Capital:* Madrid.
*Population:* 35,472,000.
*Occupation:* Agriculture: grain, rice, oil, wine. Tourism, mining, textiles, industry, shipbuilding.
*Climate:* Temperate in north, hot and dry in south. Rainfall mostly January to April. Summer storms can be violent.
*Measures:* Metric.
*Electricity:* Mainly 110–125 V a.c. 50 Hz. But 220 V in some places. Plugs: two round pins or American two-pin.
*Transport:* International airports: Madrid, Barcelona and Malaga, Palma. Direct from U.K. by B.A., Iberia, British Caledonian. Railways: link all cities. A ticket is available giving unlimited travel up to 12,000 km. Limited time period on all tickets. Roads: international driving permit. Insurance should include bail guarantee in case of accidents. Police strict, fines heavy.
*Currency:* Peseta = 100 centimos. Not

more than 50,000 pesetas may be taken in and not more than 3,000 pesetas taken out.
*Religion:* R.C.
*Visa:* No.
*Jabs:* No.
*Language:* Spanish.
*Time:* Mainland: G.M.T. + 1 (+ 2 April to September). Canaries: G.M.T. (+ 1 April to September).
*Hotels:* Tourist Board classification: five star to one star. Abundance of hotels of every kind. Many block-booked by travel operators. Plentiful camping and caravan sites. Tourist office says take internal Student Card, but it does not officially signify. The only student discount card available is for those attending a Spanish University or College and able to present a special registration card issued by the organizers of the course.
*Shop Hours:* 09.00 to 14.00 and 16.30 to 20.00. Many have special licences to remain open longer.
*Bank Hours:* 09.00 to 14.00 (until 12.00 in summer) Monday to Friday. 09.00 to 13.30 Saturday.
*British Embassy:* Calle de Fernando el Santo 16, Madrid 4; telephone 4190200. Consulates in most major cities.
*Tourist Office:* Spanish National Tourist Office, 70 Jermyn Street, London SW1; telephone 01-930 8578.

## Sri Lanka

*Area:* 65,610 km² (25,332 square miles). Connected to India by chain of flat shoals called Adam's Bridge. Mountainous with flat coast.
*Capital:* Colombo.
*Population:* 13,986,000.
*Occupation:* Agriculture: tea, rubber, tobacco, rice, coconuts, cinnamon. Shoes, mining precious stones, tourism.
*Climate:* Tropical: Colombo average from 26 to 28 °C (79 to 82 °F). Humidity 80%. Rainfall: monsoons May to September and December to February.
*Measures:* Metric, but Imperial system is still being phased out.
*Electricity:* 220 V a.c. 50 Hz. In some places, still d.c. Ask before using showers.
*Transport:* One international airport: Colombo. Airlines: B.A., Air Ceylon, U.T.A./Air France, Qantas, Aeroflot, T.W.A. Embarkation tax: 2.50–10 rupees. Railways: main towns all linked by railways. Government system. Luxury trains, air-conditioned. Book sleeping and refreshment cars on long journeys. Roads: good to excellent roads link all towns. Drive on left. Buses on every main road (state-run). Domestic air services.

*Currency:* Sri Lanka rupee = 100 cents. Local currency may not be taken in or out.
*Religion:* Buddhist and Hindu (Tamil) and Muslims (600,000).
*Visa:* No.
*Jabs:* Smallpox and typhoid. Cholera recommended. Take anti-malaria precautions.
*Language:* Official: Sinhala, Tamil, English.
*Time:* G.M.T. + 5½.
*Hotels:* No rating at present, but this is being done. Inter-Continental, Regent International, Holiday Inn, Trust Houses Forte and Oberoi (an Indian chain). Government Rest Houses, very good. Need to book in popular season.
*Shop Hours:* 08.00 to 24.00. 08.00 to 18.00 in cities. Small shopkeepers live on premises.
*Bank Hours:* 10.00 to 15.00 including Saturdays.
*British High Commission:* Galli Road, Kollupitiya, (P.O. Box 1433), Colombo 3; telephone 27611/17.
*Reference Book:* L. F. Rushbrook Williams, *A Handbook for Travellers in India, Pakistan, Nepal, Bangladesh and Sri Lanka (Ceylon),* 22nd edition (London: Murray, 1975).
*Tourist Office:* Ceylon Tourist Board (represented by Marketing Services (Travel & Tourism) Ltd.), 52 High Holborn, London WC1V 6RL; telephone 01-242 3131.

## Sudan

*Area:* 2,505,813 km² (967,498 square miles).
*Capital:* Khartoum.
*Population:* 17,757,000.
*Occupation:* Agriculture: cotton and increasing wheatlands, herding, production of gum arabic. Much untapped mineral wealth, lots of geological surveys etc., gold at Red Sea Hills.
*Climate:* Dry and very hot. Temperature range 8–46 °C (47–114 °F). Rain in north June to October. In south April to September. Best time to visit: December to April, otherwise unbearably hot.
*Measures:* Metric, Imperial and local.
*Electricity:* 240 V a.c.
*Transport:* New airports planned at Wau and Port Sudan; extension of airports at Malakal and Juba. International airport: Khartoum. Direct from U.K.: Sudan Airways. Embarkation tax. Internal air services to most main towns. Railways: Sudanese often travel on the top of the 30 m.p.h. trains (narrow gauge). A main north-south route through Khartoum with branches. Trains very slow, but with luxury first class. Roads: 15,000 km of

roads, but very few paved. Port Sudan to Khartoum Road should be open 1978/79. Drive on right. Check roads are open and inform police before travelling outside Khartoum. U.K. or international driving licence. The Kosti-tuba steamer up the White Nile can take eleven days. Most natives travel in lorries, in the cab, with freight or on top — fix price with driver: in the north, there are also donkeys, bicycles.

*Currency:* Sudanese pound = 100 piastres. Local currency may not be taken in or out.

*Religion:* Muslim in North, traditional in South. R.C. cathedral and Anglican services in Khartoum.

*Visa:* Yes: it costs £3.65 and you must present your smallpox and cholera vaccination certificates and two photos. Also, special permits if going to South. Embassy at 3 Cleveland Row, St. James's, London SW1A 1DD; telephone 01-839 8080.

*Jabs:* Smallpox and cholera. Yellow fever if from infected area. Take anti-malaria precautions and salt tablets.

*Language:* Arabic, English and many African languages.

*Time:* G.M.T. + 2.

*Hotels:* No official rating. Limited in number. At least two good ones in Khartoum. Hilton just opened. Meridium (has rats). Arab planned.

*Shop Hours:* 08.00 to 13.00 and 17.00 to 20.00 Saturday to Thursday.

*Bank Hours:* 08.30 to 12.00 Saturday to Thursday.

*British Embassy:* New Aboulela Building, Barlaman Avenue, (P.O. Box 801), Khartoum; telephone 70760.

*Tourist Office:* Tourism, Hotel and Estates Corporation, P.O. Box 2424, Khartoum.

## Surinam

*Area:* 163,265 km² (63,037 square miles).

*Capital:* Paramaribo.

*Population:* 422,000. About 90% of population live in or around Paramaribo or in coastal towns.

*Occupation:* Mining bauxite. Agriculture along coast. Timber processing. High unemployment.

*Climate:* Daily temperature range 25–29 °C (77–84 °F). Cooler at night. Very humid. Rain daily May to August and November to January.

*Measures:* Metric.

*Electricity:* 127/220 V a.c. 60 Hz. Plugs: two round pins.

*Transport:* International airport: Paramaribo. Fly via Lisbon or Amsterdam on K.L.M., Air France or Pan Am. Mini-buses and taxi. One ancient railway line inland from Paramaribo. Roads adequate, drive on left. Paramaribo City Buses run by

government: but 'wild' buses cheap and fast.

*Currency:* Surinam guilder = 100 cents. Not more than 100 Surinam guilders may be taken in or out.

*Religion:* All major ones.

*Visa:* No.

*Jabs:* Smallpox. Sleep under mosquito net, if room not air-conditioned.

*Language:* Dutch official. English widely spoken.

*Time:* G.M.T. – 3½.

*Hotels:* Several with air-conditioning in Paramaribo. Also Y.M.C.A., cheap hotels and boarding-houses. Really cheap Centraal Pension — men only.

*Shop Hours:* 07.00 to 13.00 and 16.00 to 18.00 Monday to Saturday.

*Bank Hours:* 07.30 to 12.30 Monday to Friday. 07.30 to 11.30 Saturday.

*British Consulate:* United Building, Van't Hogerhuysstraat (P.O. Box 1300), Paramaribo; telephone 72870.

## Swaziland

*Area:* 17,363 km² (6,704 square miles) in southeast Africa, surrounded north, west and south by Republic of South Africa, bounded on east by Mozambique.

*Capital:* Mbabane.

*Population:* 494,000.

*Occupation:* Agriculture (maize, sugar, cotton, citrus), mining (iron, asbestos), tourism.

*Climate:* Generally pleasant, but can be very hot in summer. Rainy season November to February.

*Currency:* Lilangeni (plural emalangeni) = 100 cents. South African currency also legal tender. 1 lilangeni = 1 rand. Restrictions as for South Africa.

*Visa:* No.

*Jabs:* Smallpox. Take anti-malaria precautions.

*Measures:* Metric.

*Electricity:* 220 V a.c.

*Religion:* 60% Christian. Rest traditional.

*Language:* Swati (Swazi), English, Afrikaans.

*Time:* G.M.T. + 2.

*Hotels:* Holiday Inn.

*British High Commission:* Allister Miller Street, Mbabane; telephone 2581.

## Sweden

*Area:* 449,964 km² (173,732 square miles).

*Capital:* Stockholm.

*Population:* 8,195,000.

*Occupation:* Machinery, iron and steel, paper, wood pulp.

*Climate:* Varied. Temperatures in Stockholm –7 to 21 °C (20 to 70 °F). North colder and drier. Summers in centre, warm. Winter November to April, very cold.

*Measures:* Metric.

*Electricity:* 220 V a.c.; sometimes d.c.
Plugs: Continental two round pins.
*Transport:* International airport:
Stockholm. Direct from U.K.: B.A. and
S.A.S. Excellent rail links to all main
towns, but fares high, reservations
compulsory. Roads: drive on right.
U.K. or international driving licence.
High fines for speeding and parking
offences. Also, strict drinking/driving
laws. It is unwise to drive after taking
any quantity of alcohol, however small.
*Currency:* Krona = 100 öre. Only coins
and notes of denomination SKr 100 or
less may be taken in or out and not
more than SKr 6,000 may be taken in
or out.
*Religion:* 99% Lutheran.
*Visa:* No.
*Jabs:* No. Cholera if from infected area.
*Language:* Swedish. English widely
spoken.
*Time:* G.M.T. + 1.
*Hotels:* No official rating. All are
expensive. Plenty of international
standard in main cities. Big chain Sara
has hotels and restaurants over the
country. Bonus Passport — buy at
travel agent — gives 20% reduction on
many hotels over a period. Student
one-room flats in Stockholm and Lund
(June to August). Motels all over.
Touring Club Lodges (cheap), open to
all. I.Y.H.A., Y.H.A. Camping sites many
and varied.
*Shop Hours:* 09.00 to 18.00 Monday to
Friday. 09.00 to 14.00 or 16.00
Saturday.
*Bank Hours:* 09.30 to 15.00. Monday to
Friday.
*British Embassy:* Skarpögatan 6–8,
S-11527 Stockholm; telephone 670140.
Also, Consulates at Göteborg
(Gothenburg); telephone 136277; and
Malmö; telephone 126625.
*Tourist Office:* Tourism Secretary, Swedish
Embassy, 23 North Row, London W1R
2DN; telephone 01-499 9500.

## Switzerland

*Area:* 41,288 km² (15,941 square miles).
Three main regions: the mountains of
the Jura, the Alps and the Midlands.
Three-fifths of the country is mountain.
*Capital:* Bern (also spelled Berne).
*Population:* 6,403,000.
*Occupation:* Machinery, instruments,
watches, tourism, finance, textiles,
food, chemicals and pharmaceuticals.
*Climate:* Cold winters, warm summers.
Temperatures −11 to 33 °C (13 to
91 °F). Daily weather reports for all
regions displayed at all major railway
stations; and outside post offices in
holiday resorts.
*Measures:* Metric.
*Electricity:* 220 V a.c. 50 Hz. Plugs: two or
three pins.

*Transport:* International airports: Zurich,
Geneva, Basle, Bern. Direct from U.K.
by B.A., Swissair and others. Railways:
all electrified, excellent fast service.
Plenty of scenic local lines in each
canton. Rail pass for eight days to a
month. Reduced Youth (under
twenty-three) and Student tickets
(student identity card). No charge
under six; half-fare six to sixteen. Also,
bargain tickets for FS 35 covering
twenty towns and cities. Roads: drive
on right. Tramline from Neuchâtel has
seventy-five-year-old bogie trams! U.K.
or international driving licence.
International insurance. Detailed road
maps from Swiss National Tourist
Office free.
*Currency:* Swiss franc = 100 centimes. No
limits on import or export.
*Religion:* R.C. and Protestant.
*Visa:* No.
*Jabs:* No.
*Language:* German, French, Italian and
Romansh. Many speak English.
*Time:* G.M.T. + 1.
*Hotels:* No official rating. Abundance of
top-rank hotels either for business or
tourist custom. Swiss Hotel
Association has yearly guide of 2,200
hotels and pensions: likewise, lists
motels. 450 approved camping sites.
Youth Hostels up to twenty-five years
of age: five days' notice required.
*Shop Hours:* Monday to Saturday until at
least 17.00. Some Monday morning
and lunch closing.
*Bank Hours:* Usually 08.00 to 16.30. Late
opening Friday. Lunch closing.
*British Embassy:* Thunstrasse 50, CH-3005
Bern; telephone 445021.
Consulates-General at Geneva
(telephone 343800) and Zurich
(telephone 471520).
*Reference Book:* Dr. Hans Bauer (ed.), *All
About Switzerland* (Swiss National
Tourist Office).
*Tourist Office:* Swiss National Tourist
Office, Swiss Centre, 1 New Coventry
Street, London W1V 3HG; telephone
01-734 1921.

## Syria

*Area:* 185,180 km² (71,498 square miles).
*Capital:* Damascus.
*Population:* 7,355,000.
*Occupation:* Agriculture: cotton, grain and
stockraising.
*Climate:* Mediterranean on coast. More
extreme inland. Hot, dry summers.
Cold winters.
*Measures:* Metric, Syrian for cloth.
*Electricity:* Damascus: 110/220 V
three-phase a.c. 50 Hz. Aleppo: 220 V
a.c. 50 Hz.
*Transport:* International airport:
Damascus. Direct from U.K.: B.A.,
Syrian Arab Airlines. Railways: from

Damascus to Beirut and to Amman.
Roads: drive on right. Breakdown and petrol services only on main roads. Must take out third-party insurance if entering by road. International driving permit.
Currency: Syrian pound = 100 piastres. Not more than 100 pounds may be taken in or out.
Religion: Muslim and Christian.
Visa: Yes. Issued at Damascus Airport or frontier crossing posts. Register with police if staying longer than two weeks. Passports with Israel visa refused.
Jabs: Smallpox. Yellow fever if from infected area.
Language: Arabic.
Time: G.M.T. + 2 (+ 3 May to August).
Hotels: Ministry of Tourism classification: de luxe, first class, second class. Most international hotels in Damascus, a few in Aleppo.
Shop Hours: 08.00 to 13.30 and 16.30 to 21.00.
Bank Hours: 08.00 to 14.30. Closed Friday.
British Embassy: 11 Kotob Building, 3rd Floor, Mohammad Kurd Ali Street, Malki Street, Damascus; telephone 332561.

## Taiwan

Area: 35,967 km² (13,887 square miles).
Capital: Taipei.
Population: 16,150,000 (end of 1975).
Occupation: Agriculture, tea and rice. Manufacture: textiles, electrical goods.
Climate: Subtropical, with long summer May to October. Rain: October to March in north, May to September in south. On the typhoon track.
Measures: Metric.
Electricity: 110 V a.c. 60 Hz.
Transport: International airport: Taipei. No direct flight from U.K., go via Hong Kong or Japan. Railways: fast trunk line through all west coast cities to Taipei. Book through travel agents, as services very crowded. Roads: international driving permit.
Currency: New Taiwan dollar. Not more than 1,000 dollars may be taken in.
Religion: Buddhist, Taoist, Muslim, Christian.
Visa: Yes. Apply to the British Passport Office, Clive House, Petty France, London SW1H 9HD; telephone 01-222 8010. Unless you hold letter of introduction from Taiwan trade service in London.
Jabs: Smallpox. Cholera if arriving from infected area.
Language: Chinese, English, Japanese.
Time: G.M.T. + 8.
Hotels: No official rating: Hilton and others of international standard. 'Single' can mean double bed, 'double' can mean twin beds. Some Buddhist

monasteries take overnight guests. There are youth hostels — very cheap bed and board.
British Embassy: None.
Tourist Office: Taiwan Tourism Bureau, 280/290 Chung-hsiao East Road, section 4, Taipei.

## Tanzania

Area: 945,087 km² (364,900 square miles) including about 52,000 km² (20,000 square miles) of lakes.
Capital: Dar es Salaam — moving eventually to Dodoma.
Population: 15,312,000.
Occupation: Agriculture: coffee, sisal, cotton, nuts, tobacco. Tourism, diamonds.
Climate: Varies. Coast: hot and humid. Central plateau: dry and arid. Northwest highlands: cool and temperate. Rain: November and December, February to May. Coolest June to September.
Measures: Metric.
Electricity: 230 V a.c. 50 Hz.
Transport: International airport: Dar es Salaam. Direct from U.K.: B.A. Railway (very slow) from Dar es Salaam to most main towns. Roads: drive on left. U.K. or international driving licence. Must get Tanzanian licence after twenty-one days. Entry by road closed to tourists from Kenya; now they must fly in and tour by Tanzanian coach or minibus. Severe fuel-saving restrictions on private cars, especially at weekends.
Currency: Tanzania shilling = 100 cents. Local currency may not be taken in or out.
Religion: Christian, Muslim.
Visa: No, but a visitor's pass is necessary: get it from the Tanzanian High Commission before you go.
Jabs: Smallpox and yellow fever. T.A.B.T. advisable if going to outlying areas. Cholera if from infected area. Take anti-malaria precautions. Swim only in sea water as there is bilharzia in most lakes and rivers.
Language: Swahili and English.
Time: G.M.T. + 3.
Hotels: No official rating. Several good ones in Dar es Salaam, on adjoining coast, and particularly in game parks.
Shop Hours: 08.00 to 17.15 or 18.00 Monday to Saturday. Lunch closing.
Bank Hours: 08.30 to 11.30 Monday to Friday. 08.30 to 10.00 Saturday.
British High Commission: 5th–8th Floors, Permanent House, Corner Maktaba Street and Independence Avenue, (P.O. Box 9200), Dar es Salaam; telephone 29601.
Tourist Office: Tanzania High Commission, Commerce and Tourism Division, 43 Hertford Street, London W1Y 7TF; telephone 01-499 8951.

*Note:* Do not photograph any public buildings, bridges, stations, etc. Best to confine photography to game parks. Dress and hairstyle should be conservative. There is a risk of mugging in Dar es Salaam.

## Thailand

*Area:* 514,000 km² (198,456 square miles).
*Capital:* Bangkok.
*Population:* 41,869,000.
*Occupation:* Agriculture (rice), tourism, tin-mining, rubber-planting.
*Climate:* Tropical. Warm in north, hot and humid in south. Monsoon: May to October. Temperatures in Bangkok: 11–41 °C (52–106 °F).
*Measures:* Metric.
*Electricity:* 220 V a.c. 50 Hz.
*Transport:* International airport: Bangkok. Served by thirty airlines. Direct from U.K.: B.A., Qantas, Singapore Airlines, Pan Am, Thai Airways International, Japan Air Lines. Rail and air links to most main towns. State railways 3,990 km (2,480 miles) of track. Roads: drive on left. International driving permit. National driving style rather risky. Excellent and cheap bus services all over, and fascinating boat links on canals and rivers.
*Currency:* Baht = 100 satang. Not more than 500 baht may be taken in or out.
*Religion:* Buddhist. Muslim minority in south.
*Visa:* Yes, if staying more than fifteen days. Issued on arrival. Do not overstay it: you face prison or fine.
*Jabs:* Smallpox, cholera and yellow fever if from infected area. T.A.B.T. recommended. Take anti-malaria precautions.
*Language:* Thai, Chinese, English.
*Time:* G.M.T. + 7.
*Hotels:* No official rating. Major international chains. Bangkok has cheap dormitory accommodation. Also Y.M.C.A. and small Chinese hotels.
*Shop Hours:* No standard hours. Usually open until 19.00 or 20.00.
*Bank Hours:* 08.30 to 15.30 Monday to Friday.
*British Embassy:* Rloenchit Road, Bangkok; telephone 2527161/9.
*Tourist Office:* Royal Thai Embassy, 30 Queen's Gate, London SW7 5JB; telephone 01-589 0173.
*Note:* Thais object to people they regard as 'hippies' (long hair, beard, or scruffily dressed). People 'improperly dressed' may be barred from temples. Men should beware of enticing approaches from 'women' who invariably turn out to be transvestite muggers.

## Togo

*Area:* 56,000 km² (21,622 square miles).
*Capital:* Lomé.
*Population:* 2,222,000, many tribal.
*Occupation:* 90% agriculture: cocoa, coffee, cotton. Main export is phosphate.
*Climate:* Tropical: hot and humid. Temperatures vary with altitude. Average 27 °C (80 °F) on coast, 30 °C (86 °F) inland. Rain: April to July, October to November.
*Measures:* Metric.
*Electricity:* 220–240 V a.c.
*Transport:* International airport: Lomé. No direct flight from U.K. Go via Paris, Air Afrique or U.T.A. Rail links from Lomé to main towns. Main roads in good condition.
*Currency:* C.F.A. franc. No limit on import but not more than 50,000 francs may be taken out.
*Religion:* R.C., traditional.
*Visa:* Yes: you have to supply four photos and it costs from £2 to £4 depending on length of stay. Exit visas too, for all who stay more than forty-eight hours. Apply to the French Consulate-General at 24 Rutland Gate, London SW7 1BE; telephone 01-584 9628.
*Jabs:* Smallpox, yellow fever. Cholera if from infected area. Take anti-malaria and tummy-upset precautions.
*Language:* French, some English.
*Time:* G.M.T.
*Hotels:* No official rating. Tourism quite well developed.
*Shop Hours:* 08.00 to 18.00 Monday to Friday. Two hours for lunch. Also Saturday morning.
*Bank Hours:* 07.30 to 11.30 and 14.30 to 15.30 Monday to Friday.
*British Embassy:* Embassy closed in 1976. Nearest representative is the British High Commission in Accra.

## Trinidad and Tobago

*Area:* 5,128 km² (1,980 square miles).
*Capital:* Port of Spain.
*Population:* 1,067,000.
*Occupation:* Coffee, sugar, rum and petroleum products.
*Climate:* Tropical. Hot and humid. Temperature range: 23–32 °C (74–90 °F). Rain: June to December. High humidity.
*Measures:* Imperial.
*Electricity:* 115 V a.c. 50 Hz (sometimes 230 V). Plugs: two flat pins.
*Transport:* International airport: Port of Spain. Direct from U.K.: B.A., B.W.I.A. Embarkation tax. Railways: none. Roads: U.K. licence for up to three months or international permit. Buses infrequent and unreliable.
*Currency:* Trinidad and Tobago dollar = 100 cents. Not more than 48 dollars may be taken in or out.

*Religion:* R.C. and Anglican with Hindu and Muslim minorities.
*Visa:* No.
*Jabs:* Smallpox. T.A.B.T. and yellow fever advisable.
*Language:* English.
*Time:* G.M.T. – 4.
*Hotels:* No official rating. Major chains: Hilton, Holiday Inn. Camping should not be contemplated.
*Shop Hours:* 08.00 to 16.00 Monday to Friday and Saturday morning. Supermarkets close Thursday afternoon.
*Bank Hours:* 08.00 to 12.30 Monday to Thursday. 08.00 to 12.00 and 15.00 to 17.00 Friday.
*British High Commission:* Fourth Floor, Furness House, 90 Independence Square, (P.O. Box 778), Port of Spain; telephone 52861/6.
*Tourist Office:* Trinidad and Tobago Travel and Trade Centre, 20 Lower Regent Street, London SW1Y 4PH; telephone 01-839 7155.

## Tunisia

*Area:* 163,610 km² (63,170 square miles).
*Capital:* Tunis.
*Population:* 5,772,000.
*Occupation:* Agriculture: grain, olives, fruit. Phosphates.
*Climate:* Mediterranean. Hot summers, mild winters. Temperature range: 2–38 °C (35–100 °F). Light rain, mostly December to March.
*Measures:* Metric.
*Electricity:* 110/220 V a.c. 50 Hz. Plugs: usually two-pin.
*Transport:* International airport: Tunis. Airlines: British Caledonian, Air France, Tunis Air. Railways: 2,021 km (1,256 miles) covering most of country. Roads: international driving permit. One of the best road networks in Africa. Links with Algeria and Libya. Efficient and regular bus services.
*Currency:* Tunisian dinar = 1000 millimes. Local currency may not be taken in or out.
*Religion:* Muslim, with Christian and Jewish minorities.
*Visa:* No. Passports with Israeli visa may be refused.
*Jabs:* Smallpox. T.A.B.T. recommended. Cholera and yellow fever if from infected area.
*Language:* Arabic, French, some English. It is hard to find interpreters.
*Time:* G.M.T. + 1 (+ 2 May to September).
*Hotels:* Tourist Board rating, four star de luxe, three star, two star etc. Some modern, some traditional architecture. Government price list for drinks should hang in the bar.
*Bank Hours:* Winter: 08.00 to 11.00 and 14.00 to 16.00 Monday to Friday.

Summer (1 July to 15 September): 07.30 to 11.00 Monday to Friday.
*British Embassy:* 5 place de la Victoire, Tunis; telephone 245100.
*Tourist Office:* Tunisian National Tourist Office, 7A Stafford Street, London W1; telephone 01-493 2952/7523.

## Turkey

*Area:* 780,576 km² (301,382 square miles).
*Capital:* Ankara.
*Population:* 39,180,000.
*Occupation:* Agriculture: tobacco, cereal, cotton, olive oil, wool.
*Climate:* Varies: long, cold winters on Anatolian Plateau in east; hot and dry on west coast. Temperature range in Ankara: –15 to 40 °C (5 to 104 °F). Rain: winter and spring. Snow: December to March in east.
*Measures:* Metric.
*Electricity:* European part: 110 V a.c. Asian part: 220 V a.c. Plugs: two round pins.
*Transport:* International airports: Ankara, Istanbul. Direct from U.K.: B.A. to Istanbul. Railway links between all main towns. Roads: drive on right. Limit 50 k.p.h. (31 m.p.h.) in towns, 90 k.p.h. (56 m.p.h.) outside. International driving permit. Private coach companies supply coaches between towns.
*Currency:* Lira = 100 kuruş. Not more than 1,000 liraşi may be taken in or out.
*Religion:* Muslim with other minorities.
*Visa:* No.
*Jabs:* Cholera and yellow fever if from infected area.
*Language:* Turkish. English taught.
*Time:* G.M.T. + 2 (+ 3 April to October).
*Hotels:* Ministry of Tourism grading: de luxe, first to fourth class. Luxury and first-class hotels in Ankara, Istanbul and Izmir. Hostels and camping sites available.
*Shop Hours:* 09.00 to 19.00 Monday to Saturday with lunch closing.
*Bank Hours:* 09.00 to 12.00 and 14.00 to 16.00 Monday to Friday.
*British Embassy:* Şehit Ersan Caddesi 46/A, Çankaya, Ankara; telephone 274310.
*Reference Book: Turkey* (Turkish Tourist Board).
*Tourist Office:* Turkish Tourism Information Office, 49 Conduit Street, London W1R 0EP; telephone 01-734 8681.

## Uganda

*Area:* 236,036 km² (19,134 square miles).
*Capital:* Kampala.
*Population:* 11,549,000.
*Occupation:* Agriculture: coffee, cotton, tea, sugar. Copper-mining.
*Climate:* Warm or very hot. Long rains: April to June. Short rains: October to November.

*Measures:* Metric.
*Electricity:* 240 V a.c. 50 Hz. Plugs: 13A three square pins or 5A two round pins.
*Transport:* International airport: Entebbe 35.5 km (22 miles) from Kampala. No direct flight from U.K. Go via Paris on Air France or via Brussels on Sabena. Railways little used for tourist traffic. Roads: drive on left. Need police permit if entering by car. Motorists face long delays. U.K. or international driving licence. Internal routes radiating from Kampala good.
*Currency:* Uganda shilling = 100 cents. Local currency may not be taken in or out.
*Religion:* Some Christian, some Muslim, most traditional.
*Visa:* Yes. Get it before leaving. You have to supply two photos.
*Jabs:* Smallpox, yellow fever. T.A.B.T. advisable. Take anti-malaria precautions. Avoid swimming in lakes and river because of bilharzia.
*Language:* Luganda (a Bantu dialect), Swahili and English. Many African languages.
*Time:* G.M.T. + 3.
*Hotels:* Several in Kampala and Entebbe. Safari lodges in National Parks.
*Bank Hours:* 08.30 to 12.30 Monday to Friday. 08.00 to 11.00 Saturday.
*British Diplomatic Mission:* None.
*Note:* Life in Uganda is subject to the volatility of President Amin. Foreigners in the country may find their situation insecure.

# U.S.S.R.

*Area:* 22,402,200 km² (8,649,523 square miles).
*Capital:* Moscow.
*Population:* 254,382,000, including 104 nationalities.
*Occupation:* All forms of industry, mining and agriculture. The economy is virtually self-sufficient.
*Climate:* Varies from subarctic to subtropical. Moscow and Leningrad: warm summers, long winters with heavy snow. Black Sea resorts: hot summers and mild winters.
*Measures:* Metric.
*Electricity:* 127/220 V a.c. 50 Hz. Plugs: Continental two pin.
*Transport:* International airports: primarily Leningrad, Kiev, Moscow, Odessa and Riga. Direct from U.K.: B.A. and Aeroflot. (Aeroflot is the world's largest airline.) Railways: to all main cities, often with sleepers. Road tax payable on entry by road. British or, preferably, international driving licence and log book necessary. Intourist (Russia's National Tourist Board) must know your itinerary. Public transport in

Moscow — flat rate. Underground excellent.
*Currency:* Rouble = 100 kopeks. Local currency may not be taken in or out.
*Religion:* Discouraged, not suppressed — mainly Russian Orthodox.
*Visa:* Yes. You need one photo and it's issued free of charge.
*Jabs:* No. Emergency medical services free, but hospitals archaic.
*Language:* Russian with 150 local languages. Interpreters and guides through Intourist.
*Time:* Twelve time zones. Moscow and Leningrad: G.M.T. + 3.
*Hotels:* All main ones are Intourist Hotels; large, international style. Prices differ for businessmen and tourists. Usually excessive central heating.
*Shop Hours:* 10.00 or 11.00 to 20.00 Monday to Saturday. Closed Sunday. Most shops close for lunch 14.00 to 15.00.
*Bank Hours:* U.S.S.R. State Bank for exchange 09.00 to 12.30 Monday to Friday. 09.00 to 11.30 Saturday. Roubles cannot be converted back. Cannot be taken in or out. Take foreign currency for shops and Intourist.
*British Embassy:* Naberezhnaya Morisa Toreza 14; telephone 231 85 11.
*Tourist Office:* Intourist, 292 Regent Street, London W1R 7PO; telephone 01-580 4974.
*Note:* The concierge person on each hotel floor can usually speak English. Some mirrors *are* two-way and there *are* some microphones. Don't break the currency regulations. Don't carry dope. Don't photograph bridges, military installations or groups of soldiers. Refer to the country as the 'Soviet Union': Russia is just one of fifteen constituent republics of the Union.

# United Arab Emirates

*Area:* 83,600 km² (32,278 square miles).
*Capital:* Abu Dhabi.
*Population:* 222,000.
*Occupation:* Economy based entirely on petroleum production. Traditional Bedouin way of life fast disappearing. Most employees work on construction.
*Climate:* Very hot and humid in summer. Mild in winter. Only 75 mm (3 inches) of rain per year.
*Measures:* Metric and local and Imperial.
*Electricity:* 220–240 V a.c. 50 Hz. Plugs: three round or flat pins.
*Transport:* International airports: Abu Dhabi, Dubai and Ras al-Khaimah. Airlines direct from U.K.: B.A. and all usual international airlines. Roads: drive on right. There is a growing network of good roads linking all major towns and connecting with Oman and Qatar.

U.S.A.

*Currency:* U.A.E. dirham = 100 fils. No restriction on import or export.
*Religion:* Muslim.
*Visa:* Yes: you may need a local sponsor. Seven-day visitor's visa obtainable on arrival if met by a sponsor. Embassy at 30 Prince's Gate, London SW7 1PT; telephone 01-581 1281.
*Jabs:* Smallpox and cholera. T.A.B.T. advisable. Take anti-malaria pills.
*Language:* Arabic. English widely spoken.
*Time:* G.M.T. + 4.
*Hotels:* No official rating. Abu Dhabi, Dubai and Sharjah have several of first-class international standard and there is a Hilton at the desert oasis of Al-Ain. No tourist industry as such exists.
*Shop Hours:* 08.00 to 12.00 and 16.00 to 19.00. Closed Friday.
*Bank Hours:* Mornings only. Closed Friday.
*British Embassy:* The Corniche, (P.O. Box 248), Abu Dhabi; telephone 41305. Tariq ibn Zayed Street, (P.O. Box 65), Dubai; telephone 31070.
*Note:* Women should not wear revealing clothes. Alcohol is available to foreigners but they must not bring it into the country.

## United Kingdom

*Area:* 244,829 km² (94,529 square miles).
*Capital:* London.
*Population:* 55,962,000.
*Occupation:* Iron, steel, engineering, chemicals, electronics, motor vehicles, aircraft, textiles, clothes and consumer goods, tourism.
*Climate:* Temperate and variable. Tourist season mid-April to mid-October. Average maximum temperatures – Edinburgh: 6 to 18 °C (43 to 64 °F), London: 7 to 21 °C (45 to 70 °F) (very variable).
*Measures:* Metric/Imperial.
*Electricity:* 220 V a.c. 50 Hz. Plugs: mostly three flat pins.
*Transport:* To Heathrow, Gatwick, Luton, direct from everywhere. B.A., T.W.A., Pan Am, Air India, El Al, Aeroflot, Icelandic, Air Canada, Lufthansa, Air France, etc. Domestic flights regular and scheduled. Vast network of railways: inter-city and branch lines. Roads: link most places, all tarmacadamed. Drive on left: international driving permit. Buses in each city or area and cross-country coaches along motorways.
*Currency:* £1 = 100 new pence. Non-residents may not take out more than £25 but there is no limit on import.
*Religion:* State religion Anglican Church of England; other denominations R.C., Methodist, Presbyterian, Baptist, Jewish, Muslim, Hindu.

*Visa:* Not for American citizens, nationals of British Commonwealth, South American, E.E.C. and most other European countries. No pets allowed in without six months' quarantine.
*Jabs:* Smallpox if arriving from an infected area.
*Language:* English: in Wales some Welsh, in Scotland some Scottish Gaelic, in Northern Ireland a little Irish.
*Time:* G.M.T. (+ 1 March to October).
*Hotels:* No official system of hotel classification. Many well-known hotel chains have come to the U.K.; Holiday Inn, Sheraton etc. Most hotels are inspected regularly for cleanliness etc. There are also inns, guest-houses, Y.M.C.A., Y.W.C.A. Y.H.A. all over the country. Motels now appearing on main motorways. Tourist Board list quite informative. 50p from British Tourist Association, St. James's St., London W1.
*Shop Hours:* 09.00 to 17.30 Monday to Friday. Except in London's Oxford Street, closed one afternoon a week. Many food shops remain open; so do small local shops. Supermarkets open until 19.30 or 20.00 Thursday and/or Friday.
*Bank Hours:* 09.30 to 15.30 Monday to Friday. Shut Saturday.

## U.S.A.

*Area:* 9,363,123 km² (3,615,116 square miles).
*Capital:* Washington, District of Columbia.
*Population:* 213,611,000.
*Occupation:* Of all kinds, but the northeast tends to industry, the south towards agriculture and the southwest to oil.
*Climate:* Every type. Cold continental in the Great Lakes region. Temperate in the eastern states. Mediterranean in southern California. Subtropical in Louisiana and Texas. Tropical in Florida. Almost without exception hot in summer.
*Measures:* U.S. weights and measures. Same names as Imperial, but measures of volume and capacity are smaller (except the fluid ounce, which is larger).
*Electricity:* 110–115 V a.c. 60 Hz. Plugs: two flat pins.
*Transport:* International airports at all major cities. Direct from U.K.: B.A., British Caledonian, Pan Am, Air India, El Al, Iran Air, T.W.A. (Heathrow and Gatwick). Supersonic London to Washington. Also Laker Skytrain: no booking, just turn up. Many internal flights for which booking is unnecessary. Roads: Drive on right. U.K. or international driving licence. The car is America's main mode of travel – in Los Angeles for example, you can be

T.C.T.–Z

stopped by police on suspicion if *walking* in a residential area.
Greyhound buses for cheap, long-distance travel. Unlimited mileage ticket for limited period.
Railways: link main towns. 250 inter-city trains every weekday over 27,000 miles of track. Lots of new rolling stock – luxurious club cars. Book. Railpasses very good value – go as you please anywhere on system.
*Currency:* U.S. dollar = 100 cents. No restrictions on import or export.
*Religion:* Mainly Protestant with large R.C., Jewish and other minorities.
*Visa:* Yes. It's free. You have to supply one photo. Visa Branch of Embassy at 5 Upper Grosvenor Street, London W1A 2JB; telephone 01-499 5521.
*Jabs:* No: medical expenses very high. Take out plenty of insurance.
*Language:* English.
*Time:* Eastern time G.M.T. – 5; Central time – 6; Mountain time – 7; Pacific time – 8; Hawaiian Islands – 10; Alaska has four zones from – 8 to – 11. Daylight saving time comes in at the end of April, until last week of October but is not used in Hawaii.
*Hotels:* No official grading. All sorts. Usually either room only or full board. B. & B. rare. Cheaper summer accommodation through universities – to be pre-booked.
*Shop Hours:* Vary – mostly 09.30 to 21.00 Monday to Saturday. In New York many shops open until midnight.
*Bank Hours:* Usually 09.00 to 15.00 Monday to Friday but many banks open earlier and close later.
*British Embassy:* 3100 Massachusetts Avenue NW, Washington, DC 20008; telephone (202) HO 2 1340.
Consulates-General: 845 Third Avenue, New York, NY 10022; telephone (211) 752 8400. Atlanta, Ga (404) 524 5856. Chicago (312) 346 1810. Most major cities.
*Reference Book: National Forest Vacations,* booklet published at irregular intervals by the Forest Service, which is part of the U.S. Department of Agriculture, and covers the National Forests of the U.S.A., giving information such as picnic areas, nature trails, sports facilities and a brief guide to each National Forest. You may be able to obtain it from the United States Travel Service, otherwise it means buying a copy when you arrive.
*Tourist Office:* United States Travel Service, 22 Sackville Street, London W1X 2EA; telephone 01-734 2203.

## Upper Volta

*Area:* 274,200 km² (105,869 square miles).
*Capital:* Ouagadougou.
*Population:* 6,032,000. 3% urban.
*Occupation:* Subsistence farming, nomadic in north, many work in neighbouring countries.
*Climate:* Tropical: hot but dry. Temperatures 25–32 °C (77–90 °F). Arid desert in north. South, cool morning and evening. Rainy season June to October.
*Measures:* Metric.
*Electricity:* 220 V a.c. three-phase 50 Hz.
*Transport:* International airport: Ouagadougou. Hotel coach from airport. Airlines: U.T.A./Air Afrique. Rail link to capital of Ivory Coast. Internal, flights operated by Air Volta. Few roads paved. International driving permit.
*Currency:* C.F.A. franc. No restrictions on import or export.
*Religion:* Traditional with Muslim and Christian minorities.
*Visa:* Yes: return ticket or repatriation guarantee required. The visa costs £6 and you have to provide two photos. Embassy at 104 Park Street, London W1Y 3RJ; telephone 01-491 7351.
*Jabs:* Smallpox, yellow fever, cholera. T.A.B.T. recommended. Take anti-malaria and tummy-upset precautions.
*Language:* French, official.
*Time:* G.M.T.
*Hotels:* Government classified: first, second and third. Two main hotels in Ouagadougou. Excellent hotel in Bobo-Diolasso.
*Shop Hours:* 08.00 to 18.00 Monday to Saturday. Three-hour lunch closing.
*British Embassy:* Refer to Ivory Coast.

## Uruguay

*Area:* 177,508 km² (68,536 square miles). Smallest independent country in South America.
*Capital:* Montevideo.
*Population:* 3,064,000.
*Occupation:* Agriculture, wool and meat export.
*Climate:* Pleasant. Average temperature range 0–21 °C (32–70 °F). Rainfall: 890 mm (35 inches) a year; wettest July and August. 200 sunny days a year on average. Spring: October and November. Autumn: April and May.
*Measures:* Metric.
*Electricity:* 220 V a.c. 50 Hz. Plugs: three flat or two round pins.
*Transport:* International airport: Montevideo. Fly from U.K.: British Caledonian, via Buenos Aires. Travel is difficult during Holy Week because of crowds. Railways link main cities and to Brazil. River-boat connection to

Buenos Aires. Good bus service to interior. Roads: international driving permit with two photos, or get ninety-day permit from Town Hall. Driving style — lacking!
*Currency:* Peso = 100 centésimos. No restrictions on import or export.
*Religion:* Mostly R.C.
*Visa:* No.
*Jabs:* Smallpox. Cholera if from infected area.
*Language:* Spanish, English, Italian, French and German.
*Time:* G.M.T. − 3 (− 2 in summer).
*Hotels:* Ministry of Tourism grading: first class, second class etc. Some international style. There are camping sites but you need police permission. Good hostel in village of Villa Serrana.
*Shop Hours:* Usually 09.00 to 12.00 and 14.00 to 19.00 Monday to Friday. 09.00 to 12.30 Saturday.
*Bank Hours:* 12.00 to 16.00 Monday to Friday.
*British Embassy:* Marco Bruto 1073, Montevideo; telephone 781865.
*Tourist Office:* Comision Nacional de Turismo, Avenida Agraciada 1409 Piso, Montevideo.

## Venezuela

*Area:* 912,050 km² (352,144 square miles).
*Capital:* Caracas.
*Population:* 11,993,000.
*Occupation:* Petroleum production and export. Mining for iron ore.
*Climate:* Tropical. Temperature varies with altitude. Caracas (990 m; 3,250 feet) mild temperatures 9−32 °C (48−90 °F). Maracaibo hot and humid. Great variation between day and night temperatures. Rain: May to November.
*Measures:* Metric.
*Electricity:* 110 V a.c. 60 Hz. Plugs: American two flat pins.
*Transport:* International airport: Maiquetia Airport, Caracas. Direct from U.K.: British Caledonian and Air France (Concorde). Railways: plan for large extension — very few at present except Barquisimeto to Puerto Cabello. Jet air transport to all main towns. Roads: excellent. Tolls on some highways. International driving permit. Must be over eighteen. Get car identity document from Venezuelan Consul if you want to bring your own car. Cheap petrol.
*Currency:* Bolívar = 100 centimos. No restrictions on import or export.
*Religion:* Mainly R.C.
*Visa:* Get a tourist landing card from your airline. You must have a return or onward ticket.
*Jabs:* Smallpox. Cholera if from infected area. T.A.B.T. jab recommended. Take anti-malaria precautions.

*Language:* Spanish, some English.
*Time:* G.M.T. − 4.
*Hotels:* Department of Tourism gradings: de luxe, first class etc. Major international chains.
*Shop Hours:* 09.00 to 13.00 and 15.00 to 19.00 Monday to Saturday.
*Bank Hours:* 8.30 to 11.30, 14.00 to 16.30 Monday to Friday.
*British Embassy:* Avenida la Estancia No. 10, Ciudad Comercial Tamanaco, (Apartado 1246), Chuao, Caracas; telephone 91 12 55.
*Tourist Office:* Conahotu, Apartado 6651, Centro Capriles, Piso 7, Caracas 105.

## Vietnam, Socialist Republic of

*Area:* 329,556 km² (127,242 square miles).
*Capital:* Hanoi.
*Population:* 45,211,000.
*Occupation:* Agriculture: tea, rubber, rice. Fishing.
*Climate:* Tropical. Hot and humid on coast. Cooler and drier in mountains. Rain: May to October.
*Measures:* Metric.
*Electricity:* 120 V a.c. 50 Hz. Plugs: two-pin.
*Transport:* Airport at Hanoi. Fly by Interflug from East Berlin or by Aeroflot from Moscow or Rangoon.
*Currency:* In the north: dông = 10 hào = 100 xu. In the south: new Vietnam piastre = 100 centimes (presumably being withdrawn). Local currency may not be taken in or out.
*Religion:* Buddhism. 3 million Catholics. Spiritualist religions with political content popular in south before reunification.
*Visa:* Yes (very hard to get).
*Jabs:* Smallpox and cholera. T.A.B.T. recommended. Take anti-malaria precautions and remedies for dysentery and prickly heat.
*Language:* Vietnamese, Chinese, French.
*Time:* G.M.T. + 7.
*Hotels:* Before reunification Saigon had excellent hotels.
*British Embassy:* 16 Pho Ly Thuang Kiet, Hanoi; telephone 2349/2510.
*Tourist Office:* Vietnamtourism, 54 Nguyen Du Street, Hanoi.

## Virgin Islands

*Area:* British Virgin Islands: 153 km² (59 square miles). Virgin Islands of the United States: 344 km² (133 square miles). Part of the Leeward Islands chain.
*Capitals:* British: Road Town, on Tortola Island. U.S.: Charlotte Amalie, on St. Thomas.
*Population:* British: 11,000. U.S.: 92,000.
*Occupation:* Tourism.
*Climate:* Winter average temperature 26 °C (78 °F), summer 28 °C (82 °F). Rain: May to November.

*Measures:* U.S. and Imperial.
*Electricity:* 120 V a.c. 60 Hz. Plugs:
American two-pin.
*Transport:* To St. Thomas and St. Croix
from New York by American Airlines.
Antilles Air Boats operate from Puerto
Rico to all islands. No railways.
Inter-island travel by launch or sloop.
Hire jeeps for exploring.
*Currency:* U.S. currency. Also British
Virgin Island coins at par with U.S.
coins. Import and export as for U.S.A.
*Religion:* Christianity.
*Visa:* British: no. U.S.: yes, same
requirements as for the U.S.A.
*Jabs:* Smallpox.
*Language:* English.
*Time:* G.M.T. − 4.
*Hotels:* Wide variety of good hotels.
*Bank Hours:* 09.00 to 14.00 Monday to
Friday. Also 16.00 to 18.00 Friday.
*British Governor:* Government House,
Tortola, British Virgin Islands.
*British Consulate:* (P.O. Box 687), Charlotte
Amalie, St. Thomas, Virgin Islands of
the United States 00801; telephone 774
0033.
*Tourist Office:* West India Committee, 18
Grosvenor Street, London W1X OHP;
telephone 01-629 6353.

## Western Samoa

*Area:* 2,842 km² (1,097 square miles). Nine
islands in South Pacific, northeast of
New Zealand (only four inhabited).
*Capital:* Apia.
*Population:* 152,000.
*Occupation:* Agriculture (copra, bananas,
cocoa beans), forestry, hunting,
fishing.
*Climate:* Tropical. Rainy season:
December to April. Cooler May to
November.
*Transport:* One international airport. Go by
Polynesian Airlines from Fiji or Tonga.
No railways. Only 130 km (81 miles) of
bitumen-surfaced roads.
*Currency:* Tala (Western Samoan dollar) =
100 sene (cents). No restrictions on
import or export.
*Visa:* No.
*Jabs:* Smallpox.
*Electricity:* 230 V a.c. 50 Hz.
*Religion:* Various forms of Evangelical
Christianity with some R.C.
*Language:* English, Samoan.
*Time:* G.M.T. − 11.

## Windward Islands

*Area:* Dominica: 751 km² (290 square
miles). Grenada: 344 km² (133 square
miles). St. Lucia: 616 km² (238 square
miles). St. Vincent: 388 km² (150
square miles). For other islands in the
Windward chain, see French West
Indies.

*Capitals:* Dominica: Roseau. Grenada: St.
George's. St. Lucia: Castries. St.
Vincent: Kingstown.
*Population:* Dominica: 75,000. Grenada:
105,000. St. Lucia: 108,000. St. Vincent:
100,000.
*Occupation:* Tourism, agriculture.
*Climate:* Subtropical with high humidity.
Best December to May.
*Measures:* Imperial.
*Electricity:* Generally 230 V a.c. 50 Hz but
220 V on Grenada.
*Transport:* International airport on St.
Lucia, served by B.A. Or via Barbados
or Trinidad. No railways. Roads: U.K.
or international driving licence. Yacht
marinas on all islands.
*Currency:* East Caribbean dollar = 100
cents. No limit on import but you can
only take out what you brought in and
declared.
*Religion:* Christianity.
*Visa:* No.
*Jabs:* Smallpox.
*Language:* English.
*Time:* G.M.T. − 4.
*Hotels:* Many luxury beach hotels: what is
called a tourist 'paradise'.
*Shop Hours:* Mostly 08.00 to 12.00 or
12.30 and 13.00 or 13.30 to 16.00.
Some close Wednesday or Thursday
afternoon.
*Bank Hours:* 08.00 to 12.00 Monday to
Friday with additional late opening
Friday (15.00 to 17.00 on Dominica,
14.30 to 17.00 on Grenada, 14.00 to
17.00 on St. Lucia and St. Vincent).
*British High Commission:* Grenada: refer
to Trinidad and Tobago.
*British Government Representative:* St.
Lucia: Office of the British Government
Representative, George Gordon
Building, (P.O. Box 227), Castries;
telephone 2484. St. Vincent: Office of
the Deputy British Government
Representative, Grenville Street, (P.O.
Box 132), Kingstown; telephone 71701.
*Tourist Office:* Eastern Caribbean Tourist
Association, Room 222, 200
Buckingham Palace Road, London SW1
9TJ; telephone 01-730 6221/2.

## Yemen, People's Democratic Republic of

*Area:* 287,753 km² (111,102 square miles)
(including islands), situated on
southeast of Arabian peninsula.
*Capital:* Aden.
*Population:* 1,630,000 (mainly Arab, with
Indian and Somali minorities).
*Occupation:* Cotton, fisheries (tuna,
lobster, green turtle), stock raising,
citrus fruit.
*Climate:* Immensely varied. Desert in north
to mountains and fertile wadis (oases).
Flat and dry round Aden. May to
September: high humidity and

temperatures. October to April: lower humidity but high temperatures.
*Measures:* Metric: still some Imperial and lots of local.
*Electricity:* 220 V a.c. 50 Hz.
*Transport:* Many foreign airlines operate to Aden: M.E.A., Kuwait Airways, U.A.A., Yemeni Airlines. No railways. Local Alyemda Airlines have many internal flights. Few tarmacadam roads. Drive on right. Inland, few roads; camels and donkeys (China and Britain are helping the country to build roads). Few buses.
*Currency:* Southern Yemen dinar = 1,000 fils. Not more than 5 dinars may be taken in or out.
*Religion:* Muslim: small Hindu and Christian minorities.
*Visa:* Yes. It costs £3.55 and you must present two photos and your cholera and smallpox vaccination certificates. Embassy at 57 Cromwell Road, London SW7 2ED; telephone 01-584 6607/9.
*Jabs:* Smallpox and cholera. Yellow fever if from infected area. T.A.B.T. advisable. Take anti-malaria pills.
*Language:* Arabic, English.
*Time:* G.M.T. + 3.
*Hotels:* At Aden, Mukalla and Seiyon.
*British Embassy:* 28 Shara Ho Chi Minh, Khormaksar; telephone 24171.
*Note:* Tourist journeys must be approved in advance by the Ministry of Culture and Tourism. Journeys up-country may only be undertaken with an official guide. Cameras may be used only with permission.

## Yemen Arab Republic

*Area:* About 195,000 km² (75,290 square miles). Boundaries ill-defined. Near southern tip of Arabian peninsula. Bounded on north and east by Saudi Arabia, southeast by South Yemen and west by the Red Sea. Mainly mountainous with fertile plateau.
*Capital:* Sana.
*Population:* 5 million, living mainly in the temperate highlands in towns and villages.
*Occupation:* Agriculture: coffee, tobacco, barley, grain, cotton, grapes, oranges, lemons, bananas, pomegranates, dates, qat (a narcotic leaf). Hunting, fishing, textiles, salt. Arab horses. Said to be the cradle of Arab civilization.
*Climate:* Coastal areas: hot, humid and dry; little vegetation (dates). Highlands: temperate, some vegetation. Rainfall in winter: 510 mm (20 inches) plateau, 810 mm (32 inches) mountains.
*Transport:* Yemen Airlines from Cairo or Kuwait. Other Arab airlines from other Arab capitals. Air services connect all towns. Road links: Hodeida to Sana, Mocha to Taiz, Hodeida to Mocha and

Taiz to Hodeida. No railways. Roads: drive on right, international driving permit. Local buses.
*Measures:* Metric.
*Electricity:* 220 V a.c. 50 Hz.
*Religion:* Muslim.
*Currency:* Riyal = 100 fils. Local currency may not be imported or exported.
*Visa:* Yes, necessary. It costs £2.25 and you have to present three photos and your smallpox vaccination certificate. Embassy at 41 South Street, London W1Y 5PD; telephone 01-629 2085.
*Jabs:* Smallpox and cholera. T.A.B.T. recommended.
*Language:* Arabic.
*Time:* G.M.T. + 3. Also sun time (set your timepiece at 12.00 each sunset).
*Hotels:* In Sana, Hodeida and Taiz. Usually heavily booked.
*British Embassy:* 13 al Qasr al Jumhuri, (P.O. Box 1287), Sana; telephone 2684/5714.

## Yugoslavia

*Area:* 255,804 km² (98,766 square miles).
*Capital:* Belgrade.
*Population:* 21,352,000.
*Occupation:* Agriculture, manufacturing industry.
*Climate:* Varied. But cool winters, hot summers on the coast. Colder winters with snow in mountains.
*Measures:* Metric.
*Electricity:* 220 V a.c. 50 Hz.
*Transport:* International airports: Belgrade, Zagreb, Dubrovnik. Direct from U.K.: B.A. and T.A.T. Railways: linked with all European countries. Roads: excellent motorways through the mountains. Beautiful coast road. U.K. or international driving licence. Green card insurance compulsory. Good ferries between the many islands in the Adriatic. Good and frequent bus connections in Yugoslavia, also to other surrounding countries. Internal and domestic lines.
*Currency:* Dinar = 100 para. Not more than 1,500 dinars may be taken in or out. Notes of denomination higher than 100 dinars may not be taken in or out.
*Religion:* Christian with large Muslim minority.
*Visa:* No.
*Jabs:* Smallpox if from infected area.
*Language:* Serbo-Croat. German is second language. English widely understood.
*Time:* G.M.T. + 1.
*Hotels:* Tourist Board rating: five stars, four stars etc. Many large tourist hotels along coast. Few are tower blocks — usually landscaped into the surroundings. Full holiday facilities. Also, tourist villages of individual villas and accommodation in private houses.

Nudist settlements along coast. Youth hostels.

*Shop Hours:* Vary: mostly 08.00 to 12.00 and 17.00 to 20.00 Monday to Friday. 08.00 to 14.00 Saturday. Markets are from about 06.00 to 12.00.

*Bank Hours:* 07.00 to 11.00 or 10.00 to 14.00. Some town banks 07.30 to 19.00.

*British Embassy:* Belgrade: Generala Zdanova 46; telephone 645-055. Zagreb: Ilica 12 (Consulate); telephone 446-333. Split: Titova Obala 7 (Honorary Consul); telephone 41-464.

*Tourist Office:* Yugoslav National Tourist Office, 143 Regent Street, London W1R 8AE; telephone 01-734 5243.

# Zaïre

*Area:* 2,345,409 km² (905,566 square miles).

*Capital:* Kinshasa.

*Population:* 24,902,000. 200 tribal groups.

*Occupation:* Forestry, agriculture, bananas, coffee, mining, copper, cobalt, diamonds.

*Climate:* Tropical: centre and west, hot and humid. East and southeast, cool and drier. Rain: southwest October to May; north September to October; equatorial all year round.

*Measures:* Metric.

*Electricity:* 220 V a.c. 50 Hz.

*Transport:* International airports: Kinshasa and Lumumbashi. Direct from U.K.: British Caledonian. Railways: from Lumumbashi to Angola and Indian Ocean. Roads: rough outside cities. International driving permit. River services: Kinshasa to Kisangani and Kinshasa to Hebo. Few buses.

*Currency:* Zaïre = 100 likuta, 1 likuta = 100 sengi. Local currency may not be taken in or out.

*Religion:* R.C. and other religions.

*Visa:* Yes: apply early. It costs £2.40 and you must present three photos. Must arrive via Kinshasa Airport. Embassy at 26 Chesham Place, London SW1X 8HH; telephone 01-235 6137.

*Jabs:* Smallpox. Yellow fever and T.A.B.T. recommended. Cholera if from infected area. Take precautions against malaria and dysentery.

*Language:* French and local languages.

*Time:* G.M.T. + 1 or 2 depending on area.

*Hotels:* No official rating. Top hotels usually heavily booked and Government can requisition blocks of rooms at short notice. Advisable to book well in advance and obtain confirmation.

*Shop Hours:* 08.00 to 12.00 and 15.00 to 18.00 Monday to Saturday. Early closing Wednesday.

*Bank Hours:* 08.00 to 11.30 Monday to Friday.

*British Embassy:* 9 avenue de l'Équateur, 5th Floor, Barclays Bank International Building, Kinshasa.

# Zambia

*Area:* 752,614 km² (290,585 square miles).

*Capital:* Lusaka.

*Population:* 4,896,000.

*Occupation:* Copper mining (accounts for 90% of export earnings), zinc, cobalt, manganese, coal — prospecting for other metals. Agriculture (provides living for 79% of population): maize, cattle, groundnuts, tobacco, wheat and sugar.

*Climate:* Tropical: modified by altitude. Average temperatures 18 to 24 °C (65 to 75 °F).

*Measures:* Metric.

*Electricity:* 220 V a.c. 50 Hz.

*Transport:* International airport: Lusaka. Zambia Airways, B.A., British Caledonian, East Africa Airlines, Botswana Airlines, Alitalia, Air Zaïre. Zambia railways — Lusaka to copperbelt towns and to Zaïre and Angola and to East African railways system. Tan(zania)-Zam(bia) railways connect the two countries (Chinese aid). Main roads metalled (many miles of unmetalled roads too).

*Currency:* Zambia kwacha = 100 ngwee. Not more than 10 kwacha may be taken in or out.

*Religion:* 25—30% nominally Christian. Rest traditional. There are Muslims and a few Hindus.

*Visa:* No.

*Jabs:* Smallpox. Yellow fever and cholera if arriving from infected areas.

*Language:* English, many African languages (including Nyanja, Bemba, Tonga, Lozi, Lunda and Luvale).

*Time:* G.M.T. + 2.

*Hotels:* Number of excellent hotels and motels. Not yet classified. National Hotels Corporation has fourteen hotels, three restaurants, six lodges in National Parks. Plans for network of cafés.

*Shop Hours:* 08.00 to 17.00 Monday to Friday. Big stores all day Saturday, small shops 08.00 to 15.00.

*Bank Hours:* 08.00 to 13.00 Monday to Friday. 08.00 to 11.00 Saturday.

*British High Commission:* Independence Avenue, (P.O. Box R.W.50), Lusaka; telephone 51122.

*Tourist Office:* Zambia National Tourist Bureau, 163 Piccadilly, London W1V 9DE; telephone 01-493 5552/5482.

# Bibliography

A completely comprehensive list of travel and guide books would fill
another volume or two, but listed below are, first, some of the leading
guide book series available in this country, followed by, in alphabetical
order of subject, books mentioned in the text and additional special
interest books. For individual guides relating to particular countries see
the Gazetteer which begins on p. 000.

## Guide Series

**A.A. publications** All, except their *Annual Handbook*, are available to
non-members. Their U.K. guides are updated annually, the others as
required.

*Guide to Hotels and Restaurants*
*Guide to Guesthouses, Farmhouses and Inns*
*Guide to Guesthouses, Farmhouses and Inns on the Continent*
*Guide to Stately Homes, Castles and Gardens*
*Guide to Camping and Caravanning*
*Camping and Caravanning on the Continent* (lists nearly 5,000 sites in 18
countries)
*Guide to Self-Catering Holiday Accommodation*
*Haunts and Haunting*
*Royal Britain*
*Continental Motoring*
*Road Book of Europe*
*Car Components Guide* (motorist's phrase book in 12 languages)
*G.B. Road Atlas*

*A.A. maps:* the A.A. publish a map of Western Europe only. They
provide a service for members whereby if you tell them where from and
to you plan to travel they will work out your best route and supply you
with strip route maps. They will cover anywhere in the world.

**ABC Travel Guides** Old Hill, London Road, Dunstable LU6 3EB

*ABC World Airways Guide*: published monthly. Gives up-to-date timetables for all the world's airlines. Comprehensive details of all through
flights and principal transfer connections. Advanced summer and
winter schedules, fares, car hire section, route maps, Hotel Guide
supplement etc.

*ABC Shipping Guide*: published monthly. Gives information on shipping lines operating passenger services throughout the world. Details of sailings and fares for all scheduled services. Includes a comprehensive worldwide cruise section.

*ABC Air/Rail Europe*: published monthly. Pocket size guide to European air and rail travel. Quick reference timetables linking 350 cities in 29 countries. Includes over 2,500 city-to-city connections, giving alternative routes.

*ABC Air Cargo Guide*: published monthly. Contains world timetables of air cargo services with general and specific commodity rates plus currency and exchange rates.

*ABC Rail Guide*: published monthly. Covers rail routes and fares from London with quick reference timetables to principal stations. Complete train service section provides concise timetables for Southern England plus shipping services. Separate inter-city section gives train services between provincial centres.

*ABC Guide to International Travel*: published quarterly. Contains worldwide information on passport and visa regulations; currency and exchange rates; health requirements and recommendations. Also customs import allowances, climate, bank holidays, business hours, languages, driving licence details, etc.

*ABC Freight Guide*: published in March and September. Lists under towns and counties general road haulage contractors in the U.K. and specialist haulers. Separate sections cover transport of goods by air, sea and rail.

*ABC Guide to Party Booking*: published annually. Covers a multitude of places of interest including zoos, river trips, cathedrals, horse racing, etc.

*Museums and Galleries*: published annually in October. Guide to over 800 collections, both large and small. Fully illustrated with a detailed subject index ranging from archeology to witchcraft. Gives details of locations, open times, admission charges and telephone numbers.

**Karl Baedeker guides** are published in Germany by the firm Karl Baedeker, 78 Freiburg im Breisgau, Rosastrasse 7, West Germany. They used to be distributed in this country by Allen and Unwin, but they are running down stocks and the only title of which they have any sizeable stock left is *Great Britain*: vol. 1 *Southern England and East Anglia* (1966), vol. 2 *Central England and Wales* (1968), vol. 3 *Northern England* (1970). Facsimile editions of the 1929 edition of *Egypt* and the 1914 edition of *Russia, with Teheran, Port Arthur and Peking* are published by David and Charles. You should contact Karl Baedeker direct for guides covering any other countries.

**Blue Guides,** published by Ernest Benn, combine practical information with a wealth of historical detail. The dates of the latest editions are given in brackets.

*Belgium and Luxembourg,* ed. John Tomes (1977)
*Crete,* ed. Stuart Rossiter (1977)
*England,* ed. Stuart Rossiter (1976)
*Greece,* ed. Stuart Rossiter (1977)
*Northern Italy,* ed. Stuart Rossiter (new edition to appear April 1978)
*London,* ed. Stuart Rossiter (1973)
*Paris and Environs,* ed. Ian Robertson (1977)
*Rome and Environs,* ed. Stuart Rossiter (1975)
*Scotland,* ed. John Tomes (1977)
*Sicily,* ed. Alta Macadam (1975)
*Spain,* ed. Ian Robertson (1975)
*Wales,* ed. Stuart Rossiter (new edition to appear 1978/79)
*Yugoslavia: The Adriatic Coast,* ed. Stuart Rossiter (1969)

**Fodor guides,** edited by Eugene Fodor and Odile Cail, are published by Hodder and Stoughton. In general they are revised yearly, though the guides covering less popular countries are not revised as frequently. The dates of the latest editions are given in brackets.

*Austria* (1976)
*Belgium and Luxembourg* (1976)
*Caribbean* (1976)
*Europe* (1976)
*Europe on a Budget* (1974)
*Europe Under 25* (1974)
*France* (1976)
*Germany* (1976)
*Great Britain* (1976)
*Greece* (1976)
*Hawaii* (1976)
*Holland* (1976)
*India* (1976)
*Ireland* (1976)

*Israel* (1976)
*Italy* (1976)
*Japan and South Korea* (1976)
*Mexico* (1976)
*Morocco* (1976)
*Peking* (1972)
*Portugal* (1976)
*Scandinavia* (1976)
*South America* (1976)
*South-East Asia* (1976)
*Soviet Union* (1976)
*Spain* (1976)
*Switzerland* (1976)

**Michelin Green Guides** These are revised every 2–3 years. They are tourist guides and give information on places of interest, museums, local customs, etc. The dates of the latest editions are given in brackets.

*Austria and the Bavarian Alps* (1974)
*Brittany* (1975)
*Châteaux of the Loire* (1974)
*French Riviera* (1975)
*Germany: West Germany and Berlin* (1974)

*Italy* (1974)
*Morocco* (1974)
*New York City* (1977)
*Normandy* (1975)
*Paris* (1977)
*Portugal* (1972)
*Pyrenees* (1974)
*Spain* (1974)
*Switzerland* (1974)

**Michelin Red Guides** These are published annually and give information on a selection of all types of hotels and restaurants.

| | |
|---|---|
| *Benelux* | *Italy* |
| *Germany* | *Paris* |
| *Great Britain and Ireland* | *Paris and Environs* |
| *Greater London* | *Spain and Portugal* |

*Camping and Caravanning in France* is also published by Michelin annually. Michelin's maps of Africa — No. 153 (North and West), No. 154 (North-East), No. 155 (Central and South) — are of special value as they show all the national parks and reserves, and roads which are dangerous and/or impassable during the rainy season. They also show the monthly average temperature and rainfall for particular places.

Their maps of Morocco, the Ivory Coast, and Algeria and Tunisia are on a larger scale than the ones mentioned above, but they do not give details of temperature and rainfall.

Michelin also publish maps of Britain, Germany, Italy, France, Spain, Switzerland and Benelux. They do not cover the Far or Middle East, Asia, or the U.S.A.

**Nagel Encyclopedia Guides** are published in Geneva and distributed in this country by Godfrey Cave Associates Ltd, 44 Great Russell Street, London WC1B 3PA. The guides are very detailed, as their name suggests, and are revised infrequently. The dates of the latest editions are given in brackets.

| | |
|---|---|
| *Algeria* (1974) | *Egypt* (1972) |
| *Austria* (1970) | *Finland* (1967) |
| *Balearic Islands* (1970) | *French and Italian Riviera* (1970) |
| *Bulgaria* (1970) | *Germany* (1974) |
| *Canada* (1975) | *Greece* (1970) |
| *Châteaux of the Loire* (1971) | *Holland* (1974) |
| *China* | *Hungary* (1973) |
| *Cyprus* (1970) | *Iceland* (1974) |
| *Czechoslovakia* (1970) | *India* (1977) |
| *Denmark and Greenland* (1956) | *Iran* (1968) |

*Israel* (1970)
*Italy* (1971)
*Japan* (1970)
*Leningrad and Its Environs* (1970)
*Mexico* (1974)
*The Moon* (1970)
*Morocco* (1970)
*Moscow and Its Environs* (1970)
*New York City* (1971)
*Poland* (1974)

*Portugal, Madeira, the Azores* (1970)
*Rome* (1968)
*Roumania* (1970)
*Spain* (1970)
*Thailand and Angkor (Cambodia)* (1971)
*Turkey* (1974)
*U.S.A.* (1972)
*U.S.S.R.* (1973)
*Yugoslavia* (1970)

**Red Guides,** published by Ward Lock, cover the U.K. in detail. They are always kept up to date.

*Bournemouth and New Forest*
*Channel Islands*
*Cornwall: South*
*Cornwall: West*
*Complete Cornwall*
*Cotswolds*
*Complete Cotswolds and Shakespeare Country*
*Explore the Cotswolds by Bicycle*
*Devon: South*
*Complete Devon*
*Dorset Coast*
*Complete Dorset and Wiltshire*
*Complete England*
*Northern Ireland*
*Isle of Wight*
*Lake District*
*London*

*London for the Disabled*
*Norfolk and the Broads*
*Peak District*
*Highlands of Scotland*
*Northern Scotland*
*Western Scotland*
*Complete Scotland*
*Complete Scottish Lowlands*
*Complete South-East Coast*
*Complete Thames and Chilterns*
*Wales, North*
*Wales, South*
*Complete Wales*
*Complete West Country*
*Complete Wye Valley, Hereford and Worcester*
*Complete Yorkshire*

**R.A.C. publications** All are available to non-members. Their two handbooks are revised annually, the other guides as necessary.

*Guide and Handbook*: lists some 4,000 R.A.C. 'appointed' hotels, motels, restaurants and grill inns, nearly 6,000 R.A.C. appointed garages and repairers, including motor cycle repairers, and includes sections on motor laws, new registration and licensing of motor vehicles, as well as maps and over 40 town plans showing parking places, meter zones and one-way systems.

*Continental Handbook and Guide to Western Europe*: covers 14 European countries and provides a mine of information, including 96 pages of town plans, details of national motoring practices, a motoring glossary and an extensive list of passes and tunnels. A map of Europe is also included loose.

*Guide to Touring in Ireland*
*Guide to Scandinavia and Eastern Europe*
*Motorist's Interpreter*: phrase book in Italian, French, German, Spanish, and Serbo-Croat.

Airport booklets: one for Heathrow and the other for Gatwick. Gives complete information on parking and garaging, car hire firms, hotels etc. In the Heathrow booklet there is a large scale map of the airport and another showing the approach roads with details of access points to the airport.

Caravan and camping sites: five books listing R.A.C. recommended sites in: England; Wales and the West Country, including the Isles of Scilly and the Channel Islands; Scotland and Northern England; Ireland; and France. They include detailed maps and complete access route information.

*Guide to British and Continental Camping and Caravanning Sites*: nearly 4,000 sites compared and located individually in the atlas section ranging from Ireland to Turkey and Portugal to Russia.

*Castles and Historic Houses*: includes gardens and other areas of interest open to the public.

Picnic sites: two booklets covering Yorkshire and the West Country. They each include a map showing location of each picnic area and approach roads.

*Great Britain Road Atlas*
*London and S.E. England Atlas*
*Road Atlas of Europe*

National and regional maps: series of 15 maps specially prepared for the touring motorist, covering: England and Wales; Scotland; Ireland; Greater London; South-East; The South; South-West; East Anglia; Midlands; South Wales; Lancashire and North Wales; Yorkshire; The North; South Scotland; North Scotland.

Local maps: series of 38 separate maps for the whole of England and Wales showing road detail with great clarity. They cover: Avon; Beds and Herts; Borders; Cambrians; Cambridge; Cornwall; North Devon; South Devon; Dorset; Downs; Essex; Fens; Humber; Kent; Lakes; North Lancs; Lincoln; London; Marches; Mersey; West Midlands; Norfolk; Oxford; Peaks; Pembroke; Potteries; Solent; Solway; Suffolk; Sussex; Trent; Tyne and Wear; Mid Wales; North Wales; South Wales; Wye; York; North Yorks.

Leisure maps: series of four illustrated district maps — South Coast, Thames Valley, Wales, East Coast — giving details of pleasure pursuits and town plans.

Motor tours: eleven illustrated booklets about the most popular holiday areas in the U.K., listing places of interest and including complete
tour maps. They cover: Cornwall; South Devon; Exmoor and North
Devon; Lake District; Drives Around London — A Day Away; Hardy
Country and New Forest; Northumbria; Scottish Locks and Highlands; North Wales; South Wales; Yorkshire.

If you are a member of the R.A.C. and are planning a trip in Europe, to
the Middle East or India they will prepare strip route maps for you
showing the best way to reach your destination. They will put members in touch with similar organizations who can help for the U.S.A.
and Australia and they will recommend publications and give as much
help as they can for trips to more out of the way places.

**Travellers' Guides,** published by Jonathan Cape, are revised every
5—8 years. The dates of the latest editions are given in brackets.

*The Travellers' Guide to Corfu and the Other Ionian Islands,* Martin Young
(1977).
*The Travellers' Guide to Crete,* John Bowman (1974).
*The Travellers' Guide to Cyprus,* Hazel Thurston (1971).
*The Travellers' Guide to Elba and the Tuscan Archipelago,* Christopher and
Jean Serpell (1977).
*The Travellers' Guide to Finland,* Sylvie Nickels (1977).
*The Travellers' Guide to Malta and Gozo,* Christopher Kininmonth
(1975).
*The Travellers' Guide to Morocco,* Christopher Kininmonth (1972).
*The Travellers' Guide to Rhodes and the Dodecanese,* Jean Currie (1975).
*The Travellers' Guide to Sardinia,* T. and B. Holme and B. Ghirardelli
(1977).
*The Travellers' Guide to Sicily,* Christopher Kininmonth (1972).
*The Travellers' Guide to Tunisia,* Hazel Thurston (1973).
*The Travellers' Guide to Turkey,* Dux Schneider (1975).
*The Travellers' Guide to Yugoslavia: Slovenia, Croatia and Bosnia, Hercego-
vina,* Sylvie Nickels (1969).

## General

*Battlefields of Europe, Guide to the,* ed. David Chandler (Hugh Evelyn,
London 1965). Volume 1 covers West Europe, Volume 2, Central and
East Europe.

Camping and caravanning
*Camping and Caravanning on the Continent,* published by the A.A. and
available to non-members, covers nearly 5,000 sites in 18 countries.
*Camping and Caravanning in France,* published annually by Michelin.

*Europa Camping and Caravanning*, published annually by Drei Brunnen
Verlag, Stuttgart, available in this country. Covers over 4,500 sites in
40 countries in Europe, the Near East and North Africa.

*Guide to British and Continental Camping and Caravanning Sites*, published
by Letts Diaries and the R.A.C., available to non-members, covers
nearly 4,000 sites ranging from Ireland to Turkey, Portugal to Russia.
The R.A.C. also publish five books listing recommended sites in:
England; Wales and the West Country, including the Isles of Scilly
and the Channel Islands; Scotland and Northern England; Ireland;
and France. Available to non-members.

*Guide to Camping and Caravanning*, published by the A.A. and available
to non-members. Covers the U.K.

## Canoeing

*Coaching Handbook* (British Canoe Union, 70 Brompton Road, London
SW3 1DT, 1977). General book on canoeing, available from the
B.C.U. to non-members.

British Canoe Union maps, available to non-members. Get them
direct from B.C.U., 70 Brompton Road, London SW3 1DT:
*Canoeists Guide to the River Wye*
*River Wye Map*
*River Severn Map*
*Canoeing Map of England and Wales*
*River Thames Map — Lechlade to Richmond*
*Broadlands Map*
*Canoe Camping*

*Car Ferries, The Lazy Way to Book Your* (Car Ferry Enquiries Ltd, 9A Spur
Road, Isleworth, Middlesex TW7 5BD). Published annually, full of ferry
booking advice.

## Castles, historic houses, gardens, etc.

*Castles and Historic Houses*, published by the R.A.C., available to non-
members. Covers the U.K. and includes gardens and other areas of
interest open to the public.

*Guide to Stately Homes, Castles and Gardens*, published by the A.A.,
available to non-members.

## Chalets

*Villa Holidays*, published by Swiss Chalet–Inter Home and distributed through the A.A., gives detailed information on chalets to
rent in 21 countries, though most are in Switzerland.

## Charter flights

*St. James's Guide to ABC [Advance Booking Charters] Flights* (St. James

Press, London) lists all ABC flights, which airlines fly where, how far in advance you have to book, how long you can stay, etc.

*Children Welcome!: The 'Happy Family' Holiday Guide*, ed. P. S. Williams (Herald Advisory Service Publications, London). Published annually.

*Country Hotels of Britain*, ed. P. S. Williams (Herald Advisory Service Publications, London). Published annually.

Cruising

*ABC Shipping Guide*, published monthly by ABC Travel Guides Ltd, Old Hill, London Road, Dunstable LU6 3EB. Gives information on shipping lines operating passenger services throughout the world. Details of sailings and fares for all scheduled services. Includes a comprehensive worldwide cruise section.

*A Lazy Man's Guide to Holidays Afloat*, booklet published annually by Boat Enquiries Ltd, 7 Walton Road, Oxford OX2 6ED, giving information and tips on cruising and boating in Britain.

Cycling

*Bicycle Touring in Europe*, Karen and Gary Hawkins (Sidgwick and Jackson, London 1974).

*Explore the Cotswolds by Bicycle*, one of the Red Guides published by Ward Lock, London.

*The Maintenance of Bicycles and Mopeds* (Reader's Digest, London 1975).

*Richard's Bicycle Book*, Richard Ballantine (Pan Books, London 1975).

*Diabetics, Holidays and Travel for*, useful brochure published by the British Diabetic Association, 3–6 Alfred Place, London WC1.

Directories and general guides to travel agents, tour operators, hotels, coach and car hire firms, railways, etc. (see also under ABC Travel Guides).

*Agents' Hotel Gazetteer*, ed. R. A. Isaacs (Continental Hotel Gazetteers, 1974). Two volumes: *Resorts of Europe* and *Tourist Cities of Europe*. Each place is described briefly with a list of hotels, their facilities and location.

*Egon Ronay's Lucas Guide* (Egon Ronay Organisation, London). Published annually. Lists and assesses hotels, inns, pensions, restaurants, wine bars, economy restaurants and pubs throughout the U.K.

*Financial Times World Hotel Directory* (Financial Times, London). Published annually. It is aimed at businessmen and lists hotels and the business facilities they offer, such as secretarial help, translation services, private entertainment and conference facilities.

*Hints to Business Men* (British Overseas Trade Board, London). These country-by-country booklets are published annually. They are available free to exporters only, not to members of the general public, but most central reference libraries stock a complete set. Apart from containing information appropriate to U.K. exporters they also cover such useful things as the social customs of each country, official public holidays, travel routes to the country concerned, hotels, restaurants and tipping, geographical features, principal cities and towns, postal, telegraph, telephone and telex facilities.

*The Holiday Guide* (St. James Press, London). Winter and summer editions. It lists tour operators and all the holiday destinations they serve, the hotels they use, the conditions of their package tours, mode of travel, place of departure, etc.

*Holiday Which?* (Consumers Association, London). Published four times a year. Gives consumer advice on tours, packages, rates of exchange, insurance, etc. This is only available to subscribers. The normal subscription will provide you with *Which?*, but you have to pay a little extra to get the *Holiday Which?* Most reference libraries, however, stock them.

*National Express Services Guide* (National Bus Company). Winter and summer editions. Gives full timetables of National Express services and those of other bus companies operating within the U.K. and to connecting services − ferry or hovercraft across the Channel. Available from any of the five areas of National Travel (N.B.C.) Ltd. Their addresses are: National Travel (SE) Ltd, Victoria Coach Station, Buckingham Palace Road, London SW1W 9TP; National Travel (E) Ltd, Frost Hill, Liversedge, Yorkshire WF15 6AU; National Travel (SW) Ltd, Coach Station, St. Margaret's Road, Cheltenham, Glos. GL50 4DX; National Travel (W) Ltd, Canada House, Chepstow Street, Manchester M1 5FU.

*Relais de Campagne et Châteaux,* published by the French government and available from French Tourist Offices. Covers a de luxe selection of hotels where you can expect attractive locations, lavish facilities, superb food and top prices. France is covered in greatest detail, but Britain, Italy, Belgium and Spain are also covered.

*Thomas Cook International Timetable* (Thomas Cook Ltd). Published monthly. Gives a complete run-down on the world's railways and local shipping services.

*Travel Directory* (St. James Press, London). Published annually. Lists all A.B.T.A. tour operators and travel agents, hotel groups, foreign hotels and their representatives in the U.K., coach and car hire firms.

*Travel Phone Guide* (St. James Press, London). A miniature of the *Travel Directory*. Lists everyone, except A.B.T.A. travel agents, giving their phone numbers only.

*Travel Trade Directory* (Morgan-Grampian Book Publishing, London). Published annually. Covers U.K. and Republic of Ireland. Lists agents, tour operators, airlines, coach and car hire firms, insurers, hotels and their representatives.

*Y.H.A. Guide to Europe*, published by the Youth Hostel Association, 29 John Adam Street, London WC2, and available to non-members, gives a country-by-country breakdown of geography, climate and history and includes information on which areas are most suitable for which outdoor activities, such as walking, sailing, camping, climbing. Each chapter covers one country, and if you don't want the complete guide you can buy the individual chapters.

## The disabled

*An ABC of Services and Information for Disabled People* by Barbara Macmorland, available from the Disablement Income Group, Attlee House, Toynbee Hall, 28 Commercial Street, London E1 6LR and local groups, provides an extensively cross-referenced catalogue of all available advice, booklets and organizations covering all handicapped needs, including holidays and travel.

Handihols, The Cottage, The Chase, Ashingdon, Rochford, Essex, is an agency for exchanging homes between disabled people.

*Holidays for the Physically Handicapped*, published by the Central Council for the Disabled, 34 Eccleston Square, London SW1V 1PD, available from them and from bookshops, is a guide to accommodation classified to show the degree of disability that can be accommodated. Hotels and guest-houses are further classified into those providing special diets, those accepting epileptics and those accepting incontinents. It covers most European countries.

## Educational travel

The Central Bureau for Educational Visits and Exchanges, 44 Baker Street, London W1M 2HJ, or 3 Bruntsfield Crescent, Edinburgh EH10 4HD, publish useful booklets jam-packed with suggestions:

*School Travel and Exchange*: basically for teachers, or parent-teacher associations. Gives information on school travel to 33 countries, including China and Albania.

*Sport and Adventure Holidays*: gives information on action holidays on offer by some 300 organizations, covering anything from overland safaris to a 15-day botanical tour of Afghanistan.

*Study Holidays*: a full and detailed listing of study courses — anything from languages to sport — available in 35 countries including the U.S.A., Russia, Poland, Mexico, Iceland and Turkey.

Farm holidays

*Farm Holiday Guide* (English, Scottish and Welsh editions), ed. D. Murdoch, published annually by Farm Holiday Guides Ltd, 18 High Street, Paisley, Renfrewshire.

*French Farm and Village Holiday Guide*, J. Herson McCartney, published by BHAM Books, 12–14 Whitfield Street, London W1, covers 1,000 moderately priced holiday houses in France.

*Guide to Guesthouses, Farmhouses and Inns*, published by the A.A., available to non-members. Covers the U.K.

*Guide to Guesthouses, Farmhouses and Inns on the Continent*, published by the A.A., available to non-members.

*Festivals and Events in Britain, B.P. Book of*, Christopher Trent (J. M. Dent, London 1973).

Fishing

*Fishing Waters*, compiled by Bill Howse, published annually by Link House Publications, Link House, Dingwall Avenue, Croydon, Surrey, covers every kind of fishing in the U.K.

*Where to Fish*, ed. D. A. Orton, Harmsworth Press, London, covers every kind of fishing in the U.K. and Ireland in detail, and also in the British Commonwealth and parts of Europe. Updated every two years or as necessary.

*Food Guide, The Good* (Consumers Association, London). Published annually. Assesses food in approved hotels and restaurants in the U.K. Mentions accommodation where it exists, but makes no judgements. Available in bookshops.

*Gay Guide, Spartacus*, available from P.O. Box 3496, Amsterdam, or from *Gay News*, 1A Normand Gardens, Greyhound Road, London W14 9SB. *Spartacus Gay Guide* gives country-by-country advice and information for homosexuals.

Games for journeys

*Fun on Wheels*, Mary Danby (Armada, London 1973).

*Games for Trains, Planes and Wet Days*, Gyles Brandreth (William Luscombe, London 1974).

*Games to Play in the Car*, Michael Harwood (Rapp and Whiting, London 1974).

*I-Spy* books, published by Polystyle Publications, distributed by Dickens Press, London, including *I-Spy on a Car Journey, I-Spy on a Train, I-Spy at the Airport, I-Spy on the Motorway, I-Spy Buses and Coaches*, and many other titles.

*How to Amuse Yourself on a Journey*, Judy Allen (Studio Vista, London 1974).

*Travel Games*, Maurice Pipard (Collins, London 1974).

*Geographical Journal* (Royal Geographical Society, 1 Kensington Gore, London SW7). Published three times a year and can be purchased from the R.G.S. by non-members. Their *Geographical Magazine* is published monthly and can be bought in most leading bookshops.

*Ghost Towns of the West*, ed. Jack McDowell, published in the U.S. by Lane Books in 1976 and distributed in this country by the Lunesdale Publishing Group, Lancaster. Covers ghost mining towns of western America, more a book to be read before you leave than one to take with you.

*Haunts and Haunting*, published by the A.A., available to non-members. Covers the U.K.

Health

*Expedition Travel and Your Health* by Dr Peter Steele, published by Bristol University, is a handy booklet giving specialized advice on travelling at high altitudes.

*Exploration Medicine: Being a Practical Guide for Those Going on Expeditions*, ed. O. G. Edholm and A. L. Bacharach (John Wright and Sons, Bristol 1965).

*Preservation of Personal Health in Warm Climates*, comprehensive booklet published by the Ross Institute of Tropical Hygiene, available from the London School of Hygiene and Tropical Medicine, Keppel Street (Gower Street), London WC1E 7HT.

*A Traveller's Guide to Health*, Lt. Col. James M. Adam (Hodder and Stoughton, for the Royal Geographical Society, London 1966).

Home swapping

Handihols, The Cottage, The Chase, Ashingdon, Rochford, Essex, is an agency for exchanging homes between disabled people.

Home Interchange Limited, P.O. Box 84, London NW8 7RR, publish a directory in December every year, with supplements in February and March. They list an average of 3,000 homes in 30 countries, covering the U.K., most of Europe, North America, Canada, Australia, New Zealand, the Far East, the Caribbean, Mexico and East Africa, available for exchange, rental or exchange hospitality, i.e. you go as a guest and your host then returns as your guest.

Homex Directory Limited, P.O. Box 27, London NW6 4HE, concentrate on exchanges between Britain and the U.S.A. and Canada. You take out a subscription, describe your home, where you want to go and when, and the information is put in the Directory. It is sent to all subscribers who then contact each other.

William Lowell Associates Incorporated, 305 South Saint Asaph Street, Alexandria, Virginia 22314, U.S.A., offer an expensive exchange service 'for professional people'. They not only supply a list of exchange names but also a security service that will take up and verify all the references each side must provide, and these are fairly stringent.

*Inns of Britain, Wayside,* ed. P. S. Williams (Herald Advisory Service Publications, London). Published annually.

Motor touring (see also under A.A. and R.A.C. publications, pp. 000 and 000).

*Europa Touring,* published by Hallwag Verlag, Bern and Stuttgart, available in this country, is an exhaustive motoring guide to Europe containing all the information you could possibly need. Includes numerous relief maps. Frequently revised.

*Museums and Galleries,* published annually in October by ABC Travel Guides, Dunstable. Guide to over 800 collections, both large and small. Fully illustrated with a detailed subject index ranging from archaeology to witchcraft. Gives details of locations, open times, admission charges and telephone numbers.

*National Parks of the West,* ed. P. C. Johnson (Lane Books, 1976, distributed by Lunesdale Publishing Group, Lancaster). Covers national parks of western America. Read it before you go, it's a little too big to take with you.

*Pets Welcome!: Animal Lovers' Holiday Guide,* ed. P. S. Williams (Herald Advisory Service Publications, London). Published annually. Lists hotels that will take pets as well as a good selection of catteries and kennels.

*Pub Guide, Egon Ronay's* (Egon Ronay Organisation, London). Published every few years. The 1977 edition covers 600 pubs, including 53 pubs on the Continent, of particular merit as regards atmosphere, amenities, architecture, etc.

*Public Holidays, The Traveller's World Guide to* (Export Times, London 1965).

Regional guides

*Africa Guide,* published annually by the Africa Guide Company, 21 Gold Street, Saffron Walden; an invaluable and exhaustive guide to some 25 African countries.

*Africa South of the Sahara* (Europa Publications, London). Published annually. Will give you background information, on political and economic aspects particularly. Read it before you go.

*The Nile Journey*, Trevor Kenworthy (Trail Finders Ltd, London 1976). Book of information and advice on travel up the Nile from Cairo to Nairobi. Available only from Trail Finders, whose address is 48 Earl's Court Road, London W8.

*Overland Through Africa*, ed. G. Crowther (B.I.T., 15 Acklam Road, London W10, 1976). Nomadic guide for the fit and sturdy travelling rough.

*Trans-Africa Motoring*, Colin McElduff (Wilton House Gentry, London 1975). Book of advice for overland travel.

*Trans-Africa Route Report*, Mike Gooley (Trail Finders Ltd, London 1975). Gives detailed advice for the independent traveller with their own vehicle travelling the trans-Saharan route to Nairobi. Available only from Trail Finders, whose address is 48 Earl's Court Road, London W8.

*Far East and Australasia* (Europa Publications, London). Published annually. Will give you background information, on political and economic aspects particularly. Read it before you go.

*Overland through India to Australia*, ed. G. Crowther (B.I.T., 15 Acklam Road, London W10, 1977). Nomadic guide for the fit and sturdy travelling rough.

*Middle East and North Africa* (Europa Publications, London). Published annually. Will give you background information, on political and economic aspects particularly. Read it before you go.

*Overland to Central and South America*, ed. G. Crowther (B.I.T., 15 Acklam Road, London W10, 1976). Nomadic guide for the fit and sturdy travelling rough.

*South American Handbook* (Trade and Travel Publications, Bath). Published annually. Essential for anybody travelling in South America; it will see you through all the bizarre situations you may well find yourself in.

*South American Survival*, Maurice Taylor (Trail Finders Ltd, London 1975). Book of advice and information on overland travel in South America. Available only from Trail Finders, whose address is 48 Earl's Court Road, London W8.

*West Indies and Caribbean Year Book* (T. Skinner Directories, London). Published annually.

*Europa Yearbook* (Europa Publications, London). Published annually. Covers every country in the world giving background, mainly political

and economic, information. Volume 1 covers international organizations (U.N., Nato, etc.) and Europe; volume 2; the rest of the world.

Retreats

The Association for Promoting Retreats, Church House, Newton
Road, London W2, whose aim is 'to foster the growth of spiritual life'
lists retreats in the U.K., the U.S.A., Canada, South Africa and New
Zealand in their journal *Vision*. Everybody is welcome.

*The Directory of Monastic Hospitality*, published by the Poor Clares of
Arundel and available from them at All Saints, London Colney, St.
Albans, Herts, lists monasteries and convents in the U.K. that offer
hospitality compatible with their traditions and their rule. There are
41 convents and 12 monasteries; charges are by donation or around £2
per day.

*Rivers of the West*, ed. Elizabeth Hogan (Lane Books, 1976, distributed by
Lunesdale Publishing Group, Lancaster). Covers rivers of western
America. Not really a book to take with you. Read it before you go.

*Royal Britain*, published by the A.A., available to non-members.

Sailing

*Boat World*, ed. Nancy Shawcross, published annually by Haymarket
Publishing, London. Lists all sailing centres round the U.K. coast and
on inland waterways.

*Self-Catering Holiday Accommodation, Guide to*, published by the A.A., available to non-members.

Sport and special interest holidays

*B.P. Book of Holidays with a Difference*, ed. Robin Dewhurst (Queen
Anne Press, London 1972). Covers all sorts of special interest and
activity holidays, including canoeing, climbing, riding, sailing, arts
and crafts, natural history, industrial archeology, film-making, antique hunting.

*Sport and Adventure Holidays*, published by the Central Bureau for
Educational Visits and Exchanges, 44 Baker Street, London W1M
2HJ or 3 Bruntsfield Crescent, Edinburgh EH10 4HD, gives information on action holidays on offer by some 300 organizations, covering anything from overland safaris to a 15-day botanical tour of
Afghanistan.

*Survival Kit Europe, Travellers*, booklet published by Vacation-Work Publications, 9 Park End Street, Oxford OX1 1HJ, is a young person's guide
to survival in Europe. Includes information on such things as where to
get free wine in France, how to get medical bills paid for you, where to get
free maps, how and where to meet the natives, how to earn money if you

are broke, how to handle the police, how the telephone systems work, and much more.

*Transport Cafés, Egon Ronay's Lucas Guide to* (Egon Ronay Organisation, London). Published annually. Assesses the cafés and their accommodation.

Working holidays and job opportunities abroad

*Employ d'Ete en France,* published annually by Vacation-Work, 9 Park End Street, Oxford OX1 1HJ. Lists thousands of vacancies in France.

The Co-ordination Committee for International Voluntary Service, 1 rue Miollis, 75015 Paris, publish a booklet of 130 organizations that arrange international work camps which they will supply if you send them three international reply coupons.

*Directory of Jobs and Careers Abroad,* ed. Roger Brown, published every two years by Vacation-Work, 9 Park End Street, Oxford OX1 1HJ. Contains a fairly extensive coverage of career and job prospects in different countries, including the Common Market, the English-speaking Commonwealth, North America, Scandinavia, Switzerland, Austria, etc., giving details on immigration, training, taxation, social security, unions, and so on.

*Summer Jobs Abroad,* ed. David Stevens, published annually by Vacation-Work, 9 Park End Street, Oxford OX1 1HJ. Lists vacancies in over 30 countries, including France, Germany, Scandinavia, Spain, Switzerland, Greece, Yugoslavia, Israel, Morocco.

*Summer Jobs in Britain,* ed. Carole Harris, published annually by Vacation-Work, Oxford. Covers everything from farm work to archaeological digs.

*Summer Employment Directory of the U.S.A.,* ed. Mynena A. Leith, published annually by the National Directory Service Inc., Ohio, distributed in this country by Vacation-Work, Oxford, gives details as to how students outside the U.S. should apply for summer work there.

*Teach Overseas,* free booklet published by the British Council, 65 Davies Street, London W1Y 2AA, gives details of one- and two-year appointments for all teachers and graduates.

*Volunteer Work Abroad,* published by the Central Bureau for Educational Visits and Exchanges, 44 Baker Street, London W1M 2HJ, or 3 Bruntsfield Crescent, Edinburgh EH10 4HD, lists organizations that need volunteers for service overseas. Many are churches or international organizations such as the Guides and Boys' Brigade.

*Working Holidays* (Central Bureau for Educational Visits and Exchanges, London and Edinburgh) is full of useful addresses and suggestions for working holidays. It gives country-by-country details and covers everything from grape picking in France to building camps for aborigines in Australia.

Y.M.C.A., 640 Forest Road, Walthamstow, London E17 3DZ and the Y.W.C.A. of Great Britain, Hampden House, 2 Weymouth Street, London W1, both publish directories listing their addresses in over 70 countries. They also give addresses for referral to doctors, lawyers, priests, consulates.

Youth Hostel Association, 29 John Adam Street, London WC2, have over 4,000 hostels in all parts of the world, many in very beautiful settings. Their *International Youth Hostel Handbook*, published annually, lists all their hostels; Volume 1 covers Europe and the Mediterranean region; Volume 2 covers the rest of the world. You have to be a member to make use of their hostels.

The Y.H.A. *Adventure Holidays* booklet, published annually, covers adventure holidays in the U.K. for sixteen-year-olds and upwards. Includes all sorts of activity holidays, from bird-watching to brass rubbing. The Eagle Holidays section offers similar activity holidays in Switzerland, Luxembourg and on the Rhine, as well as in the U.K., for 11–15 year olds. These holidays are for members only.

# Index

*See also the Gazetteer, which begins on p.289, and the Bibliography, p.359, for information on particular countries and on publications.*